EU Energy and Climate Policy after COVID-19 and the Invasion of Ukraine

AF763752

This book discusses the impact of the COVID-19 pandemic and the Russian invasion of Ukraine on the European Union's climate and energy policy.

By examining the positions of the various actors involved, the book analyses whether the COVID-19 pandemic and the Russian invasion of Ukraine has contributed to greater unity, decarbonisation, and security of energy supply, and if not, whether these crises prompted member states to turn inwards and opt for national solutions to climate and energy challenges. It thus provides a new outlook for EU energy policy in relation to the experience of the two crises.

This book will be of key interest to scholars, students and practitioners of climate and energy policy, energy security, EU policy, and more broadly to energy politics, European integration and European Union governance.

Matúš Mišík is Associate Professor in the Department of Political Science at Comenius University Bratislava, Slovakia.

Andrea Figulová is Assistant Professor in the Faculty of Social and Economic Sciences at Comenius University Bratislava, Slovakia.

Routledge Studies on the Governance of Sustainability in Europe

At the beginning of the twenty-first century the EU is faced with major economic, environmental and societal challenges. Climate change is at the forefront of these challenges having a wide-ranging impact on the economy and society. This series will examine tensions and ambiguities in European sustainable development from an interdisciplinary and multidisciplinary background, covering the impact of sustainable development policies on European integration, and sustainability issues in energy, environmental, transport, development and agricultural policies.

Series editors: *Thomas Hoerber, ESSCA School of Management, France, Jenny Fairbrass, University of East Anglia, UK, Kristina Kurze, University of Göttingen, Germany, and Helene Dyrhauge, Roskilde University, Denmark*

Comparative Renewables Policy
Political, Organizational and European Fields
Edited by Elin Lerum Boasson, Merethe Dotterud Leiren and Jørgen Wettestad

The European Environmental Conscience in EU Politics
A Developing Ideology
Edited by Thomas Hoerber and Gabriel Weber

Making the European Green Deal Work
EU Sustainability Policies at Home and Abroad
Edited by Helene Dyrhauge and Kristina Kurze

The EU in a Globalized World
Edited by Thomas Hoerber, Alexandre Bohas and Stefano Valdemarin

EU Energy and Climate Policy after COVID-19 and the Invasion of Ukraine
Decarbonisation and Security in Transition
Edited by Matúš Mišík and Andrea Figulová

EU Energy and Climate Policy after COVID-19 and the Invasion of Ukraine

Decarbonisation and Security in Transition

Edited by Matúš Mišík and Andrea Figulová

Routledge
Taylor & Francis Group
LONDON AND NEW YORK

First published 2025
by Routledge
4 Park Square, Milton Park, Abingdon, Oxon OX14 4RN

and by Routledge
605 Third Avenue, New York, NY 10158

Routledge is an imprint of the Taylor & Francis Group, an informa business

British Library Cataloguing-in-Publication Data
A catalogue record for this book is available from the British Library

ISBN: 978-1-032-62482-2 (hbk)
ISBN: 978-1-032-62481-5 (pbk)
ISBN: 978-1-032-62483-9 (ebk)

DOI: 10.4324/9781032624839

Typeset in Times New Roman
by Newgen Publishing UK

M.M. To Nada and Matilda

A.F. To Julia, Juraj and Rudik

Contents

Illustrations

Figures

Tables

Contributors

András Deák is the head of the Economics of Globalisation Research Group at at HUN-REN CERS IWE and a senior research fellow at the John Lukacs Institute, University of Public Service, both in Budapest. He received his Diploma (MA) and Doctorate (PhD) in International Relations in 1997 and 2003, respectively, both from the University of Economic Sciences, Hungary. His research fields cover economic processes in the post-Soviet space, integration into the world economy, and energy policy in particular.

Andrea Figulová is assistant professor at Institute of the European Studies and International Relations at the Faculty of Social and Economic Sciences, Comenius University in Bratislava. Her research focuses on Slovak politics and parliamentarism and foreign policy with an emphasis on energy and security issues.

Zsolt Gál is an assistant professor at the Department of Political Science, Faculty of Arts at Comenius University Bratislava, Slovakia. He holds an MA degree in Political Science and a PhD in Economics. His research interests include public finances, EU economic policies, post-communist economic transformation, and international migration.

Andrea Gatto is senior assistant professor (with tenure) in Development Economics at College of Business and Public Management, Department of Economics, Wenzhou-Kean University. He is an Adjunct Professor at Korea University (world top 70) and Visiting Researcher for several European, American and Asian universities. Gatto is part of the top 2% World Scientists list issued by Stanford University.

Ivana Gondášová is a PhD candidate affiliated with the Institute of Economic Research at the Slovak Academy of Sciences in Bratislava. Her current research focuses on scrutiny of the energy security of the EU within the framework of EU-Russia energy relations.

Petra Grigelová obtained a PhD in Political Science at the Institute of Political Science, Slovak Academy of Sciences. She works at the Institute as a researcher.

Her research focuses on the foreign policy of the Slovak Republic, Slovakia's bilateral relations and diplomacy.

Wiktor Hebda is an assistant professor in the Institute of Political Science and International Relations at the Jagiellonian University in Krakow, Poland. His research and publications concern energy policy and security, as well as energy transformation, especially in the countries of Central Europe.

Jana Kajanová is a professor at the Faculty of Management, Comenius University Bratislava. She has authored more than 180 publications. Her recognition of scientific activities is more than 200 citations, requested lectures, and participations on review processes in scientific journals. Her research interests include finance, management, and environmental aspects of economy.

Katarzyna Leśniak is a PhD candidate at the AGH University of Science and Technology in Krakow, Poland. Her research and publications concern environmental engineering, mining and energy.

Juraj Marušiak is senior research fellow at the Institute of Political Science, Slovak Academy of Sciences, Bratislava, Slovakia (since 1996). His research is focused on the comparative politics and international relations in the region of Central and Eastern Europe since 1989. In 2022 he was appointed a director of the Institute.

Raffaele Mattera holds a PhD in Econometrics at the University of Naples "Federico II". Currently, he is Assistant Professor of Statistics at the Sapienza University of Rome, Italy. His main research interest is in computational statistics and predictive analytics, with a focus on clustering and forecasting of temporal, spatio-temporal and network data.

Matúš Mišík is associate professor at the Department of Political Science at Comenius University in Bratislava. His research interests include small states and energy security in the EU. He is the author of *External Energy Security in the European Union* (Routledge, 2019), co-author of *Energy Transitions in Central and Eastern Europe* (Cambridge University Press, 2024) and has published articles in journals including *Nature Energy, Energy, Energy Policy* and *Energy Research and Social Science.*

Matej Navrátil works as a researcher at the IESIR, Comenius University and as an Associate Researcher at the ECFR. His research focus includes the EU, organisation theory, institutional theory, foreign and security policy. His work appeared in the *Hague Journal of Diplomacy, Politics and Governance* and he has co-authored book chapters in international scholarly volumes.

Andrej Nosko is an energy expert, and researcher at Matej Bel University in Banská Bystrica and serves as Co-Executive Director at PILnet, an international NGO. His academic interests include the political economy of security, energy, and issues of political and energy transition. He has advised governments, businesses, and civil society organisations, lectured, and authored papers on energy policies of Central European countries.

Veronika Oravcová is a research assistant at the Department of Political Science at Comenius University in Bratislava and a research fellow at the Slovak Foreign Policy Association. Her research interests are centered on energy transition and energy security in Central and Eastern Europe. She has published several chapters on energy transition and papers on the Slovak and Visegrad energy policy.

Demetrio Panarello is an associate professor of Political Economy at Link Campus University, Italy, dedicated to the understanding and resolution of contemporary socio-economic challenges. His research covers a diverse range of topics, including sustainable energy and behaviours, climate transition policies and the resilience of households to economic and financial shocks.

Katarína Šafaříková is an associate professor at the Theatre Faculty of the Academy of Performing Arts in Bratislava and Head of Department of Speech and Voice Training. Her research and teaching activities focus on speech technique and vocal interpretation of artistic text. As an actress, she performed on several Slovak theatre stages, in television and film work.

Marek Stolorz is a PhD candidate at the Polish Academy of Sciences in Warsaw, Poland. He is an attorney-at-law, specialising in energy law.

John Szabo is a research fellow at the Institute of World Economics, Centre for Economic and Regional Studies, HUN-REN, Budapest and an Assistant Professor at the Department of Global and Development Studies, Eötvös Loránd University, Budapest.

Jaroslav Ušiak is a professor of International Relations at Matej Bel University, specialising in security studies and international relations, including theoretical approaches and current security threats, with a focus on Central Europe. His background combines academic research and project management with over 15+ years of professional experience in scholarly research, teaching, research supervision and team leading.

Lukáš Veteška is an employee of the Department of Economics and Finance of the Faculty of Management, Comenius University Bratislava. His pedagogical focus is on the field of corporate accounting. In his research activities, he specialises mainly in the field of economy, financial management and environmentally sustainable economy.

Radka Vicenová works as a postdoctoral fellow at the Department of Political Science at the Comenius University Bratislava and as a Researcher at the Slovak National Centre for Human Rights. Her research focuses primarily on the contemporary far right, particularly in Central and Eastern Europe.

Csaba Weiner a senior research fellow at the Institute of World Economics, HUN-REN Centre for Economic and Regional Studies, Hungary, which he joined in 2003. His main research interests are the energy sector in Central and Eastern Europe and foreign direct investment in and from Russia.

Acknowledgements

This work was financially supported by the Slovak Research and Development Agency under Contract no APVV-20-0012. We would like to thank our reviewers and the publishing team at Routledge for their comments, advice and support during the production of the book.

Introduction

Matúš Mišík and Andrea Figulová

0.1 Introduction

Recently the European Union's energy and climate policies have become its two most important policies. Since 2021 there has been an unprecedented number of both European Council (both ordinary and extraordinary) and extraordinary Council of the European Union (Transport, Telecommunications and Energy Council) meetings on these policies. Never has energy and climate policy been so heavily debated, nor has there been such high levels of public interest as in the last couple of years. It is all down to the two major crises that the EU has been facing since 2020 – the COVID-19 pandemic (Mastropietro et al., 2020; Santiago et al., 2021; Steffen et al., 2020) and the Russian invasion of Ukraine (Bricout et al., 2022; Mišík, 2022). The EU has, of course, had to tackle various crises since 2008 (economic/banking, refugee, Brexit, etc.) and that sparked a debate as to whether it was facing a polycrisis or was in constant crisis mode (Wolff and Ladi, 2020; Zeitlin et al., 2019). However, when we look back at these hard times, the current two crises differ because they are linked to climate and energy policy, which is something the EU has not had to deal with previously (see below for a discussion on the 1970s and 2009 gas/oil crises). This is despite the two crises sharing very few characteristics (the first being public health crisis and the second the military invasion) and the fact that, initially, their short-term impact on energy and climate policy was radically different. Whereas the COVID-19 crisis led to a fall in energy demand and a sharp decrease in energy prices (Kuzemko et al., 2020, but see Nagaj and Korpysa, 2020 on other energy-related aspects of the pandemic), Russia's activities, including its invasion of Ukraine, generated energy shortages and sharp increases in energy prices throughout the EU (Fernández Alvarez and Molnar, 2021; Zachmann et al., 2021).

Despite this difference, the main EU actors reacted similarly to these two crises. This was mainly because although the short-term consequences of the crises on climate and energy policy were different, the long-term consequences and the proposed long-term solution are very similar. The European Commission (also the Commission) responded to both crises – and the long-term consequences – in much the same way. In both cases, the Commission suggested strengthening and supporting the EU's long-term decarbonization goals as a means of both recovering

DOI: 10.4324/9781032624839-1

from the economic recession triggered by the pandemic and reducing EU dependency on external energy suppliers generally and Russia in particular. A key element in this approach is the creation of a common EU front that will both strengthen the Union and improve energy security, whilst also helping achieve the decarbonization goal. That goal was adopted in December 2019 at the European Council summit (European Council, 2019), just a couple of months before the onset of the pandemic in March 2020. At the summit, member states agreed that the EU economy would achieve carbon neutrality by 2050 and not emit more greenhouse gasses (GHG) than can be absorbed by the environment (the 'carbon sink'; Pugh et al., 2019). The Union's aim is to prevent an absolute increase in GHGs emissions beyond 2050. The goal is extremely ambitious, and EU leaders and member states recognize that to reach this goal the EU needs to step up its decarbonization efforts. Therefore, the EU's original 2030 climate and energy goals (European Council, 2014) have been repeatedly revised to put it on a trajectory that would allow it to achieve carbon neutrality in 2050 (Mišík et al., 2022).

The Commission has not eased up on its efforts to support the EU decarbonization goal as an easy solution to the problems (for example, by supporting cheap domestic coal to restart the economy after the pandemic or reduce EU dependency on external energy supplies) but has doubled down on decarbonization efforts. Not all member states have supported this approach – just as not all of them backed a common European solution, preferring to devise their own national solutions or even openly criticize the common solutions suggested by the Commission or other member states. Such criticism was also heard during the discussions on the sanctions against Russia following its invasion of Ukraine (Hungary is a case in point, see below) as well as during the discussions on the post-pandemic recovery.

The interplay between the Commission, member states, and other actors is one of the central planks in this volume examining the changes in EU climate and energy policy in relation to the two crises. The authors attempt to answer two main research questions: Has the COVID-19 pandemic and Russian invasion of Ukraine changed EU climate and energy policy? If so, have these changes led to the deepening of European integration in these policies or have member states opted for national solutions instead? In other words, have the crises contributed to EU unity, decarbonization, and security of energy supply, or have they prompted member states to turn inwards and search for national solutions to the climate and energy challenges? In the remainder of this introduction these ideas are discussed more broadly and then the individual chapters explore the various climate and energy policy issues connected to the two crises.

0.2 A green way out of the pandemic

As COVID-19 began to take hold in the EU in March 2022, it seemed, somewhat paradoxically, to have a positive effect on the EU's energy and climate goals. Energy prices fell (in some cases dramatically) as the draconian restrictions on movement reduced energy demand to levels not seen before (the oil price turned negative) and consequently energy availability was not a problem (Chong et al., 2022). The main challenges were the supply chain disruptions caused by the lockdowns, but these were not energy related (Pujawan and Bah, 2022). Moreover, the rapid decline in mobility and economic productivity led to – albeit only in the short term – a fall in GHG emissions, which was one of very few silver linings of the pandemic (Le Quéré et al., 2021). However, once the EU began to discuss how member states' economies and societies could recover from the consequences of the pandemic both climate and energy policy took centre stage (Koasidis et al., 2022).

In summer 2020 two main options were discussed that can be called – somewhat simplistically – *cheap* vs. *clean* energy. The cheap option was based on reversing the existing policy of greater use of renewable energy sources, which would enable a return to fossil fuels (especially cheap domestic coal) by reconsidering the emission schemes and other climate policy provisions designed to raise the price of fossil fuels (Kuzemko et al., 2020). Renewables were considered to be more expensive energy sources than fossil fuels, and proponents of this solution argued that the economy needed a strong impetus to recover from the shock caused by the pandemic. This solution was particularly popular among industries that had been hit hard by the pandemic and were looking for a fast and painless way out.

In the second, clean, option the pandemic was seen as an opportunity to restart the EU's economy on green foundations and centre it around greater use of renewable energy sources and other measures that would support the EU's decarbonization goal (Barbier, 2020; Kanda and Kivimaa, 2020). The main argument was that the pandemic presented an opportunity to rethink the energy supply chain and change the way energy is produced and used. The Commission was particularly keen on this position, but many member states had adopted a similar position from the very start (Mišík and Oravcová, 2022). Back in 2020 the Commission had reached an agreement with the member states on the need to create EU funds to support the post-pandemic recovery.

Both the New Generation program and the more general Multiannual Financial Framework for 2021–2027 were revised to reflect the EU's two main post-pandemic preferences – to make society both green and digital (European Council, 2020). In collaboration with the Commission, member states created National Recovery and Resilience Plans, the blueprints for the post-pandemic recovery underpinned by EU funds. Member states had to allocate 20 per cent of these funds to activities that would encourage digitalization and 37 per cent to activities that would contribute to the decarbonization goal (de la Porte and Jensen, 2021). As buildings account for high overall share of energy consumption, many member states devoted a substantial section of their Plans to improving energy efficiency in public and private buildings (Tajani et al., 2022). The Commission provided guidance on drafting the Plans based on experiences of the National Energy and Climate Plans. These had only been formally approved once the member states had adopted its recommendations, which in turn led to a new governance system in the EU (Vanhercke and Verdun, 2022). In most cases this process was successful – at least from the Commission's perspective – as the member states revised their national energy and climate goals in line with the Commission's preferences. Similarly, the National Recovery and Resilience Plans adopted the Commission's recommendations on assigning fund levels in line with its priorities; many member countries even allocated more money from the post-pandemic recovery funds to green goals than the required 37 per cent (Mišík and Oravcová, 2022).

Thus, the pandemic seems to have contributed to the deepening of energy and climate policy integration as the Commission used existing tools to push member states into aligning their own national preferences regarding the post-pandemic recovery with those of the Commission. Although the member states themselves decided how to use the EU funds assigned to them, they still had to work within the limits set at EU level (especially on digital and climate/energy goals).

0.3 EU's energy crises

The energy crisis that started in 2021 (and is still ongoing) was not the first to affect the European Union and its member states. Nonetheless, it differs from the previous energy crises in nature and magnitude. For example, the energy crises of the 1970s related to one energy source (oil) and impacted only a handful of members of what was then the European Community (McGowan, 2011). The main lesson taken from these crises was that member states should tighten control over energy companies operating within the country. As a consequence, many energy companies were nationalized in a bid to improve energy security. This went against the Community's common approach as the member states sought solutions within their national borders. It was also a blow to international cooperation in energy security. For example, the International Energy Agency was created in 1974 as the energy importing countries' answer to OPEC (IEA, 1994). But not everybody was on board with this: France stayed out of the new energy security-focused international organization (only becoming a member in 1992).

It was not until the very end of the 1980s and the formal creation of the common energy market that the EU began liberalizing its energy sector (Matláry, 1997). Nonetheless, it took the whole of the 1990s and 2000s to create an almost completely liberalized energy market and three rounds of liberalization legislation that gradually handed government control of the energy market to competing market players and oversight authorities (Ciambra and Solorio, 2015). With its strong market focus, the liberalization left several back doors open for actors whose interests were incompatible with the market. The EU was able to close some of these (the famous Gazprom clause is an example; Goldthau and Sitter, 2014), but market developments during the second half of 2021 showed there were still some remaining security loopholes (storage being a prime example; Zachmann et al., 2021). The liberalization push of the 1990s and 2000s is therefore considered to be one of the reasons why the EU found itself in a very difficult energy security situation in the second half of 2021 and throughout 2022 and 2023.

The EU faced another energy crisis at the very beginning of 2009 and a smaller prelude at the beginning of 2006 (Stulberg, 2015). Following a dispute between Russia (Gazprom), the natural gas supplier, on the one hand and Ukraine, the transit country, on the other over the transit fees and gas price paid by Ukraine, no new contract could be agreed after the previous one expired at the end of 2008

(Kratochvíl and Tichý, 2013). The resulting dispute led to the complete cessation of gas supplies to Europe. At that time the Brotherhood pipeline was one of only two pipelines transporting Russian gas to Europe (along with the Yamal pipeline; Mišík, 2019). While the majority of the EU member states only experienced a slight blip in their gas supplies, as they had access to other sources and transit corridors, Bulgaria and Slovakia were left with no external gas sources in the middle of the heating season in a harsh winter because their only supply route (the Brotherhood pipeline) had been shut down. Moreover, in Slovakia gas storage systems were used as a back-up for gas transit, not for emergency supplies, so they could not be used to rectify the situation despite their considerable size. The lesson from this crisis was that the energy infrastructure had to be upgraded to enable diversification of natural gas and other types of energy supply (European Commission, 2009). Consequently, in 2010, the EU began to encourage the building of new energy infrastructure including interconnectors, the creation of reverse flows and the upgrading and enlargement of storage facilities (Prontera and Plenta, 2020). However, most of these projects were focused on improving interconnectedness between member states, and only a very few (the LNG terminals in particular) were aimed at enhancing EU access to non-Russian energy sources (Oravcová and Mišík, 2018).

Moreover the 2009 gas crisis did not affect all member states to the same extent (Rodríguez-Gómez et al., 2016). Apart from the two most affected countries – Bulgaria and Slovakia – the impact of the crisis on EU member states in Central and Eastern Europe was felt in the form of lower supplies (direct impact) or merely confirmed their suspicions that Russia was not a reliable energy supplier (indirect impact). Poland and Lithuania, although not directly affected, were most active in diversifying energy infrastructure and almost immediately began building LNG terminals that would give them access to global gas supplies (Mišík and Prachárová, 2016; Zarzecki, 2022). This came at a high price at the time (2014 in Lithuania and 2015 in Poland; European Commission, 2019; Schulte and Weiser, 2019) but has enabled them to substantially limit the consequences of the reduction in Russian supplies after 2021. Since most EU members were not affected by the 2009 crisis, the EU's energy security policy did not undergo comprehensive change (there was little support for a more thorough revision of the existing rules) and the focus was on improving the EU's internal mechanisms. However, in the second half of 2021 and throughout 2022 and 2023 the reduction in Russian natural gas supplies to Europe together with other factors caused energy prices to spike and generated a serious energy crisis in the EU.

In the meantime the EU's domestic natural gas sources had decreased and it had actually become more dependent on external natural gas supplies (oil import dependency has always been extremely high; European Commission, 2020). Although the EU drew up a new set of rules in response to the energy security issues by mandating mutual help among member states (Security of Supply Regulation of 2010 revised in 2017 and in 2022 with regards to gas storage), that is targeted at the internal situation. The EU has not been able to muster a common stance on its external energy suppliers as member states have favoured national solutions to their energy needs. This position was reinforced in the Lisbon Treaty adopted in 2007 (i.e. before the 2009 gas crisis) and ratified by the last member state in 2009 (Hosli et al., 2013). The Lisbon Treaty energy provisions cover the EU's approach to its internal energy market but leave the energy mixes in the hands of the member states. This gives member states all the power when deciding from where and under what conditions they will get their energy (Thaler and Pakalkaite, 2021). Consequently, agreeing common EU positions is exceedingly difficult as each member has veto power. Member states who had agreed to advantageous bilateral deals with their energy suppliers (for example, Russian Gazprom) were particularly reluctant to relinquish their favourable position by supporting common EU solutions that would mean the loss of their bilateral deals.

0.4 The 2022 crisis: Sanctions

While our preliminary analysis of the impact of the COVID-19 pandemic on EU climate and energy policy suggests that the crisis led to changes in these policies, developments related to the Russian invasion of Ukraine indicate it had only a marginal influence on EU climate and energy policy despite its severity. Natural gas prices (as well as electricity as the two are closely interconnected) had already increased in the EU during the second half of 2021, at least partly because of Russia's activities. The energy crisis was fully exposed after Russia invaded Ukraine and the EU retaliated by providing military, humanitarian, economic, and other assistance and by imposing several rounds of sanctions. Russian energy exports fell substantially, in some cases regardless of the sanctions (this is especially true of natural gas that has not been sanctioned as of April 2024). The EU's ability to adopt a common position was limited, although the Commission did suggest some long-term ideas (European Commission, 2022a) and short-term solutions (European Commission, 2022b). The proposal for reducing EU dependency on external energy sources over the long-term centres around the idea that domestic renewable energy sources are the most effective means of responding to the crisis.

On 24 February 2022 Russian military forces invaded Ukraine. This provoked a strong international response but did not deter Russia from continuing its invasion. The EU therefore joined forces with other Western actors and introduced sanctions to limit Russia's access to international goods and services as well as limit its revenue from goods sold internationally. Energy is Russia's main source of international revenue, so discussions began almost immediately on a suitable target for EU sanctions, with many actors suggesting sanctions on Russian energy in an attempt to restrict Russia's ability to raise revenue for its war efforts. Russia is dependent on revenue from energy exports, and the EU had been its main export destination before the 2022 invasion (European Commission, 2015). Voices within the EU have argued that the community had to impose sanctions in areas where they have the biggest impact – such as the energy sector. The Commission called for a common EU position on this, but member countries were not terribly supportive, arguing that energy sanctions would worsen an already difficult situation in the common energy market.

The EU is the biggest economy in the world, but it is unable to translate this economic strength into a robust bargaining position. Not, it has to be said, for want of trying – for example, the 2015 Energy Union took account of this shortcoming (Andersen et al., 2017). The main point of the initiative was to develop a common position that would make the EU stronger and thereby prevent the Russian Federation from engaging in a 'divide and rule' approach to energy negotiations (Karlsen, 2019). Indeed, the challenge of presenting a united position on external energy relations can be considered to lie at the heart of the EU's inability to come up with a set of powerful economic sanctions (Mišík and Nosko, 2023).

The first energy source to make it onto the sanctions list was Russian coal, which has been subject to full sanctions since August 2022, including an earlier transitional period. However, coal represents only a fraction of what Russia exports to the EU, compared to oil or natural gas, so coal sanctions have only a very limited impact on the main goal – which is to weaken Russia's economy and its ability to prop up the invasion. The EU has a lot of domestic coal so Russian coal can be replaced by increasing imports from other sources and, to some degree, by increasing domestic production. Besides, Russia was able to effectively divert its coal exports away from the EU, for example to India or China (Reuters, 2022), reducing the effectiveness of the sanctions. Moreover, coal has the biggest carbon footprint in the EU's energy mix and its use has been steadily decreasing owing to the Union's decarbonization goals (European Council, 2019). Despite the weak position of coal in the EU's economy, imposing sanctions on Russian coal exports was not without its problems and was the subject of difficult negotiations. Even during the first rounds of the sanctions negotiations it was clear it would be difficult to reach a common position on other energy sources.

Further problems emerged immediately after discussions began on the oil sanctions. Several member states presented strong opposing positions, arguing that Russian oil was their only option at that time as their oil industries needed extra time to adjust to supplies from other countries. Hungary and Slovakia adopted such a position and, as they were joined by Germany (for historical reasons the refineries in the former German Democratic Republic are still designed to process Russian oil), the opposition to full oil sanctions was strong (Barigazzi and Kijewski, 2022). Consequently, a system of transition periods and derogations emerged which effectively excluded Russian oil transported via pipelines. EU member states were thus not united, sending signals about the inability of the Union to agree on a sanctions regime that would most effectively target the Russian aggression.

Natural gas supplies from Russia placed the EU in an even more difficult situation. While the oil sanctions cannot be considered a success, the EU's position on the natural gas sectors vis-à-vis Russia seems to be even weaker and more reactive. Natural gas sanctions have not even been officially discussed yet (as of April 2024), and, so far, member states have only agreed on a price mechanism to prevent the spikes and market instability in evidence since late 2021. Some member states, but not all, backed the Commission's proposed natural gas price cap. There has been no deeper discussion among member states on sanctioning natural gas imports, and the steps taken so far are either internally focused (filling domestic storage tanks, reducing natural gas consumption; European Commission, 2022b) or concern alternative supplies (finding new suppliers). Moreover, many member states have 'nationalized' their energy security and have started to find ways of securing natural gas supplies or were reducing prices for domestic consumers (the most striking example is Germany). Consequently, they have become competitors on the international energy market (for example, over LNG) and shown only limited willingness to support EU-wide solutions such as voluntarily reducing gas consumption (see below). This has led to a supply situation in which Russia is playing a very active role, while the EU passively observes. Russia's demand that natural gas be paid for in roubles (breaking the existing contractual agreement) is a case in point. Similarly, Gazprom named various 'maintenance' and other 'technical' issues as reasons for disruptions to the natural gas flow via some of its pipelines in the first half of 2022 before it completely halted supplies via the Yamal and Nord Stream pipelines during the summer of 2022.

The EU has not proved very effective on energy sanctions. Even in the areas where sanctions were adopted (coal, oil), the negotiations were difficult, with some member states having the power of veto. The resulting sanction regimes came with transitional periods and exceptions (for example, oil transported by pipeline was excluded from the sanctions), which considerably reduced their effect. However, the main challenge for the EU has been the need for unanimity among member states to introduce EU-wide sanctions. Member states have been willing to use the threat of veto in pursuit of their national interests, often connected to their political interests, which in some cases go against those of the EU (and other member states'). This undermines the EU's ability to succeed and plays into Russia's hands, especially its 'divide and rule' approach.

0.5 The 2022/2023 crisis: Solidarity

The Commission suggested that member states should voluntarily reduce gas consumption in the 2022/2023 winter to lower EU gas consumption overall and thereby free up natural gas supplies for member states faced with a challenging gas supply situation (European Commission, 2022b). This voluntary mechanism was intended as a means of showing solidarity with member states having a hard time securing supplies during the most difficult period of the year for natural gas demand. It was supposed to be a gesture of goodwill and demonstrate a willingness to support those member states vulnerable to external shocks. There was no obligation to help member states in an energy emergency under the Security of Supply Regulation (see above). Nonetheless, many member states reacted negatively, and the EU level negotiations that followed the Commission proposal for this voluntary measure proved difficult. In the end many member states were able to negotiate special conditions that were nowhere near the proposed 15 per cent reduction in natural gas consumption for the winter season of 2022/2023 (Mišík and Nosko, 2023).

A few countries even managed to negotiate an increase in natural gas consumption for the 2022/2023 winter. One of the most striking cases was Slovakia, which had rejected the Commission's calls for solidarity, despite having repeatedly called for EU and member-state solidarity on energy following the 2009 gas crisis. Paradoxically, several Mediterranean EU members behaved similarly, rejecting the across-the-board reduction in natural gas consumption, despite having called for solidarity throughout the refugee crisis that began in 2015. Member states yet again showed they were incapable of agreeing a common solution for the natural gas sector, although there had been calls from the Commission – and several member states – to unite and adopt a strong common stance. A common external energy policy dimension would enable the EU to adopt a united position despite the objections of a small number of members (currently able to use their veto) and would solve at least some of the problems it currently faces. It would turn the EU's economic power (i.e. the ability to pay for energy imports in a way no other entity in the world does) into a political power, allowing the EU to pursue its own preferences (Mišík, 2022). The EU as such, however, managed to save more than the expected 15 per cent of natural gas consumption during the winter of 2022/2023. Member states even supported prolonging the voluntary gas consumption reduction program for the 2023/2024 winter, although Hungary and Poland voted against and Italy abstained (Council of the EU, 2023).

The reaction from EU actors suggests that even external shocks cannot – for now – force member states into changing their positions on common solutions to energy (and climate) problems. As the member-state competences on the energy mix lie at the heart of its problems – be they the proportion of renewable energy sources used in the country or the external energy sources required to cover national needs – policy changes are dependent on their support.

0.6 Structure of the book

This edited volume looks at the two latest crises impacting the EU (the COVID-19 pandemic and Russian invasion of Ukraine) from the perspective of energy and climate policy and how the crises have affected these. It examines the policy changes from various perspectives and contains 11 chapters (plus this Introduction and Conclusion) on diverse member states. These are grouped into three main sections that are tied together by the volume's focus on the effect of the abovementioned crises on EU energy and climate policy. This is done from a holistic perspective, studying the development of these policies in various member states, within regional groupings, but also at EU level. The book examines these issues from various angles: European studies, political science, public administration, as well as economics and public opinion. Therefore, contributions to this volume utilize various approaches which allows them to analyse their specific perspectives on the impact of the COVID-19 pandemic and the Russian invasion of Ukraine on the EU's energy and climate policy. Methodological approaches thus vary in all proposed contributions and encompass quantitative as well as qualitative methods including (among others) discursive, comparative, or regression analysis that utilize various types of data. Such perspective allows the volume to cover a whole spectrum of challenges connected to examined crises, while being tied together by the main puzzles and research questions.

However, such an approach has also its limitations, especially when it comes to the ability of the volume to stay coherent and be more than the sum of its parts. Coherence is secured by each chapter's specific contribution to solving the book's main puzzle and looking into a common set of research questions. Each chapter examines the changes to the EU's energy and climate policy caused by the pandemic and the invasion and thus contributes to two main research questions: Has the EU become (or is it on the way to becoming) decarbonized, secure, and united (Research question 1) and, if yes, have these changes led to the deepening of European integration in these policies or have member states opted for national solutions instead? (Research question 2). Each contribution reflects on these research questions and explains how its specific analytical perspective is instrumental in developing a complex explanation of the impact of the pandemic and Russian invasion of Ukraine on the EU's energy and climate policy. Moreover, the Conclusion of this volume aggregates these partial conclusions and discusses the overall answers to the book's main research questions and how the interdisciplinary nature of the volume helped to shed light on the puzzles which were examined.

Part I – EU energy transition at a crossroads – combines different economic approaches and stakeholder perspectives. Chapter 1, 'European Green Deal: Creeping supranationalism in the EU governance?' by Navrátil and Grigelová examines the Commission's strategy towards the European Green Deal goals and looks at how these are being expanded into other policy areas. In doing so it provides a broad perspective on the European integration process. Chapter 2, 'What does EU energy policy mean to you? Regional differences in EU citizens' sentiments on energy transition – socio-economic, political and environmental factors' by Mattera, Panarello, and Gatto analyses citizens' perceptions of the energy transition and the implications for creating specific energy and climate policies influenced by the crises discussed in this volume. Chapter 3, 'Role of the regions in climate and energy policy: Insight from Visegrad countries' by Oravcová and Šafaříková explores how prepared the local and regional authorities are in the Visegrad Group countries (Czechia, Hungary, Poland and Slovakia) for the challenges of the energy transition and the effects on policy. In Chapter 4, 'In Rosatom's shadow: The uncertain role of nuclear in energy transition of Central and Eastern Europe', Gál examines the limits of nuclear power in the energy transition in Central and Eastern Europe,

Part II – Russian invasion and European energy security – begins with Chapter 5 'Russia's aggression against Ukraine and its impact on the energy cooperation of Visegrad Group countries' by Marušiak and explores developments in energy security in the Visegrad Group following the Russian invasion. In Chapter 6 'Russia's gas weapon in Central and Eastern Europe: Diverging responses from three friendly states', Deák, Szabo, and Weiner present a comparative analysis of the energy policy of three Russia-friendly Central and East European countries – Bulgaria, Hungary, and Serbia. Chapter 7 'Energy transition at gunpoint' by Nosko and Ušiak studies the links between the sanctions and the transformation of the energy system and the economies of energy-dependent countries. Macroeconomic indicators and their changes in the crisis are the core focus of Chapter 8 'Structural development of the Slovak economy and the impact on the production of emissions' by Kajanová and Veteška. Chapter 9, the last chapter in this section, 'A quantitative assessment of energy security in EU member states following COVID-19 and the energy crisis' by Gondášová examines changes in energy policy during the crisis using the Energy Security Index and the z-score standardization method.

Part III – Renewables as energy security tool – addresses specific determinants of energy security and transition and contains two chapters on renewable energy. Chapter 10 'Wind energy in Poland – a successful restart or another false start?' by Hebda, Lésniak, and Stolorz looks at issues related to the employment of renewable energy from a legal perspective, utilizing Poland as a case study. The last chapter in the section, Chapter 11, 'Nativist framing of energy issues in times of crises across the Slovak political spectrum', by Figulová and Vicenová examines changes in the positions of various political actors on energy and climate using the Slovak Republic as a case study.

The conclusion summarizes the main findings of the volume, presents the limits of the current research, and suggests future research avenues. It also reflects on how each chapter contributed to answering two main research questions of the edited volume and links findings from individual chapters, so they create a coherent picture of the impact of examined crises on EU energy and climate policy.

Acknowledgements

This work was supported by the Slovak Research and Development Agency Grant No APVV-20-0012.

References

Andersen, S.S., Goldthau, A., Sitter, N., 2017. *Energy Union. Europe's New Liberal Mercantilism?* London: Palgrave Macmillan.

Barbier, E.B., 2020. Greening the post-pandemic recovery in the G20. *Environ. Resour. Econ.* 76, 685–703. https://doi.org/10.1007/s10640-020-00437-w

Bricout, A., Slade, R., Staffell, I., Halttunen, K., 2022. From the geopolitics of oil and gas to the geopolitics of the energy transition: Is there a role for European supermajors? *Energy Res. Soc. Sci.* 88, 102634. https://doi.org/https://doi.org/10.1016/j.erss.2022.102634

Barigazzi, J., Kijewski, L., 2022. *EU's Russian Oil Ban Stalls as Hungary Holds up Sanctions*. Brussels: Politico.

Chong, C.T., Fan, Y. Van, Lee, C.T., Klemeš, J.J., 2022. Post COVID-19 energy sustainability and carbon emissions neutrality. *Energy* 241, 122801. https://doi.org/10.1016/j.energy.2021.122801

Ciambra, A., Solorio, I., 2015. The liberalisation of the internal energy market: Is the EU dancing at a British tempo?, in: Tosun, J., Biesenbender, S., Schulze, K. (Eds), *Energy Policy Making in the EU. Building the Agenda*. London: Springer-Verlag.

Council of the EU, 2023. End of writen procedure. Proposal for a Council Regulation amending Regulation (EU) 2022/1369 as regards prolonging the demand reduction period for demand-reduction measures for gas and reinforcing the reporting and monitoring of their implementation. Brussels: European Commission.

de la Porte, C., Jensen, M.D., 2021. The next generation EU: An analysis of the dimensions of conflict behind the deal. *Soc. Policy Adm.* 55, 388–402. https://doi.org/10.1111/spol.12709

European Commission, 2009. The January 2009 gas supply disruption to the EU: An assessment. Brussels: European Commission.

European Commission, 2015. A framework strategy for a resilient energy union with a forward-looking climate change policy 1–21. https://doi.org/10.1017/CBO9781107415324.004

European Commission, 2019. Energy Union: EU invests to upgrade Polish Liquefied Natural Gas terminal in Świnoujście. Brussels: European Commission.

European Commission, 2020. An EU-wide assessment of National Energy and Climate Plans. Brussels: European Commission.

European Commission, 2022a. REPowerEU: Joint European Action for more affordable, secure and sustainable energy. Brussels: European Commission.

European Commission, 2022b. Save gas for a safe winter. Brussels: European Commission.

European Council, 2014. European Council conclusions, 23 and 24 October 2014. Brussels: European Commission.

European Council, 2019. European Council meeting (12 December 2019) – Conclusions. Brussels: European Commission.

European Council, 2020. Special meeting of the European Council (17, 18, 19, 20 and 21 July 2020) – Conclusions. Brussels: European Commission.

Fernández Alvarez, C., Molnar, G., 2021. What is behind soaring energy prices and what happens next? – Analysis – IEA. Paris: International Energy Agency.

Goldthau, A., Sitter, N., 2014. A liberal actor in a realist world? The Commission and the external dimension of the single market for energy. *J. Eur. Public Policy* 21, 1425–1472. https://doi.org/10.1080/13501763.2014.912251

Hosli, M., Kreppel, A., Plechanovová, B., Verdun, A., 2013. Decision-making in the European Union before and after the Lisbon Treaty. *West Eur. Polit.* 36, 1121–1127. https://doi.org/10.1080/01402382.2013.826020

IEA, 1994. *The History of International Energy Agency. The first twenty years*. Paris: OECD/IEA.

Kanda, W., Kivimaa, P., 2020. What opportunities could the COVID-19 outbreak offer for sustainability transitions research on electricity and mobility? *Energy Res. Soc. Sci.* 68 1–5 https://doi.org/10.1016/j.erss.2020.101666

Karlsen, G.H., 2019. Divide and rule: Ten lessons about Russian political influence activities in Europe. *Palgrave Commun.* 5, 19. https://doi.org/10.1057/s41599-019-0227-8

Koasidis, K., Nikas, A., Van de Ven, D.-J., Xexakis, G., Forouli, A., Mittal, S., Gambhir, A., Koutsellis, T., Doukas, H., 2022. Towards a green recovery in the EU: Aligning further emissions reductions with short- and long-term energy-sector employment gains. *Energy Policy* 171, 113301. https://doi.org/10.1016/j.enpol.2022.113301

Kratochvíl, P., Tichý, L., 2013. EU and Russian discourse on energy relations. *Energy Policy* 56, 391–406. https://doi.org/10.1016/j.enpol.2012.12.077

Kuzemko, C., Bradshaw, M., Bridge, G., Goldthau, A., Jewell, J., Overland, I., Scholten, D., Van de Graaf, T., Westphal, K., 2020. COVID-19 and the politics of sustainable energy transitions. *Energy Res. Soc. Sci.* 68, 101685. https://doi.org/10.1016/j.erss.2020.101685

Le Quéré, C., Peters, G.P., Friedlingstein, P., Andrew, R.M., Canadell, J.G., Davis, S.J., Jackson, R.B., Jones, M.W., 2021. Fossil CO_2 emissions in the post-COVID-19 era. *Nat. Clim. Chang.* 11, 197–199. https://doi.org/10.1038/s41558-021-01001-0

Mastropietro, P., Rodilla, P., Batlle, C., 2020. Emergency measures to protect energy consumers during the COVID-19 pandemic: A global review and critical analysis. *Energy Res. Soc. Sci.* 68, 101678. https://doi.org/10.1016/j.erss.2020.101678

Matláry, J.H., 1997. *Energy Policy in the European Union*. London: Macmillan Education UK,. https://doi.org/10.1007/978-1-349-25735-5

McGowan, F., 2011. Putting energy insecurity into historical context: European responses to the energy crises of the 1970s and 2000s. *Geopolitics* 16, 486–511. https://doi.org/10.1080/14650045.2011.520857

Mišík, M., 2019. *External Energy Security in the European Union. Small Member States' Perspective*. London: Routledge.

Mišík, M., 2022. The EU needs to improve its external energy security. *Energy Policy* 165, 112930. https://doi.org/10.1016/j.enpol.2022.112930

Mišík, M., Nosko, A., 2023. Each one for themselves: Exploring the energy security paradox of the European Union. *Energy Res. Soc. Sci.* 99, 103074. https://doi.org/10.1016/j.erss.2023.103074.

Mišík, M., Oravcová, V., 2022. Ex ante governance in the European Union: Energy and climate policy as a 'test run' for the post-pandemic recovery. *Energy Policy* 167, 113076. https://doi.org/10.1016/J.ENPOL.2022.113076

Mišík, M., Oravcová, V., Plenta, P., 2022. The European Union's energy policy. From market liberalisation to convergence with climate policy. In: Hoerber, T.C., Weber, G., Cabras, I. (Eds), *The Routledge Handbook of European Integrations*. London: Routledge, pp. 315–330.

Mišík, M., Prachárová, V., 2016. Before 'Independence' arrived: Interdependence in energy relations between Lithuania and Russia. *Geopolitics* 21, 579–604. https://doi.org/10.1080/14650045.2015.1113402

Nagaj, R., Korpysa, J., 2020. Impact of COVID-19 on the level of energy poverty in Poland. *Energies* 13, 4977. https://doi.org/10.3390/en13184977

Oravcová, V., Mišík, M., 2018. EU funds and limited cooperation: Energy infrastructure development in the Visegrad Group. *Int. Issues Slovak Foreign Policy Aff.* 27, 11–26.

Prontera, A., Plenta, P., 2020. Catalytic power Europe and gas infrastructural policy in the Visegrad countries. *Energy Policy* 137, 111189. https://doi.org/10.1016/j.enpol.2019.111189

Pugh, T.A.M., Lindeskog, M., Smith, B., Poulter, B., Arneth, A., Haverd, V., Calle, L., 2019. Role of forest regrowth in global carbon sink dynamics. *Proc. Natl. Acad. Sci.* 116, 4382 LP–4387. https://doi.org/10.1073/pnas.1810512116

Pujawan, I.N., Bah, A.U., 2022. Supply chains under COVID-19 disruptions: Literature review and research agenda. *Supply Chain Forum An Int. J.* 23, 81–95. https://doi.org/10.1080/16258312.2021.1932568

Reuters, 2022. China's July Russian coal imports hit five-year high as West shuns Moscow https://www.reuters.com/markets/europe/chinas-july-russian-coal-imports-hit-5-yr-high-west-shuns-moscow-2022-08-20/.

Rodríguez-Gómez, N., Zaccarelli, N., Bolado-Lavín, R., 2016. European ability to cope with a gas crisis. Comparison between 2009 and 2014. *Energy Policy* 97, 461–474. https://doi.org/10.1016/j.enpol.2016.07.016

Santiago, I., Moreno-Munoz, A., Quintero-Jiménez, P., Garcia-Torres, F., Gonzalez-Redondo, M.J., 2021. Electricity demand during pandemic times: The case of the COVID-19 in Spain. *Energy Policy* 148, 111964. https://doi.org/10.1016/j.enpol.2020.111964

Schulte, S., Weiser, F., 2019. LNG import quotas in Lithuania – Economic effects of breaking Gazprom's natural gas monopoly. *Energy Econ.* 78, 174–181. https://doi.org/https://doi.org/10.1016/j.eneco.2018.10.030

Steffen, B., Egli, F., Pahle, M., Schmidt, T.S., 2020. Navigating the clean energy transition in the COVID-19 crisis. *Joule* 4, 1137–1141. https://doi.org/10.1016/j.joule.2020.04.011

Stulberg, A.N., 2015. Out of gas? Russia, Ukraine, Europe, and the changing geopolitics of natural gas. *Probl. Post-Communism* 62, 112–130. https://doi.org/10.1080/10758216.2015.1010914

Tajani, F., Di Liddo, F., Ranieri, R., 2022. The effective use of national recovery and resilience plan funding: A methodological approach for the optimal assessment of the initiative costs. *Land* 11(10), 1812 https://doi.org/10.3390/land11101812

Thaler, P., Pakalkaite, V., 2021. Governance through real-time compliance: the supranationalisation of European external energy policy. *J. Eur. Public Policy* 28, 208–228. https://doi.org/10.1080/13501763.2020.1712462

Vanhercke, B., Verdun, A., 2022. The European semester as goldilocks: Macroeconomic policy coordination and the recovery and resilience facility. *JCMS J. Common Mark. Stud.* 60, 204–223. https://doi.org/https://doi.org/10.1111/jcms.13267

Wolff, S., Ladi, S., 2020. European Union responses to the COVID-19 pandemic: adaptability in times of Permanent Emergency. *J. Eur. Integr.* 42, 1025–1040. https://doi.org/10.1080/07036337.2020.1853120

Zachmann, G., McWilliams, B., Sgaravatti, G., 2021. *How Serious Is Europe's Natural Gas Storage Shortfall?* Brussels: OECD/IEA.

Zarzecki, D., 2022. Development of the LNG terminal in Świnoujście, Poland. In: Liuhto, K. (Ed.), *The Future of Energy Consumption, Security and Natural Gas: LNG in the Baltic Sea Region*. Cham: Springer International Publishing, pp. 191–220. https://doi.org/10.1007/978-3-030-80367-4_7

Zeitlin, J., Nicoli, F., Laffan, B., 2019. Introduction: The European Union beyond the polycrisis? Integration and politicization in an age of shifting cleavages. *J. Eur. Public Policy* 26, 963–976. https://doi.org/10.1080/13501763.2019.1619803

Part I

EU energy transition at a crossroads

1 European Green Deal

Creeping supranationalism in the EU governance?

Matej Navrátil and Petra Grigelová

1.1 Introduction

The European Green Deal (EGD) represents an ambitious and holistic set of policies designed to mitigate carbon emissions, foster sustainable growth, and safeguard biodiversity within the European Union (EU). As a strategic response to climate change, the EGD aspires to make the EU a carbon-neutral continent by 2050, surpassing the Paris Agreement's global warming limitation goal of well below 2°C. Despite contributing only around 10% of global greenhouse gas emissions, the EU has committed to reducing these emissions by at least 55% by 2030 compared to 1990 levels. Central to the EGD is the European Climate Law, proposed in March 2020, which legally enshrines the EU's emission reduction targets and establishes a framework for monitoring and reporting on progress. Since the official announcement of the EGD in 2019, scholarly attention on this topic has burgeoned. EGD has generated the creation of numerous thematic areas in which specific policies were studied in more detail, from engineering and agriculture through natural and social sciences. The EGD was the subject of discussions in relation to the potential of renewable energy sources (Brodny et al., 2020) like solar energy (Jäger-Waldau et al. 2020) or wind energy (Hrnčić et al. 2021). Authors were interested in comparing specific EU countries and the structure of their energy production (Hafner & Raimondi, 2021, Tutak et al. 2021); assessing energy management at EU level (Hafner & Raimondi, 2021; Skjærseth, 2021); discussing the EU's Climate and Energy Law (Kulovesi & Oberthür, 2020) or revealing how the European Commission and the European Parliament facilitated strategic narratives in order to obtain approval of the Climate Law (Domorenok and Graziano, 2023). Academics have explored the evolution of EU climate policies (Oberthür and von Homeyer, 2023) and scrutinised the EGD's development amid multiple crises (von Homeyer et al., 2021; Skjærseth, 2021). The EGD has been hailed as a 'paradigm shift' (Schunz, 2022) in EU sustainability, marking an ambitious breakthrough (Sachs, 2019), with transformative potential for Europe's identity (Tubiana, 2021). Yet, scepticism persists, with some viewing the EGD as an effort to extend neoliberal hegemony in EU climate policies (Samper, Schockling, and Islar, 2021).

What has received relatively little attention, and forms the focus of this contribution, is an evaluation of how the EGD has the potential to transform the EU's

DOI: 10.4324/9781032624839-3

governance system. Arguably, an investigation of the changes in the climate and energy policies against the background of crises is also the starting point of this book (see the Introduction by Mišík and Figulová). The editors ask whether the COVID-19 pandemic and the Russian invasion of Ukraine changed the climate and energy policy and, if so, have these changes led to a deepening of these policy fields or have member states decided to implement their solutions. While we see the EGD as a response to the crises, and hence reply affirmatively to the former, our objective is not to trace down member states' individual responses, nor to judge the EGD's normative goals and policies. Rather, this contribution focuses on evaluation of how the EGD has the potential to transform the EU's governance system (but see Becker, 2024).

Therefore, our goal is to examine how the European Commission's articulated goals and the ensuing implementation processes reshape institutional power dynamics in the EU and influence the integration project's future. Specifically, we employ the term 'creeping supranationalism' as articulated by Wong (2015), denoting a situation in which supranational bodies outside the state gradually acquire more functional and discretionary powers, shifting decision-making away from the state and eroding its authority. Our interest lies in uncovering who holds sway over European integration concerning EGD implementation and the ensuing repercussions. Wong sees this process to be "reactive rather than purposeful, based on short-term considerations rather than a long-term vision" (ibid. 2015, p. 236). Seeing the concept of creeping supranationalism from this perspective is indeed an important addition to the literature on processes accompanying regional integration, but it does not go beyond descriptive categories. Therefore, in order to render it's analytical utility, we suggest connecting this concept with the academic debates about the European regulatory governance literature (Majone, 1996; Heritier, 1997); debates about the role of the EU-level agencies (Majone 2005; Everson and Joerges, 2006; Pollak and Puntscher-Riekmann, 2008; Egeberg and Trondal, 2011; Egeberg et al., 2015; Ruffing, 2022; Ruffing et. al. 2023) and 'soft governance' (Scharpf, 1997; Radaelli, 2003; Maggetti, 2015, p. 255; Bocquillon et. al. 2023). These debates, steeped in insights about power struggles in EU governance, allow for a deeper understanding of the actual processes and mechanisms through which 'creeping supranationalism' operates.

This chapter unfolds in three parts. Part 1 outlines debates surrounding the concept of "creeping supranationalism" in EU governance. Part 2 delves into EGD policies, scrutinising signs of creeping supranationalisation. Part 3 explores the implications and challenges associated with the intensification of supranationalism in EU governance and focuses on how the erosion of national sovereignty undermines the authority over the 'state core powers'. The Conclusion follows.

1.2 Modes of EU's governance in the times of crisis

Over the past decade, the European Union (EU) has been meddling through a series of overlapping crises, including the post-2008 Eurozone crisis, the 2014 Ukraine crisis, the migration crisis of 2015, Brexit, the COVID-19 pandemic, and the recent Russian aggression in Ukraine. Despite this 'polycrisis' (Zeitlin et al., 2019) and persistent political turbulence, the EU has experienced considerable economic growth. This complex web of challenges has not deterred the EU from actively pursuing its ambitious plan to implement climate governance policies. Within the realm of literature exploring the EU's approach to climate governance amid such turbulent times, diverse conclusions have emerged. Some scholars posit that solutions to these crises lie in the promotion of EU energy policies (Jordan et al., 2010). Furthermore, it is argued that addressing the long-term challenges could not only foster resilience but also bolster popular support for the EU (Schulmeister, 2019). There are even suggestions that this may lead to the formulation of a new 'constitutional settlement' (Nicolaidis, 2019). However, an opposing viewpoint contends that the aftermath of the post-2008 financial and economic crisis has impeded the EU's ability to develop credible climate and environmental policies, resulting in policy stagnation and raising the possibility of complete dismantlement (Gravey & Jordan, 2020). Moreover, the advent of right-wing populism has added a layer of complexity, rendering the passage of climate-related issues and policies even more challenging (Schaller & Carius, 2019). This socio-political shift has created impediments, complicating the EU's ability to navigate and enact effective climate governance measures.

The ongoing debate has addressed the institutional dynamics and shifts in EU governance to a limited extent, particularly in response to crises. Fabbrini and Capati (2023) provide a valuable starting point for this discussion by asserting that the prevailing power dynamics within the EU's governance system have transitioned from 'unconstrained intergovernmentalism' – a governance model employed during the European financial crisis, involving an increasing number of policy decisions by member states of the euro area. They propose a shift toward what they term 'constrained supranationalism', wherein the Commission's decision-making authority is somewhat augmented (also explored by Butti and Fabbrinni, 2022). While their study illuminates the EU's distinctive logic in addressing crises with significant economic implications, we argue that the progression towards constrained supranationalism requires a more thorough exploration. For that reason, we delve into the literature on the EU governance system produced over the past decade to better grasp its institutional evolution. Our goal is to unravel the basic mechanism through which the shift towards constrained supranationalism materialises and its implications for the EU's response to crises. In so doing, we hope to stimulate further research into the interplay between institutional dynamics and crisis-induced transformations within the EU governance framework, that have been outlined in the introductory chapter by Mišík and Figulová (Chapter 1).

Over the past few decades, the process of supranationalisation has permeated the European Union's (EU) regulatory network. The European Commission has not only become part of the pre-existing transnational network of national agencies but has also played an active role in fostering the establishment of new ones (Majone 2005; Eberlein and Newman 2008; Levi-Faur 2011; Thatcher 2011). This infiltration into the regulatory landscape has facilitated the Commission's efforts to expand its authority through various channels. One avenue through which this happened was by enhancing its organisational capacity to fulfil a monitoring role over EU agencies (Groenleer, 2009). Simultaneously, agencies themselves have strategically leveraged expertise and rule-making processes, what provided them with unapparelled autonomy and a served them as a protective shield against excessive external influences (Ossege, 2016). This strategic empowerment of agencies challenges conventional state's hierarchies and underscores the complexity of the evolving regulatory environment within the EU. A noteworthy aspect, as highlighted by a study among EU agency managers, is the perception that EU agencies wield greater power compared to national ministries or their counterparts in other nations (Egeberg and Trondal, 2011). Crucially, within the supranational regulatory network of the EU, national agencies, while operating under national ministries, also contribute to the EU's multilevel administrative order (Egeberg and Trondal, 2017). This interconnectedness further complicates the dynamics of EU governance, blurring the lines between national and supranational entities. In general, a key indicator of the supranationalisation of the EU's administration is the trend towards a 'more direct' administration, with EU agencies increasingly taking on a growing number of regulatory tasks (ibid, 2017).

Given this context, we conceptualise 'creeping supranationalism' in environmental policy integration as a dynamic process with three distinct but overlapping features. First, the European Commission's *cross-sectoral strategy* aims to align EGD goals with other policies, extending its competencies into policy areas that are formally beyond its legal remit. The second approach employed by the Commission, closely connected to the first one, is that of *legal strategy* – establishing non-legislative yet legally binding acts, specifically in the form of delegated acts, thereby bypassing formal legislative procedures. Borrowing from Mann (1986, 2008), the third approach is *infrastructural strategy*. This refers to the Commission's capacity to utilise the pre-existing set of institutions, wherein power is diffused, emphasising a 'power-through' approach which, in turn, shapes and influences the normative and cognitive beliefs of other actors by deploying ideational elements. A detailed look at each strategy employed by the Commission is provided in the next part of this chapter.

In contrast to Wong's perspective (2015), our interpretation does not characterise this process as erratic but rather as path-dependent, contingent on decisions made in the past and relying on the existing web of institutions, set of practices and rules. We acknowledge the historical trajectories and decisions that have shaped the Commission's evolving role in environmental policy integration (for a brief overview see the introductory chapter of this volume). Furthermore, the Commission's actions are not haphazard; rather they are contingent on past choices, policy developments, and existing institutional frameworks. This underscores the deliberate and structured nature of the Commission's incremental expansion into policy domains traditionally outside its purview and deployment of various strategies (cross-sectoral, legal and infrastructural) to reach its objectives. In other words, the term 'creeping supranationalism' captures the gradual, yet purposeful, manner in which the Commission strategically broadens its influence across various policy sectors. The crux of this phenomenon lies in the intentional alignment of EGD objectives with disparate policy areas, fostering a more integrated and cohesive approach to environmental governance.

1.3 The European Green Deal governance

The EGD goals and policies infiltrate into various sectoral areas. The EU's attempts to govern its environmental policy can be traced to the Amsterdam Treaty. Introduced in 2019, the EGD consists of 11 initiatives. They all have unified goal: to increase the EU's Climate ambition for 2030 and 2050. This should be reached by adopting the European Climate pact and climate law. EGD has set the ambitious plan to take measures to accelerate the shift to sustainable and smart mobility, to mobilise industry for a clean and circular economy, to supply clean, affordable and secure energy, and also to build and renovate in an energy- and resource-efficient way so the EU becomes a global leader in sustainable future. Further initiatives aim to achieve zero pollution for a toxic-free environment, to finance green projects, to preserve and restore ecosystems and biodiversity, to reach a fair, healthy and environmentally friendly food system called "From farm to fork", as well as to leave no one behind (just transition) (European Commission, 2019).

What our contribution aims to do is to investigate Commission's strategies in influencing the implementation of the EGD and identify the features of 'supranationalising' tendencies in the EU's governance. In what follows we elaborate on the understanding of 'creeping supranationalism' by studying it alongside three interconnected and overlapping features or strategies mentioned above: cross-sectoral, legal and infrastructural.

1.3.1 Cross-sectoral strategy

The European Climate Law serves as a pivotal instrument in translating the EGD goals into legally binding obligations, endowing the European Commission with substantial leverage over member states in the realm of green governance. The primary objective of this legislation is to establish a robust legal foundation for the effective implementation of carbon pricing mechanisms throughout the European economy.

Central to this is the flagship initiative of revising the Energy Taxation Directive (ETD), initially adopted in 2003. The revised directive seeks to set minimum tax rates on various energy types, preventing member countries from engaging in price dumping to gain a competitive advantage. While the existing ETD predominantly focuses on internal market objectives, the proposed revision prioritises environmental impact considerations. Unveiled by the Commission on 14 July 2021, the revision of the ETD aims to align the taxation of energy products with the overarching goals of the EU's energy and climate policies. Notably, the proposed revision aims to promote clean technologies while addressing outdated exemptions and reduced tax rates that might incentivise the continued use of fossil fuels. The envisioned changes introduce a novel tax rate structure based on both the energy content and environmental performance of fuels and electricity. This approach reflects a nuanced understanding of the need to incentivise and prioritise environmentally friendly energy sources while discouraging reliance on fossil fuels. Moreover, the revised directive broadens the taxable base by expanding its scope to include additional products, thereby ensuring a more comprehensive and impactful approach to energy taxation (Kostova Karaboytcheva, 2022).

The proposal introduces a tax rate structure, that departs from the prevailing volume-based system, to align with the energy content and environmental impact of fuels and electricity. In redefining the structure of tax rates, the plan advocates for a new approach by establishing minimum tax rates that are contingent on the real energy content of products, denominated in euros per gigajoules, and their environmental performance. Departure from the conventional volume-based structure is poised to provide businesses and individuals with more transparent and informative price signals and empower them to make informed decisions that prioritise cleaner, energy-efficient, and climate-friendly choices. Under the current framework, diesel used as a motor fuel, is subject to a lower minimum tax rate as compared to gasoline that is used for the same purpose. The proposed changes seek to rectify this discrepancy, ensuring a more equitable taxation approach. By establishing new minimum rates that are linked to energy content, the proposal aims to eliminate distortions in the market, fostering fair competition and incentivising the adoption of cleaner energy alternatives.

The proposal will have a significant impact on the convergence of effective national tax rates across Member States. The harmonisation of minimum rates and the expansion of the taxable base are expected to contribute to a more uniform taxation landscape, promoting consistency and coherence in the application of energy taxes. This convergence is particularly relevant for a majority of items, further reinforcing the proposal's commitment to creating a level playing field within the European Union (European Commission, 2021). The proposed restructuring of tax rates represents an important shift towards a more transparent, equitable, and environmentally conscious taxation framework. Linking minimum rates to energy content and environmental performance, the proposal not only addresses existing imbalances, but also lays the foundation for a cohesive and harmonised approach to energy taxation across Member States.

However, a caveat exists in that the Council must unanimously agree to adopt this revision. Despite the potential workaround provided by categorising the ETD revision as an environmental concern, the ultimate approval of such a measure hinges on achieving unanimity within the Council first. At the time of writing (December 2023) it seems that member states are reluctant to proceed with the ETD any further, thus the debates are currently deadlocked, with little prospect of moving forward under the future European Council Presidencies (Kurmayer and Packroff, 2023). However, if this legislation were to be approved, a pivotal transformation would occur in the voting dynamics on taxes within this domain – shifting from unanimity to a qualified majority under the ordinary legislative procedure.

1.3.2 Legal strategy

A critical aspect of Commission's empowerment in the realm of EGD involves its responsibility to scrutinise key policy instruments (Bongardt and Torres 2021). In instances where revisions are deemed necessary, the Commission is tasked with proposing the requisite amendments. This process aims to ensure that all policies within the European Union align with the overarching goal of achieving climate neutrality. Commission possesses the authority to issue recommendations to member states whose actions diverge from the climate-neutrality objective. Member states are obliged to duly consider these recommendations or alternatively provide a clear justification for non-compliance. This authority is exercised through Delegated acts, as stipulated in Article 290 of the Treaty on the Functioning of the European Union (TFEU), which empowers the Commission to modify or supplement legislation.

System of delegated acts include that the Council and the EP jointly decide to delegate powers to the Commission, which can be controlled by each of the two institutions. Nevertheless, it would be wrong to assume that the Council and the EP join forces in scrutinising the Commission. As Brandsma (2016) reports, in the interviews conducted with EP administrators before the official scrutiny period begins, EP lacks power but can exert influence. However, once the scrutiny period starts, EP gains power but often struggles to exert influence within the short time limits agreed upon for scrutiny. This challenge was evident in a rare case where the Commission sent a controversial delegated act shortly before Christmas with a one-month veto deadline, leading to a rushed committee decision in January that ultimately avoided an objection. The current system of delegated acts instigated heightened accountability towards the EP, both de jure and de facto, notably with the EP gaining the authority to veto delegated acts for any reason, thereby introducing a politicisation of accountability for this type of measure.

Preparing phase of delegated acts is particularly important (Kaeding and Hardacre, 2010). The system's practice of deploying staff members to the Commission's expert groups empowers the EP to identify potentially contentious measures and influence decision-making within the Commission before the finalisation of delegated acts, leading to increased interaction between the Commission and the EP. Commission staff are often invited to closed-door meetings with EP committee members, such as party group coordinators, to share information about upcoming delegated acts and discuss them. During these encounters, the Commission may focus on updating EP, ensuring the smooth passage of delegated acts, and/or strategically framing the political dynamics, including implying potential blame on the EP in case the act would not pass (Brandsma, 2016). On another occasion, when the Commission introduced its initial delegated acts on energy efficiency labelling regulation, a dispute between the Council and the Commission arose due to the Commission's joint consultation with national experts alongside other experts. In this instance, the Council argued for separate consultations with member state experts and emphasised the need for drafts of delegated acts with clear explanations of which comments would be considered, revealing a "fundamental lack of trust in delegating powers to the Commission without the control member states had under the old comitology rules" (Christiansen and Dobbels, 2012).

A delegated act played a pivotal role in the process of adopting the ban on combustion engines. This measure is deemed indispensable for achieving the Commission's target of reducing emissions by 55% by 2030. Despite prompting varied responses from EU member states,[1] the act was successfully passed and ratified by the European Parliament in February 2023. Consequently, starting from 2035, all new cars entering the market are mandated to have zero CO_2 emissions, facilitating the vision of having an entire transport sector that is carbon-neutral by 2050. However, in early March 2023, the issue was tabled for a vote in the Council of the EU. Germany dissented, necessitating discussions with the Commission and Berlin to address the disagreement. The EC eventually yielded to Germany's stance and has undertaken a modification of regulations to accommodate vehicles utilising e-fuels.[2] Thus, in late March 2023, the Commission committed establish a distinct legal category for vehicles exclusively running on e-fuels. As part of this initiative, the EU executive intends to append a delegated act to the 2035 legislation, thereby exempting this new vehicle class from the zero-emissions obligation outlined in the CO_2 targets (Leali et al., 2023). This move reflects somehow adaptive response to national concerns, underscoring the sensitive relations between EU regulatory bodies and individual member states in shaping environmental policies.

1.3.3 Infrastructural and ideational strategy

Commission activities as described here resemble what Mann (1986, 1988, 2008) termed infrastructural power, i.e. the capacity of state to penetrate society and logistically implement decisions throughout its territory. In a similar manner, the existing system of EU agencies is responsible for dispersing their control/power through the society, what signifies the 'power through' approach, rather than power over. In essence, the infrastructural power relates to the capacity to have a full presence in the territories that are under its realm and are to act 'at the source', that is, to have regulative capacity without coercion (Mann, 2008).[3] For that purpose, the Commission often uses the pre-existing network of agencies, which are connected to the EU level of governance and also tapped to the member states via set of national agencies; together these create the EU's complicated multi-level governance system.

Thus, in implementing the EGD, the Commission relies on a complex network of pre-existing set of agencies and other relevant institutions that would be responsible for monitoring, implementation and evaluation of the proposed policies. One of them is the European Climate, Infrastructure and Environment Executive Agency (CINEA). The agency has undergone an interesting transformative journey marked by name changes and an expanded mandate, while maintaining consistent leadership. CINEA assumed roles ascribed to the Innovation and Networks Executive Agency (INEA) which is, in turn, the successor to the Trans-European Transport Network Executive Agency (TEN-T EA), created by the European

Commission in 2006, to manage the technical and financial implementation of its TEN-T programme.

What makes CINEA quite interesting is the fact that it is an executive agency. This has consequences when it comes to its control and accountability mechanisms, legal status or operational designs, compared to existing agencies in the EU's governance system. Executive agencies, compared to others, are *pro tempore* agencies established and closely monitored by the European Commission to perform managerial tasks, aiding in the implementation of EU financial support programmes. They have a unique structure, comprising a steering committee with five members and an executive director appointed by the Commission (see Vos, 2013). Thus, initially assigned responsibilities in managing Community programmes, executive agencies are currently effectively overseen by the Commission, with their annual activity reports appended to the relevant Commission Directorate-General reports.

CINEA is structured into four broad departments: Department A – Programme support and resources (covering overall coordination, evaluation, communication, legal affairs, external audits, administrative and operational finance, HR, IT and logistics); Department B – Sustainable networks and investments (covering the CEF Transport and CEF Energy programmes plus the Just Transition Mechanism and Renewable Energy Financing Mechanism); Department C – Green research and innovation (covering the cluster on Climate, Energy and Mobility from the Horizon Europe Programme and the Innovation Fund programmes) and Department D – Natural resources, climate, sustainable blue economy and clean energy (covering the LIFE funding instrument for the environment and climate action, sustainable Blue Economy and European Maritime, Fisheries and Aquaculture Fund programmes). From this brief glimpse at CINEA's organisational structure, it becomes evident that the agency has become, over time, intertwined in complicated web of relations and diverse portfolios. Branching out into different policy domains means that it is not under the purview of just one, but rather several of the Commission's DGs.

The agency has not only taken over full responsibility for managing ongoing TEN-T projects but has also expanded its scope to include the technical and financial management of the Connecting Europe Facility (CEF) and parts of the Horizon 2020 programme (Stephenson 2022). Since 2021, it is tasked with supporting the EGD agenda by overseeing the implementation of related delegated programmes. Another crucial tool for realising the ambitious decarbonisation objectives set forth by the EU is therefore CEF, through which the Commission seeks to channel investments into the infrastructure, innovation, and sustainable technologies, fostering an interconnected and environmentally conscious transport network. This underscores the EU's commitment to achieving decarbonisation targets and also exemplifies an effort to harmonise and propel sustainable transport initiatives across member states. The CEF, therefore, assumes a crucial role in the broader framework of the EGD, contributing substantially to the realisation of a decarbonised and sustainable future for European transportation. It serves as a mechanism facilitating the planning and execution of projects aimed at bolstering the trans-European transport network, encompassing the domains of transport, energy, and telecommunications. Operated directly by the European Commission, it is akin to other Community instruments, and assumes an important role in advancing the European Union's infrastructural objectives.

The distribution of CEF funds among Union member states is executed through calls for proposals managed by both the CINEA and DG MOVE. Notably, the legislative framework governing the CEF does not explicitly delineate the percentage distribution of resources across different modes of transport. Nevertheless, the European Commission has proactively urged member states to accord precedence to the construction and modernisation of rail corridors and other modes of 'sustainable transport'. While the legislative provisions do not prescribe specific allocations, there exists a general directive to limit road infrastructure development to a maximum of 10%, underscoring a preference for the advancement of more sustainable transportation modalities. Overall, as noted by Stephenson (2022) 'the institutional spillover' in case of the agency is quite apparent, when an increasing number of tasks and implementation activities are delegated to it and its mandate has broadened, what becomes evident is the agency's authority to delegate tasks via national intermediaries at the member state level.

1.4 Implications of the creeping supranationalism

The three abovementioned Commission strategies in the green transition do not exhaust all the possibilities through which 'creeping supranationalism' manifests its traits. Rather these strategies should be seen as complementary to the broader trend of shifting the EU's system of governance as a response to the crisis from 'unconstrained intergovernmentalism' to 'constrained supranationalism' (Fabbrini and Capati, 2023).

First, the Commission's *cross-sectoral strategy* of connecting the EGD goals to other sectoral policies means expanding its competencies to policy areas in which it has no or limited powers. In essence, the revision of the ETD, as guided by the European Climate Law, represents a crucial step towards aligning fiscal policies with environmental obligations. By incorporating clean technologies and reconfiguring tax rates based on environmental considerations, the Commission's revised directive positions itself as a key tool in realising the transformative goals set forth in the EGD. In other words, the European Commission has devised a strategy to circumvent the unanimity constraint by framing the revision of the ETD primarily as an environmental issue rather than a tax matter, given its integral role in the achieving the EGD goals. According to EU law, decisions pertaining to environmental matters can be reached through a qualified majority, thus avoiding the need for unanimous agreement. The member states bear full responsibility for tax collection and control within their territories, a vital function aimed at fulfilling budgetary requirements. It is what could be described as a state's basic prerogative to collect and set taxes, i.e. this represents its "core state" power (see Genschel and Jachtenfuchs, 2014). Beyond the economic dimension, taxation is also regarded by member states as integral to national security, particularly in critical sectors like energy supply. In this context, certain member states contend that the unanimity rule serves as a safeguard, ensuring the preservation of national sovereignty in taxation matters, acting as a bulwark against any undesirable changes imposed at the EU level. Furthermore, the unanimity principle is, in many countries, perceived as a mechanism to uphold national autonomy and prevent unwarranted alterations in taxation policies that could potentially impact critical national interests.

Second, facilitation of the *legal strategy* by the Commission disadvantages the intergovernmental Council and the EP, because increasing the pace by which the delegated acts are produced creates time shortages and the latter two institutions often lack the necessary expert capacities to assess each legislation thoroughly. Initially, the number of delegated acts was relatively modest, and the EP appeared adept at efficiently managing their scrutiny. Nevertheless, with the continual adoption of new legislation and the alignment of existing legislation with the provisions of the Lisbon Treaty, the delegated acts system is expected to be increasingly applied. In fact, according to the official EU register, the number of delegated acts between 2010–2014 was 239, between 2015–2019 it increased to 814 and just in the past three years (January 2021 – November 2023) 797 delegated acts were proposed (European Union, 2023). Consequently, with the expected intensification of the Commission's legislative activity the EP and the Council will essentially confront challenges related to manpower shortages when monitoring all delegated acts produced, making it progressively difficult to maintain effective control.

Third, the *infrastructural strategy* is intertwined with the previous two and refers to the implementation capacity to penetrate the civil society without coercive mechanism by committing to fulfil policies proposed (Mann, 1988). This includes a commitment to specific financial endowments and maintaining professional member states administrative core connected to the EU's bureaucracy (Trondal, 2010). The 'power through' highlights another trend in the process of European governance that refers to the capacity of the actors in the EU to shape and redefine the normative and cognitive beliefs of other actors through deployment of ideational elements (Carstensen and Schmidt, 2016). This usually manifests informally, via discourse or during a complicated set of deliberative processes which various consultatory and preparatory bodies of the Commission, EP or Council usually go through. The discursive practices through which the EGD is framed was evident right from the outset when the Commission President von der Leyen, speaking in front of the EP, compared the deal to "Europe's man on the moon moment". In fact, in terms of discourse, the Commission envisions itself as the main actor overseeing the realisation of the implementation the green transformation through incentives, regulations and funding programmes. Furthermore, the ideological underpinning of the EGD redefines the relationship between economic growth and environmental policies, when the social and economic policies should now serve to environmental considerations to create a sustainable living condition on Earth for the next generations. Coupled with the 'numerous ambitiously worded legislative proposals' (Schunz, 2023, 20), it is evident that the Commission strategically envisions the EU as a leading force in the drive to transform Europe into the first 'climate-neutral continent'. This vision emphasises the need for societal support, underlining the indispensability of citizen participation. The Commission reinforces this by emphasising that the EGD is designed for the benefit of the 'EU and its citizens' which in turn legitimises its 'strong governance' over this complex framework of innovations (see Molek-Kozakowska, 2023, 192).

1.5 Conclusion

The aim of this chapter is to point out different strategies through which the Commissions attempts to exert influence and ownership in early days of implementing the EGD. This can be perceived, in part, as an endeavour to reshape the Union's governance system, particularly in the context of an ambitious environmental policy. The Commission pursues a strategy of connecting the EGD goals to other sectoral policies and, by so doing, it expands its competencies to policy areas outside its legal remit, into certain extent affecting the 'state core powers' (see Genschel and Jachtenfuchs, 2014). Not only does such a 'climate policy integration' (von Homeyer, Oberthür and Jordan, 2021) cement the Commission's governing authority, but it illustrates also broader trends in the process of European integration, where the Commission has become an important agenda setter of EU policies (see Mišík and Oravcová, 2022).

The overarching goals of the EGD to achieve carbon neutrality for the continent by 2050 share a common approach – anchoring these ambitious targets through legally binding acts, specifically in the form of delegated acts, thereby bypassing formal legislative procedures. Consequently, carbon neutrality by 2050 is now legally binding for all member states that are also mandated to adapt their policies incrementally, addressing specific sectors under Commission's purview. Notably, these sectors traditionally fall within the realm of member states' responsibilities, implying a reconfiguration of power dynamics in favour of the EU's competences.

Although, at the time of writing (December 2023), there are still a lot of unanswered questions, proposals pending and, in some cases, it seems even political deadlock, we contend that the Commission's strategies alluded to in this chapter are visible even now and it becomes an intriguing prospect to observe how and to what extent they will be facilitated in fulfilling these green targets. Furthermore, it would be interesting to see whether their practical implementation in the social and economic fields influences the institutional power relations within the Union as it was suggested here.

Acknowledgements

This chapter was supported by the Slovak Research and Development Agency Grant No APVV-20-0012.

Notes

1 Objections were raised by following countries: Germany, Italy, Poland, Bulgaria, Czech Republic.

2 E-fuels are synthetic alternative to fossil fuels made from hydrogen and CO_2 that is cleaner than conventional gasoline but still emits some greenhouse gases.
3 Mann uses an example of state's ability to collect taxes every month without the need to intervene in the process.

References

Becker, S. (2024). Supranational entrepreneurship through the administrative backdoor: The commission, the Green Deal and the CAP 2023–2027. *JCMS Journal of Common Market Studies*, 62(3), 688–704. https://doi.org/10.1111/jcms.13522

Bocquillon, P., Brooks, E., & Maltby, T. (2023). Talkin' bout a revolution? Institutional change in the EU Recovery and Resilience Facility: The case of climate policy. *JCMS: Journal of Common Market Studies*, 1–21. https://doi.org/10.1111/jcms.13536

Bongardt, A., & Torres, F. S. (2021). The European Green Deal: More than an exit strategy to the pandemic crisis, a building block of sustainable European economic model. Available at: https:onlinelibrary.wiley.com/doi/10.1111/jcms.13264

Brandsma, G. J. (2016). Holding the European Commission to account: The promise of delegated acts. *International Review of Administrative Sciences*, *82*(4), 656–673. https://doi.org/10.1177/0020852315583195

Brodny, J., Tutak, M., & Saki, S. A. (2020). Forecasting the structure of energy production from renewable energy sources and biofuels in Poland. *Energies*, *13*(10), 1–31. https://doi.org/10.3390/en13102539

Buti, M., & Fabbrini, S. (2022). Next generation EU and the future of economic governance: Towards a paradigm change or just a big one-off? *Journal of European Public Policy*, *30*(4), 676–695.

Carstensen, M. B. & Schmidt, V. A. (2016). Power through, over and in ideas: conceptualizing ideational power in discursive institutionalism. *Journal of European Public Policy*, *23*(3), 318–337. https://doi.org/10.1080/13501763.2015.1115534

Christiansen, T. & Dobbels, M. (2012). Comitology and delegated acts after Lisbon: How the European Parliament lost the implementation game. *European Integration online Papers* (EIoP), Vol. 16, Article 13, 1–23. http://eiop.or.at/eiop/texte/2012-013a.htm

Domorenok, E., & Graziano, P. (2023). Understanding the European Green Deal: A narrative policy framework approach. *European Policy Analysis*, *9*(1), 9–29. https://doi.org/10.1002/epa2.1168

Eberlein, B. & Newman, A. L. (2008). Escaping the international governance dilemma? Incorporated transgovernmental networks in the European Union. *Governance*, *21*(1), 25–52.

Egeberg, M., & Trondal, J. (2011). EU-level agencies: New executive centre formation or vehicles for national control? *Journal of European Public Policy*, *18*(6), 868–887.

Egeberg, M., & Trondal, J. (2017). Researching European Union agencies: What have we learnt (and where do we go from here)? *JCMS: Journal of Common Market Studies*, *55*(4), 675–690.

Egeberg, M., Trondal, J., & Vestlund, N. M. (2015). The quest for order: Unravelling the relationship between the European Commission and European Union agencies. *Journal of European Public Policy*, *22*(5), 609–629.

European Commission (2019). European Green Deal. https://eur-lex.europa.eu/legal-content/EN/TXT/?uri=COM%3A2019%3A640%3AFIN (accessed 18 December 2023).

European Commission (2021). Revision of the Energy Taxation Directive (ETD): Questions and answers. https://ec.europa.eu/commission/presscorner/detail/en/qanda_21_3662 (accessed 19 December 2023).

European Union. Interinstitutional register of delegated acts (2023). https://webgate.ec.europa.eu/regdel/#/delegatedActs?lang=en (accessed 19 December 2023).

Everson, M., & Joerges, C. (2006). Re-conceptualising Europeanisation as a public law of collisions: Comitology, agencies and an interactive public adjudication, in H. C. H. Hofmann and A. H. Turk (Eds), *EU Administrative Governance*. Cheltenham: Edward Elgar, 521–540.

Fabbrini, S., & Capati, A. (2023). Adjustments in economic crises: The different outcome of the sovereign debt and pandemic crisis in Europe. In D. Adamski, F. Amtenbrink, & J. de Haan (Eds), *Cambridge Handbook on European Monetary, Economic and Financial Market Integration*. Cambridge: Cambridge University Press, 363–376.

Genschel, P., & Jachtenfuchs, M. (Eds) (2014). *Beyond The Regulatory Polity?: The European Integration of Core State Powers.* Oxford: Oxford University Press.

Gravey, V., & Jordan, A. J. (2020). Policy dismantling at EU level: Reaching the limits of 'an ever-closer ecological union'? *Public Administration*, *98*(2), 349–362. https://doi.org/10.1111/padm.12605

Groenleer, M. L. P. (2009). *The Autonomy of European Union Agencies*. Delft: Eburon.

Hafner, M., & Raimondi, P. P. (2021). Priorities and challenges of the EU energy transition: From the European Green Package to the new Green Deal. *Russian Journal of Economics*, *6*(4), 374–389. https://doi.org/10.32609/J.RUJE.6.55375

Heritier, A. (1997). Policymaking by subterfuge: Interest accommodation, innovation and substitute democratic legitimation in Europe-perspectives from distinctive policy areas. *Journal of European Public Policy, 4*(2), 171–189.

Hrnčić, B., Pfeifer, A., Jurić, F., Duić, N., Ivanović, V., & Vušanović, I. (2021). Different investment dynamics in energy transition towards a 100% renewable energy system. *Energy*, *237*. 1–11. https://doi.org/10.1016/j.energy.2021.121526

Jäger-Waldau, A., Kougias, I., Taylor, N., & Thiel, C. (2020). How photovoltaics can contribute to GHG emission reductions of 55% in the EU by 2030. *Renewable and Sustainable Energy Reviews*, *126*, 1–8. https://doi.org/10.1016/j.rser.2020.109836

Jordan, A. J., Huitema, D., van Asselt, H., Rayner, T., & Berkhout, F. (Eds) (2010). *Climate Change Policy in the European Union: Confronting the Dilemmas of Mitigation and Adaptation?* Cambridge: Cambridge University Press.

Kaeding, M., & Hardacre, A. (2010). The execution of delegated powers after Lisbon. *A timely analysis of the Regulatory Procedure with Scrutiny and its lessons for Delegated Acts*. Florence: European University Institute.

Kostova Karaboytcheva, M. (2022). *Revision of the Energy Taxation Directive: Fit for 55 package*. European Parliament Research Service. Available here: www.europarl.europa.eu/RegData/etudes/BRIE/2022/698883/EPRS_BRI(2022)698883_EN.pdf (accessed 19 December 2023).

Kulovesi, K., & Oberthür, S. (2020). Assessing the EU's 2030 Climate and Energy Policy Framework: Incremental change toward radical transformation? *Review of European, Comparative and International Environmental Law*, *29*(2), 151–166. https://doi.org/10.1111/reel.12358

Kurmayer, N. J., & Packroff, J. (2023). Energy Taxation Directive: Europe's key climate law stuck in a quagmire. www.euractiv.com/section/energy-environment/news/energy-taxation-directive-europes-key-climate-law-stuck-in-a-quagmire/ (accessed 19 December 2023).

Leali, G., Posaner, J., & von der Burchard, H. (2023). Germany wins Pyrrhic victory in the war to save the car engine. Available here: www.politico.eu/article/germany-pyrrhic-victory-war-save-car-engine/ (accessed 19 December 2023).

Levi-Faur, D. (2011). Regulatory networks and regulatory agencification: Towards a single European regulatory space. *Journal of European Public Policy*, *18*(6), 810–29.

Maggetti, M. (2015). Hard and soft governance. In K. Lynggaard, I. Manners, K. Löfgren (Eds), *Research Methods in European Union Studies*. London: Palgrave Macmillan, 252–265.

Majone, G. (1996). *Regulating Europe. European Public Policy Series.* London, New York: Routledge.

Majone, G. (2005). *Dilemmas of European Integration*. Oxford: Oxford University Press.

Mann, M. (1986). The Sources of Social Power: A History of Power from the Beginning to A.D. 1760. Cambridge: Cambridge University Press.

Mann, M. (1988). *States, War, and Capitalism: Studies in Political Sociology B*. Oxford, UK: Blackwell.

Mann, M. (2008). Infrastructural power revisited. *Studies in Comparative International Development*, 43(3), 355–365.

Mišík, M. & Oravcová, V. (2022). Ex Ante Governance in the European Union: Energy and climate policy as a 'test run' for the post-pandemic recovery. *Energy Policy*, 167, article no. 113076. https://doi.org/10.1016/j.enpol.2022.113076

Molek-Kozakowska, K. (2024). The hybrid discourse of the 'European Green Deal': Road-mapping economic transition to environmental sustainability (almost) seamlessly. *Critical Discourse Studies*, *21*(2), 182–199.

Nicolaïdis, K. (2019). Sustainable integration: The silver lining of a democratically challenged EU. In Twelve Stars Initiative, Bertelsmann Stiftung (Eds). *Twelve Stars: Philosophers chart a course for Europe. Gütersloh:* Bertelsmann Stiftung, 117–126.

Oberthür, S., & Von Homeyer, I. (2023). From emissions trading to the European Green Deal: The evolution of the climate policy mix and climate policy integration in the EU. *Journal of European Public Policy*, *30*(3), 445–468.

Ossege, C. (2016). *European Regulatory Agencies in EU Decision-Making*. Basingstoke: Palgrave Macmillan.

Ossewaarde, M., & Ossewaarde-Lowtoo, R. (2020). The EU's Green Deal: A third alternative to green growth and degrowth? *Sustainability, 12*, 9825. doi:10.3390/su12239825

Paul, J. S. (2022). The physical completion of the EU's single market: trans-European networks as experimentalist governance? *Journal of European Integration*, *44*(1), 99–115. doi:10.1080/07036337.2021.2011268

Pollak, J., & Riekmann, S.P. (2008). European administration: Centralisation and fragmentation as means of polity-building? *West European Politics*, *31*(4), 771–788.

Radaelli, C. M. (2003) *The Open Method of Co-ordination* (Research Report: Swedish Institute for European Policy Studies).

Ruffing, E. (2022). European (networked) agencies between independence and influence. *Journal of European Public Policy*, *29*, 1546–1567.

Ruffing, E., Weinrich, M., Rittberger, B., & Wonka, A. (2023). The European administrative space over time: Mapping the formal independence of EU agencies. *Regulation & Governance*. 1–21.

Sachs, J. D. (2019). "Europe's Green Deal." Project Syndicate. December 13. Available here: www.project-syndicate.org/commentary/europe-green-deal-is-global-beacon-by-jeffrey-d-sachs-2019-12

Samper, J. A., Schockling, A., & Islar, M. (2021). Climate politics in Green Deals: Exposing the political frontiers of the European Green Deal. *Politics and Governance, 9*(2), 8–16.

Schaller, S. & Carius, A. (2019). *Convenient Truths. Mapping Climate Agendas of Right-Wing Populist Parties in Europe*. Berlin: adelphi consult GmbH.

Scharpf, F. W. (1997). Introduction: The Problem-solving capacity of multi-level governance. *Journal of European Public Policy,* 4(4), 520–538.

Schulmeister, P. (Ed.). (2019). Closer to the citizen, closer to the ballot. *Eurobarometer Survey 91.1 of the European Parliament. A Public Opinion Monitoring Study.* Brussels: European Union.

Schunz, S. (2022). The 'European Green Deal' – A paradigm shift? Transformations in the European Union's sustainability meta-discourse. *Political Research Exchange*, *4*(1), 2085121.

Skjærseth, J. B. (2021). Towards a European Green Deal: The evolution of EU climate and energy policy mixes. *International Environmental Agreements: Politics, Law and Economics*, *21*(1), 25–41. https://doi.org/10.1007/s10784-021-09529-4

Thatcher, M. (2011). The creation of European regulatory agencies and its limits: A comparative analysis of European delegation. *Journal of European Public Policy*, *18*(6), 790–809.

Trondal, J. (2010). *An Emergent European Executive Order*. Oxford: Oxford University Press.

Tubiana, L. (2021). The Green Deal is the New Social Contract. Groupe d'Etudes Géopolitiques. Available here: https://geopolitique.eu/en/2021/09/28/laurence-tubiana-green-deal/

Tutak, M., Brodny, J., & Bindzár, P. (2021). Assessing the level of energy and climate sustainability in the European Union countries in the context of the European green deal strategy and agenda 2030. *Energies*, *14*(6), 1–33.

Von Homeyer, I., Oberthür, S., & Jordan, A. J. (2021). EU climate and energy governance in times of crisis: Towards a new agenda. *Journal of European Public Policy*, *28*(7), 959–979.

Vos, Ellen, EU Agencies: Features, Framework and Future (September 16, 2013). In *European agencies in between institutions and Member States*, Michelle Everson, Cosimo Monda, & Ellen Vos (Eds), Kluwer Law Publishing, Forthcoming, Maastricht Faculty of Law Working Paper No. 2013–3, Available at SSRN: https://ssrn.com/abstract=2326361 or http://dx.doi.org/10.2139/ssrn.2326361

Wong, R. (2015). Creeping supranationalism: The EU and ASEAN experiences. In L. Brennan & P. Murray (Eds), *Drivers of Integration and Regionalism in Europe and Asia.* (pp. 267–283). Abingdon: Routledge.

Zeitlin, J., Nicoli, F., & Laffan, B. (2019). Introduction: The European Union beyond the polycrisis? Integration and politicization in an age of shifting cleavages. *Journal of European Public Policy*, *26*(7), 963–976.

2 What does EU energy policy mean to you?

Regional differences in EU citizens' sentiments on energy transition – socio-economic, political and environmental factors

Raffaele Mattera, Demetrio Panarello and Andrea Gatto

2.1 Introduction: Navigating the EU energy transition during the *polycrisis*

The times the EU is currently experiencing can be referred to as an authentic polycrisis (Meissner and Schoeller, 2019; Schimmelfennig, 2022). In a few years, the old continent had to tackle concurring shocks – the COVID-19 outbreak, the 2022 energy crisis, the Russian-Ukrainian war and the resulting inflation (Zakeri et al., 2022; Gatto et al., 2024). These major events exacerbated existing (youth) unemployment, corruption, demographics, migration, Brexit, cohesion, bureaucratic problems and further structural issues of an experimental, sui generis and benchmarking democracy as the EU (Erokhin, 2019). This multi-layered crisis is even more complex if we consider that COVID-19 has been referred to as an ecosyndemic besides being a pandemic (Begou and Kassomenos, 2023).

All these major adverse events sum up to the vigorous strive to meet the net zero goal promoted by the EU (Caineng et al., 2021). The EU's decarbonisation ambitions have attracted great political interest and immediate policy action within the EU (Dorsch et al., 2020). In the last few years, the European Green Deal, climate change and the ecological and energy transition have become a cornerstone for global energy transitions and sustainable development. Following the first energy price fluctuations, the Russian attack on Ukraine, the energy crises and the resulting inflation, different reactions have been advocated by politicians, policymakers, analysts and academics (Steffen and Patt, 2022).

The energy transition has become a contended standing point for propaganda and cheap talks from any observer. On the one hand, (heavy) decarbonisation has been saluted as the salvific panacea for tackling environmental issues, ensuring new (green) jobs and creating more just societies. On the other hand, the new crises were seen as a chance to get rid of these avoidable expenses and get back to cheaper, more stable and consolidated fossil fuels consumption. Populisms and chauvinisms

DOI: 10.4324/9781032624839-4

found fertile terrain to proliferate in this environment as well as national individualistic mires (Riedel, 2021; Fabry, 2019; Freeman, 2021; Mišík and Oravcová, 2022; Hansen and Knolle, 2022; Nosko and Ušiak, 2023; Mišík and Nosko, 2023).

Summing up, two notable sets of multi-layered and interconnected problems arose. First, the world – especially the EU – concretely realised the myopic extent of delegating most of its energy demand to external partners, particularly non-democratic states. Thus, the new perspectives after the war outbreak changed the ongoing politics and relationships between the EU and its partners – above all economic, commercial and energy agreements with Russia. Most EU and European countries realised the risk and cost of being dependent on Russia for energy and thus promptly interrupted or gradually loosened their agreements to find new energy provisioning. This choice was not contemplated by all EU members and European countries, generating additional political instability within the EU. While for the US this decision was less painful due to their oil, gas and other reserves, this option had huge socio-economic implications for the EU. At the same time, the new business and supply agreements that were signed were with other dictatorships or autocracies and the costs of the provisions were not as favourable as those previously signed with Russia. Furthermore, cutting the previous supply agreements meant suspending large infrastructure and project investments, such as NordStream 2.

Second, these new issues popped up amidst a period of great investment, expansion and media coverage for decarbonisation and energy and ecological transition projects. So many governments and researchers wondered if it was the right moment to push investments in renewables and alternative energy sources, considering the huge financial and economic problems. These questions meant revisiting the EU's ecological agreements which had only been agreed after a great deal of effort. Any of the paths embarked on would translate into exponential sacrifices for the EU and its citizens. Nevertheless, the European Commission successfully established a blueprint to keep its decarbonisation commitment, macroeconomic policy coordination and the Recovery and Resilience Plan – regardless of the different domestic positions. These policies were initially drafted in the aftermath of the COVID-19 pandemic and were eventually consolidated against a background of war, the energy crisis and high inflation (de la Porte and Jensen, 2021; Pianta et al., 2021; Vanhercke and Verdun, 2022).

It is easy to understand that these problems constitute urgent open conundrums which are likely to determine decisions for the EU, its member states, partners and the whole continent. First and foremost, these problems imply major energy security and sovereignty directions having strong repercussions for both regional and national political stability (Mišík, 2022). To cope with this major issue, the European Commission has found it of the utmost importance to pursue its energy transition goals (European Commission, 2022). Likewise, clear trade-offs and sustainability issues have arisen since social, economic, environmental and political matters were included (Gatto, 2022).

Considering these timeliness, popularity and importance of the decisions, this situation became a hot topic for EU citizens and public discourse (Steffen and

Patt, 2022). This fact motivates the need for new explorations on EU citizens' perception of the energy transition and related socio-economic, ecological and political matters in this specific historic period. The scarcity of similar studies further highlights this research gap.

Moreover, regional differences do exist within the EU nations and possible opinion clusters. This item is of peculiar interest for a profoundly diverse region such as Europe, especially when it comes to energy mix preferences and strategies and when European integration fails (Szulecki, 2018; Thaler and Pakalkaite, 2021; Gatto and Panarello, 2022; Panarello and Gatto, 2023). This observation nudged us to conduct quantitative geographical analyses to obtain some insight into these aspects. We analyse a number of citizens' perceptions which may possibly be determinant to their interpretation of the EU energy policy. Specifically, we wonder if the transition from fossil fuels to renewables as a means of climate change mitigation and adaptation should be part of the EU energy policy agenda. To follow up on this question, we build up a statistical model to investigate regional specifications on economic, political, social and environmental variables, based on 2019 EU Eurobarometer data on Europeans' attitudes toward the EU energy policy.

While the data used in this analysis predates the 2022 Russian invasion of Ukraine and subsequent geopolitical shifts, the insights derived from this earlier period remain pertinent for understanding underlying trends and attitudes toward renewable energy and energy policy. Although public perceptions may have evolved in response to recent events, the historical context captured by this data provides valuable baseline information. The findings offer a foundational understanding of attitudes and preferences toward renewable energy sources, energy policy, and energy security before the crisis. They serve as a reference point against which potential shifts in public opinion or policy responses can be compared. Additionally, these pre-crisis insights may offer insights into enduring attitudes or trends that have persisted despite the changing geopolitical landscape.

This chapter is organised as follows: in Section 2.1, we provide an overview of the energy transition within the multidimensional crises we are living in and the importance of EU citizens' perception. Section 2.2 describes the data and methods used in this exercise – i.e., the Eurobarometer and spatial econometrics techniques, respectively. Section 2.3 presents the results of our analyses. Finally, Section 2.4 presents concluding remarks, illustrating future speculations on the subjects studied and possible policy venues.

2.2 Data and methodology

2.2.1. Data

The data under consideration is derived from the 2019 Eurobarometer 91.4 survey (ZA7575) regarding European sentiments towards the EU energy policy (European Commission, 2020). This survey stands out as one of the most pertinent inquiries conducted in recent years, specifically focusing on the perspectives of European citizens concerning the EU energy policy. It delves into its priorities, perceived significance, and the sense of responsibility it bears towards critical issues like energy security and the green transition. The survey was administered in 2019 to representative samples of citizens from all 28 EU member countries, including the United Kingdom, which was still an EU member at that time. Our analysis is conducted at the country level. In our examination, we omit the United Kingdom from the sample, to centre our focus on citizens of the current EU member states.

In this context, we scrutinise inquiries pertaining to potential factors influencing citizens' interpretations of the EU energy policy: namely, we wish to give insights into whether the transition from conventional power sources to sustainable green energy, as a strategy to combat climate change, is seen as one of the meanings of the EU energy policy. We employ this as the dependent variable and construct statistical models that encompass six independent variables related to political endorsement and public opinions regarding EU energy priorities, prerequisites for accessing secure energy, and the accountability of European-level institutions with regard to these subjects. All these variables have been converted into a binary form to facilitate the explication of the model outcomes. Table 2.1 presents the fundamental descriptive statistics of the chosen variables, which highlight the proportion of citizens who responded affirmatively (Agree/Tend to agree) to the posed queries.

Our dependent variable (denoted as "y") stems from question QB1 in the Eurobarometer survey. In this question, respondents are tasked with identifying the three most significant interpretations of the EU energy policy from a provided list of nine options. Consequently, y is assigned the value of 1 if the participant indicates "Transitioning from fossil fuels to renewable energy sources for combatting climate change" as one of the primary meanings of the EU energy policy.

Table 2.1 Descriptive statistics of the dataset (n = 26416)

Variable	*Description*	*Min*	*Max*	*% (yes)*
y	"What does EU energy policy mean to you?": Shifting from fossil fuels to renewable energy sources to combat climate change (dep. variable)	0	1	42.18%
x_1	EU energy priorities next 10 years: reduce EU energy imports	0	1	15.14%
x_2	EU energy priorities next 10 years: protect critical energy infrastructure	0	1	20.41%
x_3	Political party: centre	0	1	34.28%
x_4	Political party: right	0	1	24.00%
x_5	Access to secure energy precondition – for EU to speak with one voice	0	1	91.10%
x_6	EU responsibility – support non-EU countries towards cleaner energy	0	1	87.27%
x_7	EU responsibility – ensure competition produces affordable prices	0	1	93.04%
x_8	Gender: male	0	1	46.38%

Source: Authors based on Eurobarometer.

Variables x_1 and x_2 originate from question QB9, where respondents are required to select, from a list of nine items, the three most crucial energy issues that the European Union should prioritise over the next decade. The first variable focuses on the reduction of EU energy imports, while the second pertains to safeguarding critical energy infrastructure from external disruptions, such as cyberattacks or extreme weather events.

In question D1, participants are asked to position themselves on a political spectrum ranging from 1 (extreme left) to 10 (extreme right). We classify respondents with left-wing political inclinations if they place themselves between levels 1 and 4, centre-wing for levels 5 to 6, and right-wing for levels 7 to 10. Consequently, three binary variables are created. Among these, x_3 and x_4, which correspond to centre- and right-wing orientations respectively, are incorporated into the models, with left-wing employed as the reference category.

Variable x_5 pertains to question QB3, item number 3, where respondents express their agreement with a statement asserting that for secure energy access, it is imperative for the EU to present a unified stance when negotiating with external energy suppliers. Respondents provide their responses on a Likert scale ranging from 1 to 4 (from "Totally agree" to "Totally disagree"). Our binary variable takes the value of 1 if the respondent selects levels 1 or 2 (indicating "Totally agree" or "Tend to agree").

Finally, variables x_6 and x_7 concern the respondents' endorsement of statements positing that it is the EU's duty to assist non-EU countries in transitioning to cleaner energy systems (variable x_6, derived from question QB4, item number 5) and to ensure that heightened competition in the EU energy markets leads to greater competitiveness and affordability for consumers (variable x_7, derived from question QB5, item number 1). Similar to variable x_5, these two questions were initially coded using a Likert scale spanning from 1 to 4, where 1 signifies "Totally agree" and 4 indicates "Totally disagree". They have subsequently been transformed into binary variables that take the value of 1 if the respondent selects one of the first two levels. The last variable (x_8) is the gender of the respondent, which highlights a slightly higher proportion of females in the sample.

To address the focal issue, we adopt an econometric framework akin to the one presented in Panarello and Gatto (2023), which centres on regression modelling with a binary dependent variable:

$$y_i = \alpha + \theta_1 x_{i1} + \theta_2 x_{i2} + \theta_3 x_{i3} + \theta_4 x_{i4} + \theta_5 x_{i5} + \theta_6 x_{i6} + \theta_7 x_{i7} + \theta_8 x_{i8} + \varepsilon_i \qquad (2.1)$$

Here, the dependent variable corresponds to the response to the inquiry *"What does EU energy policy mean to you?": Shifting from fossil fuels to renewable energy sources to combat climate change*. The variables $x_i = (x_{i1}, \ldots, x_{i8})$ serve as the covariates, encapsulating the questions delineated in Table 2.1.

In this chapter, we incorporate considerations for spatial heterogeneity and clustering when determining the parameters in (2.1), as explained in the ensuing section which elaborates on the econometric model employed to discern the clustering patterns on a country level and the interrelationships among the variables.

2.2.2 Spatially clustered regression with binary dependent variables

Let us consider the regression framework with binary dependent variable:

$$y_i = f(\mathrm{x}_i, \theta) + \varepsilon_i,\ i = 1, \ldots, N \tag{2.2}$$

where $x_i = (x_{1i}, \ldots, x_{Pi})'$ is a vector of the observables $p = 1, \ldots, P$ variables for the i-th units $(i = 1, \ldots, N)$. The parameters are included in the vector $\theta = (\theta_1, \ldots, \theta_P)'$ and $f(\mathrm{x}_i, \theta)$ is the function form. The econometric specification that we consider in (2.1) leads to the following Linear Probability Model (LPM):

$$\mathrm{P}(y_i = 1 | x_i) = x_i' \theta + \varepsilon_i,\ i = 1, \ldots, N \tag{2.3}$$

The LPM can be easily estimated by means of least square or maximum likelihood (Agresti, 2015). Differently from Panarello and Gatto (2023), however, we do account for both clustering structure and spatial heterogeneity in the statistical units. As we deal with a georeferenced dataset, we assume that location information s_i, e.g., longitude and latitude, are available for the i-th unit.

In an ideal setting, we aim at identifying a set of unit-specific regression parameters θ_i. However, without imposing any structure, we cannot identify θ_i as repeated measurement on the same i-th unit is not available in the cross-sectional setting. However, if we assume that N units are divided into $G(g = 1, \ldots, G)$ groups each of the size N_g, and that the units in the same group share the same parameter values θ_g, we can develop a suitable procedure for identifying and estimating θ_g. Given the vector $g = (g_1, \ldots, g_N)$ of clustering membership, spatial heterogeneity can be easily considered in the problem by assuming that the units in the G groups are spatially clustered. Under this set of assumptions, (2.3) becomes:

$$\mathrm{P}(y_i = 1 | x_i, g = g_i) = x_i' \theta_{g_i} + \varepsilon_i \tag{2.4}$$

Notice that the group membership of each i-th unit g_i is unknown and needs to be estimated, and an algorithm is needed for this aim. In this chapter, we propose to use the algorithm developed by Sugasawa and Murakami (2021) which works as follows. Given the number of clusters G, an initial suitable spatial partition based on spatial coordinates (see Fouedjio, 2016; Mattera and Franses, 2023) is performed and the initial parameters are estimated considering separated clusterwise models, i.e. clusterwise LPM (2.4). Then, the cluster membership is updated by assigning the i-th unit to the g-th cluster maximising a penalised log-likelihood function:

$$Q = \sum_{i=1}^{n} \log f(y_i \mid x_i;\ \theta_{g_i}) + \sum_{i<j} w_{ij} I(\mathrm{g}_i = g_j) \tag{2.5}$$

where w_{ij} indicates the spatial proximity of the units i and j. While the first term in (2.5) represents the log-likelihood, the second term indicates the spatial penalty (Chavent et al., 2018; Mattera, 2022). The cluster assignment is instead given by:

$$g_i = \underset{g_i \in \{1,\dots,G\}}{\text{argmax}} \sum_{i=1}^{n} \log f(y_i \mid x_i;\, \theta_{g_i}) + \sum_{i<j} w_{ij} I\left(g_i = g_j\right) \tag{2.6}$$

In the case of LPM, $f(y_i \mid x_i;\, \theta_{g_i})$ is given by the Gaussian density. The algorithm iterates the two steps – i.e. estimation of clusterwise models and clustering assignment based on penalised log-likelihood – until convergence. The number of clusters is chosen following an iterative procedure with the aim of minimising information criteria such as the BIC. A sampling procedure follows, which assigns 200 randomly selected statistical units to each cluster. Therefore, given that we consider 27 EU countries (clusters), the final size of the estimation sample will be 200 x 27 = 5400.

2.3 Results

The resulting clustering structure is depicted in Figure 2.1. We can see that, roughly speaking, the algorithm assigns the southern and central-eastern parts of Europe to Group A (13 countries), while Western Europe (9 countries) is assigned to Group B, and Scandinavian and Baltic countries (5 countries) become part of Group C.

Group A comprises the Visegrád Group countries (Poland, Hungary, Czech Republic, and Slovakia), Italy and its neighbouring countries (Austria, Croatia, and Slovenia), as well as Romania, Bulgaria, and Greece. These nations share numerous historical, geographical, cultural and political connections. For instance, Romania, Bulgaria, and Greece are predominantly Orthodox Christian countries, which has fostered cultural and religious ties. They also collaborate on common interests related to regional stability, energy security, and infrastructure development (Andreas et al., 2018; Karamaneas et al., 2023). The Visegrád Group, often referred to as the Visegrád Four (V4), consists of four Central European countries. Geographically proximate in Central Europe, they share a rich history of political, cultural, and economic interactions (Kořan, 2012). The Visegrád Group was officially established in 1991 to promote cooperation and regional integration, primarily in pursuit of aspirations to join Western institutions like the European Union (EU) and NATO. These countries have jointly pursued common political objectives, including EU accession. Furthermore, the Visegrád countries collectively address concerns related to energy security and have collaborated on energy infrastructure projects and diversification of energy sources (Kochanek, 2021).

Group B consists of France, Germany, and the Benelux countries (Belgium, the Netherlands, and Luxembourg), often perceived as similar due to a combination of historical, geographical, economic, and political factors. These nations form the core of the European Union (EU) and have a long-standing history of economic integration. Indeed, Group B countries boast robust and advanced economies

Figure 2.1 Resulting clustering structure.

Source: Authors, created with Datawrapper (www.datawrapper.de).

compared to their European counterparts, characterised by high levels of industrialisation, trade openness, and comprehensive social welfare systems. Furthermore, France, Germany, and the Benelux countries actively collaborate on regional and international matters, participating in various regional organisations. They work jointly on issues encompassing transportation, energy, and environmental policies (Pérez et al., 2019).

Finally, in Group C we find the Baltic countries, Finland, and Sweden. The similarities among the Baltic countries (Estonia, Latvia, and Lithuania) and Finland and Sweden can be attributed to a combination of historical, geographical, cultural, and economic factors. First and foremost, the Baltic countries are situated in close geographical proximity to Finland and Sweden in Northern Europe. This results in shared cultural and historical ties (Laitinen et al., 2002). Secondly, these nations share a history of interactions and influences. Historical trade routes, alliances, and conflicts have played pivotal roles in shaping their relationships over the centuries. They have frequently found themselves part of similar political and economic structures. Additionally, the Baltic countries and Finland share linguistic and cultural affinities, with Finnish and Estonian exhibiting particularly close linguistic connections. This shared linguistic heritage has nurtured cultural exchanges and similarities in traditions. Furthermore, economic ties, including trade and investment, contribute significantly to the resemblances among these countries (Studzieniecki et al., 2022; Gatto and Sadik-Zada, 2023). They engage in substantial trade with one another and actively participate in regional economic organisations, such as those within the Baltic Sea region. Lastly, this group does not include large countries and, as such, there is a history of political cooperation and collaboration among these nations, particularly within regional organisations like the Baltic Assembly and the Nordic Council. These forums facilitate dialogue and cooperation on a wide range of issues, further reinforcing their shared interests (Sadik-Zada and Gatto, 2023). The Linear Probability Model results are presented in Table 2.2.

We can see that the first variable (EU energy priorities for the next ten years: reduce EU energy imports) does not show any statistical association with the dependent variable: therefore, this statement does not have significant effects on citizens' beliefs that one of the EU energy policy meanings is to shift from fossil fuels to renewable energy to combat climate change.

As regards the second variable (EU energy priorities for the next ten years: protect critical energy infrastructure), we notice that a statistical association is only noticeable in the third cluster (Group C, which includes Scandinavian and Baltic countries), while it is not significant when considering the full sample results (without clustering structure). Therefore, for the citizens of such countries, believing the protection of critical energy infrastructure to be one of the EU's policy priorities of the next decade also leads to a belief that one of the main objectives of the EU energy policy with a view to fighting climate change is to make the transition from fossils to renewables. We miss this evidence by overlooking the clustering structure. As regards political variables, we can see that people who support centre- and right-wing political parties are generally less likely to support the view of an EU energy policy committed to promoting the green transition, compared to left-wing political supporters. A strong statistical association is not present in two out of three clusters when considering the difference between centre- and left-wing, even though the sign is negative as expected – as left-wing supporters generally tend to be more conscious about environmental matters (Panarello, 2021).

The fifth regressor is related to the question of whether a united EU could be a prerequisite for accessing secure energy. This is positively associated with the

Table 2.2 Linear Probability Model results

	Dependent variable:			
	"What does EU energy policy mean to you?": Shifting from fossil fuels to renewable energy sources to combat climate change			
	Full sample	*Group A*	*Group B*	*Group C*
EU energy priorities next 10 years: reduce EU energy imports	-0.029 (0.019)	-0.001 (0.025)	-0.042 (0.033)	-0.065 (0.051)
EU energy priorities next 10 years: protect critical energy infrastructure	0.023 (0.017)	0.030 (0.024)	-0.037 (0.029)	0.072* (0.037)
Centre vs. left party	-0.036** (0.016)	-0.00001 (0.024)	-0.035 (0.027)	-0.109*** (0.039)
Right vs. left party	-0.077*** (0.017)	-0.048** (0.024)	-0.065** (0.033)	-0.103** (0.042)
Access to secure energy precondition – for EU to speak with one voice	0.043* (0.025)	0.056* (0.034)	0.105** (0.047)	-0.180*** (0.061)
EU responsibility – support non-EU countries towards cleaner energy	0.066*** (0.021)	0.074** (0.029)	0.020 (0.038)	0.110** (0.045)
EU responsibility – ensure competition produces affordable prices	-0.005 (0.028)	0.053 (0.038)	-0.070 (0.047)	-0.055 (0.068)
Gender (male vs. female)	0.030** (0.013)	0.040** (0.019)	0.013 (0.024)	0.011 (0.032)
Constant	0.358*** (0.033)	0.203*** (0.042)	0.468*** (0.064)	0.652*** (0.087)
Observations	5,400	2,600	1,800	1,000
F Statistic	5.849***	3.857***	1.932*	3.701***

Note: *p<0.1; **p<0.05; ***p<0.01. Robust standard errors in parentheses.

dependent variable in two clusters (Groups A and B), while it seems that citizens from Scandinavia, Estonia, Latvia and Lithuania who answer affirmatively to such questions are less likely to believe that one of the EU energy policy meanings is to combat climate change by switching from fossil fuels to renewable energy sources. This could be due to the fact that Baltic countries have made notable progress in increasing the use of renewable energy sources in their energy mix over the past decade compared with other countries, especially those placed in Group A. Moving on to the sixth variable (EU responsibility – support non-EU countries towards cleaner energy), we notice that the association with the dependent variable is generally significant and with a positive sign. The association is shown to be weaker in Group B, even though the sign is the same. Believing that it is the EU's responsibility to ensure that competition produces affordable prices does not seem to be related to believing that the EU's energy policy is related to the transition from fossil fuels to renewables.

As regards gender, males are more likely to think that switching to renewables is one of the main features of the EU's energy policy: this is significant, on average, when considering the full sample of EU citizens. Moving on to the three clusters, the association shows itself to be stronger in Group A (Western Europe), while it is no longer significant in the two other clusters at conventional statistical thresholds. This suggests that for countries placed in Groups B and C there is no significant difference between males and females in their attitude towards the EU's energy policy.

2.4 Concluding remarks and policy venues

The current *polycrisis* affecting Europe was mainly generated by the Russian-Ukrainian war resulting in, inter alia, energy price rises, energy supply issues, geopolitical frictions, political instability and an increase in inflation . This run of simultaneous adverse events is not unusual in Europe and requires both preparedness and resilience to cope with vulnerabilities and energy insecurity (Zeitlin et al., 2019; Mišík, 2019). Nonetheless, it is hard to estimate the long-term impact of this multi-layered crisis (Davies, 2022; Le Quéré et al., 2021). This controversial situation highlighted pre-existing regional integration flaws and created major uncertainties regarding the EU's stability and even its foundations and mission (Dinan et al., 2017; Herranz-Surrallés et al., 2022). The EU had to tackle contrasting voices regarding failing energy union, while enforcing new regulations and policies to meet long-standing energy transition targets (Dupont and Oberthür, 2015; Minas and Ntousas, 2018; Mete, 2019; Bäckstrand, 2022).

In this chapter, we exploit the fact that the attitude toward energy transition in Europe shows spatial heterogeneity due to factors like economic structure, resource availability, politics, culture, and history. Regions with fossil fuel dependence, conservative politics, or limited renewable resources tend to be less supportive. Conversely, areas with clean energy infrastructure, progressive values, and abundant renewables are more likely to embrace the transition. Moreover, we cannot discard the presence of latent cultural factors while investigating the problem empirically. Similarly, policymakers must consider these regional differences when planning effective energy transition strategies. To account for spatial heterogeneity, we employ a recent econometric methodology which builds on spatial clustering. In sum, by means of the spatially clustered LPM adopted, we identify European regions characterised by similar beliefs concerning the significance of EU energy policy and different citizens' attitudes towards the energy transition process.

In our investigation, we ascertain that the populace's convictions regarding the underlying significance of EU energy policy, namely the transition towards renewable energy sources as a mechanism to combat climate change, are predominantly influenced by their political affiliations, the degree of emphasis they place on a unified European Union, and the perceived interconnection between the EU and non-EU entities. Furthermore, a heightened multiplicity of determinants manifests in the Baltic, Finnish and Swedish region (Group C) in contrast to the broader European context.

Based on our findings, policymakers should consider the following strategies to enhance the transition to renewable energy sources and align with the EU energy policy. First of all, policymakers should adopt a tailored communication strategy and promote the concept of a unified EU as a vital force in tackling climate change and reducing reliance on non-EU energy sources. Moreover, it seems that policies should have a deeper regional focus. For example, recognising the unique circumstances in the Baltic, Finnish, and Swedish region and developing energy transition plans tailored to the specific concerns and priorities of each specific region. This translates into closer collaboration with local governments and stakeholders. In this context, the efforts in facilitating the cooperation between EU member states to share best practice and initiate cross-border projects that demonstrate the advantages of renewable energy adoption seem to be of crucial relevance. This knowledge exchange can indeed help regions with different attitudes to learn from one another.

These aspects clearly require, from one side, a long-term planning activity, as acknowledging shifts in public attitudes takes time. While acknowledging the possibility of evolving perceptions since the administration of the Eurobarometer questionnaire in 2019, the significance of these earlier findings lies in their role as a benchmark for evaluating changes and identifying potential areas where attitudes or policies may have shifted in response to the crisis. Future studies that incorporate post-crisis data can build upon this foundation to provide a comprehensive understanding of the dynamic relationship between geopolitical events, public perception and energy-related policies. Developing comprehensive, consistent, and long-term energy transition plans, along with consistency in policy over time, builds trust and confidence in the transition and is important for enhancing the effectiveness of energy transition in the EU. On the other hand, mechanisms to track and measure the impact of policies on public attitudes at a regional scale also need to be clarified. In this regard, regular surveys, feedback mechanisms, and public consultations enable policymakers to understand the influence of their initiatives and make adjustments as needed. By applying these strategies thoughtfully, policymakers can accelerate the adoption of renewable energy sources and garner more widespread public support for the energy transition across Europe.

Acknowledgements

The authors are indebted to Matúš Mišík, Andrea Figulová, Andrej Nosko and all participants at the conference 'A decarbonised, secure, and united EU?' – Bratislava, Slovakia, 20–21 April 2023 for their thorough comments and extended, useful discussion. Funding: The research was funded by the Internal Faculty Start-Up Research Grant of Wenzhou-Kean University Project No ISRG2023014.

References

Agresti, A., 2015. *Foundations of Linear and Generalized Linear Models*. Chichester: John Wiley & Sons.

Andreas, J.J., Burns, C., Touza, J., 2018. Overcoming energy injustice? Bulgaria's renewable energy transition in times of crisis. *Energy Research & Social Science* 42, 44–52.

Bäckstrand, K., 2022. Towards a Climate-Neutral Union by 2050? The European Green Deal, Climate Law, and Green Recovery. In *Routes to a Resilient European Union: Interdisciplinary European Studies* (pp. 39–61). Cham: Palgrave Macmillan.

Begou, P., Kassomenos, P., 2023. The ecosyndemic framework of the global environmental change and the COVID-19 pandemic. *Science of the Total Environment* 857, 159327.

Caineng, Z.O.U., Xiong, B., Huaqing, X.U.E., Zheng, D., Zhixin, G.E., Ying, W.A.N.G., ..., Songtao, W., 2021. The role of new energy in carbon neutral. *Petroleum exploration and Development* 48(2), 480–491.

Chavent, M., Kuentz-Simonet, V., Labenne, A., Saracco, J., 2018. ClustGeo: An R package for hierarchical clustering with spatial constraints. *Computational Statistics* 33(4), 1799–1822.

Davies, R., 2022. Gas Price Hike of More than 30% Stokes Home Bills Fears for Europe. *The Guardian*, January 22.

de la Porte, C., Jensen, M.D., 2021. The next generation EU: An analysis of the dimensions of conflict behind the deal. *Social Policy & Administration* 55(2), 388–402.

Dinan, D., Nugent, N., Paterson, W.E., 2017. *The European Union in Crisis*. London: Palgrave Macmillan.

Dorsch, M.J., Flachsland, C., Kornek, U., 2020. Building and enhancing climate policy ambition with transfers: Allowance allocation and revenue spending in the EU ETS. *Environmental Politics* 29(5), 781–803.

Dupont, C., Oberthür, S., 2015. *Decarbonization in the European Union Internal Policies and External Strategies*. London: Springer.

Erokhin, D., 2019. Greater Europe from Lisbon to Vladivostok: Challenges and perspectives of a Common Economic Space. *European Policy Review* 2(2), 77–88.

European Commission, 2020. Eurobarometer 91.4, 2019. GESIS Data Archive, Cologne. ZA7575 Data file Version 1.0.0. https://doi.org/10.4232/1.13429

European Commission, 2022. *REPowerEU: Joint European Action for More Affordable, Secure and Sustainable Energy*. Brussels: European Commission

Fabry, A., 2019. Neoliberalism, crisis and authoritarian–ethnicist reaction: The ascendancy of the Orbán regime. *Competition & Change* 23(2), 165–191.

Fouedjio, F., 2016. A hierarchical clustering method for multivariate geostatistical data. *Spatial Statistics* 18, 333–351.

Freeman, R., 2021. Modelling the socio-political feasibility of energy transition with system dynamics. *Environmental Innovation and Societal Transitions* 40, 486–500.

Gatto, A., 2022. The energy futures we want: A research and policy agenda for energy transitions. *Energy Research & Social Science* 89, 102639.

Gatto, A., Panarello, D., 2022. Misleading intentions? Questioning the effectiveness and biases of Eurobarometer data for energy sustainability, development and transition research. *Energy Research & Social Science* 93, 102813.

Gatto, A., Sadik-Zada, E.R., 2023. People have the power. Electricity production, renewable energy transition, and communities empowerment across 11 Nordic-Baltic countries. *Environmental Science and Pollution Research*, 30 125464–125477.

Gatto, A., Mattera, R., & Panarello, D. (2024). For whom the bell tolls. A spatial analysis of the renewable energy transition determinants in Europe in light of the Russia-Ukraine war. *Journal of Environmental Management*, 352, 119833.

Hansen, H., Knolle, K., 2022. *Germany Agrees 200 Bln Euro Package to Shield against Surging Energy Prices*. Reuters.

Herranz-Surrallés, A., Solorio, I., Fairbrass, J., 2022. *Renegotiating Authority in EU Energy and Climate Policy*. Abingdon: Routledge.

Karamaneas, A., Koasidis, K., Frilingou, N., Xexakis, G., Nikas, A., Doukas, H., 2023. A stakeholder-informed modelling study of Greece's energy transition amidst an energy crisis: The role of natural gas and climate ambition. *Renewable and Sustainable Energy Transition* 3, 100049.

Kochanek, E., 2021. The energy transition in the Visegrad group countries. *Energies* 14(8), 2212.

Kořan, M., 2012. The Visegrad Group on the threshold of its third decade: A Central European hub?. In Šabič, Z. and Drulák, P. (eds) *Regional and International Relations of Central Europe* (pp. 201–218). London: Palgrave Macmillan UK.

Laitinen, V., Lahermo, P., Sistonen, P., Savontaus, M.L., 2002. Y-chromosomal diversity suggests that Baltic males share common Finno-Ugric-speaking forefathers. *Human Heredity* 53(2), 68–78.

Le Quéré, C., Peters, G.P., Friedlingstein, P., Andrew, R.M., Canadell, J.G., Davis, S.J., ..., Jones, M.W., 2021. Fossil CO_2 emissions in the post-COVID-19 era. *Nature Climate Change* 11(3), 197–199.

Mattera, R., 2022. A weighted approach for spatio-temporal clustering of COVID-19 spread in Italy. *Spatial and Spatio-temporal Epidemiology* 41, 100500.

Mattera, R., Franses, P.H., 2023. Are African business cycles synchronized? Evidence from spatio-temporal modelling. *Economic Modelling* 128, 106485.

Meissner, K.L., Schoeller, M.G., 2019. Rising despite the polycrisis? The European Parliament's strategies of self-empowerment after Lisbon. *Journal of European Public Policy* 26(7), 1075–1093.

Mete, G., 2019. *Energy Transitions and the Future of Gas in the EU. Subsidise or Decarbonise*. London: Palgrave.

Minas, S., Ntousas, V., 2018. *EU Climate Diplomacy: Politics, Law and Negotiations*. Abingdon: Routledge.

Mišík, M., 2019. *External Energy Security in the European Union. Small Member States' Perspective*. Abingdon: Routledge.

Mišík, M., 2022. The EU needs to improve its external energy security. *Energy Policy* 165, 112930.

Mišík, M., Nosko, A., 2023. Post-pandemic lessons for EU energy and climate policy after the Russian invasion of Ukraine: Introduction to a special issue on EU green recovery in the post-Covid-19 period. *Energy Policy* 177, 113546.

Mišík, M., Oravcová, V., 2022. Ex ante governance in the European Union: Energy and climate policy as a 'test run' for the post-pandemic recovery. *Energy Policy* 167, 113076.

Nosko, A., Ušiak, J., 2023. Effects of COVID-19 on civil society voices in European energy and climate policy. *Energy Policy* 174, 113421.

Panarello, D., 2021. Economic insecurity, conservatism, and the crisis of environmentalism: 30 years of evidence. *Socio-Economic Planning Sciences* 73, 100925.

Panarello, D., Gatto, A., 2023. Decarbonising Europe–EU citizens' perception of renewable energy transition amidst the European Green Deal. *Energy Policy* 172, 113272.

Pérez, M.D.L.E.M., Scholten, D., Stegen, K.S., 2019. The multi-speed energy transition in Europe: Opportunities and challenges for EU energy security. *Energy Strategy Reviews* 26, 100415.

Pianta, S., Brutschin, E., van Ruijven, B., Bosetti, V., 2021. Faster or slower decarbonization: Policymakers' and stakeholders' expectations on the effect of the COVID-19 pandemic. *Energy Research & Social Science* 76, 102025.

Riedel, R., 2021. Green conservatism or environmental nativism? Exploring carbon dependency as populist political strategy in Poland. *Zeitschrift für Vergleichende Politikwissenschaft* 15(2), 207–227.

Sadik-Zada, E. R., Gatto, A., 2023. Civic engagement and energy transition in the Nordic-Baltic Sea Region: Parametric and nonparametric inquiries. *Socio-Economic Planning Sciences* 87, 101347.

Schimmelfennig, F., 2022. *Differentiated Integration Has Been of Limited Use in the EU's Polycrisis*. Florence: European University Institute.

Steffen, B., Patt, A., 2022. A historical turning point? Early evidence on how the Russia-Ukraine war changes public support for clean energy policies. *Energy Research & Social Science* 91, 102758.

Studzieniecki, T., Palmowski, T., Joeck, R., 2022. Territorial cooperation—A factor stimulating Baltic Sea Region energy transition. *Energies* 15(2), 436.

Sugasawa, S., Murakami, D., 2021. Spatially clustered regression. *Spatial Statistics* 44, 100525.

Szulecki, K., 2018. *Energy Security in Europe. Divergent Perceptions and Policy Challenges*. London: Palgrave Macmillan.

Thaler, P., Pakalkaite, V., 2021. Governance through real-time compliance: The Supranationalisation of European external energy policy. *Journal of European Public Policy* 28(2), 208–228.

Vanhercke, B., Verdun, A., 2022. The European semester as goldilocks: Macroeconomic policy coordination and the recovery and resilience facility. *Journal of Common Market Studies* 60(1), 204–223.

Zakeri, B., Paulavets, K., Barreto-Gomez, L., Echeverri, L.G., Pachauri, S., Boza-Kiss, B., ..., Pouya, S., 2022. Pandemic, war, and global energy transitions. *Energies* 15(17), 6114.

Zeitlin, J., Nicoli, F., Laffan, B., 2019. Introduction: The European Union beyond the polycrisis? Integration and politicization in an age of shifting cleavages. *Journal of European Public Policy* 26(7), 963–976.

3 Role of the regions in climate and energy policy

Insight from Visegrad countries

Veronika Oravcová and Katarína Šafaříková

3.1 Introduction

During the last decade, climate and energy policy within the European Union (EU) has undergone several important milestones, starting with the establishment of the 2030 targets (European Council, 2014), the commitment to achieve climate neutrality by 2050 (European Council, 2019), and the announcement of the European Green Deal (European Commission, 2019). A world economy shaken by the COVID-19 pandemic and subsequent economic recovery led the EU to first introduce the Next Generation EU instrument aimed especially at "green" recovery (European Commission, 2020) and then the Fit for 55 package which implements the policies of the European Green Deal (European Commission, 2021a). The Russian invasion of Ukraine in February 2022 revealed the risks associated with high energy dependence on Russia and the EU responded by reducing its dependency on fossil fuel imports from Russia and diversifying import routes. Furthermore, it addressed the climate crisis through energy savings and the accelerated adoption of renewable energy sources (European Commission, 2022a).

The successful implementation of all these milestones and targets of energy transformation, in alignment with the goal to reach climate neutrality by 2050, requires substantial changes not only at the national, but also the local level. This impacts economies and societies, highlighting the involvement of local and regional actors. Governance thus faces a complex challenge in climate change, which requires not only horizontal cooperation across various sectors but also vertical collaboration involving international, national, regional, and local actors. Local and regional governments are in a unique position to deliver on the net-zero emissions agenda (OECD, 2020), as regions and municipalities (Dahal et al., 2018) play vital roles in energy savings, climate mitigation, and adaptation.

This chapter assumes a comparative perspective to examine regions of the so-called Visegrad Group countries (V4; Czechia, Hungary, Poland, and Slovakia). It aims to investigate the involvement of regions as sub-national entities in the energy transition process and reaching climate neutrality by looking at regional mid-term

DOI: 10.4324/9781032624839-5

strategies until 2030. The main research goal is to examine how decarbonization and green transformation policies are reflected in V4 regional strategies. Energy and climate policies are interconnected and cover vast areas. Given the central role of energy transition in reaching climate neutrality (De La Peña et al., 2022), the chapter especially examines whether the V4 regions plan to implement climate policies and what types of renewable energy sources they intend to develop.

The chapter is structured as follows: the second section provides an overview of the role that local and regional levels play in energy transformation, while the third examines the national approaches of individual Visegrad Group countries to energy policies. The fourth section presents the research data and methodology, while the fifth explores climate policies in regional strategies while the sixth delves deeper into the regions' use of renewable energy and provides the arguments they use for further expanding these sources. The seventh section investigates plans for using other energy sources within the regions, while the eighth and final part summarizes the chapter's main findings.

3.2 Local and regional governance in climate neutrality and energy transition

Linked to the goal of achieving climate neutrality by 2050, as agreed by the EU member states (European Council, 2019), energy transition requires a complex transformation within both the energy sector and society as a whole. Although most scholarly attention has been dedicated to studying policies and processes at the EU and national level, it is crucial to recognize that meeting energy and climate objectives cannot rely only on top-down initiatives led by the EU and/or national governments, since they should be reinforced by a bottom-up approach. Changes brought about by an energy transformation are not uniform and will vary among citizens, regions, and sectors (OECD, 2020). Therefore, it is essential to examine local and regional levels, and explore their engagement and stance towards climate and energy policies.

As revealed during the COVID-19 pandemic, regions and municipalities are key partners in implementing effective solutions, not only in the case of health crises (Dvorak, 2021), but also in terms of other policies. The recent energy crisis has highlighted the readiness of regions and their energy agencies to scale up and replicate energy transition programs across Europe, ensuring the sustainability of the energy system (FEDARENE, 2023). That is because regions and cities, which often collaborate with the private sector, are better positioned to develop and implement effective solutions, including the green transition and achieving net-zero carbon emissions (Krog, 2019). All these efforts require significant investments in innovation, a large-scale adoption of innovative solutions, infrastructure development, and change of citizens' daily habits. Notably, over half of environmental and climate-related spending and roughly two-thirds of related investments originate from subnational governments, which highlights the substantial role regions and cities play in these efforts (OECD, 2019).

The EU is at the forefront of setting climate policy standards through 'shared leadership', meaning that all levels of governance, communities, municipalities, regions, and national parliaments and EU institutions, share the examples of best practices and lessons learned (European Parliament, 2020). Local and regional governance institutions thus should play a pivotal role in implementing measures for combating climate change. These cover both structural prevention, which enhances adaptive capabilities, and operational prevention, which deals with ongoing capacities (Kern, 2019; Mi et al., 2019). It has also been argued that the success of energy transitions crucially depends on successful transitions at the local level (Brugger and Henry, 2021).

While there has been fairly extensive interest in researching climate change and energy transformation in cities and municipalities (Dobravec et al., 2021; Melica et al., 2018), including, for instance, robust research on local climate planning in 885 cities across the EU (Reckien et al., 2018), studies focused on the regional level remains rather scarce. Relatively little attention persists despite the acknowledged importance of a multi-level governance approach towards various aspects of energy transition processes, such as the deployment of renewable energy (Smith, 2007; van Dijk et al., 2022). Previous research on the role of regions focused, for instance, on collaborative governance, the role of external stakeholders outside of regional institutions fostering energy transition processes (Sedlacek et al., 2020), relations between national and regional policies, including fossil fuel subsidies, and their impact on the energy transition in regions (Su and Tan, 2023), and how interactions between governance bodies influence an energy region's capacity to govern the energy transition (van Dijk et al., 2022).

Previous research showed that regions play a pivotal role in providing renewable energy sources (RES), as technological solutions will have to be adapted to individual regional contexts due to their unique geographical characteristics (Kettl et al., 2014). Investing in RES allows regions to reduce their dependence on centralized fossil fuel-based power generation and simultaneously stimulate local economies (Varela-Vázquez and Sánchez-Carreira, 2015). It has also been argued that regional efforts to set up decentralized energy systems support the need for energy self-sufficiency (Hecher et al., 2016).

Moreover, most academic attention has been dedicated to Western European countries (Hecher et al., 2016; Komendantova and Neumueller, 2020), as well as countries outside of Europe, such as Brazil (Lazaro et al., 2022) or China (Su and Tan, 2023). The Visegrad Group countries remain under-researched from this perspective, with a few exceptions focusing on coal regions in transition (Gerbelová et al., 2020) and their use of strategic planning instruments to prepare for structural change (Matern et al., 2023). Furthermore, past research highlights the role of regional joint planning in climate and energy (Brownlee et al., 2021; Krog, 2019). Although robust regional plans may fail during the implementation process (Suitner and Ecker, 2020), they set the direction of those policies that are going to be discussed and implemented. Therefore, it is crucial to study these trends further to understand regional contributions to climate and energy policies.

3.3 National approaches to energy policy in Visegrad Group countries

The Visegrad countries have many different preferences and their cooperation is based on the ad hoc convergence of preferences in areas where they align, including energy policy (Mišík and Oravcová, 2022). Even when looking at the V4's energy mix we can observe several differences (Figure 3.1). While Czechia and especially Poland have relied mainly on (domestic) coal, Hungary and Slovakia are less dependent on it. The latter two countries have been heading towards a coal phase-out in electricity production but, in the case of Slovakia, the share of coal in the overall energy mix is still relatively high, as the main steel producer runs on this source. In Czechia, the government announced a coal phase-out by 2033, which is a few years earlier than anticipated by the so-called Coal Commission established by the Czech Government, which recommends that coal be phased out by 2038 (Voříšek, 2023).

When it comes to other fossil fuels, natural gas is important for all four countries, but especially for Hungary and Slovakia where it is a pillar of the heating sector and crucial for industry as well. Similarly, oil is vital for transportation, where all four countries have been experiencing increasing demand. The V4 countries slightly differ in their use of nuclear energy. While this is a traditional source for Czechia, Hungary, and Slovakia, Poland announced the development of its first nuclear reactors only in 2018, in the updated National Energy Policy. Adopted in 2020, the Polish Nuclear Power Programme argues that the implementation of nuclear power will contribute to the country's energy security and enable the replacement of ageing high-emission baseload coal units (Republic of Poland, 2020). All four countries have a relatively low share of renewable energy sources (RES) and rely especially on biomass for heating and co-generation.

The difference between the countries analysed is even more visible when we look at their electricity mixes (Figure 3.2). Czechia's electricity production is based especially on coal and nuclear energy. Hungary is the only V4 country that substantially relies on gas-fired power plants. While coal is the dominant source

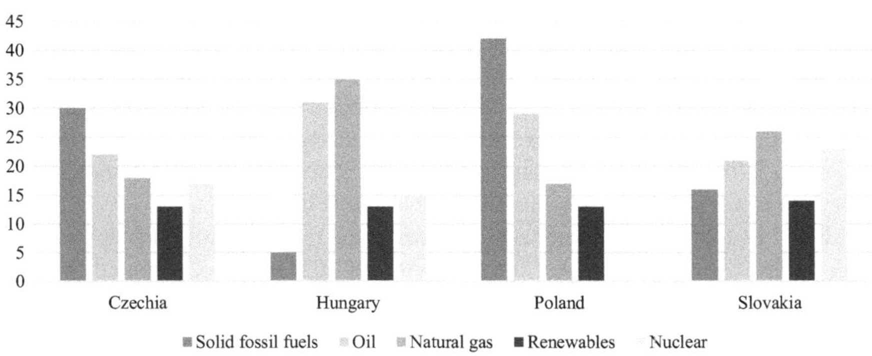

Figure 3.1 Energy mix of Visegrad Group countries (2021).

Source: Authors based on European Commission data.

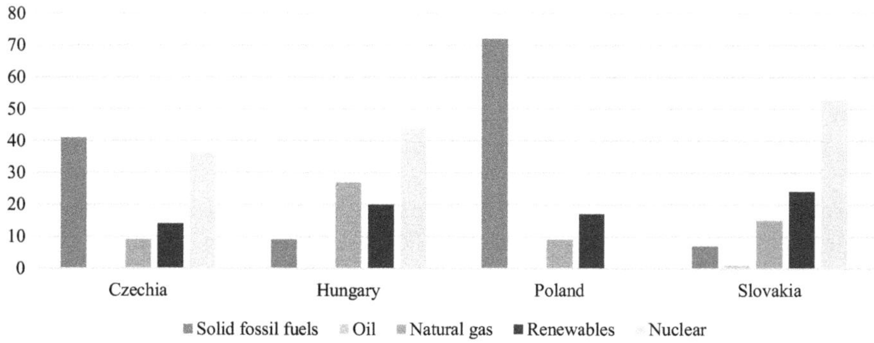

Figure 3.2 Electricity mix of Visegrad Group countries (2021).

Source: Authors based on European Commission data.

of electricity in Poland, the country also relies on renewables, especially wind energy. Renewables are important for Hungarian and Slovak electricity production, dominated by hydropower. However, both countries also rely heavily on nuclear energy, with Slovakia using nuclear for more than half of its electricity production.

The recent energy crisis which began with the post-COVID-19 economy recovery and was exacerbated by the Russian invasion of Ukraine provided a push for further EU-wide RES adoption, including V4. As energy prices increased during the crisis, the deployment of RES and energy-efficiency measures emerged as a potential solution to alleviate the pressure articulated especially within the REPowerEU initiative (European Commission, 2022a). Increasing renewable energy targets not only contributes to the V4 countries' energy independence but also offers financial benefits (Czyżak and Fox, 2023). Moreover, according to the latest findings, V4 countries have made remarkable progress towards RES deployment during the energy crisis years (Atikur Rahaman et al., 2023).

The climate and energy trajectory for the Visegrad Group countries up until 2030 could be deduced from the National Energy and Climate Plans (NECPs) prepared on the basis of Article 14 of Regulation (EU) 2018/1999 of the European Parliament and of the Council of 11 December 2018 on the Governance of the Energy Union and Climate Action (European Commission, 2018). These plans not only reveal their climate ambitions aimed at decreasing emissions, and the sources and energy efficiency measures the countries intend to deploy, but also specify the policy measures they intend to implement to achieve these goals.

All EU countries were expected to submit their revised draft NECPs by June 2023, aligned with the goals set for the period of 2021–2030. Compared to their 2020 version, the NECPs 2023 updates have encountered more ambitious targets and unique challenges also at the EU level, as they aim to increase the share of renewables in the EU energy mix to 42.5% by 2030. Poland is among the countries that did not submit its updated 2023 NECP draft by the end of 2023. Czechia and Hungary reflect the increased ambition of further EU-wide RES deployment in

Table 3.1 Renewable energy targets in Visegrad Group countries (in %)

	2020 targets	*2020 values*	*2030 targets NECPs 2019 (draft I)*	*2030 targets NECPs 2020 (final I)*	*2030 targets NECPs 2023 (draft II)*
Czechia	13	17.3	20.8	22	30
Hungary	13	13.9	20	21	29
Poland	15	16.1	21	21–23	N/A
Slovakia	14	17.3	18	19.2	23
EU	20	22	30.4–31.9	32	42.5*

Source: Authors, based on European Commission data.

* Note: 42.5% is the EU-wide target as defined by the REPowerEU Strategy.

their updated NECPs drafts, while Slovakia's contribution remains rather modest (Table 3.1).

All three revised NECPs submitted by V4 acknowledge the importance of the local and regional level in the energy transition and climate policies. The Czech NECP sees the role of local and regional authorities in the implementation of smart strategies and smart projects at the municipal and city level, and the development of renewable energy communities, in which the role of local and regional actors is key for citizens' participation in and acceptance of these projects (Ministry of Industry and Trade of the ČR, 2023). Similarly, Hungary sees the role of local and regional authorities in developing energy communities, but especially in implementing energy efficiency measures and the energy management system, including energy audits (Ministry of Innovation and Technology of Hungary, 2023).

The Slovak NECP also acknowledges the pivotal role of the regional and local level by elaborating on the concept of Regional Energy Centres, which primarily focus on supporting and enhancing energy efficiency in public administration and building capacities for high-quality energy task performance for regions, towns, and municipalities. These centres are intended for planning, coordinating the decarbonization process, and providing support during its implementation, which includes identifying key investment activities and projects. They will also engage in activities aimed at increasing regional partners' awareness of energy efficiency and renewable energy sources (Ministry of Economy of the SR, 2023).

Although Poland has not yet submitted its 2023 NECP, in the 2020 version of the document, the country acknowledges that RES development is crucial for local and regional economies and the stimulation of the labour market. The document also focuses on cooperation between the national government, regions and municipalities in decreasing emissions in the heating and transport sector, as well as air pollution. Moreover, it highlights the need for collaboration between local and regional authorities on the transition of coal regions in order to gain public acceptance of that process (Ministry of State Assets of Poland, 2019).

Finally, the V4 local level has gained visibility at the EU level. In June 2020, the mayors of the V4 capitals – Bratislava, Budapest, Prague, and Warsaw – sent an open letter to the Council of the EU in which they emphasized the central role of cities in the ecological transformation. Referring to the escalating climate crisis, the mayors urged the EU to set a more ambitious emissions reduction target for 2030. They called for an EU-wide agreement to reduce emissions by at least 55% of 1990 levels by 2030 and asked for EU-wide measures to support the cities' climate action (Reuters, 2020). Indeed, the target was raised one year later, as part of the Fit for 55 package presented by the European Commission in July 2021.

3.4 Data and methodology

To investigate the regional approach to climate policies and the energy transition, we chose to examine the strategies of the regions within the Visegrad Group countries. In contrast to previous studies that utilized a case study approach (Hoppe and Miedema, 2020; Tàbara, 2011), we have opted for a comparative approach and selected all regions across the four countries. The main research question is how decarbonization and green transformation policies are reflected in V4 regional strategies. Our objective was twofold: first, to look at the climate policies of the regions and second, to identify the primary energy sources they aim to develop further, along with the supporting arguments for such initiatives. To achieve this, we conducted a content analysis of primary documents related to regional development in V4. We analysed regional approaches to climate and energy policies in four steps: firstly, we selected the regions; secondly, we identified their main strategies; thirdly, we conducted content analyses by coding the documents for climate and energy topics, and finally, we delved deeper into the plans of individual regions to develop energy sources.

By "regions" we understand 14 higher-level territorial self-governing units in Czechia, 20 counties in Hungary, 16 voivodships in Poland, and eight higher territorial units (self-governing regions) in Slovakia. In the case of Czechia and Hungary, such administrative divisions also include the capitals: Prague and Budapest. Therefore, we incorporated the remaining V4 capitals, Warsaw (Poland) and Bratislava (Slovakia), to create our dataset (see Table 3.2 for an overview). We collected a total of 60 strategic documents (one for each region) as the foundation for our analysis.

We analysed the main development strategies of a given region. These are medium-term strategic documents that, based on knowledge of the territory, social conditions, and EU and national development trends, define the basic strategic objectives for the region. They also formulate the measures and activities for achieving these objectives. Serving as fundamental strategic documents, the self-governments of the regions rely on them when deciding on the appropriateness of plans, projects, and activities applying for regional support. As such, they are umbrella documents that define the most significant problems, tasks, and challenges crucial for the development of the region in all aspects in the medium-term holding relevance for the public sphere, as well as the business, academic, and non-profit sector. Moreover, they serve as the basis for arguments during negotiations with

Table 3.2 List of regions and capital cities in Visegrad Group countries

Slovakia	*Czechia*	*Poland*	*Hungary*
regions (NUTS 3)	*regions (NUTS 3)*	*regions (NUTS 2)*	*counties (NUTS 3)*
Banská Bystrica	Central Bohemian	Greater Poland	Bács-Kiskun
Bratislava	Hradec Králové	Kujawy-Pomerania	Baranya
Košice	Karlovy Vary	Lesser Poland	Békés
Nitra	Liberec	Lower Silesia	Borsod-Abaúj-Zemplén
Prešov	Moravian-Silesian	Łódź	Csongrád-Csanád
Trenčín	Olomouc	Lublin	Fejér
Trnava	Pardubice	Lubusz	Győr-Moson-Sopron
Žilina	Plzeň	Masovia	Hajdú-Bihar
	South Bohemian	Opole	Heves
Capital	South Moravian	Podlaskie	Jász-Nagykun-Szolnok
Bratislava	Ústí nad Labem	Pomerania	Komárom-Esztergom
	Vysočina	Silesia	Nógrád
	Zlín	Subcarpathian	Pest
		Świętokrzyskie	Somogy
	Capital	West Pomerania	Szabolcs-Szatmár-Bereg
	Prague	Warmia-Masuria	Tolna
			Vas
		Capital	Veszprém
		Warsaw	Zala
			Capital
			Budapest

Source: Authors.

central authorities and for strategic decision making by entrepreneurs, investors, universities, etc. In general, all these documents consist of two main parts: an analytical section examining the current state and a strategic section outlining future development. We reviewed each document, primarily focusing on the strategic section, as this is expected to define subsequent steps in climate and energy development.

The development and approval (by the regional parliaments) of the strategic documents are also among the conditions for providing subsidies from the state budget and additional resources, such as the European Regional Development Fund (ERDF), including the Interreg programme which encompasses the Czech, Hungarian, and Slovak NUTS 3 level, and the Polish NUTS 2 level (European Commission, 2023a). These documents were drafted, written, and approved during the preparation of the new EU programming period 2021–2027. These proved to be very turbulent times from a climate and energy policy perspective (Figure 3.3). The majority of regional documents (30 strategies) were approved in 2021, followed by 13 strategies in 2020 and nine strategies in 2022. In total, six strategies were approved before the Commission announced the European Green Deal in December 2019. The oldest strategy dates back to 2015 (the City of Warsaw),

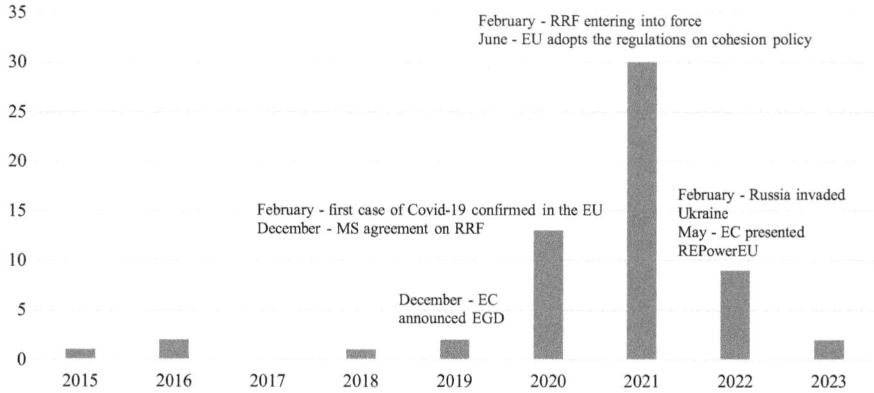

Figure 3.3 Adoption of current regional strategies in Visegrad Group countries by year.
Source: Authors.

while two strategies were approved in 2023 (the Slovak Trnava Region and the Czech Plzeň Region).

When it comes to the limitations of our methodology, it is important to acknowledge that there are numerous other regional strategies. For instance, the Territorial Energy Concept is a conceptual regional development document addressing energy issues in the territory of the Czech Regions in connection with the state energy concept, including energy measures concerning the region's property, processed with regard to the fulfilment of Act no. 406/2000 Coll. on energy management. However, to create a comparable dataset across all the V4 regions we decided to focus solely on the main regional documents.

Following that, we coded the main topics related to climate and energy policies in the regional strategies. We examined whether climate and energy topics were present in the following categories (also the main categories of the European Green Deal (European Commission, 2019)): achieving climate neutrality; adaptation measures; the development of (clean) energy sources; circular economy; energy efficiency measures in buildings; sustainable transport; ecological agriculture; biodiversity protection; and measures against air pollution. Additionally, we assessed if the strategies were referring to key EU green transformation documents (such as the European Green Deal and the Recovery and Resilience Plans).

In the final step, we examined in detail the regions' plans to develop RES. We focused on the types of RES each region opted for (biogas, biomass, geothermal, hydro, solar, wind) and looked at the plans for their development, as well as the energy systems (such as batteries) needed for this type of infrastructure. Additionally, we examined plans to develop hydrogen, as well as their attitudes towards traditional fossil fuel sources (coal, natural gas) and the use of waste for energy purposes. We examined the plans for the further use of these sources, considering which sources were to be developed and the primary arguments supporting their further development.

3.5 Overview of climate policies in V4 regional strategies

Most of the regional strategies were developed in accordance with the new programming period 2021–2027 for the use of EU funds. Therefore, they develop their priority policies and measures in accordance with the new cohesion policy, which stands on five pillars: a more competitive and smarter Europe; a greener, low-carbon transitioning towards a net-zero carbon economy; a more connected Europe by enhancing mobility; a more social and inclusive Europe; and a Europe closer to its citizens by fostering the sustainable and integrated development of all types of territories (European Commission, 2021b). Many policies and measures are tied with EU priorities to obtain EU funding from national or other programmes, such as Interreg or EU horizontal programmes (for instance Horizon Europe or LIFE).

Not every region mentioned the most important EU climate policies and plans (Figure 3.4); Czech regions, in particular, alluded to them only scarcely. The connection to the Recovery and Resilience Plan is found in 28 strategies but is missing from 15 strategies approved after 2020. The connection to the European Green Deal is present in 27 but absent from 26 strategies approved after 2019. Not all the regions acknowledge the need to reach climate neutrality, mentioned in 29 strategies.

Some of the regions (e.g. the Polish Lubusz Region) mention in their documents that while the EU commits to reaching climate neutrality by 2050, they themselves do not. Other Polish regions see the climate neutrality goal mostly in the context of shifting away from coal and plans to support activities related to changing and improving the qualifications of people employed in the mining sector (Lublin Region, 2023) or emphasize the need to reach that goal in connection to the energy system transformation and education (Lesser Poland Region, 2020). However, even those regions that do not explicitly mention climate neutrality present their strategies on how to deal with climate change (which they all acknowledge) and the transition to a low-carbon economy.

Figure 3.4 Number of references to the main EU policies in regional strategies of Visegrad Group countries.

When it comes to the specific areas of the European Green Deal that we looked at (achieving climate neutrality including adaptation measures, the development of (clean) energy sources, circular economy, energy efficiency measures in buildings, sustainable transport, ecological agriculture, biodiversity protection, and measures against air pollution), we found that all regions included these policies in their mid-term plans. They especially emphasized adaptation measures, specifically water management, and developments towards a circular economy in connection to a given region's waste management. In terms of energy efficiency, there are many detailed plans for building renovation (especially in Hungarian regions). Biodiversity protection, mostly in connection with ecological agriculture, was also included. Air pollution policies were part of a more complex picture related especially to coal use (Czechia and Poland), individual heating, and the transport sector. When it comes to the latter, all regions tend to emphasize public transport, with Poland very much focusing on railway modernization and development. However, the development of e-mobility and the charging infrastructure in particular are missing from nine strategies across the Visegrad Group countries. Nevertheless, almost all regions have strategies for public transport development and plan to expand their renewable energy sources (see the next part).

3.6 Renewable energy policies in V4 regional strategies

All the regions without exception are generally supportive of renewables deployment; however, there are substantial differences stemming from the geographical conditions, current energy mix, political vision, and financial possibilities of individual regions. The majority of regions remark on the particular RES they aim to develop, except the Bratislava and Prague capitals, the Polish Opole Region, and the Slovak Žilina Region, which do not specify their choice of energy sources. The Polish Podlaskie Region also fails to specify its further use of renewable energy sources, but does include "energy revolution and circular economy" as one of its main region-specific aims (Podlaskie Region, 2020). Regional strategies not only highlight the benefits of renewables but also acknowledge their drawbacks. This is evident in the case of the Czech Plzeň and Vysočina Regions, which emphasize that, despite the increasing use of RES for electricity production, their construction and utilization must not adversely affect the environment, the aesthetic value of the landscape, or landscape management (Plzeň Region, 2023).

Figure 3.5 presents specific RES. We have included only those regions that express support (positive values) or non-support (negative values) for the further development of a particular energy source. If a specific source is not mentioned at all in the regional strategy, it has not been included in the figure. Solar energy (47 supportive regions) is the most popular, followed by biomass (43 supportive regions). However, in the case of biomass, two Czech and two Slovak regions maintain a rather negative stance. On the other hand, hydro (22 supportive regions) and wind energy (24 supportive regions) enjoy lower levels of support.

Attitudes towards biomass are rather mixed. On the positive side, it is highlighted as advantageous in villages compared to larger towns and cities (Central Bohemian

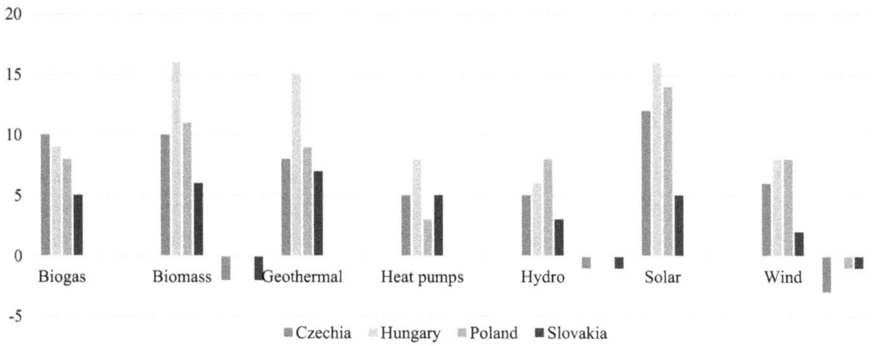

Figure 3.5 Development of renewable energy sources in regional strategies of Visegrad Group countries.

Source: Authors.

Region, 2022). The use of biomass in Czechia and Slovakia is understood especially as the use of firewood. On the negative side, biomass is seen as contributing to air pollution through inappropriate heating (using wet wood together with coal, waste) and emphasis is placed on measures leading to the proper burning of solid fuels in local heating systems (Prešov Region, 2021). However, Polish regions point out that the further use of biomass also entails fisheries and forestry, as well as the by-products of agricultural activities (Łódź Region, 2021).

The arguments for the further use of biomass vary across regions; for instance, many Czech and Polish regions consider biomass crucial for coal replacement and aim to develop its further potential use. Similarly, the Czech Hradec Králové and South Bohemian Regions see biomass as having the largest potential among all RES. In Slovakia it has been argued that biomass has the largest technically usable potential, especially in heat production (Trnava Region, 2023). The further use of biomass is supported by assisting low-income households to change their heating furnaces through the Czech programme Boiler subsidies V and in the Slovak Žilina Region. The crucial importance of replacing and monitoring heating furnaces more frequently is often highlighted (Ústí Region, 2016).

Solar energy is the most supported RES in regional strategies, with 47 out of 60 regions calling for its promotion. This is in alignment with the EU strategy which considers solar energy key for a clean energy transition, as it can reduce dependence on fossil fuels and at the same time be economically competitive (European Commission, 2023b). Regarding the innovative use of solar energy, the Czech Olomouc Region plans to develop solar energy infrastructure for agricultural use, specifically through agrophotovoltaics (Olomouc Region, 2020). Conversely, some regions have expressed a desire to develop solar energy while also addressing its potential negative effects. The Czech Vysočina Region, for instance, points out that excessive and unregulated construction of wind or solar power plants poses a threat, especially when it comes to the social and aesthetic aspects of cultural monuments, as solar panels may impact the appearance of cultural monuments or other individual interests inconsistent with the surrounding environment, both natural and urbanized (Vysočina Region, 2020). The Polish Świętokrzyskie Region emphasizes the importance of employing technologies that protect against the "water mirror" effect (which affects birds) and advocates fencing that facilitates the movement of small animals (Świętokrzyskie Region, 2023).

The decarbonization of heating systems in V4 presents a particular challenge, with biogas and geothermal energy appearing to be fitting solutions according to 32 and 39 regional documents, respectively. Heat pumps are mentioned to a much lesser degree (in only 21, mostly Hungarian strategies). Several regions emphasize the development of geothermal energy in heating systems, citing the need for more decentralized sources, and research and development in this field (Ústí Region, 2016). The role of geothermal together with biomass is particularly highlighted (Central Bohemian Region, 2022). However, negative stances are also articulated, such as the low efficiency of heat pumps in cold weather conditions (Somogy Region, 2021), or the risk of geothermal development jeopardizing the quantity and quality of groundwater in the case of poor quality and unprofessional drilling for wells and heat pump installations (South Bohemian Region, 2021).

When it comes to hydro use, all regional strategies rely on water management in their landscapes. However, only a few of them (22) mention this source as suitable for energy use and development by emphasizing its further development in line with nature protection. Regions arguing in favour of this source mention the role of hydro as adding flexibility to electricity. For instance, the Vysočina Region considers the continued maintenance of hydropower crucial, also because of the presence of the Dukovany nuclear power plants in the region (Vysočina Region, 2020).

Attitudes toward wind energy are rather mixed, with only 24 regions planning to support its development. For example, the Czech Liberec Region emphasizes potential issues with the further development of large solar wind parks due to nature protection but supports small-scale wind parks (Liberec Region, 2020). Concerns about large-scale wind parks are also evident in the Ústí Region, particularly in proximity to woods and buildings. On the other hand, Slovakia takes a more friendly approach to wind energy and considers it currently insufficiently mapped and hindered by legislation and national-level policy, despite significant investor interest in this type of energy (Prešov Region, 2021). One exception is the Trnava Region, which emphasizes limited wind potential due to insufficient wind blowing, constraining the production capacities of turbines (Trnava Region, 2023).

As the only V4 country with access to the sea, Poland sees its future in wind development. Offshore wind farms are crucial not only for future energy development but also for the overall economic potential based on supply chains in renewables (Pomerania Region, 2021). However, it also acknowledges limitations, especially the need for developing distribution systems. The West Pomerania Region is one of the most inclined towards wind development but sees the problem of further development, arguing that it makes investments in wind power plants less profitable and their location more difficult (West Pomerania Region, 2019). Although in the Polish Łódź Region wind currently constitutes the largest share of regional RES, there are plans to decrease its use due to its negative impact on urbanized areas (such as the reduction of land value and noise nuisance) and the reduction of scenic values, given the flat nature of the region (Łódź Region, 2021).

In connection to RES development, only a few regions emphasize the importance of energy storage and the development of infrastructure to integrate clean sources. Among these, there are plans to develop an Innovation Centre with smart technologies, with energy as its backbone (Olomouc Region, 2020), to create a system of good practices in RES, energy efficiency, and energy management systems (Subcarpathian Region, 2020), ensure the region's role as an aggregator for the flexibility of smart energy networks (Moravian-Silesian Region, 2019; Nógrád Region, 2021), develop battery storages as a priority (Trnava Region, 2023), strengthen cross-border interconnectors (Győr-Moson-Sopron Region, 2021), and focus on cybersecurity for energy systems in connection to energy security (Lubusz Region, 2021). Several Hungarian and Polish regions also highlight developments towards prosumers.

3.7 Further development of other energy sources

Of course, regions do not want to develop renewable energy exclusively; rather, they also aim to develop other energy sources. We examined four of them, as summarized in Figure 3.6. Hydrogen is the only energy source that cannot be considered 'traditional'. Indeed, the EU sees it as an important part of decarbonization and the efforts are being put into research and development, as it is currently almost entirely produced from fossil fuels (European Commission, 2023c). Developing hydrogen is also of greater interest to regional authorities in the Visegrad countries, as more than one-third of the regions (24) anticipate its use. They aim to develop a hydrogen ecosystem by 2040 (Greater Poland Region, 2020) or the Hydrogen Valley, intended to transform the region from relying mainly on heavy industry and metallurgy to being engaged in smart technologies, advanced

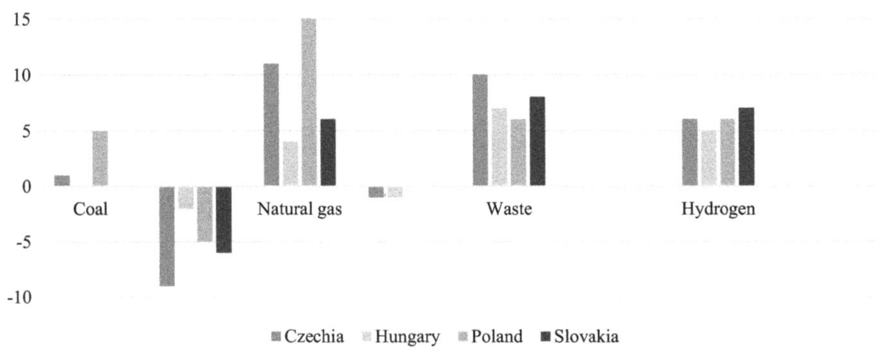

Figure 3.6 Development of other energy sources in regional strategies of Visegrad Group countries.

Source: Authors.

engineering, or technologies with high added value (Moravian-Silesian Region, 2019). There are also plans to modify the existing gas infrastructure to use pipelines for transporting hydrogen from Ukraine (Košice Region, 2022) and ambitions to produce hydrogen from RES (Csongrád-Csanád Region, 2021).

Hydrogen is primarily seen as an important part of cleaner mobility, as regions aim to develop hydrogen filling stations and buses (Moravian-Silesian Region, 2019). In Poland, hydrogen is produced in a refinery in Gdansk, but there are plans for further production using nuclear energy that is currently being developed in Poland and wind energy surpluses (Pomerania Region, 2021). Some regions see hydrogen as a complex energy carrier of the future (Greater Poland Region, 2020) or plan to blend it into the heating system and develop it alongside biomethane and synthetic methane (Łódź Region, 2021).

As discussed in the third section of the chapter, coal remains a significant part of the energy mix in Czechia and, especially, Poland. However, as Figure 3.6 illustrates, regions generally express a negative stance towards this source and propose various policies and measures to transition away from it. In the case of Hungary, coal is almost entirely absent from the documents, with the Baranya Region considering it to be a nineteenth-century source of energy (Baranya Region, 2021). In the case of Slovakia, there are few arguments against its further use, as coal is mainly seen as a source of air pollution which should therefore be replaced by natural gas and renewables (Prešov Region, 2021).

Most Czech regions view the shift away from coal as an inevitable process. Several of them focus on the recultivation of the country due to the fact that extensive areas have been degraded by brown coal mining (Ústí Region, 2016). The Karlovy Vary Region highlights the positive effects of coal phase-out on nature: with the gradual cessation of mining and cultivation the environment in the region undergoes positive transformations to maintain the high quality of the natural environment. It should be noted, however, that this region is one of the three Czech regions that are part of the Initiative for Coal Regions in Transition established on the basis of the Government Resolution No 826 of 19 October 2015 (Ministry of Industry and Trade of the ČR, 2023) and thus also enjoys financial support provided by the European Commission.

In many Czech regions, a shift away from brown coal is anticipated in local furnace areas (Pardubice Region, 2021), while Prague emphasizes the importance of collecting precise data on households using coal, which is the first step in setting more effective city policies (Capital City of Prague, 2016). Some regions, however, find that heating properly is important for having clean air and consider coal crucial in the upcoming years (Plzeň Region, 2023).

Poland acknowledges environmental problems associated with coal use. However, it is not always clear which policies should be implemented to eliminate this source of energy (Masovia Region, 2022) and the coal-based Polish national energy strategy is often blamed (Opole Region, 2021). Regions point to the air pollution problem, which is attributed mainly to old furnaces (Lower Silesia, Pomerania). Other coal regions highlight the importance of coal mining and do not anticipate any substantial changes by 2030 in terms of coal mining and extracting (alongside with natural gas) for the overall industry of the region (Lower Silesia Region, 2018). Silesia acknowledges the strong position of coal in the industry and wants to continue coal mining activities by implementing more efficient methods of coal mining and processing. At the same time, however, it relies on the Just Transition Fund, considering it crucial in the process of regional transformation (Silesia Region, 2020).

Similarly, Polish regions tend to place more emphasis on the need to shift away from coal towards low-carbon sources under the Just Transition Fund rather than the role of mining activities in the economy (Lesser Poland Region, 2020), not only because of environmental harm caused by coal mining activities, especially problems with water shortages due to mining activities, but also the negative social, health, and economic effects of mining (Greater Poland Region, 2020).

When it comes to the use of natural gas, we can expect it to remain an important source, as 36 strategies acknowledge its continued use in the future, emphasizing the improvement of accessibility and maintenance of gas infrastructure, as well as its modernization and further development. Even in regions with progressive renewable policies, plans are in place to expand gas infrastructure to users who currently do not have access to it (Greater Poland Region, 2020). Polish regions also foresee future developments in increasing gas storage, considering it crucial for the country's energy security (Kujawy-Pomerania Region, 2020) and aim to become an important gas hub in the region, which is supported by the presence of an LNG port (Pomerania Region, 2021). Hungarian strategies mention the further development of natural gas only scarcely, also because they have the largest share of gas in heating among the Visegrad Group countries (Kerekes et al., 2023). However, some of them acknowledge the importance of a developed gas infrastructure (Baranya Region, 2021).

Czech and Polish regions consider natural gas an important means of decreasing emissions from coal in heating. The V4 regions highlight the role of gas in the future, especially in the context of developing a centralized heating system over individual heating. For example, in the Central Bohemian Region, a priority in the energy sector is to review the number of "dead connections" in the gas sector and explore the possibilities of their revival, with particular emphasis on developing the district heating system (Central Bohemian Region, 2022). Additionally, there are plans to incorporate natural gas into the transport sector through the use of CNG buses due to their lower emissions and benefits for local air quality (Liberec Region, 2020). Natural gas in transport is seen as a future prospect, especially in Czechia and Poland.

Conversely, not every region views gas as a potential energy source. The Czech capital places emphasis on e-mobility as a means to decrease dependence on natural gas and oil (Capital City of Prague, 2016). In regions where natural gas constitutes a substantial part of the energy mix, the future leans more towards biogas (Zlín Region, 2020) and geothermal energy (Borsod-Abaúj-Zemplén Region, 2021), arguing that further construction of the gas distribution network is unprofitable (Nitra Region, 2022).

Finally, the regions are rather divided on the issue of using waste for energy purposes. For instance, Bratislava City wants to preserve the existing incinerator, while simultaneously aiming to modernize it and use less waste for energy purposes. More than half of the regions (31) acknowledge the importance of using waste for energy purposes and want to expand current capacities or build new incinerators including industrial waste (Baranya Region, 2021). Poland is the most cautious about the use of waste for energy purposes, while Czechia embraces this source the most. However, it is important to add that all regions have their own strategies for waste management, mainly focused on a circular economy approach, recycling, and decreasing the percentage of landfill waste.

3.8 Conclusion

The aim of this chapter was to examine how regions within the Visegrad Four countries respond to challenges posed by climate change and energy transition by analyzing the strategies of 60 regions, including capital cities. In general, all regions acknowledge climate change and aim to transition toward sustainable and low-carbon energy systems and deploy climate policies. In their future development, regions emphasize measures that fit within the European Green Deal areas, such as building renovation, sustainable transport, biodiversity protection, ecological agriculture, measures against air pollution, circular economy, and adaptation to climate change. A notable divergence exists among the V4 countries regarding their acknowledgment and alignment with EU climate policies and plans, including reaching climate neutrality, the Recovery and Resilience Plan, and the European Green Deal. Slovakia stands out as the country where almost every region explicitly mentions these policies, while Czech regions refer to them more sparingly.

By looking into the further use of energy sources, we can see that the V4 regions opt for diverse approaches to the energy transition. All regions express general support for RES, but there are differences in their preferred types based on geographical conditions, current energy mix, political preferences, and financial possibilities. Solar energy enjoys the most support, followed by biomass and geothermal; on the other hand, regions plan to develop wind energy, hydro and heat pumps to a much smaller degree. Moreover, there are also negative stances toward wind energy, particularly in Czechia. Regions of the Visegrad Group countries express negative stances toward coal and propose policies to transition away from it, with notable exceptions in Hungary and Slovakia, which barely mention coal in their strategies. In Czech regions, the shift away from coal is viewed as inevitable, while Polish regions opt for slightly different approaches, with some emphasizing the importance of coal mining for the local economy. The Just Transition Fund plays a crucial role in the transformation process, providing financial support for regional projects and activities leading to a coal phase-out.

We can conclude that from a climate and energy policy perspective, the studied regions are characterized by Europeanization (Sturm and Dieringer, 2005), as there is recognition of EU climate efforts (climate neutrality goal, European Green Deal policies), mainly because of the strategies which are especially aligned with the

Interreg programme priorities and the new EU funds period. The importance of EU funds is emphasized in all the documents. However, many strategies are in the shadow of policy developments at the national level as they lack their own ambitions (Hoppe and Miedema, 2020) and the majority of regions appear to facilitate rather than drive the transition towards renewable energy (Smith, 2007).

Future research should build upon these findings and look closer not only at the specific strategies of the regions in the field of climate and energy policies (for instance, energy strategies), but especially at their implementation. To successfully implement ambitious plans, several crucial factors must be researched, primarily the regions' capacities as, despite robust plans, there is a risk of failure due to a lack of administrative capacities and political leadership (Suitner and Ecker, 2020). Another potential area of study is the barriers to climate policy development at the local level within V4 which, include the lack of citizen involvement, general attachment to the status quo, dependency on external financial support, as well as the lack of awareness about funding opportunities and complex interrelations with frameworks in neighbouring regions and at the national level (Hat et al., 2022). Addressing these barriers in research is crucial also for the successful advancement of climate policies and energy transformation in V4.

Acknowledgements

This work was supported by the Slovak Research and Development Agency Grant No APVV-20-0012. The authors would like to thank Nada Kujundžić for the language editing.

References

Atikur Rahaman, M., Bin Amin, M., Taru, R.D., Ahammed, M.R., Rabbi, M.F., 2023. An analysis of renewable energy consumption in Visegrád countries. *Environ Res Commun* 5, 105013. https://doi.org/10.1088/2515-7620/acff40

Baranya Region, 2021. Baranya Megyei Területfejlesztési Program [Online Document]. URL www.baranya.hu/dokumentum/1471 (accessed 16.1.24).

Borsod-Abaúj-Zemplén Region, 2021. Borsod-AbaBorsod-Abaúj-Zemplúj-Zemplén Megye Területfejlesztési Programja 2021–2027 [Online Document]. URL https://baz.hu/media/2206_0_teruletfejlesztesi_program_21_27_strategiai_programresz_836.pdf (accessed 16.1.24).

Brownlee, T.D., Camaioni, C., Magaudda, S., Mugnoz, S., Pellegrino, P., 2021. The INTERREG Italy-Croatia Joint_SECAP Project: A collaborative approach for adaptation planning. *Sustainability* 14, 404. https://doi.org/10.3390/su14010404

Brugger, H., Henry, A.D., 2021. Influence of policy discourse networks on local energy transitions. *Environ Innov Soc Transit* 39, 141–154. https://doi.org/10.1016/j.eist.2021.03.006

Capital City of Prague, 2016. Strategický plán hlavního města Prahy [Online Document]. URL https://iprpraha.cz/stranka/27 (accessed 12.11.23).

Central Bohemian Region, 2022. Strategie rozvoje územního obvodu Středočeského kraje na období 2019 – 2024 s výhledem do 2030 [Online Document]. URL https://stredoceskykraj.cz/web/uzemni-planovani/strategicke-dokumenty (accessed 12.11.23).

Csongrád-Csanád Region, 2021. CsongraCsongrád-Csanád-Csanád Megye Területfejlesztési Programja 2021–2027 [Online Document]. URL www.csongrad-megye.hu/teruletfejlesztes/Csongrad-Csanad_TFP_2021-2027_STRATEGIAI.pdf (accessed 16.1.24).

Czyżak, P., Fox, H., 2023. In it together: The road to a cleaner, cheaper CEE power system [Online Document]. EMBER. URL https://ember-climate.org/insights/research/in-it-together-cee-power-system/ (accessed 12.7.23).

Dahal, K., Juhola, S., Niemelä, J., 2018. The role of renewable energy policies for carbon neutrality in Helsinki Metropolitan area. *Sustain Cities Soc* 40, 222–232. https://doi.org/10.1016/j.scs.2018.04.015

De La Peña, L., Guo, R., Cao, X., Ni, X., Zhang, W., 2022. Accelerating the energy transition to achieve carbon neutrality. *Resour Conserv Recycl* 177, 105957. https://doi.org/10.1016/j.resconrec.2021.105957

Dobravec, V., Matak, N., Sakulin, C., Krajačić, G., 2021. Multilevel governance energy planning and policy: A view on local energy initiatives. *Energy Sustain Soc* 11, 2. https://doi.org/10.1186/s13705-020-00277-y

Dvorak, J., 2021. Response of the Lithuanian municipalities to the first wave of COVID-19. *Baltic region* 13. https://doi.org/10.5922/2079-8555-2021-1-4

European Commission, 2018. National energy and climate plans [Online Document]. URL https://commission.europa.eu/energy-climate-change-environment/implementation-eu-countries/energy-and-climate-governance-and-reporting/national-energy-and-climate-plans_en (accessed 12.7.23).

European Commission, 2019. The European Green Deal [Online Document]. URL https://ec.europa.eu/commission/presscorner/detail/en/ip_19_6691 (accessed 12.10.23).

European Commission, 2020. Recovery plan for Europe [Online Document]. URL https://commission.europa.eu/strategy-and-policy/recovery-plan-europe_en (accessed 12.12.23).

European Commission, 2021a. Fit for 55 [Online Document]. URL www.consilium.europa.eu/en/policies/green-deal/fit-for-55-the-eu-plan-for-a-green-transition/ (accessed 12.12.23).

European Commission, 2021b. Priorities for 2021–2027 [Online Document]. URL https://ec.europa.eu/regional_policy/policy/how/priorities_en (accessed 12.7.23).

European Commission, 2022a. REPowerEU [Online Document]. URL https://commission.europa.eu/strategy-and-policy/priorities-2019-2024/european-green-deal/repowereu-affordable-secure-and-sustainable-energy-europe_en (accessed 12.7.23).

European Commission, 2022b. State of the energy union 2022 – snapshots per EU country [Online Document]. URL https://energy.ec.europa.eu/publications/state-energy-union-2022-snapshots-eu-country_en (accessed 15.1.24).

European Commission, 2023a. EU regional and urban development [Online Document]. URL https://ec.europa.eu/regional_policy/in-your-country/programmes_en (accessed 15.1.24).

European Commission, 2023b. Solar energy [Online Document]. URL https://energy.ec.europa.eu/topics/renewable-energy/solar-energy_en (accessed 16.1.24).

European Commission, 2023c. Hydrogen [Online Document]. URL https://energy.ec.europa.eu/topics/energy-systems-integration/hydrogen_en (accessed 16.1.24).

European Council, 2014. European Council (23 and 24 October 2014) Conclusions on 2030 Climate and Energy Policy Framework [Online Document]. URL www.consilium.europa.eu/uedocs/cms_data/docs/pressdata/en/ec/145356.pdf (accessed 1.8.24).

European Council, 2019. European Council meeting (12 December 2019) – Conclusions [Online Document]. URL www.consilium.europa.eu/media/41768/12-euco-final-conclusions-en.pdf (accessed 12.12.23).

European Parliament, 2020. European climate pact [Online Document]. URL www.europarl.europa.eu/RegData/etudes/BRIE/2020/659303/EPRS_BRI(2020)659303_EN.pdf (accessed 20.9.23).

FEDARENE, 2023. Regions Repower Europe [Online Document]. URL https://fedarene.org/repowereu/ (accessed 9.20.23).

Gerbelová, H., Spisto, A., Giaccaria, S., 2020. Regional energy transition: An analytical approach applied to the Slovakian Coal Region. *Energies (Basel)* 14, 110. https://doi.org/10.3390/en14010110

Greater Poland Region, 2020. Strategia rozwoju województwa wielkopolskiego do 2030 roku [Online Document]. URL https://bip.umww.pl/292---k_91---k_207---strategia-rozwoju-wojewodztwa-wielkopolskiego-do-2030 (accessed 12.12.23).

Győr-Moson-Sopron Region, 2021. Győr-Moson-Sopron Megye Stratégiai Program [Online Document]. URL www.gyms.hu/data/files/2021/teruletfejlesztes_anyagok/GYMS_StrategiaiProgram_3.0_20210907_01.pdf (accessed 16.1.24).

Hat, K., Gorny, H., Gaupp-Berghausen, M., Schuh, B., Barroso, S., 2022. EU regions in the transformation towards a climate-neutral future. www.europarl.europa.eu/RegData/etudes/STUD/2022/699628/IPOL_STU(2022)699628_EN.pdf (accessed 16.1.24).

Hecher, M., Vilsmaier, U., Akhavan, R., Binder, C.R., 2016. An integrative analysis of energy transitions in energy regions: A case study of ökoEnergieland in Austria. *Ecological Economics* 121, 40–53. https://doi.org/10.1016/j.ecolecon.2015.11.015

Hoppe, T., Miedema, M., 2020. A Governance approach to regional energy transition: Meaning, conceptualization and practice. *Sustainability* 12, 915. https://doi.org/10.3390/su12030915

Kerekes, L., Horváth, G., Loskot-Strachota, A., Oravcova, V., Sklenář, O., Kotek, P., Takácsné Tóth, B., 2023. Decarbonisation of the Household Heating Sector in the Visegrad Countries [Online Document]. Rekk. https://rekk.hu/downloads/academic_publications/V4_decarbonisation_of%20heating_2023.pdf (accessed 16.1.24).

Kern, K., 2019. Cities as leaders in EU multilevel climate governance: Embedded upscaling of local experiments in Europe. *Env Polit* 28, 125–145. https://doi.org/10.1080/09644016.2019.1521979

Kettl, K.-H., Niemetz, N., Eder, M., Narodoslawsky, M., 2014. Optimal renewable energy systems for regions. *J. Sustain. Dev. of Energy, Water Environ. Syst.* 2, 88–99. https://doi.org/10.13044/j.sdewes.2014.02.0008

Komendantova, N., Neumueller, S., 2020. Discourses about energy transition in Austrian climate and energy model regions: Turning awareness into action. *Energy & Environment* 31, 1473–1497. https://doi.org/10.1177/0958305X20907086

Košice Region, 2022. Program hospodárskeho rozvoja a sociálneho rozvoja KSK na roky 2023–2027 [Online Document]. URL https://web.vucke.sk/sk/uradna-tabula/rozvoj-regionu/phrsr-ksk-roky-2022-2027/ (accessed 12.12.23).

Krog, L., 2019. How municipalities act under the new paradigm for energy planning. *Sustain Cities Soc* 47, 101511. https://doi.org/10.1016/j.scs.2019.101511

Kujawy-Pomerania Region, 2020. Strategia rozwoju województwa kujawsko-pomorskiego do 2030 roku – Strategia Przyspieszenia 2030+ [Online Document]. URL https://kujawsko-pomorskie.pl/35295-prace-nad-strategia-2030 (accessed 12.12.23).

Lazaro, L.L.B., Soares, R.S., Bermann, C., Collaço, F.M.A., Giatti, L.L., Abram, S., 2022. Energy transition in Brazil: Is there a role for multilevel governance in a centralized energy regime? *Energy Res Soc Sci* 85, 102404. https://doi.org/10.1016/j.erss.2021.102404

Lesser Poland Region, 2020. Strategią Rozwoju Województwa "Małopolska 2030" [Online Document]. URL www.malopolska.pl/strategia-2030 (accessed 12.12.23).

Liberec Region, 2020. Strategie rozvoje Libereckého kraje 2021 – 2027 [Online Document]. URL https://regionalni-rozvoj.kraj-lbc.cz/page1874/krajske-koncepcni-dokumenty (accessed 12.11.23).

Łódź Region, 2021. Strategia Rozwoju Województwa Łódzkiego 2030 [Online Document]. URL https://strategia.lodzkie.pl/strategia-rozwoju-wl-2030/ (accessed 12.11.23).

Lower Silesia Region, 2018. Województwa Dolnośląskiego strategia rozwoju [Online Document]. URL https://umwd.dolnyslask.pl/fileadmin/user_upload/Rozwoj_regionalny/SRWD/projekt_strategii/SRWD_2030_calosc_druk.pdf (accessed 12.12.23).

Lublin Region, 2023. Doradztwo Energetyczne [Online Document]. URL www.lubelskie.pl/doradztwo-energetyczne/ (accessed 12.7.23).

Lubusz Region, 2021. Strategia rozwoju województwa lubuskiego 2030 [Online Document]. URL https://files.lubuskie.pl/sites/1/wiadomosci/19771/files/strategia_wojewodztwa_lubuskiego_2030.pdf (accessed 12.11.23).

Masovia Region, 2022. Strategia rozwoju województwa mazowieckiego 2030+ [Online Document]. URL www.dialog.mazovia.pl/aktualnosci/informacje/582-strategia-rozwoju-wojewodztwa-mazowieckiego-2030-innowacyjne-mazowsze-przyjeta-przez-sejmik-wojewodztwa-mazowieckiego (accessed 12.12.23).

Matern, A., Špaček, M., Theuner, J., Knippschild, R., Janáček, J., 2023. Strategies for energy transition and regional development in European post-coal mining regions: Ústí Region, Czechia, and Lusatia, Germany. *Territ Politic Gov* 1–22. https://doi.org/10.1080/21622671.2023.2231972

Melica, G., Bertoldi, P., Kona, A., Iancu, A., Rivas, S., Zancanella, P., 2018. Multilevel governance of sustainable energy policies: The role of regions and provinces to support the participation of small local authorities in the Covenant of Mayors. *Sustain Cities Soc* 39, 729–739. https://doi.org/10.1016/j.scs.2018.01.013

Mi, Z., Guan, D., Liu, Z., Liu, J., Viguié, V., Fromer, N., Wang, Y., 2019. Cities: The core of climate change mitigation. *J Clean Prod* 207, 582–589. https://doi.org/10.1016/j.jclepro.2018.10.034

Ministry of Economy of the SR, 2023. Draft update of the Integrated National energy and climate plan for 2021–2030 [Online Document]. URL https://commission.europa.eu/system/files/2023-09/SLOVAKIA%20-%20DRAFT%20UPDATED%20NECP%202021-2030_EN.pdf (accessed 20.9.23).

Ministry of Industry and Trade of the ČR, 2023. Update of the Czech National Plan of the Republics in the field of energy and climate [Online Document]. URL https://commission.europa.eu/publications/czech-draft-updated-necp-2021-2030_en (accessed 12.7.23).

Ministry of Innovation and Technology of Hungary, 2023. National Energy and Climate Plan [Online Document]. URL https://commission.europa.eu/publications/hungary-draft-updated-necp-2021-2030_en (accessed 12.7.23).

Ministry of State Assets of Poland, 2019. The National Energy and Climate Plan for 2021–2030 [Online Document]. URL https://commission.europa.eu/energy-climate-change-environment/implementation-eu-countries/energy-and-climate-governance-and-reporting/national-energy-and-climate-plans_en#national-energy-and-climate-plans-2021-2030 (accessed 12.7.23).

Mišík, M., Oravcová, V., 2022. The myth of homogeneity: The Visegrad Group's energy transition. pp. 1–24. https://doi.org/10.1007/978-3-030-74380-2_28-1
Moravian-Silesian Region, 2019. Strategie rozvoje Moravskoslezského kraje pro období 2019–2027 [Online Document]. URL www.msk.cz/cs/temata/cestovni_ruch/strategicke-dokumenty-2425/ (accessed 12.11.23).
Nitra Region, 2022. Program hospodárskeho rozvoja a sociálneho rozvoja NSK do roku 2030 [Online Document]. URL www.unsk.sk/Zobraz/Sekciu/program-hospodarskeho-rozvoja-a-socialneho-rozvoja-nsk-do-roku-2030 (accessed 12.12.23).
Nógrád Region, 2021. Nógrád Megye Területfejlesztési Programja 2021–2027 [Online Document]. URL www.nograd.hu/files/terfejl/program/TFP-2021-27.pdf (accessed 16.1.24).
OECD, 2019. Financing environmental and energy transitions for regions and cities: creating local solutions for global challenges [Online Document]. URL www.oecd.org/cfe/regionaldevelopment/Schoenmaker-Schramade-2019-Financing-Environmental-Energy-Transitions.pdf (accessed 20.9.23).
OECD, 2020. Managing Environmental and Energy Transitions for Regions and Cities [Online Document]. URL https://www.oecd-ilibrary.org/urban-rural-and-regional-development/managing-environmental-and-energy-transitions-for-regions-and-cities_f0c6621f-en (accessed 20.9.23).
Olomouc Region, 2020. Strategie rozvoje územního obvodu Olomouckého kraje pro období 2021–2027 [Online Document]. URL www.olkraj.cz/strategie-rozvoje-uzemniho-obvodu-olomouckeho-kraje-cl-537.html (accessed 12.11.23).
Opole Region, 2021. Strategia rozwoju województwa opolskiego – Opolskie 2030 [Online Document]. URL www.opolskie.pl/region/rozwoj-regionalny/strategia-rozwoju-wojewodztwa-opolskiego-opolskie-2030/ (accessed 12.12.23).
Pardubice Region, 2021. Strategie rozvoje Pardubického kraje 2021–2027 [Online Document]. URL www.pardubickykraj.cz/strategie-rozvoje-pardubickeho-kraje-2021-2027 (accessed 12.11.23).
Plzeň Region, 2023. Program rozvoje Plzeňského kraje 2022+ [Online Document]. URL www.plzensky-kraj.cz/navrh-dokumentu-program-rozvoje-plzenskeho-kraje- (accessed 12.11.23).
Podlaskie Region, 2020. Strategia Rozwoju Województwa Podlaskiego 2030 [Online Document]. URL https://strategia.wrotapodlasia.pl/pl/strategia_rozwoju_wojewdztwa_podlaskiego_2030/ (accessed 12.11.23).
Pomerania Region, 2021. Strategia Rozwoju Województwa Pomorskiego 2030 [Online Document]. URL https://strategia2030.pomorskie.eu/wp-content/uploads/2021/06/Zalacznik-do-uchwaly_SWP_376_XXXI_21_SRWP2030_120421.pdf (accessed 12.11.23).
Prešov Region, 2021. Program hospodárskeho rozvoja a sociálneho rozvoja PSK na roky 2021–2030 [Online Document]. URL www.po-kraj.sk/sk/samosprava/vyzvy-granty/programove-obdobie-2021-2027/phrsr-psk-2021-2030.html (accessed 12.11.23).
Reckien, D., Salvia, M., Heidrich, O., Church, J.M., Pietrapertosa, F., De Gregorio-Hurtado, S., D'Alonzo, V., Foley, A., Simoes, S.G., Krkoška Lorencová, E., Orru, H., Orru, K., Wejs, A., Flacke, J., Olazabal, M., Geneletti, D., Feliu, E., Vasilie, S., Nador, C., Krook-Riekkola, A., Matosović, M., Fokaides, P.A., Ioannou, B.I., Flamos, A., Spyridaki, N.-A., Balzan, M. V., Fülöp, O., Paspaldzhiev, I., Grafakos, S., Dawson, R., 2018. How are cities planning to respond to climate change? Assessment of local climate plans from 885 cities in the EU-28. *J Clean Prod* 191, 207–219. https://doi.org/10.1016/j.jclepro.2018.03.220

Republic of Poland, 2020. PAA in the Polish Nuclear Power Programme [Online Document]. URL www.gov.pl/web/paa-en/Polish-Nuclear-Power-Program (accessed 12.7.23).

Reuters, 2020. Mayors of central European capitals call for tougher EU climate goals [Online Document]. URL www.reuters.com/article/business/energy/mayors-of-central-european-capitals-call-for-tougher-eu-climate-goals-idUSL8N2DU3H5/ (accessed 12.12.23).

Sedlacek, S., Tötzer, T., Lund-Durlacher, D., 2020. Collaborative governance in energy regions – Experiences from an Austrian region. *J Clean Prod* 256, 120256. https://doi.org/10.1016/j.jclepro.2020.120256

Silesia Region, 2020. Strategia rozwoju województwa Śląskiego "Śląskie 2030" [Online Document]. URL www.slaskie.pl/content/strategia-rozwoju-wojewodztwa-slaskiego-slaskie-2030 (accessed 12.12.23).

Smith, A., 2007. Emerging in between: The multi-level governance of renewable energy in the English regions. *Energy Policy* 35, 6266–6280. https://doi.org/10.1016/j.enpol.2007.07.023

Somogy Region, 2021. Somogy Megye Területfejlesztési Programja [Online Document]. URL www.som-onkorm.hu/static/files/Megyei_Területf_21-27/Somogy%20Megye%20Területfejlesztési%20Program.pdf (accessed 16.1.24).

South Bohemian Region, 2021. Program rozvoje Jihočeského kraje na období 2021 – 2027 [Online Document]. URL www.kraj-jihocesky.cz/cs/krajsky-urad/odbor-regionalniho-rozvoje-uzemniho-planovani-stavebniho-radu (accessed 12.11.23).

Sturm, R., Dieringer, J., 2005. The Europeanization of regions in Eastern and Western Europe: Theoretical perspectives. *Regional & Federal Studies* 15, 279–294. https://doi.org/10.1080/10438590500223251

Su, X., Tan, J., 2023. Regional energy transition path and the role of government support and resource endowment in China. *Renew. Sustain. Energy Rev.* 174, 113150. https://doi.org/10.1016/j.rser.2023.113150

Subcarpathian Region, 2020. Strategia rozwoju województwa – Podkarpackie 2030 [Online Document]. URL www.podkarpackie.pl/images/pliki/RR/2022/Strategia_rozwoju_wojew%C3%B3dztwa_-_Podkarpackie_2030_-_Sejmik_WP_28.09.2020_r.pdf (accessed 12.11.23).

Suitner, J., Ecker, M., 2020. "Making energy transition work": Bricolage in Austrian regions' path-creation. *Environ Innov Soc Transit* 36, 209–220. https://doi.org/10.1016/j.eist.2020.07.005

Świętokrzyskie Region, 2023. Gospodarka odpadami [Online Document]. URL www.swietokrzyskie.pro/category/urzad-marszalkowski/departamenty/departament-rozwoju-obszarow-wiejskich-i-srodowiska/oddzialy-departament-rozwoju-obszarow-wiejskich-i-srodowiska/oddzial-gospodarki-odpadami/gospodarka-odpadami/ (accessed 12.7.23).

Tàbara, J.D., 2011. Integrated climate governance in regions? Assessing Catalonia's performance using the 'climate learning ladder.' *Reg Environ Change* 11, 259–270. https://doi.org/10.1007/s10113-010-0135-3

Trnava Region, 2023. Program hospodárskeho rozvoja a sociálneho rozvoja Trnavského samosprávneho kraja 2023–2030 [Online Document]. URL www.enviroportal.sk/sk/eia/detail/program-hospodarskeho-rozvoja-socialneho-rozvoja-trnavskeho-samospravn-2 (accessed 12.11.23).

Ústí Region, 2016. Strategie rozvoje Ústeckého kraje do roku 2027 [Online Document]. URL www.kr-ustecky.cz/strategie-rozvoje-kraje/ms-274628/p1=274628 (accessed 12.11.23).

van Dijk, J., Wieczorek, A.J., Ligtvoet, A., 2022. Regional capacity to govern the energy transition: The case of two Dutch energy regions. *Environ Innov Soc Transit* 44, 92–109. https://doi.org/10.1016/j.eist.2022.06.001

Varela-Vázquez, P., Sánchez-Carreira, M. del C., 2015. Socioeconomic impact of wind energy on peripheral regions. *Renew Sustain Energy Rev* 50, 982–990. https://doi.org/10.1016/j.rser.2015.05.045

Voříšek, M., 2023. Evropské uhlí dohání vysoké provozní náklady, nikoliv vládní termíny pro konec uhlí. OENERGETICE. [Online Document]. URL https://oenergetice.cz/uhli/evropske-uhli-dohani-vysoke-provozni-naklady-nikoliv-vladni-terminy-pro-konec-uhli (accessed 12.12.23).

Vysočina Region, 2020. Strategie rozvoje Kraje Vysočina (2021–2027) [Online Document]. URL www.kr-vysocina.cz/regionalni-rozvoj/ds-305235/p1=122461 (accessed 12.11.23).

West Pomerania Region, 2019. Pomorze Zachodnie Strategia 2030 [Online Document]. URL https://eregion.wzp.pl/sites/default/files/srwz_2030_en_size.pdf (accessed 12.11.23).

Zlín Region, 2020. Strategie rozvoje Zlínského kraje 2030 [Online Document]. URL https://zlinskykraj.cz/strategie-a-koncepce-zlinskeho-kraje (accessed 12.12.23).

4 In Rosatom's shadow

The uncertain role of nuclear in energy transition of Central and Eastern Europe

Zsolt Gál

4.1 Introduction

Less than a week after the full-scale Russian invasion of Ukraine had started – and a day after the European Union (EU) had closed its airspace to Russian airlines and private jets as a response – an Ilyushin Il-76 cargo aircraft, belonging to Russian cargo airline Volga-Dnepr, took off in Moscow and flew across Belarus and Poland to land in Bratislava, Slovakia (Pandey, 2023). About a month later, a Russian aircraft of the same make flew even further into neighbouring Hungary – the planes (as well as several other similar deliveries) – were exempt from the ban because they were shipping critical nuclear fuel for Hungarian and Slovak Soviet-designed VVER[1] nuclear reactors. Both countries have a very high share of nuclear power in their electricity mix (Figure 4.1). Since the construction of their nuclear power plants (NPPs) both countries have been fully dependent on nuclear fuel from Russia and therefore highly vulnerable to any supply disruptions. Getting rid of this dependency is impossible in the short-term and is likely to be slow, technically difficult, and costly in the longer-term (Dolzikova, 2023; Lorenz, 2022). This largely explains the two country's opposition to impose EU sanctions on the Russian nuclear holding Rosatom and their desperate attempts to secure fuel to their reactors during the extraordinary war times.

This episode may serve as an illustration of the difficulties many Central and Eastern European (CEE) countries have been facing since the Russian aggression of February 2022. Although the EU-wide discussion and policymaking regarding the reduction of energy-dependence from Russia almost entirely concentrated on fossil fuels, mostly crude oil and natural gas; it seems to be that the decoupling from Russian nuclear fuel supplies is going to be by far the hardest challenge, especially for some CEE member states. Before and during the full-scale military aggression, it was the Russian gas monopoly, Gazprom that the Putin regime heavily utilised as its main energy weapon against the EU. Correspondingly, it attracted large-scale media coverage.

Meanwhile, the nuclear dependence remained largely hidden from the public, while Moscow maintained the status quo by not abusing Rosatom's leverage in a similar way to Gazprom's. At least not against EU countries and not until early

DOI: 10.4324/9781032624839-6

2024. While the EU sanctioned and stopped the import of Russian coal entirely and the import of Russian oil and gas drastically declined, Rosatom's nuclear exports – untouched by any sanctions or restrictions – continued to flourish. Indeed, Russia even managed to increase its nuclear exports in 2022 (Dolzikova, 2023). Regarding the EU, there was no substantial decline in Russian nuclear exports after the invasion and Euratom Supply Agency (ESA) data showed increased nuclear fuel supplies for the bloc's Russian-designed VVER reactors in 2022 which, according to Agency officials, was likely to be repeated in 2023 as the five member states concerned tried to increase their inventories of fresh fuel (Baczynska, 2023; ESA, 2023).

Despite all these difficulties, not only does the overwhelming consensus for maintaining existing nuclear capacities prevail across the CEE region, but almost all governments are sticking to their original plans of building new nuclear facilities. On the one hand, the green energy transition is unthinkable without the existing nuclear sources, and even without new nuclear capacities in some countries (for example, Poland). On the other hand, the prevailing nuclear enthusiasm raises serious questions since almost all new NPPs face massive construction delays and cost overruns worldwide. Additionally, nuclear energy is not a risk-free option, considering its vulnerability due to the overreliance on one or two NPPs and their 100 per cent dependence on foreign fuel supplies. Especially as the supplier is the Putin regime which tends to utilise the 'energy weapon' increasingly, even against its most loyal and profit-bringing long-term customers.

The aim of this chapter is to examine the importance of nuclear energy in the energy mixes of CEE countries especially regarding its potential role in the green energy transition while pointing at the exceptional character of the region within the developed world. We also describe how the region is coping with its dependence on Russia and how most countries are trying to decouple from this dependence, turning to alternative investors and nuclear fuel suppliers. Finally, we address the issue of feasibility regarding the numerous ongoing and planned new nuclear projects. Although we concentrate on the 11 post-socialist member states of the EU[2] (EU-11), the perspective of the chapter is often widened to include two more countries, Finland and Ukraine, since they share the common heritage of Russian dependence, and their recent developments may serve as a valuable lesson for CEE countries.

4.2 Central and Eastern Europe's nuclear exceptionality

CEE countries have been unique considering the importance of nuclear energy in their electricity and, consequently, energy mixes for quite a long time. In no other part of the world has the share of nuclear in the electricity mix been so high in so many countries. In 2022, of the top 10 countries in the world with the highest share of nuclear in their electricity production, six were post-socialist countries from the former Eastern Bloc and the Soviet Union, namely Slovakia, Hungary, Slovenia, Czechia, Bulgaria, and Ukraine (Figure 4.1). When the Russian aggression against

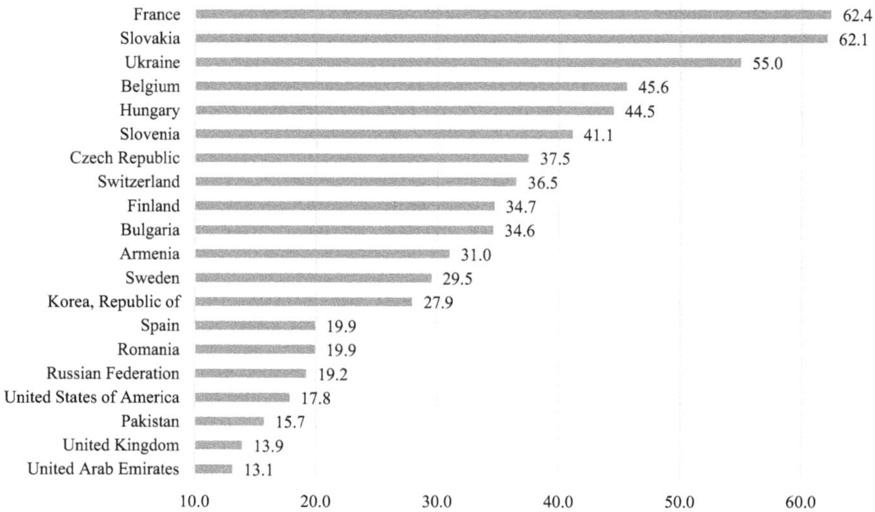

Figure 4.1 Twenty countries in the world with the highest share of nuclear in their electricity mix (2022 in %).

Ukraine started on 24 February 2022, among the ten global nuclear leaders, six countries were entirely or partially dependent on the fuel supplies of TVEL, a subsidiary of Rosatom: Slovakia, Hungary, Czechia, Bulgaria, Finland and Ukraine (Table 4.1). Five of those – except for Ukraine – are EU member states. In addition, four of them – except Finland – were entirely reliant on TVEL's supplies. Naturally, it creates dependence and a high vulnerability to supply shocks. Additionally, nuclear energy production is heavily concentrated in the relatively small CEE countries: usually they have one single or two NPP sites, the only exception being Ukraine with four (Table 4.1). This level of concentration further exacerbates the vulnerability of the energy system.

Another factor, which is unique in the region, has been the enduring high level of support for nuclear energy among the political elites, public opinion, and the community of technicians (Polanecký and Haverkamp, 2011). While the attitudes towards nuclear energy have been quite changeable in Western and Southern Europe, in CEE countries, we have continued to see a high level of support. None of the countries in the region decided to close down existing reactors (before the end of their life cycle) or phase out nuclear energy ; on the contrary, most of them are considering extending the operating lifetimes of their existing reactors and/or are planning new nuclear facilities (Schneider and Froggatt, 2023). We do not consider the closedown of several older Soviet-type reactors, viewed as unsafe by the EU, in Bulgaria, Lithuania and Slovakia here, since their phase out and decommissioning has been conditional in the EU-accession process of these countries (Mišík and Prachárová, 2021).

Table 4.1 Large commercial nuclear reactors closed, in operation, under construction or planned in CEE countries, Finland and Ukraine in 2023

Country	*Status*	*Number and capacity of reactors*	*NPP site and reactors*	*Reactor type*	*Year of shutdown, grid connection or planned start*	*Fuel supplied by*	*Mean age in years*
Bulgaria	decommissioning	4 (1620 MW)	Kozloduy 1-4	VVER-440/V230	2002, 2002, 2006, 2006	-	
	in operation	2 (2006 MW)	Kozloduy 5-6	VVER-1000/V-320	1987, 1991	TVEL	33,8
	planned	1 (1000 MW)	Kozloduy 7	AP1000	?	alternative	
Czechia	in operation	6 (4212 MW)	Dukovany 1-4	VVER-440/V-213	1985, 1986, 1986, 1987	TVEL	32
			Temelín 1-2	VVER-1000/V-320	2000, 2002	TVEL	
	planned	1 (1200 MW)	Dukovany 5	EPR, APR1000 or AP1000	2036	alternative	
Finland	in operation	5 (4394 MW)	Loviisa 1-2	VVER-440/V-213	1977, 1980	TVEL	35,7
			Olkiluoto 1-2	ABB-III, BWR-2500	1978, 1980	alternative	
			Olkiluoto 3	EPR	2022	alternative	
Hungary	in operation	4 (1916 MW)	Paks 1-4	VVER-440/V-213	1982, 1984, 1986, 1987	TVEL	38
	planned	2 (2400 MW)	Paks 5-6	VVER-1200/V-527	2032?	TVEL	
Lithuania	decommissioning	2 (2370 MW)	Ignalina 1-2	RBMK-1500	2004, 2009	-	
Poland	planned	3 (3750 MW)	Lubiatowo-Kopalino 1-3	AP1000	2033	alternative	
Romania	in operation	2 (1300 MW)	Cernavoda 1-2	CANDU 6	1996, 2007	alternative	21,5
Slovakia	decommissioning	3 (900 MW)	Jaslovské Bohunice A1	heavy water GCR	1977	-	

(*Continued*)

Table 4.1 (Continued)

Country	*Status*	*Number and capacity of reactors*	*NPP site and reactors*	*Reactor type*	*Year of shutdown, grid connection or planned start*	*Fuel supplied by*	*Mean age in years*
			Jaslovské Bohunice V1 1-2	VVER-440/V230	2006, 2008	-	
	in operation	5 (2308 MW)	Jaslovské Bohunice V2 1-2	VVER-440/V-213	1984, 1985	TVEL	25,1
			Mochovce 1-3	VVER-440/V-213	1998, 1999, 2023	TVEL	
	under construction	1 (471 MW)	Mochovce 4	VVER-440/V-213	2025?	TVEL	
	planned	1 (1200 MW)	Jaslovské Bohunice	N/A	after 2035	alternative	
Slovenia	in operation	1 (688 MW)	Krško 1[a]	WE 212	1981	alternative	41,7
Ukraine[b]	in operation	15 (13107 MW)	Rivne 1-2	VVER-440/V-213	1980, 1981	TVEL and alternative	34,4
			Rivne 3-4 Khmelnitsky 1-2 South Ukraine 1-3	VVER-1000/V-320 VVER-1000/V-320 VVER-1000/V-302/338/320	1986, 2004, 1987, 2004 1982, 1985, 1989		
			Zaporizhzhya 1-6	VVER-1000/V-320	1984-87, 1989, 1995		

Sources: Schneider and Froggatt (eds) The World Nuclear Industry Status Report 2023; World Nuclear Association, 2023. Country Profiles.

Notes: [a]jointly owned by Croatia's Hrvatska elektroprivreda (HEP Group) and Slovenia's GEN Energija, each owning 50% of the operator Nuklearna Elektrarna Krško (NEK) and accordingly dividing the total output. [b]Only operating/operable reactors in Ukraine. Reactor types: ABB-III – type of boiling water reactors (BWRs) designed mainly by Swedish ASEA-Atom, now a part of Westinghouse; AP1000 – type of pressurised water reactors (PWRs), designed by American Westinghouse; APR1000 (Advanced Power Reactor) – a PWR design developed in the Republic of Korea; CANDU – pressurised heavy water reactor (PHWR) developed in Canada; EPR (European Pressurised Reactor) – third generation PWR design developed mainly by French Framatome and EDF (Électricité de France), and by German Siemens; heavy water GCR – Soviet designed gas-cooled reactor (GCR); RBMK – Soviet design light water graphite-moderated reactor (LWGR); VVER – Soviet designed PWRs, WE212 – American Westinghouse designed PWR.

This enduring CEE support is in sharp contrast to the development in some European countries. Shaken by the Chernobyl and Fukushima accidents, countries such as Germany, Belgium, Spain, and Switzerland announced their intention to phase out nuclear power (Brugidou and Bouillet, 2023). Although the energy crisis triggered by the war in Ukraine resulted in the postponement of this phase out – in the case of Belgium by ten years – in Germany it added just few months to the original deadlines (ibid.). With Germany ending nuclear electricity generation in 2023, a nuclear-free axis from Italy to Denmark was born dividing pro-nuclear CEE countries and France. Additionally, if Spain phases out nuclear power in 2035, the whole Mediterranean part of the EU, from Portugal to Greece is going to be nuclear free as well. On the contrary, from the 11 post-communist EU members, only the three small Baltic countries neither have nor plan to have traditional large NPPs, but even they are considering building Small Modular Reactors (SMR). Although as it is on Slovenian territory, the Krško NPP is jointly owned by Slovenia and Croatia, therefore we consider Croatia as a nuclear country here.

Generally, the world's nuclear fleet has been shrinking and the share of nuclear in electricity generation has been in decline for more than two decades now; this is especially true for developed countries. As of 1 July 2023, a total of 407 nuclear reactors were operating in 32 countries – 31 below the 2002 global peak. The share of nuclear in global electricity production declined from 17.5 to 9.2 per cent between its peak in 1996 and 2022 (Schneider and Froggatt, 2023: 45–50). Considering that during the last two decades most reactor closures have happened in developed countries, especially in the West, while the vast majority of new startups happened in developing countries, especially in China, the decline in the Western world has been much more drastic (ibid.). Again, our EU-11 group is quite exceptional since the decline by eight reactors between 2002 and 2009 (due to the closure of above-mentioned 'unsafe' reactors related to EU-accession) has been largely compensated by seven new reactors that connected to the grid between 1996–2023 (Table 4.1). An additional reactor – Mochovce-4 in Slovakia – is expected within two years. Therefore, on average, the role of nuclear has not changed much in the region.

The enduring wide support for nuclear energy has been the consequence of various factors. Some narratives and arguments regularly appear in the public debate of CEE countries. In Czechia, Poland and Slovakia, for example, the following were often mentioned. First, nuclear energy is seen as a domestic source of power contributing to energy self-sufficiency and energy independence from outside powers, reducing 'strategic vulnerability' and enabling countries to freely determine the preferred own energy mix. Second, nuclear energy is a modern, stable, clean and safe source representing an environmentally sound alternative to fossil fuels and thus necessary for green transition. Third, the trusted scientific authorities, industry technicians and professionals, as well as public institutions, support nuclear energy. Four, nuclear is opposed by 'radicals' and the opposition from some countries (notably Germany and Austria) is mistaken, irrational and emotional (Kratochvíl and Mišík, 2020; Osička and Černoch, 2017; Żuk, 2023). It is also important to mention the vested interests of influential power utility companies lobbying for nuclear energy, often with personal and ownership ties to the governments (Osička and Černoch, 2017). Additionally, energy systems in general, and nuclear energy in particular, are subject to path dependence, where 'history matters' due to several technological, infrastructural, institutional, socio-economical and behavioural lock-in effects (Lee and Gloaguen, 2015).

Another key factor connected to the support for nuclear energy has been favourable public opinion. International polls that include CEE states and enable cross-country comparisons concerning nuclear energy are quite rare, but all confirm that most CEE countries are among the leading nuclear supporters (OECD, 2010). For example, an EU-wide Special Eurobarometer survey in 2009 showed that, regarding all survey questions, most CEE respondents expressed above- average positive attitudes towards nuclear energy (European Commission, 2010). A more recent poll in eight countries (including France, the UK, US, Germany and Japan) found the highest support for nuclear energy in Poland, the only CEE country included in the sample (ClearPath et al., 2023). The results of the Project Europe Research in 2022, conducted by Hungarian think tank Századvég, also demonstrated that the group of most pro-nuclear countries within the EU is dominated by CEE countries with the notable exception of the Baltic States (Századvég, 2023).

It is thus not surprising that CEE countries – with the notable exception of the Baltics – have been strong advocates of nuclear energy on the international stage, entering all possible informal and formal alliances to ensure that atomic energy is considered a substantial part of the green transition process. Pushing the Commission to approve the inclusion of nuclear energy in the taxonomy of sustainable investments, in 2021 ministers from Visegrad Group (Hungary, Slovakia, the Czech Republic and Poland) met in Paks – where the Hungarian NPP is situated – and demonstrated their unity. State Secretary at the Ministry of Economy of the Slovak Republic Karol Galek claimed that '[w]ith my colleagues, we agreed that without nuclear power it will not be possible to achieve the goals of climate neutrality', adding that there had been a strong consensus that 'the EU needs to create a supportive and transparent framework for investment in all technologies capable of reducing greenhouse gas emissions, including nuclear energy' (WNN, 2021). Similarly, the declaration launching an alliance for nuclear power in Europe at an EU Council meeting in February 2023 signed by 11 countries (Bulgaria, Croatia, Czechia, Finland, France, Hungary, the Netherlands, Poland, Romania, Slovakia, and Slovenia) stated that '[n]uclear energy is one of many tools to achieve our climate goals, to generate baseload electricity and to ensure security of supply' (Simon, 2023). Except for the main initiators, France and the Netherlands, the group consisted of countries from the CEE region and Finland. The same group plus Ukraine was part of the group of more than 20 countries that launched a 'Declaration to Triple Nuclear Energy by 2050' at the 28th United Nations Climate Change Conference, often referred to as COP28, held in Dubai in December 2023 (Department of Energy, 2023).

As these few examples demonstrate (we could find many more), CEE countries were surfing the wave of increasing international support for nuclear energy. During the last few years globally an increasingly consensual attitude has emerged that various ambitious emissions targets trying to mitigate climate change are likely to be out of reach without the substantial use of nuclear energy. The view that it is next to impossible to achieve energy decarbonisation without utilising nuclear power has been widely shared not only by scientific and industry experts, companies, and organisations like the International Energy Agency, but also the United Nations' Intergovernmental Panel on Climate Change (IPCC) which counts nuclear power as part of future decarbonised power systems (Bohdanowicz et al., 2023; IEA, 2022; IPCC, 2022). The Technical Expert Group on Sustainable Finance, advising the European Commission on Taxonomy, also referred to the positions of IPCC and OECD when acknowledging nuclear as a low-carbon energy source in the so-called EU Taxonomy Complementary Climate Delegated Act (European Commission, 2022). This opened the way to recognise 'certain nuclear and gas activities' as 'transitional' in EU sustainable finance policy, meaning that they 'contribute to climate change mitigation and with the potential to play a major role in the transition to a climate-neutral economy, in line with EU climate goals and commitments' (ibid.).

This green label basically enables investors to distinguish and finance nuclear investments under strict conditions: new, 'Generation III+' technology, nuclear power plant projects until 2045 (date of approval of construction permit); and lifetime extension of existing nuclear installations until 2040 (date of approval by competent authority). The fact that the European Parliament failed to block the legislation in July 2022 resulted in deep regrets from many of its members (MEPs) but warm welcome from most CEE countries. Actually, two of the European Parliament's lead committees rejected the Commission's proposal previously in June and in the plenary more MEPs voted against (328) it than in favour (278) – with 33 abstaining – but it was still short of the absolute majority of 353 MEPs needed for the veto (Patricolo, 2022). On the contrary, Slovak Prime Minister Eduard Heger joined the Commission in welcoming the results saying that '[w]e've worked hard for this over the last two years', while Klaus Iohannis, the President of Romania declared that he was 'glad that Romania's constant efforts on considering gas and nuclear as part of progressive decarbonisation were reflected in the EP's final decision' (ibid.).

Considering the uncertainty and volatility of renewable energy generation in both the short and long-term, nuclear energy, providing a low-carbon, secure and reliable baseload supply of electricity and the ability to fill the gaps of changing supply, especially in long-term and thus balancing and stabilising the grid, may be complementary to the large-scale utilisation of renewables (Judah et al., 2023). CEE countries, by joining various alliances, most notably with France and some other Western European countries, have been successful in convincing the Commission to follow this logic, which resulted in the inclusion of nuclear energy in the EU taxonomy. The path for CEE countries to replace the fossil fuels, at least partially with nuclear power, be they reactor capacity expansions, lifetime extensions, large new reactors or small modular reactors and combine it with the deployment of renewables has been created (Gherasim, 2023).

Apart from the rising international acceptance of nuclear energy and its traditionally strong position in CEE countries there has been another objective factor, namely the limited utilisation and potential of renewables in the region. Not only have the installed solar and wind capacities and their share in electricity generation been lower compared to the EU average, but so has the realistic, i.e., cost-effective renewable energy potential (IRENA, 2018). This is mostly because many CEE countries lack coastlines for offshore wind and appropriate solar resources (Judah et al., 2023). This is especially true for the V4 countries: Czechia, Hungary and Slovakia are landlocked and Poland is still overly reliant on coal. However, when looking at the total share of renewables in gross final energy consumption (where other sectors like industry, heating, and transport as well as other sources like hydro and biofuels are also included) in the last few years, the region has become much more diverse. Some smaller countries, most notably the Baltic States and Croatia, have been well above the EU average (23% in 2022), while others, such as Slovenia, Bulgaria and Romania have been average, while the V4 has been lagging behind (Eurostat, 2023).

Overall, CEE countries secured the ways to fully utilise their – existing and potential – nuclear capacities in the green energy transition. However, the full-scale Russian invasion of Ukraine in February 2022 completely changed the situation. The countries suddenly faced another huge challenge: how to keep nuclear power but decouple from Russia.

4.3 Decoupling from Russia but not from nuclear energy

Prior to the full-scale invasion of Ukraine, Rosatom had been in the best position to exploit its leverage over the CEE region. No other company in the world had the capacity to be a 'one stop nuclear shop' for all needs, able to provide an ' all-inclusive package' on a global scale for so many partners (Szulecki and Overland, 2023). And no other region in the world had been so dependent on Rosatom like the former socialist countries from Eastern Europe. Created by Vladimir Putin in 2007 as a state holding, Rosatom includes about 300 enterprises and organisations employing a total workforce of more than 290,000, and it covers the whole fuel cycle from raw uranium mining, conversion, enrichment, fabrication of nuclear fuel assemblies, to their installation, maintenance to reprocessing and waste management (Dolzikova, 2023; Lorenz, 2022). The same applies for the reactor life cycle: from design, construction, operation, maintenance to decommissioning – with very lucrative conditions offered to foreign clients, including the cheap financing of the investment.

According to the data gathered by Szulecki and Overland (2023), upon Russia's invasion of Ukraine, Rosatom boasted as many as 73 different projects in 29 countries, although at very different stages of development from power plants in operation; to planned investments and involvements in tenders. A more detailed picture is less impressive since many of the projects have been stuck at the planning stage or were merely visions laid out in non-committal memorandums of understanding (ibid.). Additionally, Rosatom's ability to deliver all the projects it agreed has been seriously questioned by some studies (e.g., Thomas, 2018). Finally, the economic benefit for Rosatom in the case of some investment projects abroad raised questions as well. The leading Russia-focused investigative journal, *The Insider* (2022) argues that Rosatom's foreign expansion has more political than economic significance for Russia.

Moscow usually provides incredibly attractive contract terms, that other countries never offer, like a system of government loans that cover up to 100% of the project cost, sometimes with no interest and supports the project at all stages: from design to decommissioning, as it was the case of the Akkuyu NPP in Turkey. 'Nowhere in the world are nuclear power plants built according to the "build-own-operate" principle with a fixed electricity sales price in dollars set for 25 years in advance. And not a single government export credit agency (USA, France, Korea, etc.) offers its money for free: the loan rate today is at least 4–5%' argues Bulat Nigmatullin, former Deputy Minister of Atomic Energy of Russia, who demanded that the agreement with Turkey should be terminated (ibid.). In exchange the Kremlin expects and most often receives political favours from the client countries, like not introducing sanctions against Russia and not condemning its steps in various international organisations. Despite all its problems, Rosatom has been the unquestioned global leader of nuclear investments and fuel supplies abroad; no other company has been involved in so many projects in so many countries and supplied so many reactors worldwide with nuclear fuel. As of mid-2023, Rosatom has been involved in building 24 out of the 58 nuclear reactors being constructed around the world, and between 2019 and mid-2023 all 11 construction that started outside China were carried out by the Russian industry giant (Schneider and Froggatt, 2023: 158, 162).

At the start of full-scale Russian aggression against Ukraine, all 18 of the Soviet-designed VVER reactors in five EU member states and about half of the 15 reactors in Ukraine are still running on nuclear fuel from Rosatom's subsidiary, TVEL (Table 4.1, Lorenz, 2022). Additionally, Russia has been involved in several new NPP investments from Finland to Hungary – although at various stages and intensity (discussed below). This is not to say that diversification efforts did not exist before, however, they haven't been very successful; this is especially true for fuel supplies as explained in the following session.

The gradual decoupling process from Russian energy sources including nuclear started well before 2022. Previous aggressive foreign policy and military steps, like the annexation of Crimea in 2014, and the challenges of various gas crises (2006, 2009) were serious warning signs and led to diversification efforts across CEE. The 2009 gas crisis has been a major turning point also in developing EU-wide energy security policy although with limited success and concentrating mostly on fossil fuel import dependencies on Russia (Mišík, 2022). After the adoption of the European Energy Security Strategy (EESS) in May 2014, the EU has been also supporting its member states to reduce the dependence upon external suppliers (Vlček, 2016). From 2013 the Euratom Supply Agency's Annual Reports expressed the concern about '100% reliance on a single supplier for VVER fuel fabrication'. In December 2013, Euroatom opened a call to support the licensing of Western nuclear fuel for VVER reactors, later won by Westinghouse (ibid.). However, these efforts ended up being unsuccessful, with Czechia and Finland, previously trying the only real alternative supplier, the American Westinghouse in their Temelín (2000–2009) and Lovisia (1998–2007) NPPs. This ran into serious technical challenges, and the diversification was seen as so uneconomical that they switched back to TVEL (Pan, 2023; Vlček, 2016). Simply, there has been no real competitor, in economic terms, to the more reliable, cheaper, and more effective fuel from TVEL. Additionally, Rosatom secured its positions by developing its third-generation fuel that would increase the reactors' efficiency and signed a set of long-term fuel contracts with CEE countries up to the late 2020s further complicating attempts to switch suppliers (ibid.).

Meanwhile, Russia faced only partial setbacks in the CEE region. Rosatom was explicitly excluded from the tender for the new reactor of the Dukovany NPP in Czechia in 2021 following news of Russian intelligence involvement in a 2014 explosion at a Czech ammunition depot (Szulecki and Overland, 2023). But the only country from the region which has been working systematically to decouple from fuel supplies is Ukraine, which faced Russian military aggression since 2014. Ukraine first managed to switch from TVEL to US-Canadian Westinghouse its South Ukraine NPP with three VVER-1000 reactors from 2015 using an improved design RWFA – Robust Westinghouse Fuel Assembly (Lorenz, 2022). By the time of the invasion Westinghouse was supplying fuel for around half of the country's 15 reactors and in June 2022, Ukranian Energoatom and Westinghouse were able to sign a contract covering the fuel supply for all Ukrainian reactors (Schneider and Froggatt, 2023: 530).

The main argument here is that Russia – despite its aggressive foreign policy steps and the utilisation of 'energy weapon' in various gas crises – with very high probability would maintain its position as the only supplier of nuclear fuel to VVER reactors in EU countries. However, the 2022 invasion became a turning point radically accelerating the decoupling efforts, leading to the opposite outcome. Russia is likely to lose most of its positions in the region. But again, the decoupling is expected to be a slow, technically difficult, and costly process. On the other hand, decoupling, when it happens, is likely to be definite. Nuclear energy partnerships are inherently long term and every new contract with an alternative vendor further locks in Rosatom's exclusion from the region (Pan, 2023).

Apart from the unprecedented invasion, Russian troops and Rosatom provided many more reasons for CEE countries to leave behind their Russian dependence for good. Rosatom staff have taken over the management at Ukraine's Zaporizhzhya NPP occupied by Russian forces and assisted the military in pressuring the staff by detention, torture, kidnapping, threatening with firing or conscription into the Russian army as part of an effort to induce them to sign work contracts with Rosenergoatom, Rosatom's nuclear utility wing (Digges, 2023: 5; Dolzikova, 2023: 3). During the summer of 2022

> the plant was the focus of particularly heavy shelling that repeatedly cut it off from outside power, leaving it to rely on diesel backup generators to keep its reactor cooling and safety systems operating. Witness reports from Ukrainian workers have since suggested that Rosatom staff at the plant helped guide

> those attacks as part of an effort to permanently isolate the plant from the Ukrainian grid.
>
> (Digges, 2023: 5)

This time the reaction from most CEE countries has been swift and decisive. Ukraine, as mentioned above, completely switched to Westinghouse – formerly the top export destination for Russian nuclear reactor fuel was not importing any at all after the end of February 2022 (Dolzikova, 2023: 11). Czechia, Slovakia, and Bulgaria have all stepped up efforts to end their dependence on Russian nuclear fuel (Dolzikova, 2023; Pan, 2023) and later Finland joined them. Czechia secured Western supplies to all its reactors from 2024: all four VVER-440 reactors at Dukovany are to be supplied with fuel manufactured by Westinghouse, and at Temelín a consortium of French Framatome and Westinghouse should provide the fuel for at least ten years from 2024 onwards (Schneider and Froggatt, 2023: 499). The Czech government also managed to regain control in the Škoda JS factory, which is of strategic importance regarding the CEE nuclear sector. Škoda JS has been responsible for the maintenance of all Czech, Slovak and Hungarian reactor units, involved as the main contractor in the construction of Mochovce-3 and 4 units in Slovakia, as well as in the modernisation of Paks 1-4 units and in the development of planned Paks II units for document evaluations, and inspections (Lorenz, 2022: 19). In 2004 the formerly Czech nuclear company, was bought by OMZ, the Russian heavy machinery manufacturer, itself owned by Gazprombank, a private bank owned by Russian state-controlled gas monopoly Gazprom (ibid. 18). In June 2022 the ČEZ Group, the largest utility and biggest public company in CEE with a 70% Czech government ownership managed to buy back Škoda JS; thanks to this the company has been removed from U.S. sanction lists on which it had been included due to its former Russian owners (Schneider and Froggatt, 2023: 502).

In Bulgaria and Slovakia the switch might take longer, but is on the way. Bulgaria, despite having a fuel contract with TVEL until 2025, in December 2022 signed a ten-year contract with Westinghouse to supply the Kozloduy 5 reactor by 2024 and announced the intention to supply Unit 6 in the same NPP with fuel from Framatome from 2025 to 2034 (ibid.: 495). In May 2023, Slovak power utility Slovenské elektrárne (SE) signed a Memorandum of Understanding with Framatome to cooperate on the provision of '100% European' fuel for VVER-440 reactors (ibid.: 518). In August 2023, SE also signed a deal with Westinghouse for future fuel deliveries for Slovak VVER 440 design reactors: the Westinghouse Electric Sweden AB company should supply the fuel approximately one year after the licensing process is finished (Slovenské elektrárne, 2023). Finally, Finland joined the group despite previous declarations that until existing operating licenses with TVEL last (2027 and 2030) it would continue purchasing fuel from Russia (Schneider and Froggatt, 2023: 470). However, in January 2024, Finnish climate and environment minister Kai Mykkänen announced that '[t]he Loviisa reactors are no longer dependent on new nuclear fuel from Russia' and that the Loviisa NPP owned by majority-state-owned energy firm Fortum, is in the process of switching to western-produced fuel (Yle News, 2024). Effectively meaning that no new shipments of Russian nuclear fuel are expected, Finland is going to use the existing stockpiles and then switch to Western ones.

Finnish reaction was much faster regarding the 1170 MW Hanhikivi 1 NPP planned by the Fennovoima consortium with the involvement of Rosatom. After the Russian invasion, Finland's Minister for Economic Affairs said that he would not be granting a construction permit under the current circumstances and, in May 2022, Fennovoima announced that the contract of plant delivery with Rosatom's RAOS Project subsidiary was terminated 'with immediate effect' starting a lengthy legal battle between stakeholders (Schneider and Froggatt, 2023: 472; World Nuclear Association, 2023). By 2024 Hungary remained the only EU country that has no declared intention to replace TVEL with Western fuel suppliers and continues in the project of Paks II NPP with Rosatom. The original bilateral contract between Hungary and Russia on Paks II even included exclusive provision of fuel by TVEL for 30 years but, due to the pressure of the European Commission, this was reduced to 10 years with the possibility of prolongation (Haverkamp, 2019).

The CEE switch to alternative fuels is likely to be a longer, more complicated, and costlier process than political statements and press declarations might indicate. There are many obstacles in the way, perhaps the largest challenge being the licencing process. CEE utilities have been previously reluctant to switch to alternative suppliers because of technical challenges and risks, bureaucratic procedures, and economic losses due to reduced reactor performance. The latter springs from the fact that licencing usually requires some operational experience, either with Lead Test Assemblies or with live operation of the fuel licensed in another reactor; during the test period, the chosen reactors are working with reduced capacity leading to economic losses (Vlček, 2016: 81). On the supply side, Western nuclear fuel production lines need to be adapted and expanded to produce VVER fuel, and these processes altogether can take years (Dolzikova, 2023: 8). Regarding the large number of CEE NPPs turning to Western suppliers almost at the same time, it is questionable if those can meet the increased demand. Additionally, Framatome has no experience at all in providing fuel for Soviet-designed VVER reactors and Westinghouse's record is rather mixed. As discussed above, some CEE utilities switched back to TVEL after facing technical difficulties including fuel-related malfunctions and resulting revenue losses due to outages when using alternative fuel from Westinghouse (Pan, 2023; Vlček, 2016).

Only Ukraine has been determined to continue but it has been forced to do so for geopolitical and strategic reasons. Moreover, even there it took over a decade to gradually replace TVEL. To make things worse, unlike in Ukraine, most reactors in the EU – 15 from 19 – are VVER 440 type (and not VVER 1000), where Westinghouse has no fresh experience with fuel supply. The single episode dates back to 2001–2007 when Westinghouse (then owned by British Nuclear Fuel Limited) supplied fuel for seven reloads to Finland's Loviisa NPP with VVER 440 reactors (Schneider and Froggatt, 2023: 470). Ultimately, Russia has always been a reliable partner in nuclear fuel supply for EU members and the Kremlin has never used Rosatom against them as an energy weapon similarly to Gazprom.

Nevertheless, nobody guarantees that the Putin regime will continue to do so. Thus, until the switch to Western fuel is completed, Russia is to maintain its leverage over the region and CEE countries should be aware of this risk. The Russian manipulation does not have to be an overt 'switching off the light'-style action but rather a pretended malfunction leading to supply disruptions as has happened several times with gas supplies or the 2005 incident in which TVEL allegedly supplied the Ukrainian Energoatom with defective fuel assemblies (Szulecki and Overland, 2023; The Insider, 2022).

Despite all the problems related to Russian dependence and the decoupling from it, CEE governments are not short of ambitious nuclear development projects. Almost all countries – except for the Baltic ones – are planning or at least considering building new nuclear reactors (Table 4.1; World Nuclear Association, 2023). Indeed, a study from Mezősi et al. (2020) examining V4+ countries (V4 plus Bulgaria and Romania) demonstrated that if ambitious nuclear plans are realised in the region, NPPs will compete for the limited export opportunities available, which will be most acute in times of seasonal renewables production (periods with the highest hours of solar irradiation and/or wind). New announcements have further underlined this hypothetical risk. In an unexpected move, in January 2024, the Czech government stated that in its long-running nuclear tender it would seek binding bids from South Korea's KHNP and France's EDF to build up to four NPP units instead of the originally planned one (ČT24, 2024). If all or most planned NPPs are built, there is a high probability it will lead to excess supply of electricity in the region. However, this is highly unlikely given the nature of large NPP construction projects.

Ambitions are one thing; reality is another and much more sobering: during the last 16 years only one single reactor (Mochovce-3 in Slovakia in 2023) has been added to the CEE nuclear fleet. A second one might follow soon (Mochovce-4 maybe in 2025) but one must be cautious with predictions. Originally, the construction of the two Mochovce units started in 1985 but it was suspended in 1993; it was restarted in 2008/2009 with announced budget of €2.8 billion and a planned completion date in 2012/2013 (Schneider and Froggatt, 2023: 513–514; World Nuclear Association, 2023). When the third unit was finally connected to the grid in January 2023 after an 11-year delay, the bill increased to €6.2 billion, more than a twofold increase. Considering that it was not a completely new NPP project but the restart of a conserved one, the cost overrun and the construction delay is very high even by industry standards, which is a financial disaster itself. There is an extensive international literature pointing to empirical evidence that massive cost overruns and construction delays are not the exception but the rule considering new NPP projects (Locatelli, 2018; Portugal-Pereira et al., 2018).

Moreover, NPPs are most vulnerable to delays and cost overruns even among construction megaprojects (Sovacool et al., 2014) and, historically, the costs and time spans are on the rise (Haas et al., 2019; Schneider and Froggatt 2023). According to the World Nuclear Industry Status Report of 2023 from the 58 reactors under construction worldwide (as of 1 July 2023) almost half (28) are delayed or are likely to be delayed (Schneider and Froggatt 2023: 61). However, it is important to add that most of the remaining reactors nominally on time have begun within the past three years or have not yet reached projected startup dates, making it difficult to assess whether they are on schedule. Between 2020–2022, only two reactors (Tianwan-4 and 5 in China) of 18 connected to the grid in seven countries started up on time (ibid. 63). It is not an exaggeration to state that, with very high probability, all new projects outside China are going to end up like this. According to Haas et al., '[r]ealized costs has always been higher than forecast costs and construction times promised have almost never been met' (2019: 97). Another good illustration of the magnitude of the problems is the interesting fact that the Mochovce-4 reactor in Slovakia with its initial construction start dating back 38 years was almost a world record in 2023. Only the Bushehr-2 reactor in Iran could beat it; this was started in 1976, over 47 years ago, and restarted in 2019, after a 40-year-long suspension (Schneider and Froggatt 2023: 62).

Ambitions might be further curbed financially by the recent performance of the two major potential investors in CEE, Westinghouse and Framatome. Both have been involved in new nuclear projects at home and abroad and are notoriously known for massive cost overruns and delays. Like Vogtle 3&4 in Georgia, US or Flamanville-3 (France) and Olkiluoto-3 (Finland) with reactor types offered to CEE countries like AP1000 and EPR (Pan, 2023; World Nuclear Association, 2023). It seems that these, the so-called Generation III+ reactors, experience much longer delays compared to their predecessors (Haas et al., 2019: 111). It is not clear how Western energy giants are willing to ensure lower costs and time spans in the CEE region where they have no experience with large-scale investments at all so far.

One would think that Hungary is better off sticking to the previously agreed co-operation with Rosatom regarding the Paks II NPP but nothing could be further from the truth. The agreement between Hungary and Russia's Rosatom triumphally but unexpectedly signed in Moscow on 14 January 2014 in the presence of Hungarian prime minister, Viktor Orbán and Russian president, Vladimir Putin on the construction of two new VVER-1200 reactors at the Paks site has been often referred to as the 'greatest deal ever' and the 'investment of the century' by Hungarian officials (Szabó, 2024). Originally intended to operate from 2023, later postponed to 2025/2026, the investment was supported by a €10 billion financing deal with Russia to cover 80% of the anticipated project cost, with Hungary to repay the loan over 21 years of operation, starting in 2026 (Schneider and Froggatt 2023: 503–508; World Nuclear Association, 2023). An endless list of problems, legal battles, bureaucratic licencing procedures and contract revisions with Russia followed. The investment was legally challenged by the European Commission (getting the green light in 2016), than by the Austrian government (European General Court ruling allowed to proceed with conditions in November 2022); later the German government was accused of blocking the delivery of the parts of control-command systems by Siemens (2023), both the investment and the financing agreement with Russia was rewritten, the start of operation was postponed to 2032 with loan repayments to 2031 – just to mention a few (ibid.)

The (most important) construction license application was submitted to the Hungarian Atomic Energy Authority (HAEA) only at the end of June 2020 and the license issued – after breaking all possible legal deadlines – only in August 2022 (ibid.). However, this was only a temporary, conditional licence allowing some related works like building the underground waterproof wall to proceed but not the construction of reactor itself (Szabó, 2024). All in all, more than 10 years after the triumphant announcement, there is no finalised licence permit, the construction of the reactors has not started and therefore all major nuclear organisations keep Paks II in the 'planned' category and not in 'under construction'. It is important to note that the most complicated parts of the NPP investment just start with the construction. A further problem is the complete lack of transparency. The 2014 agreement was born in secret, without any public or political consultations, impact assessment, tender or parliamentary debate, the details of the contract, both the original and the new one have been kept confidential, and there have been many personal changes both in the Hungarian project management team and in the HAEA. It does not look like 'greatest deal ever', rather it has high chance of becoming a never-ending NPP project with a questionable outcome.

4.4 Conclusion

Generally pro-nuclear CEE countries taking part in various alliances were able to convince the European Commission that nuclear energy as a supplementary of renewables can play a crucial role in the green energy transition. The inclusion of the nuclear projects in the EU Taxonomy opened the way for the cheap financing of these investments. However, only investments to the existing NPPs, like operating lifetime extensions and upgrades look economically feasible currently, being competitive even with renewable energy generation, which now enjoys famously low costs (Judah et al., 2023). While CEE governments are not short of ambitious plans about nuclear projects, most of the recent NPP investments have run into serious construction cost overruns and delays in developed countries leading to high project risk perception, hampering further investment decisions (IAEA 2023: 4). This applies to all recent projects in the countries discussed here: Mochovce-3 and 4 in Slovakia, Olkiluoto-3 in Finland and Paks II in Hungary.

Before entering into new nuclear megaprojects, CEE countries should think twice and rather make up for lost ground in renewables, where many of them have been lagging behind the rest of the EU. Here the investments have just the opposite characteristics: they are much cheaper, construction time spans are much shorter, large cost overruns and delays are unusual and private capital is pouring to the area without government guarantees or massive public subsidies. During the last few years, the pace of development and deployment of renewable energy has accelerated while investments in new nuclear projects became marginal compared to them. During 2022, the total investment in non-hydro 'new' renewables globally was a record US$495 billion of which the individual investments in wind and solar were US$174 billion and US$307 billion respectively while investments to new nuclear projects were estimated to only US$35.1 billion (Schneider and Froggatt 2023: 412). In percentage terms, according to REN21, calculations the investment in the power sector in 2022 was 74 per cent renewables, 19 per cent fossil fuels and 8 per cent nuclear, the same level as coal (ibid.).

The difference is even more striking in the advanced economies. While the cost of new renewables drastically declined in the last two decades, the cost of nuclear power went up becoming the most expensive utility-scale power source for the first time – the Levelized Cost of Energy (LCOE) for nuclear was estimated to be 2 to 7 times higher than different sources of solar and wind power (ibid. 414). These circumstances seriously question the CEE's nuclear enthusiasm. Traditional new NPPs may have some rationale only in countries with limited renewable potential and without existing nuclear capacities that largely rely on fossil fuels and are determined to drastically reduce greenhouse gas emissions. From our sample, only Poland would fit into this category assuming strong determination to mitigate climate change. The so-called Small Modular Reactors can be a breakthrough drastically changing the energy landscape but the whole world is waiting for the first one to be connected to the grid and starting commercial operation. To sum up, the future of nuclear energy in CEE countries is rather uncertain.

What is, however, certain is that it would be foolish to continue considering Russia as a reliable partner after its 2022 invasion of Ukraine and energy war against the EU. Most CEE governments understood the lesson and started the process of decoupling from Rosatom. It is expected to be slow, technically difficult, and costly, and we can't exclude the possibility that some countries may step back depending on the actual political developments. But if the switch to Western nuclear fuel is completed, it is likely to be definite, given the inherently long-term nature of nuclear partnerships. It is almost certain that Russia has lost its dominant position on the CEE nuclear market and the Kremlin can only blame itself for this.

Acknowledgements

This work was supported by the Slovak Research and Development Agency Grant No APVV-20-0012.

Notes

1 A type of pressurised water reactor originally developed in the Soviet Union, VVER stands for "water-water energy reactor", i.e. water-cooled water-moderated energy reactor derived from Russian acronym ("vodo-vodyanoi enyergeticheskiy reactor").

2 The 11 post-communist Central and Eastern European member states of the European Union are the following: the Baltic states, namely Estonia, Latvia and Lithuania, the Visegrad four (V4) countries, Czechia, Hungary, Poland and Slovakia; Slovenia joined in 2004, Bulgaria and Romania joined in 2007 and Croatia joined in 2013.

References

Baczynska, G., 2023. Exclusive: EU nuclear agency sees some Russia imports up again in 2023 from before Ukraine war. Reuters, 1 December 2023. Available online: www.reuters.com/world/europe/eu-nuclear-agency-sees-some-russia-imports-up-again-2023-before-ukraine-war-2023-12-01/

Bohdanowicz, Z., Łopaciuk-Gonczaryk, B., Gajda, P., Rajewski, A., 2023. Support for nuclear power and proenvironmental attitudes: The cases of Germany and Poland. *Energy Policy* 177, 113578. https://doi.org/10.1016/j.enpol.2023.113578

Brugidou, M., Bouillet, J., 2023. A return to grace for nuclear power in European public opinion? Some elements of a rapid paradigm shift. Policy Paper European issues No 662, Foundation Robert Schuman.

ClearPath, Potential Energy, RePlanet, Third Way, 2023. The world wants new nuclear. Findings from a comprehensive evaluation of the world's understanding and support for advanced nuclear. Available at: https://thirdway.imgix.net/The-World-Wants-New-Nuclear.pdf

ČT24, 2024. Vláda chce až čtyři nové jaderné bloky, žádá uchazeče o závazné nabídky, in: ČT24, January 31, 2024. Available at: https://ct24.ceskatelevize.cz/clanek/domaci/vlada-chce-az-ctyri-nove-jaderne-bloky-zada-uchazece-o-zavazne-nabidky-345529

Department of Energy, 2023. At COP28, countries launch declaration to triple nuclear energy capacity by 2050, recognizing the key role of nuclear energy in reaching net zero. Washington, DC: U.S. Department of Energy. Available at: www.energy.gov/articles/cop28-countries-launch-declaration-triple-nuclear-energy-capacity-2050-recognizing-key

Digges, Ch., 2023. Rosatom's Role in the War in Ukraine. Working paper, 2023, Bellona Foundation, Vilnius.

Dolzikova, D., 2023. Atoms for Sale: Developments in Russian Nuclear Energy Exports. RUSI Special Report, Royal United Services Institute for Defence and Security Studies, London.

ESA, 2023. ESA Annual Report 2022. Luxembourg: Euratom Supply Agency, European Commission.

European Commission, 2010. Europeans and nuclear safety. Special Eurobarometer 324. Brussels: European Commission, Directorate-General for Communication and TNS Opinion & Social.

European Commission, 2022. Questions and answers on the EU Taxonomy Complementary Climate Delegated Act covering certain nuclear and gas activities. Brussels: European Commission. Available at: https://ec.europa.eu/commission/presscorner/detail/en/QANDA_22_712

Eurostat, 2023. Renewable energy statistics. Available at: https://ec.europa.eu/eurostat/statistics-explained/index.php?title=Renewable_energy_statistics

Gherasim, D. P., 2023. *The Europeanisation of the Energy Transition in Central and Eastern EU Countries: An Uphill Battle that Can Be Won.* Paris: Notes de l'Ifri, Ifri (French Institute of International Relations).

Haas, R., Thomas, S., Ajanovic, A., 2019. The historical development of the costs of nuclear power. In: Haas, R., Mez, L., Ajanovic, A. (eds), *The Technological and Economic Future of Nuclear Power. Energiepolitik und Klimaschutz. Energy Policy and Climate Protection.* pp. 97–115. Wiesbaden: Springer VS. https://doi.org/10.1007/978-3-658-25987-7_5

Haverkamp, J., 2019. *Nuclear Energy – The Looming Dependency on Rosatom in the EU.* Written in commission for The Greens/EFA in the European Parliament, WISE International, Amsterdam.

IAEA, 2023. *Energy, Electricity and Nuclear Power Estimates for the Period up to 2050,* Reference Data Series No. 1, 2023 Edition. Vienna: International Atomic Energy Agency.

IEA, 2022. Nuclear Power and Secure Energy Transitions. Paris: International Energy Agency. Available at: www.iea.org/reports/nuclear-power-and-secure-energy-transitions

IPCC, 2022. Summary for Policymakers, in: Intergovernmental Panel on Climate Change (IPCC) (Ed.), Climate Change 2022 – Mitigation of Climate Change: Working Group III Contribution to the Sixth Assessment Report of the Intergovernmental Panel on Climate Change. Cambridge University Press, Cambridge, pp. 3–48. https://doi.org/10.1017/9781009157926.001

IRENA, 2018. Renewable Energy Prospects for the European Union International Renewable Energy Agency and European Commission. www.irena.org/-/media/Files/IRENA/Agency/Publication/2018/Feb/IRENA_REmap_EU_2018.pdf

Judah, B., Rizzo, R., Pouget-Abadie, T., Allen, J., Shin, F., 2023. *How to Strike a Grand Bargain on EU Nuclear Energy Policy*. Washington, DC: Atlantic Council. Available at: www.atlanticcouncil.org/in-depth-research-reports/report/how-to-strike-a-grand-bargain-on-eu-nuclear-energy-policy/

Kratochvíl, P., Mišík, M., 2020. Bad external actors and good nuclear energy: Media discourse on energy supplies in the Czech Republic and Slovakia. *Energy Policy,* 136, 111058. https://doi.org/10.1016/j.enpol.2019.111058

Lee, R. P., Gloaguen, S., 2015. Path-dependence, lock-in, and student perceptions of nuclear energy in France: Implications from a pilot study. *Energy Research & Social Science* 8, 86–99, https://doi.org/10.1016/j.erss.2015.05.001

Locatelli, G., 2018. Why are Megaprojects, Including Nuclear Power Plants, Delivered Overbudget and Late? Reasons and Remedies, Report MIT-ANP-TR-172, Center for Advanced Nuclear Energy Systems (CANES), Massachusetts Institute of Technology, Cambridge, MA.

Lorenz, P., 2022. Russian Grip on EU Nuclear Power. Vienna: Vienna Ombudsoffice for Environmental Protection (Wiener Umweltanwaltschaft – WUA). Available at: https://wua-wien.at/images/stories/publikationen/russian-grip-on-eu-nuclear-power.pdf

Mezősi, A., Felsmann, B., Kerekes, L., Szabó, L., 2020. Coexistence of nuclear and renewables in the V4 electricity system: Friends or enemies? *Energy Policy,* 140, 111449. https://doi.org/10.1016/j.enpol.2020.111449

Mišík, M., 2022. The EU needs to improve its external energy security. *Energy Policy,* 165, 112930. https://doi.org/10.1016/j.enpol.2022.112930

Mišík, M., Pachárová, V., 2021. Perfect compliance? Nuclear power in Central and Eastern Europe and the EU membership. In Mišík, M., Oravcová, V. (eds), *From Economic to Energy Transition: Three Decades of Transitions in Central and Eastern Europe*. Cham: Palgrave Macmillan, pp. 429–456.

OECD, 2010. *Public Attitudes to Nuclear Power, Nuclear Development*. Paris: OECD Publishing. https://doi.org/10.1787/9789264097933-en

Osička, J., Černoch, F., 2017. Anatomy of a black sheep: The roots of the Czech Republic's pro-nuclear energy policy. *Energy Research & Social Science,* 27, 9–13. https://doi.org/10.1016/j.erss.2017.02.006

Pan, Y., 2023. Managing the atomic divorce: The challenges of East Central Europe's nuclear energy decoupling from Russia. *The Electricity Journal,* 36/1, 107241. https://doi.org/10.1016/j.tej.2023.107241

Patricolo, C., 2022. European Parliament backs green label for gas and nuclear, in: CEENERGYNEWS, July 6, 2022. Available at: https://ceenergynews.com/eu-affairs/european-parliament-backs-green-label-for-gas-and-nuclear/

Polanecký, K., Haverkamp, J. (Eds.). 2011. *Energy of the Future? Nuclear Energy in Central and Eastern Europe*. Praha: Heinrich Böll Stiftung.

Portugal-Pereira, J., Ferreira, P., Cunha, J., Szklo, A., Schaeffer, R., Araújo, M., 2018. Better late than never, but never late is better: Risk assessment of nuclear power construction projects. *Energy Policy,* 120, 158–166. https://doi.org/10.1016/j.enpol.2018.05.041

Schneider, M., Froggatt, A. (Eds.). 2023. *The World Nuclear Industry Status Report 2023.* Paris: Mycle Schneider Consulting Project.

Simon, F., 2023. Eleven EU countries launch alliance for nuclear power in Europe, in: Euractiv, March 1, 2023. Available at: www.euractiv.com/section/energy-environment/news/eleven-eu-countries-launch-alliance-for-nuclear-power-in-europe/

Slovenské elektrárne, 2023. Strengthening Slovakia's energy security: Slovenské elektrárne concluded a fuel supply agreement with Westinghouse. Press release, August 25, 2023. Available at: www.seas.sk/en/press-releases/slovenske-elektrarne-nuclear-fuel-westinghouse/

Sovacool, B. K., Gilbert, A., Nugent, D., 2014. An international comparative assessment of construction cost overruns for electricity infrastructure. *Energy Research & Social Science,* 3, 152–160. https://doi.org/10.1016/j.erss.2014.07.016

Szabó, M. I., 2024. Paks II.: az évszázad beruházásától az elherdált évtizedig, in: Szabad Európa, January 15, 2024. Available at: www.szabadeuropa.hu/a/paks-ii-az-evszazad-beruhazasatol-az-elherdalt-evtizedig/32771246.html

Századvég, 2023. Public support for nuclear energy in Europe is growing. Századvég, Budapest. Available at: https://szazadveg.hu/en/cikkek/public-support-for-nuclear-energy-in-europe-is-growing/

Szulecki, K., Overland, I., 2023. Russian nuclear energy diplomacy and its implications for energy security in the context of the war in Ukraine. *Nature Energy,* 8, 413–42. https://doi.org/10.1038/s41560-023-01228-5

The Insider, 2022. Weaponized Rosatom. How Russia uses its nuclear plants abroad for blackmail and political pressure. In: *The Insider,* 10 November 2022. Available at: https://theins.ru/en/economics/256858

Thomas, S, 2018. Russia's nuclear export programme. *Energy Policy,* 121, 236–247. https://doi.org/10.1016/j.enpol.2018.06.036

Vlček, T., 2016. Critical assessment of diversification of nuclear fuel for the operating VVER reactors in the EU. *Energy Strategy Reviews,* 13–14, 77–85. https://doi.org/10.1016/j.esr.2016.08.006

WNN – World Nuclear News, 2021. V4 countries reiterate support for nuclear. *World Nuclear News,* 19 November 2021, Available at: www.world-nuclear-news.org/Articles/V4-countries-reiterate-support-for-nuclear

World Nuclear Association, 2023. Country profiles. Available at: www.world-nuclear.org/information-library/country-profiles.aspx

Yle News, 2024. Minister: Loviisa plant cuts dependence on Russian nuclear fuel. *Yle News,* January 13, 2024. Available at: https://yle.fi/a/74-20069301

Żuk, P., 2023. Soft power and the media management of energy transition: Analysis of the media narrative about the construction of nuclear power plants in Poland. *Energy Reports,* 9, 568–583. https://doi.org/10.1016/j.egyr.2022.11.192

Part II

Russian invasion and European energy security

5 Russia's aggression against Ukraine and its impact on the energy cooperation of Visegrad Group countries

Juraj Marušiak

5.1 Introduction

The Visegrad Group (V4) is an informal regional cooperation structure that brings together the Czech Republic, Hungary, Poland, and Slovakia. It has been an important factor in the transformation of these Central European states, their integration into the EU, and their EU participation in the first years after its enlargement in 2004. The similar structural characteristics of the participating states and their closely related strategic objectives even allow one to speak of a specific Visegrad model of post-communist transformation. This model is based on principles linked to "anchored neoliberalism", legitimized in a largely materialistic way, by mitigating the social consequences of the introduction of a market economy through various forms of compensation (Bohle and Greskovits, 2012: 81–82). The Visegrad model of transformation was oriented towards the rapid integration of these states into Western integration and security structures – the EU and NATO (Aslund, 1997: 468). It has also been a model of close cooperation between neighbouring states, reminiscent of the Benelux or the Nordic Council (Švec, 2003; Drulák, 2003).

In the first stages of Visegrad cooperation in the 1990s, but also immediately after EU accession in 2004, the V4 agenda was primarily political. It focused on EU enlargement, the accession of new member states to the Schengen area, and the formation of the EU's Common Eastern Policy. After EU enlargement occurred, cooperation at the sectoral level began to strengthen. Overall, a growing differentiation became present within the V4 in the post-accession period, regarding a preference for flexible alliances, which resulted from the diversity present in the European agenda and the large number of EU member states. Exceptions have included the common position of the V4 states during the 2015–2016 refugee crisis (Nyzio, 2018). A number of important factors exist, however, that differentiate the V4 countries. This situation has resulted in diverse preferences and a reduction in bloc cohesion (Cianciara, 2019: 5), and so even the refugee crisis did not contribute to the V4's renewed position as a political bloc, as was the case before 2004 or in the first ten years after the EU's eastern enlargement.

The Visegrad Group, in the form it took after a revival of its activities in 1998–1999, is analysed here as a structure following the principles of the "new

DOI: 10.4324/9781032624839-8

regionalism". Thus, it has no formal interstate regional organizations; on the contrary, it rejects such institutionalization. Instead, it is characterized by "multidimensionality, complexity, fluidity and non-conformity" (Söderbaum, 2003: 1). The group's activities are not based on any treaty or legal document, but on political declarations. The only institution operating within the group is the International Visegrad Fund, which permits the involvement of non-state actors. Complexity and multidimensionality are guaranteed by sectoral cooperation and by the involvement of both governmental, parliamentary, and non-state actors. The principle of fluidity enables the V4+ format to work, as it allows other states outside of the group to cooperate with the group's individual activities. This form of Visegrad cooperation, while sticking to the four participating states, thus has an inclusive, extroverted character, and therefore meets the criteria for being classified as a "new regionalism" project (Söderbaum, 2003: 5). This flexible nature also allows Visegrad Group countries to participate in other forms of regional cooperation that do not overlap with the V4's activities, or to cooperate with only a few, not all, of the group's states. Therefore, in several cases, it is more appropriate to speak of cooperation in the Visegrad area instead of the activities of the Visegrad Group. This chapter's aim will be to identify the level of Visegrad cooperation in dealing with the mentioned challenges, focusing on the question of how Russia's aggression against Ukraine has affected this cooperation. A further question considered in this chapter is the extent to which the weakening of political aspects of Visegrad cooperation has translated into cooperation in other areas, such as energy. This chapter's primary focus is less on the choice of specific policies and the technocratic aspects of energy transition, and much more on the V4's functioning as a regional cooperation structure, that is, the extent to which the Visegrad countries have been able to act together in the field of energy policy.

The chapter also maps Europeanization processes in relation to the V4 states' energy policy amid the energy transition, and also considers the context of breaking away from unilateral dependence on Russia for energy raw materials. Europeanization is understood here as the "construction, diffusion and institutionalization of formal and informal rules, procedures, policy paradigms, styles, ways of doing things, shared beliefs and norms, which are first defined and consolidated in the EU policy process and then incorporated in the logic of domestic (national and subnational) discourse, political structures and subnational policies" (Radaelli, 2004: 4). Yet this chapter does not view this process as unidirectional and irreversible. Within the EU, on some issues, opposed, de-Europeanizing processes may be taking place, "in which the previous impetus to converge with EU norms and the willingness to get involved in EU policies slows down and can even take an opposite direction" (Soler and Lecha, 2008; Jańczak, 2010: 99). One specific case of de-Europeanization is counter-Europeanization, resulting in the "reverse (slowing down, stopping or regress) of European transformation of a system" (Jańczak, 2010: 110).

Within Europeanization and de-Europeanization, we can identify different strategies chosen as regards energy policy. These strategies may be situationally conditioned, or they may indicate the long-term strategic priorities of individual

EU member states or of the whole group. Besides the "adaptationist" strategy inherited from the pre-accession period, consisting in the automatic adoption of EU rules, it is possible to speak of "integrationist" approaches based on taking advantage of the state's deep integration, with choices made from a range of alternative options. Finally, the third strategy is "sovereigntist", that is, it places the subjectivity of the own state and its interests at the top of the list of priorities (Cichocki, 2009: 4–6). This chapter seeks to identify how the Visegrad Group states have applied these strategies to address specific EU energy policy challenges, particularly amid Russian aggression against Ukraine. It examines the extent to which they have been interested in a common approach or have been able to reach a common approach, and the extent to which they have been able to assert their interests and ideas in intra-EU cooperation, or, on the contrary, have come into conflict with the majority of EU member states and their institutions.

In the next part, the chapter traces the development of Visegrad cooperation a year before Russia's open aggression against Ukraine began in February 2022. The third part analyses the evolution of the V4 states' understanding of energy security and the policy of building broader alliances in this area in the EU and beyond. Particular attention is paid to the V4 response to the EU's green transition. All of the above sections are essential for understanding the V4's responses to the Russian Federation's invasion of Ukraine in 2022, and how this war has affected the V4 states' energy policies and the overall nature of Visegrad cooperation. The issue of energy transition is not only part of the agenda of interstate relations; it is also becoming increasingly relevant in the internal political discourse of the V4 states, which is why a separate section has been devoted to it. The final section provides answers to research questions concerning the implications of the ongoing war in Ukraine for Visegrad cooperation, with a focus on the energy sector.

5.2 The Visegrad Group in the post-accession period

While the V4 countries were able to act in unison during the pre-accession process and in their efforts to gain an equal status to the original members of the EU as quickly as possible, efforts to make the V4 speak with "one voice" (PAP, 2018), in terms of developing common priorities, were much less successful. Yet the relationship between the V4 and the rest of the EU has gradually evolved. The possibilities of the already mentioned original adaptationist strategies (Cichocki, 2009: 3–5), gradually started to run out. This became evident, however, only a few years after accession, with the "habit of automatic adoption of rules" continuing for a longer period. The 2015–2016 refugee crisis was a turning point in this respect. Yet, differences in priorities between the old and new member states had already begun to emerge, precisely on energy issues. The V4 articulated the interests of its member states in a different way precisely during negotiations on climate and energy packages in 2008–2009. The different interests articulated by group members were due to different inherited energy mixes. Previously, Poland and the Czech Republic had been largely dependent on hard coal and lignite, while Hungary was dependent on natural gas at a level comparable to that of large West

European gas-producing countries (e.g., the Netherlands, the UK). This difference played an important role in the formulation of Hungary's energy policy priorities (Nosko et al., 2010; Mišík, 2010).

Key V4 documents adopted in the post-accession period also show that its representatives at that time viewed the role of the group, besides fostering cohesion among both the EU and V4 and enhancing their competitiveness, primarily as an example of successful transformation and as actors supporting the process of further EU enlargement to include the states of South East and Eastern Europe. For example, the 2004 Kroměříž Declaration declared "shaping and implementing the European Union's policies towards the countries of Eastern and Southeastern Europe" as one of the V4's priorities, while the 2011 Bratislava Declaration stated that the priority was to facilitate the process of enlarging the area of stability and democracy in the EU neighbourhood and actively contribute towards the implementation of European and Euro-Atlantic ambitions of the countries of Eastern Partnership and continue to support the Western Balkans countries in their EU and NATO integration (Visegrad Group, 2004, 2011b).

The V4's role was thus closely linked to the region's Europeanization, understood as the transfer of EU values and rules. Increasing differentiation practices regarding how EU positions are formulated, especially given the criticism of European institutions addressed to the governments of Hungary and Poland with regard to reforms of the judiciary and control over public media after 2010, have resulted in the group's Europeanization potential weakening. The V4 stopped being held up as an example to follow because of internal political problems of the participating states. This issue escalated after 2017, when, in the context of rule of law discussions, EU officials started to push for proposals to take away voting rights in EU institutions from Hungary and possibly from Poland, too (Boffey and Davies, 2017). There was also talk of splitting the V4 into two informal subgroups (the V2+ 2 format). Unlike Hungary and Poland, neither Slovakia nor the Czech Republic were interested in confronting EU institutions (Janebová and Hloušek, 2023). Viktor Orbán started to present the V4 as a potential alternative to the EU, for example, when he spoke of the need for a cultural counter-revolution in Europe (Krekó and Enyedi, 2018) in 2016. Slovakia and the Czech Republic, however, rejected such an alternative. Thus, for example, Fico still claimed in 2017 that the V4 was not an alternative to the EU, and in response to Poland's and Hungary's threat to veto both the EU Recovery Package and the Multiannual Financial Framework 2021–2027 the prime minister of Slovakia, Igor Matovič (2020–2021), stated that "Slovakia will not be the slave of the V4" (TASR, 2017; Strážay, 2021: 118).

The V4 countries' internal political crisis ran parallel not only to the refugee crisis but also to the crisis in EU–Russia relations, especially because of the developments in Ukraine and Russia's annexation of Crimea in 2014. Support for Ukraine's European integration has thus conflicted with the Russian Federation's interests. For instance, the Russian Federation put up resistance to the Eastern Partnership programme, especially in relation to the signing of a Ukraine–EU Association Agreement. Indeed, the issue of Ukraine's territorial integrity and the geographical location of the V4 states on the EU's eastern border have meant that the EU is gradually ceasing to behave as a soft, transformative power and is becoming a geopolitical actor in its relations with the states of Eastern and South East Europe. In a situation where some of the V4 states are now in conflict with EU institutions and a large number of its member states, the V4 has lost its role as an instrument of regional transformation.

The gas crises due to the Russian–Ukrainian gas disputes in 2006 and 2009 and the refugee crisis in 2015–2016 focused the V4 states' attention on security issues. This agenda became a key priority in that period, overshadowing other issues. This has changed in light of further developments in Ukraine. The issue of the relationship with Russia contributed to the reconfiguration of the Visegrad area and its dividing lines, first into a subgroup of states more actively supporting the sanctions imposed by the EU and US against the Russian Federation after 2014. This included the Czech Republic and especially Poland, while Slovakia and especially Hungary were critical of the sanctions.

Slovakia's position changed briefly after the 2020 parliamentary elections, when the coalition led by the Smer-SD party headed by Robert Fico was replaced by a coalition of centre-right parties. By 2023, the Slovak government had similar positions to Poland and the Czech Republic. The interpretation of the causes of the Ukraine War, but especially Hungary's position on providing military aid to Ukraine after the outbreak of Russia's open aggression in February 2022, caused an informal split that resulted in the V3+1. The member states' position on the redistribution of refugees among EU member states and the introduction of appropriate quotas has not fundamentally changed since the 2015–2016 refugee crisis, nor has the negative attitude towards a greater influx of non-European migrants changed, despite the various governments. An example of this is the Civic Platform's position. They formed the government in Poland after the parliamentary elections on 15 October 2023, when this party replaced the national-conservative Law and Justice Party, which had been in power for eight years. This issue's relevance, however, has diminished in the light of the war in Ukraine.

The Russian Federation's aggression against Ukraine, and the fact that Russia was (and in many aspects remained, even in early 2024) a major source of energy raw materials, especially fossil fuels (oil, natural gas, coal), but also nuclear fuel for Central Europe, threatens the countries of the V4 not only in terms of the security of raw material resources, but also in terms of the transport routes that run through Ukraine. Moreover, the war in Ukraine has coincided with the EU's green transformation, the strategic goal of which is to achieve EU carbon neutrality by 2050. The goals resulting from this initiative are particularly challenging for the highly energy-intensive economies of the post-communist states, especially Poland and the Czech Republic. The V4 countries thus face similar challenges in energy policy.

5.3 The Visegrad Group and security of supply of energy raw materials

Energy cooperation became part of the Visegrad cooperation agenda after the EU accession of the V4 states in 2004. It focused mainly on two aspects – diversification of energy sources and transport routes for energy raw materials, and climate change issues.

The V4 countries inherited an energy infrastructure from the socialist period, which created a unilateral dependence on the Russian Federation through the Brotherhood gas pipeline and the Druzhba oil pipeline. While the construction of these pipelines was a geopolitically motivated investment, after 1989 the V4 states' political elites viewed energy relations with the Russian Federation primarily as a commercial issue. Two interruptions in natural gas supplies from the Russian Federation via Ukraine in 2006 and 2009, because of commercial and partly political disputes between the two states, caused the issue to become securitized. The search for new sources of natural gas and transport routes to diversify the unilateral dependence on the Russian Federation was primarily the initiative of the president of Poland, Lech Kaczyński (2005–2010) (Grochmalski, 2018), although the 2009 natural gas supply shortfall affected Slovakia, Hungary, and Bulgaria most severely. In his projects, Kaczyński relied on cooperation with Ukraine, the South Caucasus, and Central Asia. But the adoption of an agreement on the construction of transport routes bypassing the territory of the Russian Federation at an energy summit in Krakow in May 2007 failed because of Kazakhstan's lack of interest (Bielawska, 2007; Socor, 2007). Although Kaczyński's idea of an energy pact drew attention to the need to develop the EU's Caspian Sea policy, the summit was attended by representatives of the EU member states, with only the heads of state of Poland, Romania, and Lithuania attending. Therefore, it did not have immediate consequences, such as the creation of a new format for energy cooperation between the EU and the Central Asian states. The summit thus demonstrated the limits of strategies that Marek Cichocki has called "sovereigntist"; in this case initiatives implemented at the level of nation states or groups of nation states.

More successful, however, was the Regional Energy Security Summit in Budapest on 24 February 2010, organized in a V4+ format (that is, with representatives of non-V4 countries participating, in this case Austria, Croatia, Serbia, Bosnia and Herzegovina, and Romania). The result was an agreement to initiate the construction of interconnectors between the gas pipeline systems of the Central European states, and to enable the reverse flow of gas between the region's states. The intention behind these interconnectors' construction was to enable the pipeline systems to become linked in a north–south direction and to link the planned liquified natural gas (LNG) terminals in Poland (Świnoujście) and Croatia (Krk). The next step was to reverse the flow of gas in the existing pipelines and to build gas storage. The participants also expressed support for the construction of an LNG terminal in Constanta (Romania). Unlike Poland's previous initiatives, the summit stressed the need to link regional cooperation in the energy field with the EU institutional framework, to involve the region's countries in building the EU internal gas and electricity market, and the need to finance these initiatives from EU funds. The gradual reduction of dependence on the Russian Federation, albeit while continuing to focus mainly on fossil fuels, also resulted from the shale gas revolution and the increased use of LNG technology, which has made the United

States a major exporter of natural gas (Figulová and Wertlen, 2021: 324; Visegrad Group, 2010).

Later, at the Bratislava summit on 25 January 2011, the Declaration of V4 Energy Ministers confirmed the need to build interconnectors to ensure links between Central European countries in a north–south direction. The declaration also addressed the crude oil sector; it was deemed necessary to enact measures to diversify oil supplies beside the ongoing supply from the Druzhba oil pipeline (Trubalska, 2019: 74). Such possibilities might include upgrading the existing Adria pipeline or increasing the capacity of the TAL (Transalpine) pipeline. Nuclear energy became another aspect to the cooperation, at least in the framework of research and development (Visegrad Group, 2011a). During the group's Polish presidency, a road map towards a regional V4 gas market was adopted in June 2013 (Trubalska, 2019: 75). Since 2013, projects for the construction of interconnectors linking the gas pipeline systems of Central European countries have been included in the EU list of projects of common interests. This list also includes projects to link electricity systems between Central European countries (European Commission, 2013).

The escalation of the Russia–Ukraine conflict in 2014 triggered the creation of the Central and South Eastern Europe energy connectivity (CESEC) group on 15 February 2015, with Austria, Bulgaria, Croatia, Greece, Hungary, Italy, Romania, Slovakia, and Slovenia participating. The CESEC group's main target is the diversification of natural gas supplies in the region and the integration of the Central and South East European gas and electricity markets (Visegrad Group, 2010; Sadik-Zada and Gatto, 2021: 495). The Budapest Summit's participants were later joined by Ukraine, the Republic of Moldova, Serbia, the Republic of North Macedonia, Albania, Bosnia and Herzegovina, Kosovo (in line with UNSCR 1244 and the ICJ's advisory opinion on the Kosovo declaration of independence), and Montenegro. Original cooperation over the interconnection of gas pipeline systems was expanded after the Fourth CESEC ministerial meeting in Bucharest in September 2017. This cooperation included additional areas, namely a joint approach to electricity markets, energy efficiency, and renewable development, a list of priority projects to build an interconnected regional electricity market, and specific actions to boost renewables and investment in energy efficiency in a region with vast growth potential in these areas (European Commission, 2022a).

The North–South Gas Corridor project has thus become a flagship project for V4 energy cooperation. Certain V4 experts interpreted it as a project of geopolitical importance (Ćwiek-Karpowicz and Kalan, 2013; Zaniewicz, 2019). Its results included the completion of the LNG terminals in Świnoujście (Poland) and Krk (Croatia), and interconnectors linking the region's countries. The Gdansk LNG terminal (Poland), which is included in the 5th PCI list, is expected to be completed during 2025 and will strengthen the security of gas supply for the Baltic States and Finland (European Commission, 2022b).

Less effective was opposition to the Nord Stream 2 pipeline project, which was an extension of the capacity of the existing Nord Stream pipeline, transporting natural gas from Russia to Germany along the Baltic Sea bed, bypassing Ukraine and other former Soviet bloc states respectively. Slovakia was one of the pipeline's main opponents. The V4 countries, along with Estonia, Latvia, Lithuania, Bulgaria, Romania, and Italy drew up a joint letter against the implementation of the Nord Stream 2 project (Lewkowicz, 2021). Although the V4 countries were nominally critical of the project, both for geopolitical reasons (together with the Baltic States) and for commercial reasons (Slovakia, Hungary, and, to some extent, Poland together with Italy) because the pipeline threatened their gas transit revenues, Gazprom gradually succeeded in neutralizing the opposition of Central European countries by promising to transit gas through their territory in a southerly and easterly direction, respectively (Szalai, 2019a).

The North–South Gas Corridor, as one of the most significant results of the cooperation between Visegrad participants, is an example of a successful implementation of the "integrationist" strategy of using the benefits of EU membership to secure the strategic interests of their states, in this case, the interconnection of previously isolated gas pipeline systems in Central Europe to ensure a greater flexibility of natural gas supply. This region's countries have used their EU membership and participation in EU institutions to implement their national and regional priorities in the field of energy policy. The follow-up activities to the 2010 V4+ Energy Security Summit are also an example of the Europeanization of initially national security priorities, which were later "uploaded" to the EU level. The Visegrad Group has also become a format whose fluid character has made it possible to involve other countries in the region in gas security projects, including non-EU countries such as Ukraine, Moldova, and the former Yugoslav states.

5.4 The Visegrad Group and the EU's green transition

The second aspect to V4 cooperation in the energy sector included the issues of carbon neutrality and the EU's green transition, where the V4 states were actors that hindered this process. Their economies are largely dependent on fossil fuels, which did not change even after the fall of the communist regimes in Central Europe in 1989 and after EU accession. This has also been facilitated by the activities of the "old" member states in building new pipelines. The reduction of the share of fossil fuels in favour of green energy – that is, energy from renewable sources – was met with a negative public reaction. For example, in the Czech Republic after 2005, the public blamed solar energy subsidies, often allocated in a non-transparent manner, for high energy prices.

In other countries, unfavourable legislation was an obstacle to increasing the share of renewables. Hungary passed a law in 2016 banning the siting of wind turbines within a 12-kilometer radius of populated areas. Up until 2023, this legislation left Hungary with no areas in which new wind energy capacities could be installed. Similar restrictive legislation was also adopted by the Polish parliament during the same period. In doing so, EU initiatives in favour of a green transition were rejected, including via arguments about the sovereignty of member states (Ámon, 2018; Szőke, 2023).

The V4 countries' elites believed the energy transition could threaten their economic growth and thus their economic convergence with the older members of the EU (Riepl and Zavarská, 2023: 17). Their position was also adopted by the Baltic States (Lithuania, Latvia, and Estonia), Bulgaria, and Romania. They criticized the EU's overly ambitious plans to reduce CO_2 emissions by 20 percent from 1990 to 2020, and the EU's plan to sell all emission rights in the energy sector at special auctions from 2013 onwards, a plan discussed in October 2008 at the time of the global financial crisis. They also called on the EU to refrain from actions that "do not take into account the differences in the economic potentials of the Member States." Furthermore, they warned of possible negative consequences, such as sharp increases in electricity prices. Italy echoed their arguments (Euractiv.pl, 2008).

The V4 countries, together with Romania and Bulgaria, also criticized the EU package on climate, clean air, and the transition to a waste-based economy ahead of the 2014 European Council meeting. In the case of the EU's climate and energy policy framework for 2030, they declared support for only one target – a 40 percent reduction in greenhouse gas emissions. They did not declare support for a 27 percent increase in the share of renewables in each country's total energy consumption, or for a non-binding target of a 30 percent increase in energy efficiency. They called for respect for the principle of solidarity and the creation of financial support mechanisms for countries whose industries would be most at risk of relocating production if tougher environmental measures were adopted. The V4 representatives also called for respect for the right of each member state to choose its energy mix (Visegrad Group, 2014). It is the fear of jeopardizing economic growth by meeting ambitious climate targets that is now a significant source of Euroskeptic sentiment in the V4 countries. A negative attitude towards the green transition was common to all the V4 countries. For example, the Czech Republic's government referred to it as an existential threat to the country (Riepl and Zavarská, 2023: 17).

The V4 also took a skeptical view towards the objective of achieving a climate-neutral EU by 2050. In October 2019, they did not support a proposal by the environment ministers of Denmark, France, the Netherlands, Latvia, Luxembourg, Portugal, Spain, and Sweden to set a more ambitious climate target of a 55 percent reduction in carbon dioxide emissions by 2030 (Euractiv.sk, 2019). Despite an initially united position, however, the V4 countries have not acted together. In October 2019, at the Environment Ministerial Council in Luxembourg, one V4 country – Slovakia – did not support blocking the adoption of increased climate targets (Detersová and Morgan, 2019), unlike the other group members as well as Bulgaria, Estonia, Lithuania, Malta, Croatia, Hungary, and Greece. Nevertheless, the majority of the V4 countries have maintained their rejection or skepticism of the EU's climate goals. Its flexible, fluid character has allowed the V4+ group to form alliances with Bulgaria, Romania, the Baltic States, and other EU states. The aim of this alliance, formed within the EU, has been to protect the sovereignty of its participants vis-à-vis the EU in choosing their own climate and energy policies.

5.5 Hesitant responses to the EU's climate targets

Given the limited possibilities available to prevent the adoption of the climate agenda, the V4 states have attempted to find a common response to the EU's climate goals. The Czech V4 Presidency 2019/2020, with the motto "V4 Reasonable Europe" (V4 Reasonable Europe, 2019), initiated a regional consultation to develop the National Energy and Climate Plans required by EU Regulation 2018/1999 on the Governance of the Energy Union and Climate Action. A common priority, however, was to support the development of nuclear energy. The issue of the green transition was addressed most intensively by Poland. The priorities of the Polish Presidency of the Visegrad Group (July 2020–June 2021) were reindustrialization and the strengthening of the V4's economic dimension. It advocated a "just transition" of the energy sector towards a climate-neutral economy, including regarding regions economically dependent on coal mining (Visegrad Group, 2022a). The V4 states pointed to their different starting position compared to higher-income EU member states and demanded respect for member states' right to determine the conditions under which their own energy mix would be used; in other words, the right to make a choice between the different energy sources. They also called for an increase in compensation for low-income member states from the Modernization Fund as part of the green transition's Fit for 55 set of proposals.

Its implementation, specifically the introduction of the new emissions trading system (ETS), including in the building and road transport sector, was identified as a threat contributing to the growth of energy poverty in the region. The key outcome of the Polish V4 Presidency's 2020/2021 activities in the energy field, however, was an "urgent call to ensure a true level playing field for nuclear power in the EU without excluding it from EU climate and energy policies." This resulted from a letter the V4 prime ministers addressed to President von der Leyen and Executive Vice President Frans Timmermans, dated 19 March 2021. As regards this demand, the V4 received support from France, Slovenia, and Romania (Visegrad Group, 2021). The V4 governments' policies considered the interests of key domestic business actors in the oil and gas sector. They also raised the possibility of increased use of biogas and biomethane (Jurkovič, 2021). During the winter of 2021, part of the V4 response was to promote the production and use of low-carbon hydrogen as an energy storage tool for the energy sector, as a carbon-neutral fuel for mobility, as feedstock for industry, and as an energy carrier for heating systems in buildings, heavy industry, and the power sector, all of which was in line with the European Commission's intentions, expressed by the EU Hydrogen Strategy for a Climate Neutral Europe adopted in 2020 (European Commission, 2020). In response, all V4 countries adopted their national hydrogen strategies in 2021. Besides the production of hydrogen from renewable sources, however, they also advocated the production of blue hydrogen from natural gas (Jenčová, 2021; Kochanek, 2022; Marzec, 2023).

Poland was the main opponent to the green transition, and it was also one of the countries with the lowest growth in the share of renewable energy sources (Moore et al., 2021). This was also linked to rapidly rising natural gas prices in 2021–2022, which triggered increased demand for coal (Kompała, 2022b). Poland even proposed a major reform of the ETS given the rising energy prices, as price rises are spiralling out of control and hitting the family budgets of EU citizens. According to the Prime Minister of Poland Mateusz Morawiecki (2022), it "threatens the financial security of ordinary people who have already suffered as a result of the pandemic. Above all, it undermines citizens' confidence in the EU's climate policy approach". Representatives of the Czech Republic, too, have criticized the situation on the market for emission allowances and have called for an increase in the number of allowances. Unlike Poland, however, they have not considered leaving the system, nor has the Hungarian prime minister, Viktor Orbán (Krzysztoszek and Zachová, 2021).

In contrast, the Slovak environment minister, Ján Budaj, then declared that "Slovakia is capable of achieving a 55 percent reduction in emissions by 2030", although the Slovak government also expressed concern about rising energy prices and the extension of the ETS to the transport and construction sectors. Although the Visegrad countries share an interest in slowing the pace of the climate transition, which they can pursue together, they are approaching concrete changes through their own priorities. This is also reflected in their voting patterns in EU institutions (Kompała, 2022a). The considerations of some Visegrad states, especially Poland, about potentially opting out of the EU green transition are examples of de-Europeanization tendencies present in the V4. A predominantly sovereigntist mindset can be identified in V4 countries' approaches to the EU climate target. However, this approach is associated with integrationist approaches, as they seek to achieve the possibility of sovereign action through negotiation within EU institutions. In this case, too, the V4 has been successful in building alliances within the EU. For instance, in the case of support for nuclear energy, it has been able to win over countries such as France, Slovenia, or Romania.

5.6 The Visegrad area and the war in Ukraine

The V4 states have pursued largely common interests in the field of EU energy policy, but the start of the war in Ukraine on 24 February 2022 elicited the deep differences between them in terms of their relations with Russia and toward EU institutions. In the early days of the war, their governments had to cope with an influx of refugees from Ukraine and deal with the issue of the diversification of energy sources. Indeed, with few exceptions, these issues have not been the subject of multilateral negotiations within the group.

Shortly before the war broke out, on 8 February 2022, the foreign ministers of the Slavkov Triangle – a loose cooperation between the Czech Republic, Slovakia, and Austria – visited Kyiv to declare their solidarity with Ukraine amid the threat of a Russian invasion. The attending ministers were Jan Lipavský from the Czech Republic, Ivan Korčok from Slovakia, and Alexander Schallenberg from Austria. The reason for Hungary's omission was its strained relations with Ukraine over legislation on education in minority languages, and its close relations with the Russian Federation (Hrabovská Francelová, 2022). The outbreak of war highlighted the differences between the V4 countries. At a summit with the prime minister of the United Kingdom in London on 8 March 2022, the prime ministers of the Visegrad Group states condemned the Russian aggression against Ukraine, stating that "[t]he actions of Russia, and those who enable them, represent an egregious violation of international law and the UN Charter that undermines European security and stability". They also announced the creation of a support package of €1 million to help Ukraine via the International Visegrad Fund, with a focus on improving the situation of Ukrainian refugees in the V4 countries, including vulnerable groups such as children (Visegrad Group, 2022c). The above declaration, however, was the only step the Visegrad Group was able to take multilaterally amid the war in Ukraine up until early 2024.

A meeting of the defence ministers, set to take place on 30–31 March 2022 in Budapest, was cancelled because the representatives of Poland and the Czech Republic refused to attend due to Budapest's lukewarm support for action against Moscow. Although Hungary voted in favour of all four packages of EU sanctions imposed on Russia, it has vehemently opposed sanctions targeting energy imports and has stated it would not let weapons destined for Ukraine, which it borders, to pass through its territory. Budapest has also vehemently rejected calls to ban Russian energy exports (Krzysztoszek et al., 2022). Hungary's position on the war in Ukraine resulted in Poland's decision to announce the end of its previously close political cooperation with Hungary. The meeting of the V4 foreign affairs committees of the national parliaments on 22 April 2022, which hoped to favour political, humanitarian, and defence aid, thus strengthening Ukraine's defence capabilities, did not result in any joint action (Visegrad Group, 2022a). Although the European Affairs Committees of the national parliaments of the V4 countries on 24 April 2022 were also dominated by the issue of the immediate response to the start of the war in Ukraine, it was at this forum that the issues of cooperation in the field of energy were most raised. However, this was not seen as a Visegrad Group agenda, but as an EU agenda. They stressed the need to start without any delay, with a view to the next winter, the refilling of gas storage across the Union. They also spoke of the need to diversify sources of energy raw materials and to rapidly complete and improve gas and electricity interconnections through the EU. On the issue of the Green Deal, they stressed the need for a technology-neutral approach in policy aiming to reduce the emission of greenhouse gases. The inclusion of nuclear energy in the green taxonomy of financing the EU remained a common priority (Visegrad Group, 2022b).

Representatives of Central European states demonstrated support for Ukraine in other forms, for example, through a meeting between the Prime Ministers Petr Fiala (Czech Republic), Mateusz Morawiecki (Poland), and Janez Janša (Slovenia), with the President of Ukraine, Volodymyr Zelensky, in Kyiv on 16 March 2022 (Gijs, 2022).

The V4 countries have therefore reacted to the conflict with Russia in different ways. Poland refused the Russian company Gazprom's demand for payments of gas supplies in roubles, so Russia stopped gas supplies to the country in April 2022 (Sawicki, 2022). Thanks to the LNG terminal in Świnoujście, Poland was able to detach itself relatively quickly from the Russian Federation's natural gas supplies. Throughout 2022, the share of Russian gas in its total gas imports fell from 61 percent (2021) to almost zero. From November 2022, Poland has imported gas via the new Baltic Pipe, a pipeline from Norway (EIU, 2023). Coal supplies from Russia have created a more serious problem for the country. In 2020 Poland imported 10 million tonnes of coal from Russia (Ciobanu, 2022). The Czech Republic stopped importing natural gas from Russia in the first quarter of 2023, although before the start of the invasion, Russian gas accounted for 97 percent of total gas imports (EIU, 2023). The Czech Republic has replaced supplies from Russia with gas from Norway transported via German territory, and shipments of LNG via ports in Belgium and the Netherlands. Hungary continued its energy orientation towards Russia in 2023; gas from Russia accounts for 80 percent of its imports. By the end of 2022, Slovakia had reduced Russia's share of gas imports to 60 percent, but was taking steps to diversify through Poland's pipeline network, and via negotiations with Italian and German companies as well as discussions with Lithuania (EIU, 2023; Berardi, 2022). The completion of an interconnector linking the Slovak and Polish pipeline systems in 2022 also helped Slovakia, with construction beginning before the war began.

An important impetus for the change in Visegrad states' energy policy priorities was the approval of a sixth package of sanctions by the European Council in June 2022 (European Council, 2022). This included a ban on the import of crude oil and certain oil products from Russia into the EU with a phasing out from six months for crude oil and eight months for other refined petroleum products. Hungary threatened a veto if the EU banned imports of Russian oil. Slovakia, Hungary, and the Czech Republic were granted a temporary exception because of their geographic situation and high dependence on Russian supplies without other viable alternatives. In 2023, Slovakia and Hungary pushed for an extension to this exception (Jack, 2023; Zachová, 2023). Unlike oil, supplies of natural gas and nuclear fuel to EU countries are not part of the sanctions package. The process of substituting Russian nuclear fuel is also a challenging one, and so the Czech Republic, Slovakia, and Hungary have obtained exemptions for aviation imports of nuclear fuel. Hungary has continued to import nuclear fuel from the Russian Federation, while the Czech Republic and Slovakia have initiated negotiations to import it from a US supplier, Westinghouse, and from France's Framatome (EIU, 2023).

Nevertheless, after the announcement of an EU embargo on seaborne Russian oil imports, Hungary declared its interest in preserving energy relations with the Russian Federation in an effort to prevent a sharp increase in fuel and gas prices by strengthening energy transport routes through Serbia. Hungary also agreed for Gazprom to reroute gas shipments to Hungary away from Ukraine and Slovakia, which had previously agreed to run at a rate of 1 billion cubic metres per year in 2021 (Afanasiev, 2022).

The geopolitical divergences between the V4 countries have also emerged in their building of nuclear power plants. In 2021, the Czech government excluded Rosatom (Russia) and CGN (China) from the tender for security reasons and announced its intention to provide financial guarantees for the construction.

Westinghouse, EDF, and KHNP are bidding to build new nuclear power plants in the Czech Republic (Trade.gov, 2023). In March 2023, Westinghouse Electric Company and ČEZ signed an agreement for the supply of VVER-440 fuel assemblies from next year for the Dukovany nuclear power plant as it switches from Russian-supplied fuel (WNN, 2023).

Poland, the only V4 country that does not yet have a nuclear power plant, signed an agreement in September 2023 with the US companies Westinghouse and Bechtel for the construction of its first nuclear plant at the Lubiatowo-Kopalino site, with plans to start up the first unit in 2033. In the words of the then Prime Minister, Mateusz Morawiecki, nuclear power is set to replace coal as the main source of energy in the future. The Slovak company Slovenské elektrárne has also signed a nuclear fuel supply contract with Westinghouse (Larson, 2023; Money.pl, 2023). Hungary is moving in the opposite direction, pushing for stronger energy cooperation with the Russian Federation. In August 2014, it signed an agreement with the Russian company Rosatom for the construction of the new Paks II nuclear power plant, with project implementation beginning in August 2023 (Rosatom, n.d.). Hungary continued this cooperation even after the war broke out, with Rosatom receiving permission to build two units of the plant in August 2022 (Sadecki, 2022).

Hungary has also distanced itself politically from the other V4 countries, especially from the Czech Republic and Poland. One example of this was when it opposed Ukraine's progressive integration into the EU, using the threat of a veto (Sadecki, 2023). During a meeting with President Vladimir Putin on 17 October 2023 in Beijing, on the sidelines of the Belt and Road Forum organized by China, Viktor Orbán referred to the war against Ukraine as a "military operation". He was the first EU member state representative to meet Russia's president since March 2023 when the International Criminal Court issued an arrest warrant for Putin. Indeed, Orbán was also the second EU leader, after Austria's chancellor, to have met Putin after Russia launched its invasion of Ukraine in February 2022 (Sadecki and Rudnik, 2023). While Poland, after the outbreak of the war, chose the path of closer cooperation within the EU, as confirmed by its 2023 parliamentary elections, Hungary is opting for a more de-Europeanizing, sovereigntist strategy in terms of political rhetoric, but also in its rejection of military aid to Ukraine. Similarly, after the parliamentary elections in Slovakia at the end of September 2023, a coalition of parties came to power that was critical of the sanctions policy against the Russian Federation and has stopped non-commercial arms supplies to Ukraine (Cienski and Melkozerova, 2023). Despite the ongoing rapprochement with Russia, Hungary and Slovakia are simultaneously taking steps to increase the security of the gas supply, with EUSTREAM (Slovakia) and FGSZ having announced a 50 percent increase in gas transmission capacity from Hungary to Slovakia from July 2024 (Potočár, 2024).

The war in Ukraine has thus reconfigured Visegrad cooperation significantly, with the V2+2 format replacing the previous V3+1 format, given Hungary's different reaction to the war in Ukraine, choosing to continue political and energy cooperation with the Russian Federation. The possibilities for cooperation in the V4 format have narrowed considerably, to the extent that after the outbreak of Russia's open aggression against Ukraine, it is more appropriate to speak of cooperation in the Visegrad area rather than of Visegrad cooperation.

5.7 Cooperation – but in which areas?

The weakening of the political dimension to Visegrad cooperation was also visible in the programmes of the presidencies of Slovakia (July 2022–June 2023) and the Czech Republic (July 2023–June 2024). Slovakia identified mitigating the consequences of the ongoing humanitarian crisis in Ukraine as a priority. Cooperation in 2022–2023 was to focus on four areas – interconnection, economy, sustainability, and people. Energy issues were at the top of the agenda, under a heading titled "Interconnections". The V4 for Future Programme of the Slovak Presidency of the Visegrad Group (July 2022–June 2023) (V4 for Future, 2022) was to focus on developing regional energy infrastructures, including projects of common EU interest, and the effective deployment of clean technologies, including hydrogen, nuclear, and renewable energy sources. Rather than concrete actions, the Slovak presidency in the field of energy envisaged mutual consultations, for instance, in sharing examples of good practices in the development and implementation of energy efficiency and renewable energy among the V4 countries, in discussing suitable EU instruments that contribute to the global reduction of emissions and climate mainstreaming, and in synchronizing laws and regulations to ensure combined positive effects on the climate and cooperation over the preparation of national climate laws.

The Slovak presidency also envisaged cooperation in phasing out the dependency on Russian oil and gas and further gas infrastructure development. At the same time, Slovakia declared its efforts to continue work on defining natural gas as an important transition fuel and on creating appropriate market conditions for all types of decarbonized gases. The Slovak presidency's program also included coordinating the preparation and implementation of the REPowerEU plan, discussing possible measures at the EU level to address the causes and impact of high energy prices.

As political cooperation within the V4 has dwindled, no ministerial meetings on energy topics have been held since Russia's open aggression against Ukraine began. The political instability associated with the collapse of the government coalition in Slovakia, however, combined with the deprioritization of Visegrad cooperation, meant that, at the end of the Slovak Presidency, for the first time since its reestablishment in 1999, no annual report was issued to evaluate the group's activities in 2023. The politicization of the recovery plans, whose implementation in the case of Hungary and Poland has been conditional on meeting EU requirements regarding the rule of law, has meant that this issue has dropped off the Visegrad agenda.

The Czech presidency (V4 citizens, 2023), which started in July 2023, did not bring any significant changes to the Visegrad agenda either. Besides the emphasis on supporting the inclusion of nuclear energy in the EU taxonomy of environmentally sustainable economic activities, the Czech Republic declared its interest in facilitating an exchange of views on the implementation of the REPowerEU Plan. With the motto "V4 citizens", the Programme of the Czech Presidency of the Visegrad Group also plans to begin coordinating activities related to the implementation of the V4 countries' national hydrogen strategies. The priority areas include the use of hydrogen in transport, the construction of hydrogen refuelling stations, and the possibility of putting low-carbon hydrogen on an equal footing with renewable hydrogen. A project of special importance to the V4 countries is Corridor E of the European Hydrogen Backbone Initiative, especially the Central European Hydrogen Corridor, which should bring renewable hydrogen produced in Ukraine to Central Europe and Germany by repurposing existing natural gas pipelines into hydrogen and the construction of new pipelines dedicated to hydrogen (Kochanek, 2022; CEH2C, n.d.). Similarly, as with Slovakia, the group's Czech presidency can only speak of minimal activities at the political level.

Instead of multilateral cooperation, bilateral cooperation has developed with greater success. The beginning of the war was the impetus for the revival of bilateral Polish–Czech cooperation, which had earlier become disrupted by the construction of a brown coal mine in Turów. After a meeting between Prime Ministers Mateusz Morawiecki and Petr Fiala in April 2022, the two countries agreed to support the construction of the Stork II gas pipeline linking the two countries. This project was already included on the PCI list but was dropped in 2016 when Poland identified it as unnecessary and prioritized the Baltic Pipe pipeline project (Tramba, 2022; Derewenda, 2023). However, the war in Ukraine and the resulting need to build new energy transport routes have revived the project's relevance. In contrast, Slovakia cooperates more closely with Hungary on diversifying its oil supply, as the Bratislava-based Slovnaft refinery is owned by the Hungarian MOL group.

The liquidity and fluidity of regional cooperation in the Visegrad area is visible in changes to Slovakia's foreign policy made after the parliamentary elections in September 2023. Before the elections, the party Smer – SD, which went on to win, was advocating the revival of Visegrad cooperation. Its leader, Robert Fico, was openly supported in the campaign by Viktor Orbán. The second official foreign visit of the newly appointed Prime Minister Fico was to Budapest in January 2024. Fico supported Orbán in his dispute with the EU institutions, but also admitted skepticism about the future of the V4, stating that it was turning into the V2 (Madro, 2024). Indeed, the war in Ukraine has shown the vulnerability of Visegrad cooperation. This has been confirmed by the programmes of the Slovak (2022–2023) and Czech (2023–2024) presidencies. Attempts to identify areas of potential cooperation, including on energy issues, are formulated in a very awkward manner in them.

5.8 The political aspect of the climate agenda – a conflictual factor in V4 societies

EU climate policy is becoming a political factor in the V4 countries. It is becoming a factor of internal political mobilization and polarization, but also a potential source of conflict between states in the region. For example, at the EU climate summit, that is, a European Council meeting in December 2019, the President of the Czech Republic, Miloš Zeman, spoke of "climate madness" and referred to the non-election of Frans Timmermans, an advocate for increasing the EU's climate targets, as president of the European Commission, stating that this was a success for the Visegrad Group. The Polish President, Andrzej Duda, spoke of a need for "a fair transition without a drastic rise in household energy prices and without a radical increase in unemployment" (Gabrižová, 2019).

Environmental issues have become a point of contention between two V4 countries – Poland and the Czech Republic. In March 2021, the Czech Republic launched an action against Poland concerning the expansion of the Turów open-pit lignite mine and brought it before the EU Court of Justice. The main reason raised in the action was the negative impact of the mine on the border regions, where the groundwater level has decreased. In addition, Poland allegedly failed to offer the Czech side until 2026 full information linked to the procedure for issuing a mining permit (Business Insider Polska, 2021). The dispute, which resulted in the Polish ambassador to the Czech Republic withdrawing, led to active political mobilization in both states. It was not settled until early February 2022, but complaints from residents of the Czech border regions about the environmental damage caused by coal mining on the Polish side continued into 2023 (Molga, 2023). The Polish–Czech agreement also sparked discontent among environmental activists in the Czech Republic (Krzysztoszek and Zachová, 2022).

The issue of the energy transition is also becoming part of internal political conflicts. In Poland, after the 2023 parliamentary elections, the issue of wind energy has become the subject of a conflict between the new government led by Donald Tusk and the opposition represented by the Law and Justice Party. While the ruling coalition has announced a more active policy regarding the deployment of renewables, the former ruling Law and Justice Party refuses to do so. It is blocking, for example, the passage of legislation that would liberalize the installation of new wind turbines, arguing, among other things, for the protection of jobs in the coal mining sector (Elżbeciak, 2023). Hungary remains skeptical about the possibility of achieving a 90 percent reduction in net greenhouse gas output across the EU by 2040, although the new Polish government has signed up to this target (Hodgson, 2024). The previous Morawiecki Government even considered rejecting the Green Deal altogether (Rankin, 2019).

For example, while in 2019 the Slovak prime minister, Peter Pellegrini, declared his skepticism about the EU's climate targets, the Slovak president, Zuzana Čaputová, warned of the consequences of the climate crisis in her first presidential speech in June 2015 (Szalai, 2019b). In 2023, renewables were not the subject of an intensive election campaign; nevertheless, all relevant parties, with the exception of Progressive Slovakia, supported the construction of a new nuclear power plant. Progressive Slovakia was also the only party that advocated an accelerated shift away from Russia as a supplier of natural gas (Jenčová, 2023).

Environmental issues, including the issue of energy transition, are thus becoming the subject of not only common action but also conflicts between the V4 countries.

These conflicts also influence internal political developments. While national-populist and conservative parties reject the energy transition, more liberal-oriented groups, on the contrary, support it or formulate their criticism of specific actions in a less radical way.

5.9 In lieu of a conclusion: The fragmented Visegrad group in conditions of war

Russia's aggression against Ukraine, which became open war from 24 February 2022 onwards, has contributed to the V4's fragmentation. The complexity and fluidity of regional cooperation, built on the principles of the New Regionalism, has shown its strengths and weaknesses. Although the group was able to build alliances involving several EU member states before the war, the different perceptions of risks arising from the war in its neighbourhood caused the V4's atomization and a decline in political cooperation. The differentiation processes within the group are not recent, but the war has contributed to the group's reconfiguration, and by early 2024, views about the V4's dysfunctionality already appeared in some political leaders' statements about the participating states. Although some analysts, such as Tomas Strážay, have postulated its continuation solely on non-political issues (Strážay, 2023: 116–118), it is precisely its depoliticization that has led to the group's deprioritization and the weakening of top-level political contacts and the closely linked sectoral-level contacts. This is because the group's activities, including the energy and climate transition, are primarily political in nature and cannot be implemented without direct support from governments. Given the weakening of Visegrad cooperation, it is becoming more appropriate to talk about cooperation in the Visegrad area.

The V4 countries have responded to the challenges of the energy transition in a way that reflects both domestic political factors and their economic capacities. The different structure of their energy mixes, with the same carbon costs for all countries, regardless of their dependence on fossil fuels, also supports arguments against these states cooperating on climate policy issues. The V4 countries have sought, through EU institutions, that their problems be considered, and they have tried to obtain the maximum possible benefits. Yet they have also favoured domestic solutions over European ones, for example, by opting for sovereigntist procedures. This has been particularly pronounced in the case of Poland and, to a lesser extent, Hungary. On the contrary, the war in Ukraine has weakened sovereigntist approaches in Poland, while Hungary has strengthened its course of moving away from the EU mainstream. In response to the EU's strategic intention to minimize economic relations with the Russian Federation, Hungary prefers not only to de-Europeanize but also to counter-Europeanize. Using energy policy as an example, it can be concluded that the V4 countries' cooperation has been more effective at achieving set goals when they have preferred integrationist strategies, instead of sovereigntist ones. When pursuing the latter, the potential for regional cooperation is also weakened.

Acknowledgements

This work was supported by the Slovak Research and Development Agency Grant No APVV-20-0012.

References

Afanasiev, V., 2022. Hungary strengthens energy ties with Russia and Serbia. Upstream, October 14. www.upstreamonline.com/politics/hungary-strengthens-energy-ties-with-russia-and-serbia/2-1-1334324

Ámon, A., 2018. V4 dáva prednosť megalomanským projektom pred čistou energiou. Euractiv.sk, July 31. https://euractiv.sk/section/buducnost-eu/opinion/v4-dava-prednost-megalomanskym-projektom-pred-cistou-energiou/

Aslund, A., 1997. Possible future directions for economies in transition. In Nelson, J. M., Tilly, Ch., Walker, L. (Eds.) *Transforming Post-Communist Political Economies.* Washington, DC: National Academy Press: 453–470.

Berardi, L., 2022. Energy remix. Late Visegrád Allies' hard path to independence. Reset: Dialogues on Civilizations, May 6. www.resetdoc.org/story/energy-remix-late-visegrad-allies-hard-path-to-independence/

Bielawska, A., 2007. How to reduce energy dependence on Russia? Radio Polonia, May 11.

Boffey, D., Davies, C., 2017. Poland may be stripped of EU voting rights over judicial independence. *Guardian*, July 19. www.theguardian.com/world/2017/jul/19/poland-may-lose-eu-voting-rights-over-judicial-independence

Bohle, D., Greskovits, B., 2012. *Capitalist Diversity on Europe's Periphery*. London/Ithaca: Cornell University Press.

Business Insider Polska, 2021. Spór Polski i Czech o Turów. O co chodzi w tym konflikcie? May 21. https://businessinsider.com.pl/wiadomosci/spor-polski-i-czech-o-turow-o-co-chodzi-w-tym-konflikcie/kckcmpf

CEH_2C, n.d. Project vision. Central European Hydrogen Corridor. www.cehc.eu/cehc-project/

Cianciara, A., 2019. Visegrad Four & differentiation in the European Union. Policy Paper. Prague: Europeum. https://europeum.org/data/articles/policy-paper-en-3.pdf

Cichocki, M., 2009. Polskie strategie w UE. *Przegląd Zachodni*, 3, 3–15.

Cienski, J., Melkozerova, V., 2023. Why Slovakia's Fico hates Ukraine. Politico, October 19. www.politico.eu/article/slovakia-new-prime-minister-robert-fico-ukraine-war/

Ciobanu, C., 2022. Ukraine war exposes extent of Poland's obsolete energy policies. Balkan Insight, September 20. https://balkaninsight.com/2022/09/20/ukraine-war-exposes-extent-of-polands-obsolete-energy-policies/

Ćwiek-Karpowicz, J., Kalan, D. (Eds) 2013. *North-South Gas Corridor: Geopolitical Breakthrough in Central Europe*. Warsaw: PISM.

Derewenda, F., 2023. Poland and Czechia to strengthen energy cooperation, following high-level meetings. CE Energy News, May 29. https://ceenergynews.com/oil-gas/poland-and-czechia-to-strengthen-energy-cooperation-following-high-level-meetings/

Detersová, K., Morgan, S., 2019. Ambicióznejšie klimatické ciele zablokovalo desať krajín Únie, Slovensko nie. Euractiv.sk, October 8. https://euractiv.sk/section/klima/news/ambicioznejsie-klimaticke-ciele-zablokovalo-desat-krajin-unie-slovensko-nie/

Drulák, P., 2003. Benelux. In Vykoukal, Jiří (Ed.) *Visegrád: možnosti a meze středoevropské spolupráce*. Praha: Dokořán: 299–313.

EIU, 2023. Central Europe makes progress towards energy independence. Economist Intelligence Unit, September 8.

Elżbeciak, T., 2023. Co ma polska wojna o wiatraki do globalnego kryzysu wiatrowego? Wysokie Napięcie, December 8. https://wysokienapiecie.pl/95173-co-ma-polska-wojna-o-wiatraki-do-globalnego-kryzysu-wiatrowego/

Euractiv.pl, 2008. Grupa Wyszehradzka o pakiecie energetyczno–klimatycznym, November 4. www.euractiv.pl/section/gospodarka/news/grupa-wyszehradzka-o-pakiecie-energetyczno-klimatycznym/

Euractiv.sk, 2019. Osem štátov žiada výraznejšie zníženie emisií, chýbajú medzi nimi Nemecko a V4, October 8. https://euractiv.sk/section/klima/news/osem-statov-ziada-vyraznejsie-znizenie-emisii-chybaju-medzi-nimi-nemecko-a-v4/

European Commission, 2013. Commission Delegated Regulation (EU) No 1391/2013 of 14 October 2013 amending Regulation (EU) No 347/2013 of the European Parliament and of the Council on guidelines for trans-European energy infrastructure as regards the Union list of projects of common interest. https://eur-lex.europa.eu/legal-content/EN/TXT/?uri=CELEX:32013R1391

European Commission, 2020. EU Hydrogen Strategy for a Climate Neutral Europe, July 8. https://energy.ec.europa.eu/system/files/2020-07/hydrogen_strategy_0.pdf

European Commission, 2022a. Central and South Eastern Europe Energy Connectivity. Projects of Common Interest in energy infrastructure in the Central and South-Eastern region, December 15. https://energy.ec.europa.eu/topics/infrastructure/high-level-groups/central-and-south-eastern-europe-energy-connectivity_en#documents

European Commission, 2022b. Communication from the Commission to the European Parliament, the European Council, the European Economic and Social Committee and the Committee of the Regions REPowerEU Plan. COM 2022 230 final, May 18. https://eur-lex.europa.eu/legal-content/EN/TXT/?uri=COM%3A2022%3A230%3AFIN&qid=1653033742483#footnote13

European Council, 2022. European Council conclusions on Ukraine, May 30. www.consilium.europa.eu/en/press/press-releases/2022/05/31/european-council-conclusions-on-ukraine-30-may-2022/

Figulová, A., Wertlen, D., 2021. Between energy security and energy transition: Visegrad Gas Hub. In Mišík, M., Oravcová, V. (Eds) *From Economic to Energy Transition Three Decades of Transitions in Central and Eastern Europe*. Cham: Palgrave Macmillan: 315–340.

Gabrižová, Z., 2019. Klimatická kríza vs klimatické šialenstvo. Summit prezidentov V4 ukázal jednotu aj odchýlky. Euractiv.sk, October 3. https://euractiv.sk/section/buducnost-eu/news/klimaticka-kriza-vs-klimaticke-sialenstvo-summit-prezidentov-v4-ukazal-jednotu-aj-odchylky/

Gijs, C., 2022. Leaders of Poland, Czech Republic, Slovenia to visit Kyiv on Tuesday. Politico, March 15. www.politico.eu/article/leader-poland-czech-republic-slovenia-visit-kyiv/

Grochmalski, P., 2018. Testament geopolityczny Prezydenta. *Polska Zbrojna*, November 10. www.polska-zbrojna.pl/home/articleshow/26848

Hodgson, R., 2024. Poland's new government commits to join EU 'fight' against climate change. Euronews, January 15. www.euronews.com/green/2024/01/15/polands-new-government-commits-to-join-eu-fight-against-climate-change

Hrabovská Francelová, N., 2022. Slovak minister teams up for Ukraine visit with Czech and Austrian counterparts. *Slovak Spectator*, February 8.

Jack, V., 2023. Slovakia asks EU for extra year to kick Russian oil addiction. Politico, November 20. www.politico.eu/article/slovakia-asks-eu-for-extra-year-to-kick-russian-oil-addiction/

Jańczak, J., 2010. De-Europeanization and counter-Europeanization as reversed Europeanization. In Jańczak, J. (Ed.) *Search of Categorization, in: Policies and Politics of the European Union*. Poznań: Adam Mickiewicz University: 99–110.

Janebová, P., Hloušek, V., 2023. Community of fate? Visegrád cooperation viewed from Bratislava and Prague. *Europe-Asia Studies*, 75(6), 947–971.

Jenčová, I., 2021. Krajiny V4: Nechceme sa obmedzovať na obnoviteľný vodík. Euractiv.sk, June 1. https://euractiv.sk/section/energetika/news/krajiny-v4-nechceme-sa-obmedzovat-na-obnovitelny-vodik/

Jenčová, I., 2023. Energetika pred voľbami: Renovácie domov aj nový jadrový zdroj. Euractiv.sk, September 13. https://euractiv.sk/section/dekarbonizacia-priemyslu/news/energetika-pred-volbami-renovacie-domov-a-novy-jadrovy-zdroj/

Jurkovič, P., 2021. Pre krajiny V4 je dôležité prepájanie plynárenských systémov, plyn ako prechodné palivo, aj princíp technologickej neutrality. Slovgas, September 16. www.slovgas.sk/aktuality/pre-krajiny-v4-je-dolezite-prepajanie-plynarenskych-systemov-plyn-ako-prechodne-palivo-aj-princip-technologickej-neutrality

Kochanek, E., 2022. The role of hydrogen in the Visegrad Group approach to energy transition. *Energies*, 15, 7235. https://doi.org/10.3390/en15197235

Kompała, M., 2022a. Państwa Grupy Wyszehradzkiej obwiniają ETS za wysokie ceny energii. Co stoi za ich wzrostem? Euractiv.pl, February 27. www.euractiv.pl/section/instytucje-ue/news/eu-ets-ets-energia-ceny-energii-frans-timmermans-viktor-orban-fit-for-55-mateusz-morawiecki-zbigniew-ziobro-czechy-polska-slowacja-wegry-v4-grupa-wyszehradzka/

Kompała, M., 2022b. Polska hamulcowym europejskiej polityki klimatycznej? Nasz kraj odpowiada za 1/3 unijnego prądu z węgla. Euractiv.pl, February 1. www.euractiv.pl/section/energia-i-srodowisko/news/ember-energia-odnawialna-oze-fotowoltaika-wegiel-polska-unia-europejska-co2-emisje-gaz/

Krekó, P., Enyedi, Z., 2018. Explaining Eastern Europe: Orbán's laboratory of illiberalism. *Journal of Democracy*, 28(3), 39–51.

Krzysztoszek, A., Zachová, A., 2021. Czech minister would support Poland's call for suspension of EU ETS. Euractiv.com, December 13. www.euractiv.com/section/politics/short_news/czech-minister-would-support-polands-call-for-suspension-of-eu-ets/

Krzysztoszek, A., Zachová, A., 2022. Unexpected Poland, Czechia mine deal upsets activists and experts. Euractiv.com, February 4. www.euractiv.com/section/politics/short_news/unexpected-poland-czechia-mine-deal-upsets-activists-and-experts/

Krzysztoszek, A., Zachová, A., Yar, L., Makszimov, V., 2022. V4 meeting cancelled over Hungary's Ukraine policy. Euractiv.com, March 29. www.euractiv.com/section/politics/short_news/v4-meeting-cancelled-over-hungarys-ukraine-policy/

Larson, A., 2023. Westinghouse will supply nuclear fuel for Russian-designed reactors in Slovakia. Powermag, August 25. www.powermag.com/westinghouse-will-supply-nuclear-fuel-for-russian-designed-reactors-in-slovakia/

Lewkowicz, Ł., 2021. Slovakia resists construction of the North Stream 2 gas pipeline. Institute of Central Europe Commentaries, November 30. https://ies.lublin.pl/en/comments/slovakia-resists-construction-of-the-nord-stream-2-gas-pipeline/

Madro, P., 2024. Premiér Fico sa v Budapešti zastal Orbána. Tvrdí, že je Európskou úniou trestaný za svoje názory. *Pravda*, January 16.

Marzec, J., 2023 The hydrogen policy of the Visegrad countries: A comparative study. *Rocznik Instytutu Europy Środkowo-Wschodniej*, 21(2), 73–90. https://doi.org/10.36874/RIESW.2023.2.4

Mišík, M., 2010. Prečo sa krajiny strednej a východnej Európy stavajú kriticky k cieľom EÚ v oblasti obnoviteľných zdrojov energie? DenníkN – blog, 26 July. https://dennikn.sk/blog/2481304/preco-sa-krajiny-strednej-a-vychodnej-europy-stavaju-kriticky-k-cielom-eu-v-oblasti-obnovitelnych-zdrojov-energie/

Molga, T., 2023. Wraca "wojna" na linii Czechy-Polska. Będą chcieli odszkodowań. WP Wiadomości, December 10. https://wiadomosci.wp.pl/morawiecki-zawarl-ugode-i-wyplacil-nie-pomoglo-czesi-szykuja-nowy-spor-o-turow-6971545667684992a

Money.pl, 2023. Elektrownia jądrowa w Polsce. Kluczowa umowa podpisana, September 27. www.money.pl/gospodarka/elektrownia-jadrowa-w-polsce-kluczowa-umowa-podpisana-6946036223851264a.html

Moore, Ch., Brown, S., Alparslan, U., Cremona, E., Alster, G., 2021. *European Electricity Review, 6-month update H1–2021*. London: Ember.

Morawiecki, M., 2022. PM Morawiecki: The EU ETS system driven by speculators must be reformed. Euractiv.com, January 3. www.euractiv.com/section/emissions-trading-scheme/opinion/pm-morawiecki-the-eu-ets-system-driven-by-speculators-must-be-reformed/

Nosko, A., Orban, A., Paczynski, W., Cernoch F., Jaros, J., 2010. *Energy Security Policy Paper for Visegrad Security Cooperation Initiative*. Bratislava: ATA-SAC.

Nyzio, A., 2018. The second revival? The Visegrád Group and the European migrant crisis in 2015–2017. *Politeia*, 50 (5): 47–98. https://doi.org/10.12797/Politeja.14.2017.50.03

PAP, 2018. "Tylko mówiąc jednym głosem będziemy, wiarygodni i słyszani w UE". Wizyta szefa MSZ Czech w Polsce, November 9. www.sejm.gov.pl/sejm8.nsf/komunikat.xsp?documentId=6E6D9AB6953BC2C5C12583400078BEE6

Polish Presidency in the Visegrad Group (July 2020 – June 2021). Presidency Programme. Visegrad Group, 2020. www.visegradgroup.eu/documents/presidency-programs/2020–2021-polish

Potočár, R., 2024. Môže prísť viac plynu v smere z Maďarska. Plynári zvyšujú prepravnú kapacitu o 50 %. Energie-portál, February 14. www.energie-portal.sk/Dokument/plyn-madarsko-eustream-110647.aspx

Radaelli, C. M., 2004. Europeanisation: Solution or problem? European Integration online Papers (EIoP), 8(16). http://eiop.or.at/eiop/texte/2004–016a.htm

Rankin, J., 2019. European Green Deal to press ahead despite Polish targets opt-out. *Guardian*, December 13.

Riepl, T., Zavarská, Z., 2023. Towards a Greener Visegrád Group. Progress and challenges in the European Green Deal. Policy Notes and Reports, 64. Vienna: The Vienna Institute for International Economic Studies.

Rosatom, n.d. Cooperation with Hungary. https://rosatom-centraleurope.com/rosatom-in-country/history-of-cooperation/hu/

Sadecki, A., 2022. Węgry: zielone światło dla Rosatomu w Paks. Warsaw: Centre for Eastern Studies, August 31. www.osw.waw.pl/en/node/30567

Sadecki, A., 2023. Orbán's blackmail: Hungary threatens to block Ukraine's integration with the EU. Warsaw: Centre for Eastern Studies, May 12. www.osw.waw.pl/en/publikacje/analyses/2023–12–05/orbans-blackmail-hungary-threatens-to-block-ukraines-integration-eu

Sadecki, A., Rudnik, F., 2023. The Orbán–Putin meeting in Beijing: Hungary drifting away from the West. Warsaw: Centre for Eastern Studies, October 19. www.osw.waw.pl/en/publikacje/analyses/2023–10–19/orban-putin-meeting-beijing-hungary-drifting-away-west

Sadik-Zada, E. R., Gatto, A., 2021. Energy security pathways in South East Europe: Diversification of the natural gas supplies, energy transition, and energy futures. In Mišík, M., Oravcová, V. (Eds.) *From Economic to Energy Transition Three Decades of Transitions in Central and Eastern Europe*. Cham: Palgrave Macmillan: 491–514.

Sawicki, B., 2022. Gazprom zakręcił Polsce kurek z gazem. Premirer potwierdza groźby. *Rzeczpospolita*, April 26.

Soccr, V., 2007. Krakow Pro-Western Energy Summit outmaneuvred by Putin in Central Asia. *Eurasia Daily Monitor*, 4 (94), May 14. https://jamestown.org/program/krakow-pro-western-energy-summit-outmaneuvered-by-putin-in-central-asia/

Söderbaum, F., 2003. Introduction: Theories of new regionalism. In Söderbaum, F., Shaw, T. M. (Eds) *Theories of New Regionalism. A Palgrave Reader*. Basingstoke: Palgrave Macmillan: 1–21.

Soler and Lecha, E., 2008. *Turkey's reluctant involvement in ESDP: Europeanisation as a round trip*, Second Global International Studies Conference (WISC) Ljubljana, July 23–26.

Strážay, T., 2021. The newcomers versus the old guard? Regional cooperation in Central Europe. In Brezáni, P. (Ed.) *The Yearbook of Slovakia s Foreign Policy 2020*. Bratislava: SFPA: 112–123.

Strážay, T., 2023. Central European challenges in Slovak foreign policy. In Brezáni, P. (Ed.) *The Yearbook of Slovakia s Foreign Policy 2022*. Bratislava: SFPA 2023: 105–118.

Švec, L., 2003. Balticko-severský prostor. In Vykoukal, J. (Ed.) *Visegrád: možnosti a meze středoevropské spolupráce*. Praha: Dokořán: 269–298.

Szalai, P., 2019a. Šéf Eustreamu: Nord Stream 2 nie je pre Slovensko problém. Euractiv.sk, November 26. https://euractiv.sk/section/energetika/news/sef-eustreamu-nord-stream-2-nie-je-pre-slovensko-problem/

Szalai, P., 2019b. Uhlíková neutralita v roku 2050? Slovensko hovorí (zatiaľ) nie. Euractiv.sk, June 17. https://euractiv.sk/section/klima/news/uhlikova-neutralita-v-roku-2050-slovensko-hovori-zatial-nie/

Szőke, E., 2023. Hungary presents new rules to advance wind energy deployment. *CE Energy News*, December 18. https://ceenergynews.com/renewables/hungary-presents-new-rules-to-advance-wind-energy-deployment/

TASR, 2017. Fico: V4 nie je pre Slovensko alternatívou k Európskej únii, April 3. www.teraz.sk/slovensko/fico-sr-nemecko-a-cr-sa-sustredia-na/252554-clanok.html?mostViewedArticlesInSectionTab=2

Trade.gov., 2023. Czech Republic – Country Commercial Guide. Energy. International Trade Administration. www.trade.gov/country-commercial-guides/czech-republic-energy

Tramba, D., 2022. Proč nemáme plynovod do Polska? Viníků je celá řada, nejen kritizovaný Babiš. Ekonomický deník, May 5. https://ekonomickydenik.cz/proc-nemame-plynovod-do-polska-viniku-je-cela-rada-nejen-kritizovany-babis/

Trubalska, J., 2019. The prospects for energy cooperation in the Visegrad Group. Annales Universitatis Mariae Curie-Skłodowska Lublin – Polonia, Section M, vol. IV, 6 – 79. https://doi.org/10.17951/m.2019.4.69–79

V4 citizens, Programme of the Czech Presidency of the Visegrad Group 2023/2024. Visegrad Group, 2023. www.visegradgroup.eu/documents/presidency-programs/v4-program-20232024

V4 for Future. The Programme of the Slovak Presidency of the Visegrad Group (July 2022 – June 2023). Visegrad Group, 2022. www.visegradgroup.eu/documents/presidency-programs/programme-of-the-slovak

V4 Reasonable Europe. Programme of the Czech Presidency of the Visegrad Group 2019/2020. Visegrad Group, 2019. www.visegradgroup.eu/documents/presidency-programs/programme-cz-v4-pres

Visegrad Group, 2004. Visegrad Declaration 2004 (Kroměříž Declaration), May 12. www.visegradgroup.eu/documents/visegrad-declarations/visegrad-declaration-110412-1

Visegrad Group, 2010. Declaration of the Budapest V4-Energy Security Summit, February 24. www.visegradgroup.eu/2010/declaration-of-the

Visegrad Group, 2011a. Declaration of V4 Energy Ministers, January 25. www.visegradgroup.eu/2011/declaration-of-v4-energy

Visegrad Group, 2011b. The Bratislava Declaration of the Prime Ministers of the Czech Republic, the Republic of Hungary, the Republic of Poland and the Slovak Republic on the occasion of the 20th anniversary of the Visegrad Group, February 15. www.visegradgroup.eu/2011/the-bratislava

Visegrad Group, 2014. Joint Statement on the 21st of the Ministers of Environment of the Visegrad Group Countries, the Republic of Bulgaria and Romania, September 30.

Visegrad Group, 2021. Joint Letter by Seven State Leaders to EU Commission on the Role of the Nuclear Power in the EU Climate and Energy Policy, March 19. www.visegradgroup.eu/documents/official-statements/joint-letter-by-seven

Visegrad Group, 2022a. Joint Statement of the Energy Ministers of the Visegrad Group countries, February 7–8. www.visegradgroup.eu/documents/official-statements/joint-statement-v4–220210

Visegrad Group, 2022b. Conclusions of the Meeting of European Affairs Committees of V4 Parliaments, April 24. www.visegradgroup.eu/calendar/conclusions-of-the

Visegrad Group, 2022c. V4 + United Kingdom Joint Statement of Prime Ministers, March 8. www.visegradgroup.eu/v4-united-kingdom-prime

WNN, 2023. Westinghouse to supply fuel to Czech Republic's Dukovany. World Nuclear News, March 30. https://world-nuclear-news.org/Articles/Westinghouse-to-supply-fuel-to-Czech-Republic-s-Du

Zachová, A., 2023. Hungary wants Russia sanctions exemption extended, ensure oil exports to Czechia. Euractiv.com, July 4. www.euractiv.com/section/politics/news/hungary-wants-russia-sanctions-exemption-extended-ensure-oil-exports-to-czechia/

Zaniewicz, M., 2019. New Gas Pipeline Geopolitics in Central and Eastern Europe. Warsaw Institute, December 21. https://warsawinstitute.org/new-gas-pipeline-geopolitics-in-central-and-eastern-europe/

6 Russia's gas weapon in Central and Eastern Europe

Diverging responses from three friendly states

András Deák, John Szabo and Csaba Weiner

6.1 Introduction

Russia's gas supply halt was widely understood as the most powerful energy policy development of the reinvigorated Russia–Ukraine war after February 2022. This followed Russia's rising role in Europe's natural gas market in recent years, as European production declined, and few competitive alternatives emerged. However, this supply fell by more than 80 per cent from its peak during 2022, making this the largest energy supply challenge Europe has faced since the 1973 oil embargo (Elliott, 2023; Schramm, 2024). Gazprom cut supplies to Bulgaria, the Baltic states, and Poland, amongst others, as they had condemned Russian aggression and supported Ukrainian defensive efforts. Meanwhile, the Kremlin was more lenient towards those that took a seemingly neutral or pro-Russian stance, such as Hungary, which continues to receive the volumes set in its long-term supply contract (Gavin, 2023). This chapter explores the intended and realised effect of Russia's 'natural gas weapon' in various socio-political contexts. We assess three cases from Central and Eastern Europe – Bulgaria, Hungary, and Serbia – with relatively pro-Russian politics prior to the war and trace their responses to the (potential) suspension of natural gas supply flows.

Russia suspended natural gas supplies to Bulgaria, while it made Hungary's and Serbia's access conditional and contingent. Even if Serbia and Hungary could buy Russian gas via Gazprom's Electronic Sales Platform until autumn 2021, they cannot access non-contracted volumes since. This has forced them to conduct political negotiations to access volumes inked into long-term supply contracts and bargain for additional supplies. The Kremlin's interventions were driven by the aim to trigger policy reactions in these targeted countries (i.e. the 'receivers' of the sanctions), shaping domestic politics and the international affairs of respective governments. In this chapter, we do not focus on the sanctions the 'West' levelled at Russia, but rather focus on the sanctions Russia deployed by wielding its 'energy weapon' – with Russia becoming the 'sender' of the sanctions in our case, through its threat to embargo gas supplies. We were intrigued by how it deployed its natural gas weapon to shape the actions of smaller states with which it had maintained close, friendly relations. On the face of it, the Kremlin had very good relations

DOI: 10.4324/9781032624839-9

with Bulgaria, Hungary, and Serbia before the war, but one may ask why Russia's actions and responses were substantially different in these three cases. This is the gap in the scholarship that this chapter seeks to address.

The approaches of European governments to the threat of Russia suspending natural gas flows have varied across a wide spectrum, reflecting a complex interaction of international and domestic politics. This chapter contributes to the general topic of the book by theorising how Russian intervention had different intentions in various socio-political contexts and led to substantially different outcomes. It explores how key themes of the book – decarbonisation, security, and integration – both shaped and were shaped by the Kremlin's threats, as governments relied on their integration into the EU and alternative sources of energy to dampen the emerging threat. Our research is animated by the following questions: What was the effect of Russia's natural gas suspension in different political contexts? How did different states respond? We deploy Crawford and Klotz's (1999) four models of influence – 'compellance', 'normative communication', 'resource denial', and 'political fracture' – to theorise how states tailor modes of influence (e.g. Russia's threat of deploying a natural gas embargo) to the specific context and what responses this prompts. This taxonomy offers a tool to structure our understanding of state responses in the cases we explore, but we suggest that there are overlaps in the taxonomical categories and compellance is universally present.

The comparability of the three cases is due to their strong reliance on Russian natural gas which they also see as a benign form of dependence. Russia was generally seen in a positive light by the governments of these countries and their populations. All three states were also relatively receptive to Russian strategic ambitions and influence, meaning that governments, elites, and the general public saw Russia as a partner. Their historical relations and geopolitical orientation differ, as did their responses to the cutoff. This allows them to be assessed as counterfactuals, given the comparable points of departure but substantially different actions following the outbreak of the war. Moreover, by including EU and non-EU countries, the chapter speaks to the book's theme of the role of EU integration and the bloc's ambition to lead decarbonisation. Temporally, the cases begin with Gazprom's decision to taper supplies to Europe during the second half of 2021, albeit the bulk of its analysis is geared to 2022 and 2023. Following this introduction, we elaborate on our theoretical framework, which is followed by the analysis of the three cases in three separate sections. In the final section, we compare the cases and discuss how they relate to our theoretical framework. Based on this, we also underscore the chapter's theoretical contributions and its broader applicability and hint at policy implications.

6.2 Theory: Sanctions and models of influence

The central role of energy in the functioning of most societies has led the energy sector to become frequent object of economic statecraft. Those who deploy sanctions aim to inflict substantial damage by targeting the 'Achilles heel' of many modern economies. Accordingly, the literature on the matter is quite rich. The failed oil sanctions against Italy in response to its Abessynian aggression and the US oil embargo against Japan during World War II are very early case studies in sanctions literature (Anderson, 1975; Strang, 2008). This shows that sanctioning the energy sector is quite similar to sanctions in general; their deployment can follow various objectives and logics and they can be targeted to include related financial flows and assets (Fischhendler et al., 2017). What may make energy sanctions unique is their highly asymmetric nature that need not be linked to economic might – a frequent prerequisite in deploying economic sanctions. For instance, the relatively small Arab OPEC countries inflicted substantial economic damage on large economic powers dependent on imported oil by deploying the so-called 'oil weapon' (Paust and Blaustein, 1974) in the 1970s. The senders of sanctions can thus target the sectoral vulnerabilities of states or other entities (i.e. receivers) that may be deemed economically more powerful, and their interventions can lead to highly disruptive outcomes.

The sanctions literature has largely foregone the investigation of how variegated intentions and responses the same intervention may entail. Recent energy sanctions literature has gravitated towards the impact of sanctions in single cases (Jones, 2015) and any adaptation by those receiving them (Elliott, 2005; Tierney, 2005; Peterson, 2020). Various streams of scholarship have also explored how small powers have had a disproportionately large impact when imposing sanctions (Cranmer et al., 2014; Rühl, 2022). However, most of these inquiries focus on sectoral questions and draw theoretical conclusions by exploring how one or a few receivers responded to sanctions. When looking at multiple cases, responses and the theorisations of actions tend to focus on commonalities, but we are curious as to why nation-states may act quite differently to the same (or very similar) set of sanctions or the threat thereof. In a similar vein, the sanctions literature that emerged in response to the war in Ukraine also tends to assess how effective Western sanctions are on Russia or how Russia responds to these forms of economic statecraft (Bergeijk, 2022). Economic statecraft was, however, not one-sided, as the Kremlin cut or reduced natural gas supplies to several European countries. And, based on the definition of economic sanctions 'as actual or threatened withdrawal of economic resources to effect a policy change by the target' (Chan and Drury, 2000, p. 2), the Kremlin deployed sanctions when suspending natural gas flows to a number of countries, which it undertook with different intentions and which prompted significantly divergent responses.

Our point of departure is Galtung's (1967) seminal study arguing that sanctions imposed by the sender may fail to deliver results because of their naïve expectations regarding the receiver's submission. This insight transpired into the sanctions literature, by considering target countries' reactions as a factor that the sender reflects upon when exerting economic statecraft. Galtung criticised the conventional and what he saw as an oversimplified view of international political theory, suggesting that receivers' political concessions are proportionate to the economic impact of sanctions (Galtung, 1967). In contrast, he identifies a variety of reasons societies may tolerate higher economic sacrifices. For the sender to reach its expected outcome, 'it is not sufficient that the sanctions are perceived as an evil; alternative courses of action must also be perceived as lesser evils' (Galtung, 1967, p. 392), while the specific socio-political context of the sanctions also needs to be carefully considered by the sender. Galtung demonstrated this point by collecting a handful of factors – moral aspects, a sense of justice and disapproval of sanctions, successful redistribution of welfare, and diversifying the national economy – that shaped the actions of the receiver, in this case, Rhodesia. His analysis highlights the importance of such factors that senders may need to consider when designing sanctions.

Scholarship further elaborated Galtung's argument by drawing on communication-related research and 'linkage diplomacy' to explicate receivers' responses. Borrowing from cognitive psychology, economic statecraft theory incorporated how the success of sanctions depends on the receiver's interpretation of external pressure and its relation to the society which it governed. The concept of cognitive links was extensively instrumentalised along Galtung's (1971) 'structural violence' of imperialism theory, which underlines that the more advanced forms of imperialism do not rely on sheer military force but exert influence through communication and culturally reshaping the subjugated society. For this to happen, 'penetration' needs to be undertaken (Scott, 1982; Morgan and Schwebach, 1996), which, in this context, entails that the penetrated society's consent with demands is reached latently, through various informal channels, actors, and is effectively woven into the fabric of society. Penetration focuses on the stability of the political regime of a receiving society, as the sender must consider whether there is a stable, robust government with deep roots in society. The presence or absence of this shapes which actors sanctions will target.

Kelman (1958, p. 52) noted that 'new attitudes will depend on their cognitive links, i.e., the particular attitude structure [of the receiver]' and goes on to differentiate three ways of receiving external pressure: 'compliance', 'identification', and 'internalisation'. Li (1993, p. 354) proposes questions to identify which form is employed: 'How much does it cost[?]' to achieve compliance, 'Who makes the demand[?]' to understand identification, and 'What are the demands[?]' to identify internalisation. Expanding on Li's approach, in the case of compliance, the receiver accepts and adheres to the intended influence, because it seeks a favourable reaction from the sender. It seeks reward or to avoid punishment, without being persuaded substantively regarding the subject matter of the sanctions (Lacy and Niou, 2004). This largely overlaps with the international political theory deployed before the widespread adoption of Galtung's insights as it tends to focus on the *quid pro quo* inherent in most economic statecraft. Compliance has been widely identified as a tool used by the sender when designing and implementing sanctions (Hufbauer et al., 2009), as in many cases the receiver had already been systematically penetrated and its dominant ideological orientation was consistent with that of the senders. In such cases, Baldwin (1985) speaks of 'anticipated reactions', given that sanctions are effectively met without resistance. This is not to say that compliance always materialises, but has long been understood as one of the main forms of economic statecraft (McLean and Whang, 2010).

To add further nuance and explicate the impact of sanctions, Kelman identified that internalisation entails that the sender's demands are consistent, or at least not contradictory, to the receiver's original stance and value system, triggering the approval of external pressure. Lastly, identification leads the receiver to accept and adhere to the demands of the sender, because it seeks to maintain pre-existing good relations, irrespective of the costs and benefits involved. Scholars widely employed identification, because it offered insight into how states complied if they were subject to structural dependence on other states, as proposed by dependence theory (Caporaso, 1978). The division of core and periphery in the world system suggests the latter's strong asymmetrical dependence on the former – not necessarily limited to economic dependence (even if this was highly influential) – extends to include norms and values. These prompt a broad range of actors to agree or empathise with the sender's objectives, leading the receiver to respond to sanctions as intended by the sender.

This three-pronged taxonomy lends analytical clarity to explicate the design and reception of sanctions, but the method of its application remained relatively vague as highlighted by Crawford and Klotz (1999). Kelman's taxonomy helps understand why receivers act in a specific manner quite generally, without providing the tools to assess specific factors that strongly influence the sanctions' forms and their impact. This contributed to the emergence of a third wave of sanctions and linkage literature that explored why sanctions were effective (Drury, 2000; Elliott, 2005; Drezner, 2012; Jones, 2015). Crawford and Klotz draw on this and propose that the systemic analysis of 'actors', 'mechanisms of influence', 'conditions for success', and 'primary site of influence' allow for a deeper understanding on the intentions and the outcomes of sanctions. By reflecting on questions such as 'Who do the sanctions target?', 'How do they have an effect?', 'What preconditions need to be met for their efficacy?', and 'Where are they effective?', one is better able to understand the guiding logic of sanction design and deployment. Accordingly, Crawford and Klotz pivot in the guiding rationale structuring their analytical toolkit from preceding efforts that focus on 'whether sanctions are successful' (Kirshner, 1997, p. 32) by gathering numerous cases (Hufbauer et al, 2009; The Global Sanctions Data Base, 2023) to narrowing in on 'how they work' (Kirshner, 1997, p. 32). Therefore, Crawford and Klotz focus on the reactions of the receiving societies and governments and the logic of their interactions with the sender.

Based on these questions and the analysis of mechanisms and targets, Crawford and Klotz (1999) develop their four-pronged taxonomy to include 'compellance', 'normative communication', 'resource denial', and 'political fracture' (see Table 6.1). Compellance is the most widely held view of how sanctions should work: 'A rational decision-making elite ought to re-evaluate the costs of pursuing its goals in light of the costs of actual or anticipated sanctions' (Crawford and Klotz, 1999, p. 26). These need to be designed and deployed to make alternative courses of actions more costly for the receiver, coercing them to govern in alignment with the sender. Normative communication 'suggests that elites and populations respond to moral arguments' (Crawford and Klotz 1999, p. 27) and leads the sender to take action based on what is presumed to be the alignment of norms. The sender may take to resource denial when compellance and normative communication did not work, leading to 'declining capabilities prevent[ing the]

Table 6.1 Crawford and Klotz's taxonomy of sanctions

	Actors	*Mechanism of influence*	*Conditions for success*	*Primary site of influence*
Compellance	decision making elite is rational	increase costs and/or decrease benefits	at least partial economic and military interdependence	elite decision makers
Normative Communication	decision making elite cares about norms	persuasion	elites clearly understand normative arguments	elite decision makers
Resource Denial	elites are stubborn: states need material capabilities	decrease target capabilities by limiting important resources	the behaviour sanctioners seek to alter requires material resources; at least partial economic and military interdependence	institutional structures of the target government; economy
Political Fracture	government depends on elite and popular support	foster a legitimation crisis that leads to increased dissent or revolution	fragile elite; external ability to support groups that oppose the target government	elite decision makers and civil society

Source: Adapted from Crawford and Klotz, 1999, p. 27.

pursuit of objectionable policies; sanctions work by depriving the state of its ability to act' (Crawford and Klotz, 1999, p. 28). Impacts are thus more forceful and aim to overthrow governance regimes or governments, while generally shifting government compositions and institutional structures to align with the interests of the sender. Finally, cases of political fracture target society and institutions at large as opposed to the government in an attempt to instigate political change in a context where the ruling elite's penetration of society is low.

Crawford and Klotz offer a taxonomy that we see as applicable to the energy scene with one minor alteration: not all mechanisms and aims are created equal. We propose that their taxonomy offers nuance, but the results of various sanctions may materialise simultaneously (McKibben, 2010; Meierding and Sigman, 2021). That is, while our perceptions of reality are inherently messy, the literature also suggests that a simultaneous materialisation of these responses is common. In addition, we have found that compellance is effectively always present. Imposing economic sanctions with which the sender presumes some rationality of decision-makers and uses material means (e.g. access to energy, commodities, financing) to influence the actions of the receiver. Given the intertwined nature of the global economy and the rarity of entirely isolated states, the precondition that there should be partial economic and military interdependence is typically met. The other three forms – normative communication, political fracture, and resource denial – emerge in tandem with compellance and are crucial considerations in sanction design that the sender needs to consider when deploying economic statecraft.

6.3 Normative communication: Hungary

Hungary has been ruled by a robust, monolithic, effectively one-party government with deep penetration into society. The Viktor Orbán-led Fidesz has secured four consecutive constitutional majorities since 2010 with few oppositional forces to jeopardise this position. The country is an EU and NATO member, deeply integrated into European economic value chains. Nevertheless, the government has taken on a non-mainstream course of action that goes against Western 'liberal' values, consolidating a self-proclaimed 'illiberal democracy' and nationalist rhetoric. It has positioned itself in opposition to EU institutions, leading to confrontation over issues including migration, LGBTQ+ and human rights, as well as, more broadly, the political status quo. Public sympathy towards Russia has been limited, given the rather negative historical memories dating back to the 1956 revolution and the negative facets of Moscow-led communism during the second half of the twentieth century. However, Prime Minister Orbán and President Putin have developed cordial relations, as the former's so-called 'Eastern Opening' has also included developing good relations with autocratic regimes who mirror the illiberal values for which Orbán stands. This has extended into domestic politics as well, as the state-controlled media that allows the government to lead the narrative has also promulgated pro-Russian messages, establishing a more positive sentiment among the populace.

Hungary is deeply reliant on imported energy carriers, given the scarcity of domestic deposits. The majority of this originates from Russia and nowhere is this more acute than with regard to natural gas. This is the largest energy source in gross inland and final energy consumption because of its dominant share in derived heat generation and residential demand. This makes it politically sensitive, as the government has framed Russia as being essential for cheap energy supplies, a central component of Fidesz' 'utility price reduction' programme that helped secure its electoral victories (Weiner and Szép, 2022). As we will elaborate below, rhetorically the government has not sought to move away from Russian natural gas imports, but – hand-in-hand with the EU – it has developed some strategies to dampen any shocks. It has established gas interconnections with all neighbouring countries, except Slovenia, by 2021, secured import capacities at the Krk LNG terminal in Croatia, and has managed substantial commercial and strategic storage capacities. Instead of diversifying and moving away from Russian natural gas, low utility prices encouraged demand – climbing to 11.1 billion cubic metres (bcm) by 2021 (MEKH and FGSZ, 2023) – which the public utility sought to meet via a ten-plus-five-year supply contract for 4.5 bcm per annum it signed in 2021 with Gazprom. Deliveries are mainly channelled through the Balkan Stream pipeline, circumventing Ukraine, but sustaining Hungary's import dependence.

Russia's February 2022 invasion of Ukraine took the government by surprise, forcing it tread water in its balancing act between the EU and Russia. The government has had a relatively free hand in tuning foreign policy as the war has unfolded, as its control over the media allowed it to shape the domestic media narrative according to its strategic ambitions. Energy import dependencies constituted a strong barrier to action and communication with the public tended to underscore the need to maintain good relations with Russia to keep natural gas flowing. The government took a seemingly neutral, 'pacifist' sentiment, calling for peace, which allowed it to avoid siding with the pro-Ukrainian stance adopted by most of the 'West' and to appease the Russian leadership, thus avoiding any political or economic retaliation. The government has criticised EU sanctions as being counterproductive, has sought continuous exemptions for Hungary and, on occasion, has threatened to veto if certain passages were not altered or removed. The sheer threat of natural gas suspensions imposed by Gazprom has driven the cost–benefit calculations of Hungarian elites; they maintain a strong pro-Russian approach, but sympathies cut deeper.

Hungary's leadership has also been persuaded on normative grounds, as it shares some of the values of Russian leaders. The illiberal regime that also introduced tightening control and weakening democracy has materialised in Hungary's standoff with the European Commission on issues over the rule of law in Hungary and access to Cohesion as well as Recovery and Resilience Funds. This has weighed on its relations with most other European states and institutions. In parallel, the government's relationship with the Russian leadership remains unchanged, with high-level meetings organised regularly, unlike in other EU countries. It also refuses to support Ukraine's forces with arms deliveries and criticises the EU's financial support for the Zelensky government. The Hungarian government's position offers a continuation of its former normative and political orientation. As a part of this, energy may be important, but relations with Russia are frequently decoupled from such considerations in official statements, reflecting the internalisation of aligned values.

The government responded to the threat of Russia suspending natural gas flows by enhancing cooperation with Gazprom and introducing a policy that would alter consumption. Halting Russian flows or refusing to pay in roubles was off the table, as the government downplayed the supply risk. However, seeing the suspension of flows to friendly states (e.g. Bulgaria) certainly kept the Hungarian government aware that the Kremlin could halt supplies to force its will. Nonetheless, the government's actions reflected little awareness of the energy security threat as the presumption of sustained friendly relations remained pervasive. Government-led measures remained meagre, apart from the decision to revamp the utility price reduction programme by charging much higher prices for above-average gas and power consumption. It paired this with demand-side measures, such as reducing temperatures in schools, public institutions, and companies. These 'last resort' measures became necessary due to supply and financial constraints alike, with the national public utility company having to absorb immense losses. Measures proved to be relatively successful. Like the EU, Hungary exceeded the EU's voluntary gas consumption reduction targets of 15 per cent between August 2022 and March 2023 compared to average consumption over the past five years. Natural gas use dropped by 17.7 per cent in the EU, and 20.2 per cent in Hungary, impacting all sectors (Eurostat, 2023; MEKH, 2022–2023, 2023). Fidesz' deep penetration of society even allowed it to weather disruptions in one of its focal policies – utility price reductions – an action that indicated there was little will to pivot from Russian imports that aligned with a pro-Russian foreign policy more broadly.

Hungarian energy policy neither pursues a conscious diversification away from Russia nor does it refuse alternatives. In a sense, both pathways are open. The deeply engrained presumption leading action is a belief in shared values, which is communicated pervasively. However, this is embedded in a techno-economic context that provides Hungary with some supply security through access to alternative imports, if need be, which makes it easier for the state to access alternative imports in times of crisis. That being said, the government took little action to diversify, with actions including short-term purchases of minor volumes from Azeri SOCAR and Turkish Botaş. At the same time, relatively long-term plans have been drafted to increase imports from Azerbaijan, as well as to secure LNG deliveries from Qatar via Croatia and from a Polish LNG terminal project in Gdansk, along with pipeline gas from Romania's Neptun Deep Black Sea project. To a great extent, diversification has been left open, while no strategic decisions have been made as the government seeks to avoid any hard commitments that lead it away from its normative alignment with Russia.

6.4 Political fracture: Bulgaria

Bulgaria's energy history is quite typical of countries in the region: it pursued industrialisation under communist leadership since the 1950s while relying on a limited resource base to support this ambition. The country may have had substantial coal reserves, but this was not sufficient to meet skyrocketing demand, driving its dependence on Soviet resources and, in many cases, technologies and know-how (Tchalakov and Mitev, 2019). Leaders in Sofia explored Soviet natural gas imports as Soviet oil supply became limited in the 1970s (Szabo and Deak, 2021). It imported natural gas through Romania and used this to meet industrial demand – cement, fertiliser, ceramics, and glass production – and to a lesser extent district heating systems in and near Sofia. Demand grew through the 1980s, peaking at 6.3 bcm in 1990, followed by a decline in the 1990s, and stabilising within a band of 2.4–3.4 bcm per annum thereafter (Energy Institute, 2023). Soviet strategy was quite successful in tying Bulgaria to its sphere of influence through this sector as, until recently, its leadership failed to introduce alternative import routes. Economic relations were closely intertwined with political cooperation, as Bulgaria, a Warsaw Pact signatory, maintained strong ties with the Soviet Union. The Kremlin has since maintained the presumption that broader society is nostalgic towards communism and thus generally views Russia favourably.

Natural gas does not play a prominent role in Bulgaria's energy system in absolute terms, but the lack of alternatives and its role in heating households makes it politically sensitive. 112,000 households are connected to the district heating network (EWRC, 2020, p. 50) and providing energy at a low price is a top political priority. The 2013 protests against the first Boyko Borisov cabinet clearly showed that energy prices can become the spark igniting public protest and also highlighted the volatility of the Bulgarian leadership. Substituting natural gas was not topical in the slow-moving energy affairs of Bulgaria and its substitution is challenging; the rising costs of carbon are rendering coal uncompetitive, while nuclear is running at full steam and renewable energy's diffusion has been slow. Historically, governments sought to tread a fine line between maintaining close ties with Russia and supporting projects that diversify imports using EU funds. They pounced on every opportunity to better energy security through integration and the opening of new import channels (e.g. projects delivering natural gas from Azerbaijan), while also hastily supporting Russian political objectives, such as Gazprom's South Stream (Bowden, 2019).

Bulgaria's infrastructural and socio-political predisposition led the Kremlin to believe that it could achieve compliance through sanctions. It seemed that Bulgaria had few alternatives to Russian natural gas and rational economic calculations suggested that, were Gazprom to cut supplies, the government would align itself with the Kremlin's policies. In parallel, the basis of the Kremlin's sanctions was that 58 per cent of the population reported a positive attitude toward Russia and President Putin before the war, even though this was balanced by a strong pro-Western orientation that materialised through actions such as joining the EU or NATO (Zankina, 2023). In addition, the Bulgarian Socialist Party (BSP) has been a bulwark of pro-Russia policy in domestic politics and, despite its weakening position, still has substantial influence. Thus, Russia presumed that, if it were to impose an embargo on natural gas, it would still be supported by the broader populace and segments of leadership, which could help the parties cut a deal to relaunch flows in return for Bulgaria's continued support. What is more, Bulgaria has been in a state of continuous political instability as governments have rapidly followed one another only to lose votes of no confidence or fail to secure re-election. The state's penetration of society has thus been volatile, limiting the efficacy of sanctions solely targeting leadership, but offering an opening for the Kremlin to orchestrate change through political fracture.

Russia launched Ukraine's invasion just over two months after Kiril Petkov of the centrist 'We Continue the Change' party took office. Following the outbreak of the war, he and his government overtly and covertly supported Ukraine. Measures ranged from welcoming refugees to calling for the resignation of Minister of Defence Stefan Yanev due to the latter's reluctance to call Russia's actions war – in line with Putin's rhetoric. Bulgaria secretly supplied Ukraine with weapons and fuel following the invasion; these were revealed later as Bulgarian arms exports increased by 200 per cent in 2022, driven by supplies to Ukraine through intermediaries (Kotseva and Nikolov, 2023). These 'strong policies' (Roth, 2022, n.p.) against Russia paved the way for Gazprom's suspension of natural gas exports to Bulgaria in April 2022 after the fourth round of EU sanctions.

Compellance had a limited effect on Bulgaria as the elites did not fold in the face of threats to suspend the natural gas flow, leading Russia to up the ante. Instead, Bulgarian leaders gambled that flow from the EU would help meet demand, so Petkov's government responded with pro-Ukraine and pro-Europe 'technocratic' agendas, lessening reliance on Russian natural gas. The Kremlin acted on Bulgarian society's favourable view of Russia and its political instability to precipitate political rupture through the embargo. The suspension of flows precipitated the fall of Petkov's coalition government, after the Slavi Trifonov-led 'There Is Such a People' party's withdrawal from the coalition and subsequent vote of no confidence in June 2022 led to the government's collapse. Trifonov cited disputes over the budget and North Macedonia's EU accession to be the leading causes of the break, but his party also unsuccessfully pushed for an agenda that would reinstate natural gas imports from Russia, indicating a pro-Russia stance. In addition, Petkov's already-frail coalition was weakened by a handful of parties pursuing pro-Russia agendas, while pervasive corruption and instable government institutions enabled Russia's influence (Tcherneva, 2023).

The effects of this political fracture emerged with the Galab Donev-led caretaker government succeeding Petkov's administration, and the new leadership looking to reconcile relations with Russia and relaunch natural gas flows. This, in principle, would have come to meet the Russian state's calculations, but the broader population's support for Russia and Putin declined between 2021–2022, with 30 per cent now seeing Russia as a security threat (up from zero a year prior). However, 57 per cent still do not consider Russia to be a threat, while 30 per cent think of it as a partner. Anti-NATO and anti-EU positions have also strengthened (Kazaz and Smilov, 2022). Thus, society remains divided and there was no clear indication of whether the political fracture would tip politics to support a pro-Russia stance. Further limiting the effect of voters turning to support pro-Russian parties was that Bulgaria was able to weather the winter, in part due to its integration into

European and international gas markets. The Donev government was unable to fortify a pro-Russian agenda and the general environment inhibited the relaunching of Russian natural gas imports. Meanwhile, the 2023 spring elections led to a power-sharing agreement between the 'GERB'–'Society of Democratic Forces' (GERB–SDS) and 'We Continue the Change'–'Democratic Bulgaria' (PP–DB), all of which maintain pro-European positions, keeping the pro-Russian extreme right 'Revival' party and the BSP from power. The Kremlin's sanctions may offer a case of political fracture, but the availability of alternative gas supplies and a normative orientation towards the EU inhibits it from achieving its set goals of reinstating a pro-Russian government.

6.5 Resource denial: Serbia

Serbia offers a case where a number of systematic pressures applied by great powers – China, the EU, Russia, the USA – confront one another in a highly visible manner, compounded by complex socio-political dynamics. Towards the end of the 2010s, the EU's share in Serbian foreign trade stood firmly at around 60 per cent, with a similar proportion observed for foreign direct investment from the EU (RBS, 2023). As an EU candidate country, it receives a large amount of technical assistance to facilitate further integration. Despite such structural embeddedness and unlike other countries in the region, public preferences do not reflect these strong economic ties to the EU. In December 2022, only 18 per cent of respondents chose the EU as Serbia's closest foreign policy partner, while 51 per cent opted for Russia and 19 per cent for China (Vuksanovic et al., 2022). Russia is not only seen as a partner, but also a magnanimous 'friend'. It was characterised as the least interest-driven partner by the public,[1] reflecting a strong identification with Russia's cause. This heavily draws on the anti-Western and nationalistic sentiments, reinforced by the Yugoslav civil war, the 1999 NATO bombing of Serbia, and the secession of Kosovo. The pro-Russian public sentiment provides fertile ground in support of Russian action and, in its extremity, penalises anti-Russian narratives. Party politics also follow geopolitical vectors (Vuksanovic, 2021a), with a handful of Serbian parties, most notably the Socialist Party of Serbia (SPS) and the right-wing opposition (POKS, Serbian Party Oathkeepers), harbouring strong pro-Russian attitudes.

Foreign relations and domestic sentiment are inseparable from Russia's main form of material influence, energy. Gazprom Neft bought the core of the Serbian oil industry, NIS, in 2008 at a 'preferential' price in the wake of international recognition of Kosovo's independence. Natural gas imports historically originate almost exclusively from Russia, while Serbia also became a transit state for Russian gas with the commissioning of the TurkStream–Balkan Stream connection in 2020.[2] Though decisions in Serbian–Russian energy relations are formally taken by heads of state, several entities are influential in respective governance. Russia's primary pillars of influence have been the Ministry of Energy, the Foreign Ministry, as well as Srbijagas (the national gas monopoly) through the control of the Socialist Party of Serbia. This has changed with the weakening position of the SPS as of 2020, but Russia continues to be able leverage domestic policy divisions to further its interests, penetrating and advocating its local partners into selected policy fields (foreign policy, intelligence, energy industry, etc.). Subjugated entities have also profited from their Russian connections, as has the government in a sense because it was able to secure or sustain favourable trade relations.

Natural gas had a 12.6 per cent share of Serbia's total energy demand in 2020. Industrial consumption constituted the bulk of consumption while residential and commercial demand remained marginal. Russia provides more than 85 per cent of natural gas, which it now supplies through Turkey instead of Ukraine. Serbia has also been playing an important transit role by forwarding volumes to Hungary from Bulgaria. Natural gas relations were strained when Gazprom introduced a more restrictive export policy from mid-2021, following the conclusion of the ten-year supply agreement (2011–2021) between the two parties. Gazprom did not sign another long-term contract, only offering President Vučić a six-month extension during his visit to Moscow in November 2021. The company also demanded a shift away from oil indexation to include TTF prices in the formula, suggesting a significant increase in export prices (Vuksanovic, 2021b). The extension was due to expire by the end of May 2022, forcing contracting parties to negotiate in a more complex environment – the war in Ukraine had begun and Vučić was still looking for a coalition partner after the 2022 April elections. Moscow resisted signing a contract to maintain Russia's leverage over the country.

This was the Kremlin's attempt to introduce resource denial by simultaneously drawing on its ability to shape politics and government structures. In principle, the Serbian government was fairly successful in arranging a new, three-year gas contract in May 2022, at a time when Gazprom had already begun to break contracts with other European partners (A'Hearn, 2022). Terms were also relatively preferential, as Serbia managed to sustain oil indexation despite a substantial price increase. Both sides could announce that they had agreed to a contract with favourable conditions, a demonstration of their true friendship. Volumes (2.2 bcm per annum) were also sufficient to cover most of the country's demand, but the slight deficit still granted Russia some leverage over Serbia in the future. The effects of Gazprom withholding supplies and Russia's political pressure materialised through Serbia's approach to the EU's sanction regime and the forming of the government coalition. Serbia did not join the Western drive for sanctions and refused to take any measures against Russia. This is in line with public sentiment in Serbia, but the government's penetration was key to support, as it had to resist considerable Western pressure on the matter. Vučić also chose the pro-Russia Socialist Party of Serbia as its coalition partner. This may seem logical, given the historical cooperation, but he had other palatable and politically feasible options. Intense negotiations were indicated by the fact that the new government was only formed in the fall of 2022, when SPS's Ivica Dačić was nominated as foreign minister.

It seems that Russia has entrenched its position in the Serbian natural gas sector, but it may have triggered a pivot. The Ministry of Energy remained in control of Vučić's Serbian Progressive Party (SNS) and intensified its efforts to find alternatives to Russian imports. By the summer of 2022, Serbia had committed to the

Bulgaria–Serbia interconnector with 1.8 bcm per annum capacity. President Vučić personally visited both this construction site and the inauguration of the Greece–Bulgaria interconnector in October 2022, signalling a high level of dedication to natural gas import diversification. The initiation of a natural gas-based cooperation with Hungary and the establishment of joint trade companies also serves as a connection to Western markets, as does access to storage capacities in Hungary (Grbić, 2023). In light of these actions, the three-year contract is interpreted as providing Serbia with a timeframe to construct infrastructure to enable alternative imports, thereby providing the government with bargaining chips vis-à-vis the Kremlin. Western pressure, from both the EU and the US, provides further push for this agenda. The EU's presence and involvement with harmonising law is evident, but punitive pressure, such as the US sanctioning the pro-Russian chief of intelligence, Aleksandar Vulin, instigates political change. Russia's influence in institutional decision-making and its ability to withhold key resources may inhibit the Vučić government's anti-Russian actions, but strong Western ties and influence disable cooperation.

6.6 Concluding thoughts

The three cases reveal key differences in 'how sanctions work' in various socio-political contexts. The Kremlin pursued similar objectives in all three countries: minimising the target country's contribution to Ukraine's war efforts and Western sanctions while maintaining cooperation with Russia. Domestic affairs, energy politics, and the characteristics of their energy systems, as well as the receiver's role in a broader web of international relations, all deeply shaped the design of sanctions, their effects, and the receiver's responses. Penetration was especially pertinent in shaping the design and impact of the sanctions. The given state's penetration of domestic society and, thereby, its ability to control narratives is crucial and shapes how the sender of sanctions selects the receiver. The Orbán governments' deep control over society led leaders in Moscow to primarily sanction the ruling elites. This forced political leaders to weigh the costs and benefits of their actions. However, it was their alignment on normative grounds that led the Hungarian leaders to support Russia's actions within the confines posed by a broader geopolitical matrix. The Hungarian government, meanwhile, presumed that it would have access to Russian supplies, given its positive response to the Kremlin's persuasion, which has resulted in the continuance of natural gas flows and a high-level of political dialogue. With this, Hungary has introduced little change in terms of its natural gas supply practices, while taking on a more confrontational position with the EU when sanctions imposed on Russia are discussed in the European Council. In a sense, the Kremlin's actions were the most effective in this case, as it brought Hungary closer to Russia and distanced it from its Western allies.

Bulgaria's and Serbia's responses to the Kremlin's sanctions both differed substantially as they pivoted away from Russia. Bulgaria's case reflects one of low penetration, where the government's position has been volatile. The natural gas embargo was aimed to destabilise the Petkov government and allow a pro-Russian coalition to take office. The Kremlin's actions thus targeted change through what was presumed to be a pro-Russian political consensus amongst the populace. This was a miscalculation, as Bulgaria's ability to turn to European natural gas and international LNG markets for supplies to meet demand lessened the impact of Russian sanctions. Apart from a brief interregnum, the leadership also did not change course in its support for Ukraine and an anti-Russian sentiment began to take shape. A legitimation crisis may have taken place in Bulgaria, but not necessarily with the outcome the Kremlin had intended. Finally, the sanctions aimed at Serbia were directed to shape party politics and the behaviour of various key economic actors, which was, in part, due to the limited penetration of the government in power and Russia's deep role in current governing institutions. Resource denial led the Vučić government to maintain its course of action, in that it continued to maintain close political relations with Russia; however, the threat of an embargo has driven the government to pursue alternative natural gas import routes and sources, allowing the country to lessen its reliance on Russia.

These cases offer three examples that can be placed in Crawford and Klotz's taxonomy, but none of them are clear cut. Cases can fall into multiple categories, even though we argue that a predominant one can be identified. The exception is compellance, which is universally applied. Accordingly, our cases suggest that compellance emerges in all sanction cases to a varying degree. The mere mention of the introduction of sanctions typically leads governments to make some rational calculations about their impact and consider what alternative courses of action they can pursue; this deeply influences their decisions.

This was vital in our cases, since the threat of the 'gas weapon' has loomed large for decades and has led most European nation-states to integrate energy systems and diversify imports. Serbia clearly had the least room to change in this sense, while Hungary's deep reliance also posed a substantial barrier that impeded its ability to contest Russian action. Compellance is thus omnipresent but, in and of itself, does not offer a deeper explanation of the dynamics that shape senders' and receivers' actions. It is typically tied to one of the other three forms of sanctions – normative communication, resource denial, or political fracture – the form of which is largely shaped by the penetration of the given government in its respective society, the senders' penetration of the targets' society, and the normative positions that leaders have adopted.

The three countries are a good demonstration of the role of non-sectoral, predominantly political considerations in short-term policy adaptation within the natural gas industry. Russia and Gazprom were well aware of the limitations of their 'political gascraft'; they developed their instruments selectively, elaborating variegated country designs. The receivers' also reacted according to their sectoral and political setups, often along the anticipated line of action, though sometimes changing their expected course (mostly Bulgaria). Nonetheless, mid- and long-term policy choices are more influenced by market realities and perceptions of supply security. In these two respects, Russian supply became problematic. The necessity of constructing alternative supply routes in other parts of Europe where Russia has cut off natural gas, such as Germany, Poland, Italy, and other countries in Western Europe, is obvious. The Russian gas supply has become extremely unreliable, partly due to Russia's actions and partly due to these new transit and political risks. All these developments will test the political factors in sectoral decision-making, in the longer term potentially ending the 'Russian gascraft' potential within these societies.

Acknowledgements

This chapter was supported by the National Research, Development and Innovation Office of Hungary under Grant No. FK-138317.

Notes

1 27.5 per cent of respondents saw it as interest driven, unlike 56.3 per cent in the case of the EU (Vuksanovic et al., 2022).
2 Previously, Serbia's role was limited to transmitting minor amounts of Russian gas, which arrived through Ukraine and Hungary, to Bosnia and Herzegovina.

References

A'Hearn, B., 2022. Serbia signs new gas supply contract with Gazprom. Argus, 30 May. www.argusmedia.com/en/news/2336504-serbia-signs-new-gas-supply-contract-with-gazprom (accessed 28 September 2023).

Anderson, I.H., 1975. The 1941 de facto embargo on oil to Japan: A bureaucratic reflex. *Pac. Hist. Rev.* 44(2), 201–231.

Baldwin, D.A., 1985. *Economic Statecraft.* Princeton University Press, Princeton, NJ.

Bergeijk, van P.A.G., 2022. Sanctions against the Russian war on Ukraine: Lessons from history and current prospects. *J. World Trade.* 56(4), 571–586. https://doi.org/10.54648/trad2022023

Bowden, J., 2019. SE Europe gas markets: Towards integration. OIES Paper NG 150. Oxford Institute of Energy Studies, Oxford, UK. www.oxfordenergy.org/publications/se-europe-gas-markets-towards-integration/ (accessed 7 April 2021).

Caporaso, J.A., 1978. Dependence, dependency, and power in the global system. *Int. Organ.* 32(1), 13–43.

Chan, S., Drury, A.C., Eds, 2000. *Sanctions as Economic Statecraft: Theory and Practice.* Palgrave Macmillan, Basingstoke, UK, and New York, NY.

Cranmer, S.J., Heinrich, T., Desmarais, B.A., 2014. Reciprocity and the structural determinants of the international sanctions network. *Soc. Networks.* 36, 5–22. https://doi.org/10.1016/j.socnet.2013.01.001

Crawford, N.C., Klotz, A., 1999. How sanctions work: A framework for analysis, in: Crawford, N.C., Klotz, A. (Eds), *How Sanctions Work: Lessons from South Africa.* Macmillan Press Ltd., London, UK, pp. 25–42.

Drezner, D.W., 2012. An analytically eclectic approach to sanctions and non-proliferation, in: Solingen, E. (Ed.), *Sanctions, Statecraft, and Nuclear Proliferation.* Cambridge University Press, Cambridge, UK, pp. 154–173. https://doi.org/10.1017/CBO9780511862380.008

Drury, A.C., 2000. How and whom the US president sanctions: A time-series cross-section analysis of US sanction decisions and characteristics, in: Chan, S., Drury, A.C. (Eds), *Sanctions as Economic Statecraft*. Palgrave Macmillan, London, UK, pp. 17–36. https://doi.org/10.1057/9780230596979_2

Elliott, K.A., 2005. Trends in economic sanctions policy: Challenges to conventional wisdom, in: Wallensteen, P., Staibano, C. (Eds), *International Sanctions: Between War and Words in the Global System*. Frank Cass, Abingdon, UK, pp. 3–14.

Elliott, S., 2023. IEA cuts European gas demand forecast for 2023, now sees 7% decline. S&P Global, 18 July. www.spglobal.com/commodityinsights/en/market-insights/latest-news/natural-gas/071823-iea-cuts-european-gas-demand-forecast-for-2023-now-sees-7-decline (accessed 18 July 2023).

Energy Institute, 2023. Statistical review of world energy data; Statistical review of world energy. www.energyinst.org/statistical-review/resources-and-data-downloads (accessed 4 October 2023).

Eurostat, 2023. Supply, transformation and consumption of gas – monthly data. https://ec.europa.eu/eurostat/databrowser/view/NRG_CB_GASM__custom_7435897/default/table?lang=en (accessed 19 September 2023).

EWRC, 2020. Annual report to the European Commission. Energy and Water Regulatory Commission (EWRC), Sofia. www.dker.bg/uploads/2020/report_EC_2020_EN.pdf (accessed 11 September 2023).

Fischhendler, I., Herman, L., Maoz, N., 2017. The political economy of energy sanctions: Insights from a global outlook 1938–2017. *Energy Res. Soc. Sci.* 34, 62–71. https://doi.org/10.1016/j.erss.2017.05.008

Galtung, J., 1967. On the effects of international economic sanctions: With examples from the case of Rhodesia. *World Polit.* 19(3), 378–416.

Galtung, J., 1971. A structural theory of imperialism. *J. Peace Res.* 8(2), 81–117.

Gavin, G., 2023. Hungary to ramp up Russian gas imports for winter, says Gazprom. Politico, 13 November. www.politico.eu/article/hungary-ramp-up-russian-gas-imports-winter-gazprom-alexey-miller/ (accessed 17 November 2023).

Grbić, T.M., 2023. Serbia establishes joint gas company with Hungary. Euractiv, 21 June. www.euractiv.com/section/politics/news/serbia-establishes-joint-gas-company-with-hungary/ (accessed 28 September 2023).

Hufbauer, G.C., Schott, J.J., Elliott, K.A., Oegg, B., 2009. *Economic Sanctions Reconsidered*. Peterson Institute for International Economics, Washington, DC.

Jones, L., 2015. *Societies under Siege: Exploring How International Economic Sanctions (Do Not) Work*. Oxford University Press, Oxford, UK.

Kazaz, J., Smilov, D., 2022. GLOBSEC Trends 2022: Bulgaria. Globsec, Bratislava. www.globsec.org/what-we-do/publications/globsec-trends-2022-bulgaria (accessed 4 October 2023).

Kelman, H.C., 1958. Compliance, identification, and internalization: Three processes of attitude change. *J. Conflict Resolut.* 2(1), 51–60.

Kirshner, J., 1997. The microfoundations of economic sanctions. *Secur. Stud.* 6(3), 32–64. https://doi.org/10.1080/09636419708429314.

Kotseva, A., Nikolov, K., 2023. Bulgarian weapons exports up 200% since Ukraine war. Euractiv, 18 July. www.euractiv.com/section/politics/news/bulgarian-weapons-exports-up-200-since-ukraine-war/ (accessed 10 September 2023).

Lacy, D., Niou, E.M.S., 2004. A theory of economic sanctions and issue linkage: The roles of preferences, information, and threats. *J. Polit.* 66(1), 25–42. https://doi.org/10.1046/j.1468-2508.2004.00140.x

Li, C-p., 1993. The effectiveness of sanction linkages: Issues and actors. *Int. Stud. Q.* 37(3), 349–370. https://doi.org/10.2307/2600812

McKibben, H.E., 2010. Issue characteristics, issue linkage, and states' choice of bargaining strategies in the European Union. *J. Eur. Public Policy.* 17(5), 694–707. https://doi.org/10.1080/13501761003748682

McLean, E.V., Whang, T., 2010. Friends or foes? Major trading partners and the success of economic sanctions. *Int. Stud. Q.* 54, 427–447. https://doi.org/10.1111/j.1468-2478.2010.00594.x

Meierding, E., Sigman, R., 2021. Understanding the mechanisms of international influence in an era of great power competition. *J. Glob. Secur. Stud.* 6(4), 1–18. https://doi.org/10.1093/jogss/ogab011

MEKH, 2022–2023. Monthly market monitoring reports: natural gas. www.mekh.hu/publications (accessed 18 September 2023).

MEKH, 2023. Annual natural gas balance 2014–2022. www.mekh.hu/download/c/59/51000/3_2_annual_natural_gas_balance_2014_2022.xlsx (accessed 31 October 2023).

MEKH, FGSZ, 2023. Data of the Hungarian natural gas system 2022. Hungary's Energy and Public Utility Regulatory Authority (MEKH), FGSZ Földgázszállító, Budapest. www.mekh.hu/download/c/19/51000/FGR_2022.pdf (accessed 19 October 2023).

Morgan, C.T., Schwebach, V.L., 1996. Economic sanctions as an instrument of foreign policy: The role of domestic politics. *Int. Interact.* 21(3), 247–263. https://doi.org/10.1080/03050629508434868

Paust, J.J, Blaustein, A.P., 1974. The Arab oil weapon: A threat to international peace. *Am. J. Int. Law.* 68(3), 410–439.

Peterson, T.M., 2020. Reconsidering economic leverage and vulnerability: Trade ties, sanction threats, and the success of economic coercion. *Confl. Manag. Peace Sci.* 37(4), 409–429. https://doi.org/10.1177/0738894218797024

RBS (Statistical Office of the Republic of Serbia), 2023. Exports and imports. https://data.stat.gov.rs/Home/Result/170301?languageCode=en-US (accessed 30 September 2023).

Roth, A., 2022. 'I fear Bulgaria will become a soft state': Kiril Petkov on threat of Russia. *The Guardian*, 23 June. www.theguardian.com/world/2022/jun/23/i-fear-bulgaria-will-become-a-soft-state-kiril-petkov-on-threat-of-russia (accessed 10 September 2023).

Rühl, C., 2022. Energy sanctions and the global economy: Mandated vs unilateral sanctions. *Int. Econ. Econ. Policy.* 19(2), 383–399. https://doi.org/10.1007/s10368-022-00542-9

Schramm, L., 2024. Some differences, many similarities: Comparing Europe's responses to the 1973 oil crisis and the 2022 gas crisis. *Eur. Political Sci. Rev.* 16(1), 56–71. https://doi.org/10.1017/S1755773923000255

Scott, A.M., 1982. *The Revolution in Statecraft: Intervention in an Age of Interdependence*. Duke University Press, Durham, NC.

Strang, G.B., 2008. 'The worst of all worlds': Oil sanctions and Italy's invasion of Abyssinia, 1935–1936. *Dipl. Statecr.* 19, 210–235. https://doi.org/10.1080/09592290802096257

Szabo, J., Deak, A., 2021. The CEE energy transition: Recurring fifty-year-old dynamics?, in: Mišík, M., Oravcová, V. (Eds), *From Economic to Energy Transition: Three Decades of Transitions in Central and Eastern Europe*. Palgrave Macmillan, Cham, pp. 63–96. https://doi.org/10.1007/978-3-030-55085-1_3

Tchalakov, I., Mitev, T., 2019. Energy dependence behind the Iron Curtain: The Bulgarian experience. *Energy Policy.* 126, 47–56. https://doi.org/10.1016/j.enpol.2018.11.008

Tcherneva, V., 2023. Easy prey? Russia's influence in Bulgaria. European Council on Foreign Relations, 8 February. https://ecfr.eu/article/easy-prey-russias-influence-in-bulgaria/ (accessed 4 October 2023).

The Global Sanctions Data Base, 2023. www.globalsanctionsdatabase.com/ (accessed 4 November 2023).
Tierney, D., 2005. Irrelevant or malevolent? UN arms embargoes in civil wars. *Rev. Int. Stud.* 31(4), 645–664. https://doi.org/10.1017/S0260210505006674
Vuksanovic, V., 2021a. Systemic pressures, party politics and foreign policy: Serbia between Russia and the West, 2008–2020. PhD thesis. London School of Economics and Political Science, London, UK. http://etheses.lse.ac.uk/4323/ (accessed September 3, 2023).
Vuksanovic, V., 2021b. Russia's gas gift to Serbia comes with strings attached. Euronews, 4 December. www.euronews.com/2021/12/04/russia-s-gas-gift-to-serbia-comes-with-strings-attached-view (accessed 25 September 2023).
Vuksanovic, V., Steric, L., Bjelos, M., 2022. Public perception of Serbian foreign policy in the midst of the war in Ukraine. Belgrade Centre for Security Policy, Belgrade. https://qkss.org/images/uploads/files/WBSB-2022_Serbia-Report-1_Dec-2022_%281%29.pdf (accessed 30 September 2023).
Weiner, C., Szép, T., 2022. The Hungarian utility cost reduction programme: An impact assessment. *Energy Strategy Rev.* 40, 100817. https://doi.org/10.1016/j.esr.2022.100817
Zankina, E., 2023. Pro-Russia or anti-Russia: Political dilemmas and dynamics in Bulgaria in the context of the war in Ukraine, in: Ivaldi, G., Zankina, E. (Eds), *The Impacts of the Russian Invasion of Ukraine on Right-wing Populism in Europe. European Center for Populism Studies*, European Center for Populism Studies, Brussels, pp. 48–63. https://doi. org/10.55271/rp0012

7 Energy transition at gunpoint?

Andrej Nosko and Jaroslav Ušiak

7.1 Introduction

The 2020–2023 period was marked by turbulence in the European Union (EU) energy sector, leading to questions of whether rapid progress towards decarbonisation is possible and whether Russia's war on its neighbour could speed up the EU's energy transition (BP 2023; IEA 2022). The strict lockdowns that radically disrupted industry during the first wave of the COVID-19 pandemic showed that a rapid reduction in greenhouse gas (GHG) emissions was possible. A 25 per cent reduction in GHG emissions (CAMS 2020) was observed from March 2020 to July 2021, but this was achieved by greatly reducing – at times even completely stopping – mobility and economic activity. And the economic and political consequences confirmed that the 'solution' was socially unsustainable, if not outright inconceivable, in the long term. Another example of radical reduction of emissions is offered by Eastern European countries as they succeeded in reducing emissions in the early 1990s, also largely through drastic measures (Zugravu et al. 2008). The pandemic brought the unimaginable within reach of the possible, even if the durability of this change was short-lived. Could Russia's war on its neighbour and the resulting sanctions on Russia's fossil fuel exports bring about, or accelerate more sustained end of fossil fuel consumption in Europe?

This chapter focuses on the impact and potential of sanctions against Russia to accelerate the EU's energy transition. The effects of sanctions on sanctioned countries have been extensively studied (Sonnenfeld et al. 2022; Rácz et al. 2023), nonetheless, we do not assess the effects of sanctions on Russia itself in this chapter. Instead, we are interested in whether the sanctions imposed by countries influence their own economies and energy systems. The stated goal of sanctions is not to influence the energy transition path of EU countries. Nonetheless, it is a relevant question to ask whether the imposition of sanctions can in effect be a policy reform tool helping 'enlightened elites' push through energy transitions (Nosko and Ušiak 2023). Using the contribution of the wave of moral panic and fear, to oblige society to accept the higher economic and social costs of speedy energy transitions.

The second section of this chapter focuses on potential impact of sanctions on the EU's initial restructuring of economy and energy systems in response to Russia's

DOI: 10.4324/9781032624839-10

attack on Ukraine. It considers the data complexities and challenges regarding the impact of sanctions on EU energy imports. The third section focuses on the influence of sanctions on the EU's energy mix and transition to determine whether sanctions can lead to reduced fossil fuel use or effective source substitution. Finally, we evaluate the role of sanctions in driving the EU's energy transition, bearing in mind their effects on EU cohesion, member state reactions, and broader climate and energy strategies. This section presents a quantitative assessment of changes in energy flows and the energy mix based on EU and Russian (2019–2023) statistical data and political documents to assess the links between sanction measures, the decarbonisation progress of EU member states, and the impact of sanctions on the EU's energy transition. In conclusion, we focus on the implications of these sanctions for Russia's energy exports and their potential role as indirect catalysts in accelerating the EU's shift towards renewable energy sources.

7.2 Sanctions as tools for economic warcraft and European Union sanctions on Russia

Due to Russia's aggression towards Ukraine, Russia became the country with the most sanctions imposed on it in history (18,772 sanctions imposed by 33 countries (Castellumai 2023). Despite at least nominal unity across the EU, energy imports have become a bone of contention. Crude oil and natural gas represent the bulk of Russian exports and are an important source of revenue for the country. However, abundant and affordable energy sources were and continue to be important for the EU as it emerged from the post-pandemic slowdown, combined with the unprecedented price shock in the summer of 2021. The price shock, caused by several factors was, according to Nosko (2021), fostered and exacerbated by Russia's market manipulation in preparation for the aggression on Ukraine and to enable Russia to blackmail the EU.

The imposition of sanctions exerts pressure to redirect trade flows away from the sanctioned country, but also affects trade flows into the country imposing the sanctions, as we also show in this chapter. The imposition of an unprecedented number[1] and scale of sanctions on Russia in the wake of the massive Russian attack on Ukraine can be seen as an example of the EU making a significant geopolitical move. Given the EU's perception of itself as a global soft power (Lucarelli 2007), the imposition of sanctions was seen within the EU as the morally *right thing* to do as illustrated by a speech from the EU Parliament's president (Roberta Metsola 2022). Moreover, it was seen as the *right thing* to do *because* it entailed costs and would demonstrate Europe's willingness to make sacrifices for its values, but stop short of it taking up arms to defend those values (Roberta Metsola 2022).

Given that gas was and (in December 2023) remains unsanctioned, the oil sanctions have proven relatively painless for the member states that depend heavily on piped Russian crude oil and for the EU overall. In this complicated geopolitical quagmire, the line between sanctioning as a moral imperative and sanctioning as a strategic measure has become blurred as the EU struggles to maintain a coherent position that reflects its founding principles while guarding its energy security and economic interests. This ambiguous position is interesting because it encapsulates the balance between upholding popular values and navigating the complex realities of transnational politics.

The EU has imposed massive and unprecedented sanctions against Russia in response to the war of aggression against Ukraine, which started on 24 February 2022 and the illegal annexation of Ukraine's Donetsk, Luhansk, Zaporizhzhia and Kherson regions. They add to existing measures imposed on Russia since 2014 following the annexation of Crimea and the non-implementation of the Minsk agreements. Sanctions include targeted restrictive measures (individual sanctions), economic sanctions and visa measures. (European Council 2023b)

The objectives of sanctions are specified quite comprehensively. European Council argues that '[t]he aim of the economic sanctions is to *impose severe consequences* on Russia for its actions and to *effectively thwart Russian abilities to continue the aggression*' (European Council 2023b; emphasis added). The wording used by the European Parliament to present sanctions is even more explicit in identifying the moral foundations: 'Outraged by Russia's illegal and unprovoked full-scale invasion of Ukraine in February 2022, European Union countries swiftly adopted unprecedentedly tough sanctions' (European Parliament 2023a). This unambiguous moral language reflects the EU's efforts to align its foreign policy instruments and tone with its image as a normative power promoting a rule-based transnational order. While no one could reasonably claim that the imposed sanctions are inconsequential, since they clearly have consequences for international trade and Russia's economy, whether these consequences are sufficiently severe and whether they effectively thwart Russian abilities to continue the war remain uncertain. Given that March 2024 marked a decade since the first restrictive measures were imposed and Russia's ability to wage aggressive war on its neighbour has not been thwarted; although the unprecedented scale of sanctions and restrictive measures was reached only since 2022 (European Council 2023a).

The EU has imposed six rounds of sanctions and restrictive measures since the illegal annexation of Crimea in 2014 until 2022 (see Table 7.1). After Russia's full-scale invasion of Ukraine in February 2022, the EU imposed 11 additional sanctions on Russia (European Commission 2023). At the time of writing (December 2023), a twelfth package of sanctions was proposed, but besides the objective to 'tighten the oil price cap and to counter circumvention of EU sanctions', no further details about sanctioning other energy sources emerged (EEAS 2023). In terms of energy, Russian coal was sanctioned in the fifth round of sanctions in April 2022, and oil was sanctioned in the sixth round in May (decision) and June (effect) 2022 (European Council 2023a; European Parliament 2023a). However, many measures allowed piped oil to be imported until late 2024, and exceptions for specific cases remain in force.

Gas is currently[2] not sanctioned, despite discussions about limiting imports of liquified natural gas (LNG) from Russia using non-sanction tools, as was attempted in the case of imposing a price ceiling on Russian gas, which did not have the intended effect because the price remains sufficiently high to provide ample funding

Table 7.1 Overview of the main sanctions and measures taken by the EU on energy sector

Date of adoption	*Sanctions package*	*Key energy sector measures*
8 April 2022	Fifth Package	An import ban on all forms of Russian coal.
3 June 2022	Sixth Package	Oil import restrictions (embargo on crude and refined oil) Oil transport services ban (EU operators prohibited from insuring and financing oil transport to non-EU countries)
21 July 2022	Maintenance and Alignment Package	Exemptions for transactions related to agricultural products and oil transport to non-EU countries
5 October 2022	Eighth Package	Implementation of the G7 oil price cap (restrictions on transport of Russian oil to non-EU countries under a pre-set price cap)
16 December 2022	Ninth Package	Restrictions on exports of drone engines and additional measures against the Russian energy and mining sectors
25 February 2023	Tenth Package	New import bans on Russian high-revenue goods Financial sector measures affecting Russian banks
23 June 2023	Eleventh Package	Energy measures including the end of the possibility to import Russian oil by pipeline for Germany and Poland Targeted derogations for specific export bans

Source: European Council, 2023b.

for Russia (European Parliament 2023b). Since the focus of this chapter is not on the effects of sanctions on Russia, despite the stated objectives of the sanctions, we focus on their effects on EU countries. The strategic move towards a more flexible and resilient energy structure in the EU, in the face of these sanctions, reflects the EU's adaptive capacity and its determination to transition to a more sustainable energy future. How do we perceive and assess the effects of sanctions on energy transition? We explain this in the next section.

7.3 Effects of EU-imposed sanctions on EU energy imports

Observing and measuring the impact of sanctions requires robust data collection and analysis, ideally over a sufficiently long period to allow also for measuring the durability of the trend, as we have seen in the case of energy and industrial changes during the pandemic and in the post-pandemic period. The absence of dependable data is a genuine challenge in making informed policy decisions and conducting academic exploration. Initially, in this chapter, we wanted to observe the effect of energy sanctions on both Russia and the EU, but obtaining Russian statistical information proved problematic. The post-invasion shutdown of Russian online data sources, combined with Russia's decision to classify trade data, increased the opacity surrounding its trade activities. Even the utility of virtual private networks (VPNs[3]) was limited, since, in May 2020, Russia classified relevant trade statistics, made them unavailable to academics and the public, and instead started publishing statistics that cannot be verified and may serve internal political objectives regarding import substitution or demographics (Russian Federal State Statistics Service 2023). The standard challenge with energy statistics in the EU is the relatively long lag, as complex energy statistics are published with at least six months and, not uncommonly, more than a year's delay. The combination of these two factors makes it difficult to assess the full effect of restrictions and sanctions on Russian trade volumes (Mitrova 2022).

Besides the incomplete data, an additional challenge is the confluence of multiple factors that forms what Torkington (2023) called a polycrisis, and Ferguson at the 2023 World Economic Forum in Davos referred to, mockingly, as 'just history happening' (Homer-Dixon 2023). However, given that so much history is currently happening, it is challenging to attribute causes correctly to observed effects. After the initial reduction in GHG emissions facilitated by the global pandemic, economic activity took off in 2021; a commensurate increase in energy consumption followed. In the summer of 2021, the EU experienced an unprecedented price shock. With the benefit of hindsight, we can now say that Russia, in preparation for the full-scale invasion of Ukraine, was putting the European energy market under pressure. Russia weaponised its market presence, focused its energy gunsight on the EU, and used its energy exports as leverage to achieve political objectives even at the cost of economic ones. Russia, with its extraordinary importance as both an exporter of natural gas and a significant player in the domestic EU market, had a sizeable involvement in the storage of natural gas in Europe. Consequently, Russia reduced supplies via traditional transit routes through Belarus and Ukraine. This reduction meant that Europe's gas storage facilities were not being filled to their usual levels. When this happened, a perfect storm of factors on both the demand and supply sides of the gas market sent natural gas prices skyrocketing. On the demand side, the increase in consumption was linked to the post-pandemic economic recovery, and the unusually long winter that preceded it, followed by a cold spring and a hot summer. On the supply side, less wind resulted in lower production from renewable sources in northern Germany (Nosko 2021).

Russia, even before it issued its ultimatum (Roth 2021), seemed to be gearing up for the invasion, taking a path that Europeans could not fathom was imaginable. Russia tried to extort the EU, especially the German authorities to approve the new Nord Stream 2 pipeline faster, with Russia's president noting that they would be able to 'increase gas supplies by an additional 17.5 billion cubic metres (about 10% of annual EU supplies) through the new pipeline the day after regulators approve Nord Stream 2' (Seddon and Sheppard 2021). Russia was also trying to use this situation as an opportunity for the EU to highlight the risks of the spot market (in which Russia, unlike other major gas suppliers, was directly involved through the control or ownership of gas storage facilities) and to contribute to the growing European public's scepticism about green transformation.

As the COVID-19 pandemic hit the EU in 2020 and 2021, the Russia-nourished price shocks of 2021 preceded the aggressive Russian invasion of Ukraine in 2022. A combination of sanctions on some Russian imports, Russian-induced 'technical' disturbances in the natural gas supply, and concerns regarding potential gas shortages collectively influenced market dynamics and led to additional surges in natural gas prices. It is crucial to dissect these factors separately to understand their individual and cumulative impacts. They all, combined with the lower output of nuclear power plants (due to hot summers, prolonged maintenance and shutdowns, and reduced hydropower generation connected to the exceptionally hot and dry summer of 2022 in many EU countries), significantly affected the European electricity market, with a notable escalation in electricity prices.

To analyse the effects of sanctions on trade flows and imports, we considered the available data, including Standard International Trade Classification (SITC[4]) data developed and maintained by the United Nations (UN). SITC is a standardised way of classifying and organising information about trade across international borders. Trade transactions should be reported in a standard way by exporting and importing countries, but discrepancies are common and have been closely analysed (Nosko 2007). Crude oil is categorised under subcode SITC 33, and natural gas is categorised under subcode SITC 34. In 2019, these energy exports represented about 48 per cent (or $231 billion) of total Russian exports ($474 billion). For comparison, the total budget of the Russian Federation in 2019 was around $240 billion (TASS 2016).

An increase in the emergence of backdoor trade and sanctions avoidance was evident in the statistics, as well as informal, off-the-record, chats with traders. An easy way to illustrate this is to analyse the overall number of imports and changes in the compositions of source countries' import profiles. We observed an increase in the value of trade reported by not elsewhere specified (NES) countries,[5] as illustrated in Figure 7.1, which lists specific EU outlier countries. The nine countries displayed in the chart did not have high imports of oil (SITC code 33) from non-specified countries in 2019, but their imports from those countries rapidly increased after the Russian invasion and the imposition of embargos on Russian oil. We observed an increase in imports from 'unknown countries' in the year after the invasion, perhaps in the expectation of trade restrictions, given that other trade with Russia was already being restricted. The EU placed restrictions on imports of Russian crude oil from December 2022, and refined petroleum products from February 2023, with limited exceptions. Regarding the average imports from these 'unknown countries', Romania and Bulgaria witnessed unprecedented increases in 2020 and 2021 (Romania) and 2022 (Bulgaria). In Croatia, rapid increases occurred in 2012 and 2022, and in Czechia, there was a visible increase in 2021. Most surprising were increases in these imports in Croatia, Cyprus, Denmark, Slovenia, and, most visibly, Slovakia (220%) and Portugal (390%) after the oil trade embargo was enforced. While these amounts are not significant absolute amounts for the countries concerned, they could represent sanctions avoidance or sloppy data collection.

For gas, this trend was not so widespread. Although imports of Russian gas were not subject to sanctions, we observed an unusual increase in gas imports from

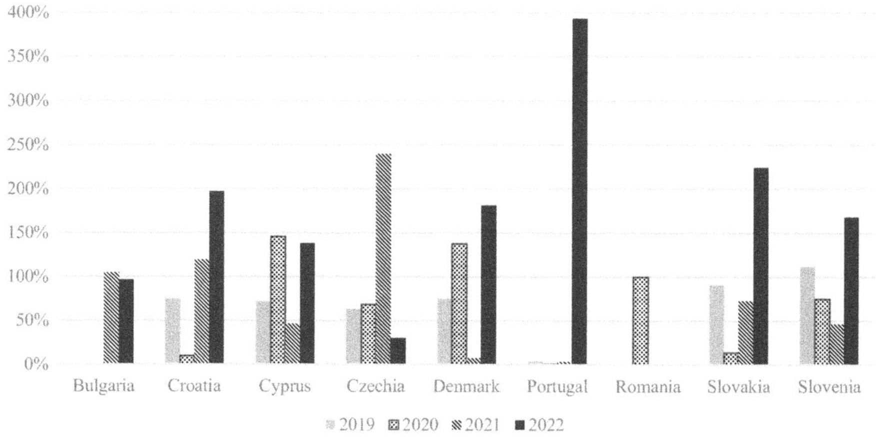

Figure 7.1 Proportions of oil imports from NES countries compared to average imports from NES countries in 2019–2022.

an 'unknown country' in Slovakia, which did not import gas from NES countries between 2019 and 2021, but which, in 2022, suddenly represented 17.89 per cent of the value of world imports of gas, accompanied by a corresponding decrease in the value of imports from Russia. These data limitations and apparently increasing creativity in reporting the sources of gas and oil arriving in Europe seriously affected the research presented in this chapter. Nonetheless, despite these limitations, we can present at least an initial reflection, accepting that some of our conclusions may need to be revised in the coming months and over the midterm. Based on the available data, there was a slight decrease in imports of natural gas from Russia to Europe, as illustrated by the statistical review of world energy in Figure 7.2. So Figure 7.2 shows a gap between the total reported exports and exports of LNG via pipelines to the Commonwealth of Independent States (CIS) and European countries, which also indicates a diversification (and reduction) of exports from Russia.

In the absence of statistical and trade data covering the most recent period, which would have shown the effects of sanctions imposed in 2022 that took effect as late as the end of 2023, we relied on alternative high-quality data used to monitor fossil fuel exports from Russia: the Centre for Research on Energy and Clean Air's (CREA's) Russian Energy Export Tracker (CREA 2023).[6] We were aware that measuring energy flows only through aggregated valuations would pose serious challenges, especially for such a volatile period as 2019–2023, but given the limitations in other statistics, we consider this an important and timely energy flow data available to use. The CREA data revealed that the value of coal imports from Russia to most of the EU countries decreased in 2022, except for those to the Netherlands, Germany, Italy, Spain, and Belgium, as shown in Figure 7.3.

Regarding oil imports, we observed reductions between 2021 and 2022 only in Spain, Lithuania, Finland, and Sweden. Denmark, Malta, Portugal, and Austria

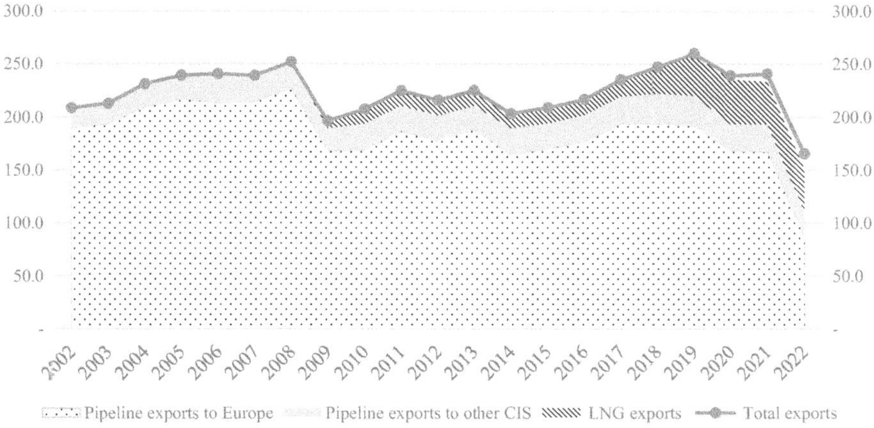

Figure 7.2 Russia's exports of natural gas (in bcm).

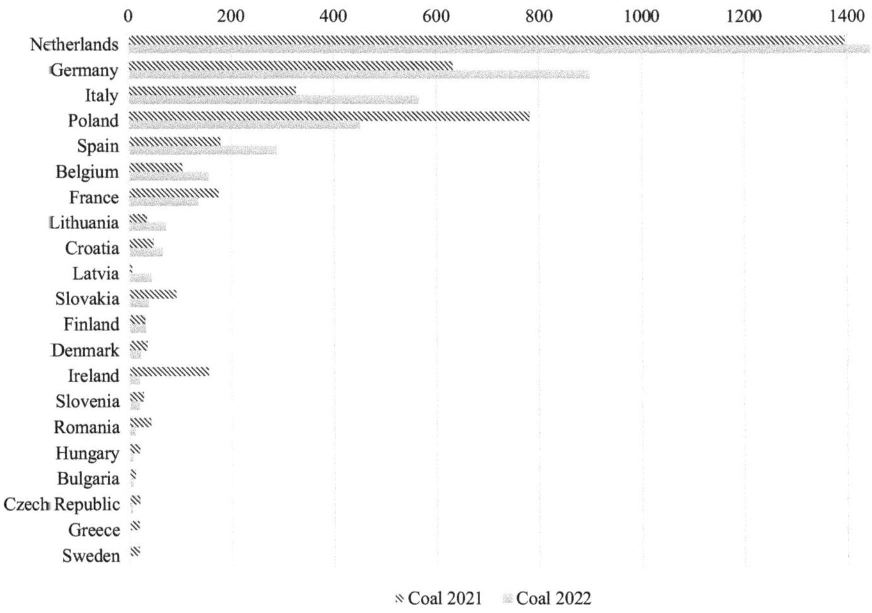

Figure 7.3 Coal imports from Russia (in million euro).

also showed decreases but, in absolute terms, they were insignificant. Although we obtained data for the first nine months of 2023 and have included it in Figure 7.4, both the incomplete data coverage and the previously high imports from Russia warrant cautious interpretation. Nonetheless, the trend seemed to be an overall

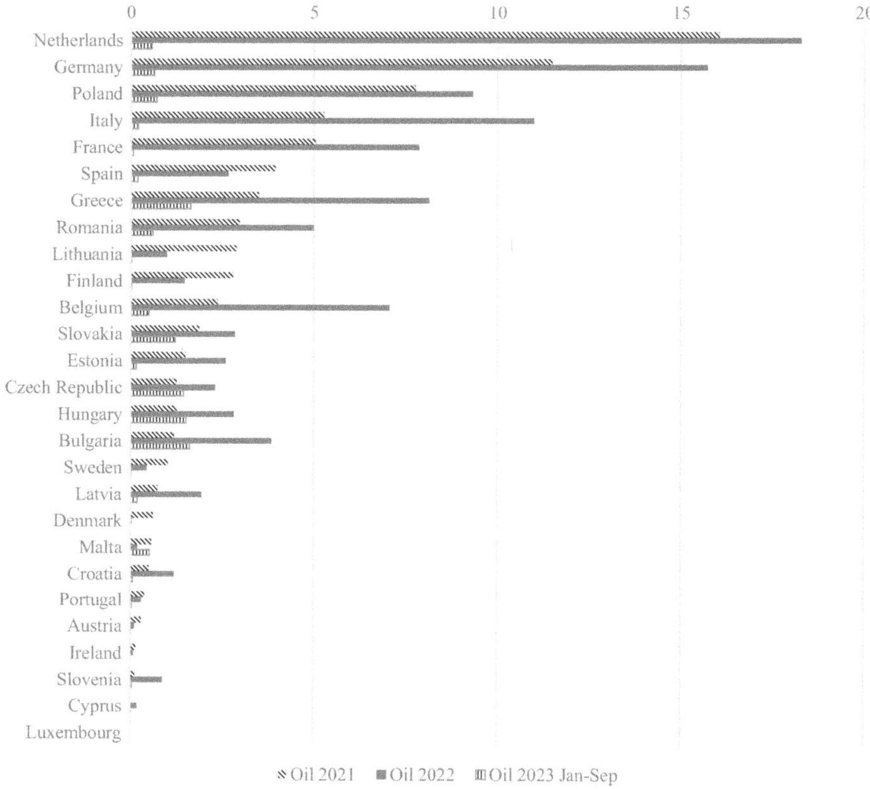

Figure 7.4 Oil imports from Russia (in billion euro).

decrease, reflecting that overt imports were the subject of sanctions or severely restricted (with notable derogations for Bulgaria, Croatia, Slovakia, Hungary, and Czechia for piped crude oil), although various creative and less creative ways of rebranding crude oil have been widely documented, including ship-to-ship transfers, location spoofing, and various other deceptive means of obfuscating the true origins of crude oil (Danis 2022; Perkins 2022; Triebert et al. 2023).

The picture of natural gas imports based on CREA data is particularly interesting. The value of gas imports in 2021–2022 increased across the board, except for Poland and Italy, reflecting rapid price increases rather than an increase in volume – a paradox that is visible when comparing the figures for values of imports (Figures 7.4 and 7.5) with figures for volume of imports (Figures 7.6 and 7.7). Similar, though much less significant, decreases were apparent for Denmark, Latvia, and Finland. For all other EU countries, there was an increase in the value of gas imports. As for natural gas, we obtained only partial data for imports of gas in the first nine months of 2023, with the same caveats noted in the case of oil. At

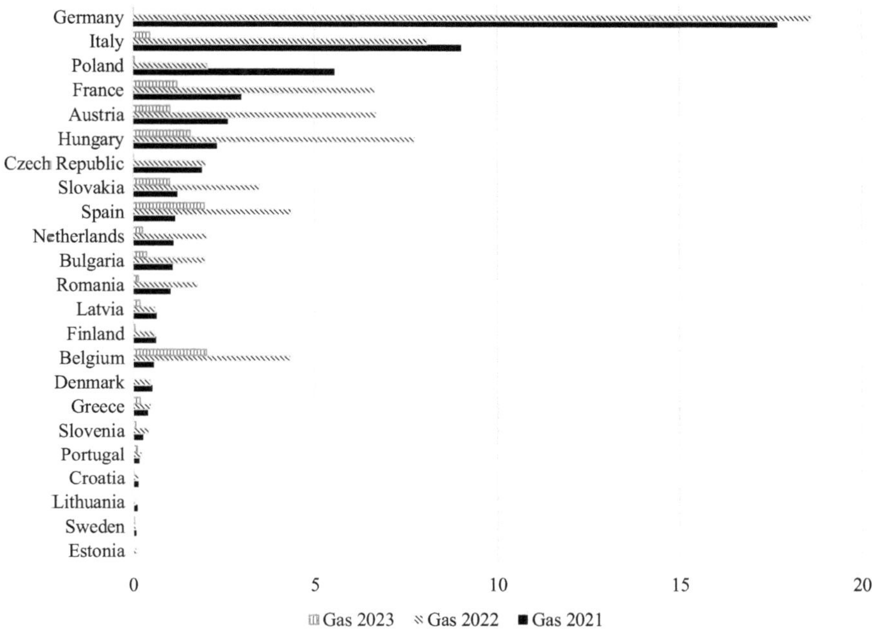

Figure 7.5 Gas imports from Russia (in billion euro).

least for Germany, Poland, Czechia, Finland, and Denmark, we can assume that the trend of no imports of Russian gas in the first half of 2023 is significant.

7.4 Effect of EU-imposed sanctions on the EU energy mix and energy transition

Changes in imports from Russia were quite visible in some EU countries. The relevant question is whether these imports from Russia were replaced by imports of fossil fuels from other countries, indicating that the sanctions were inconsequential to the EU energy transition. Therefore, it is necessary to consider the EU energy mix.

Starting with the overall imports of natural gas to Europe, we examined the developing trend in imports of natural gas and LNG from Russia and compared it with the trend over the past decade. We clearly observed a decrease in imports from Russia, reflected in the overall decrease in piped imports of gas, but we also noted an increase in LNG imports; thus, overall imports were 5 per cent higher than average over the past 10 years (right axis shows the comparison with the decade average).

We further considered the development of the EU energy mix, as shown in Figure 7.7. Only in 2021 did natural gas consumption decrease as a function of

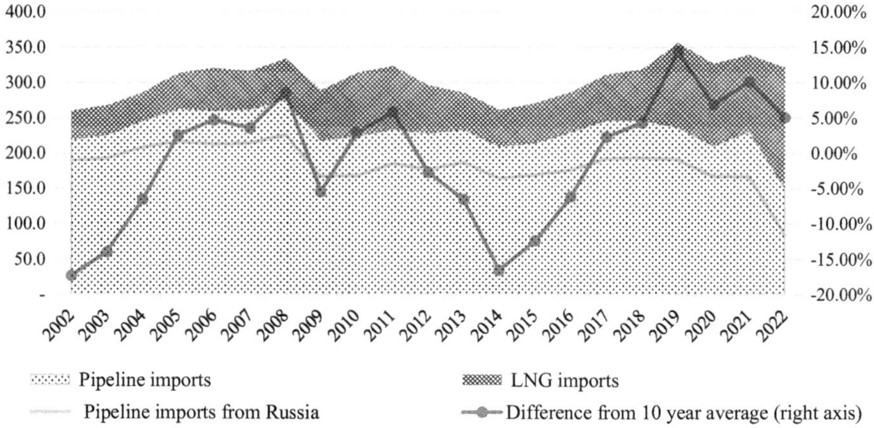

Figure 7.6 Imports of natural gas to Europe (in bcm).

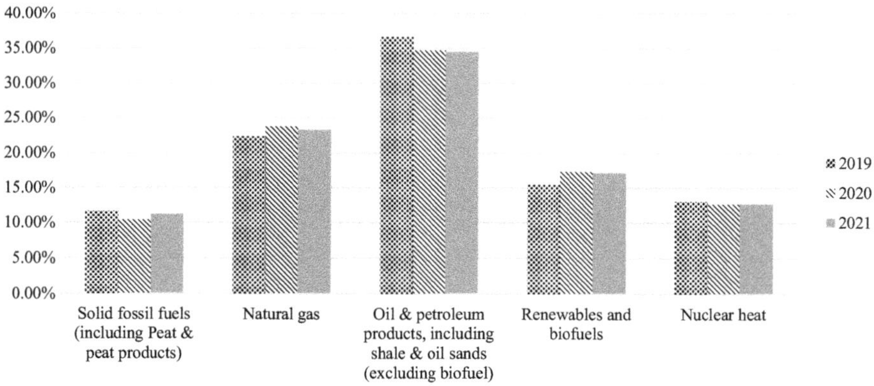

Figure 7.7 EU composition of gross available energy (energy mix).

price and effective policy measures at the EU level. We observed a steady decline for oil and, conversely, steady increases for renewables and biofuels, which can be considered a positive trend on the low-carbon energy transition path.

We also observed an increase in the consumed amounts across all three major fossil primary energy sources. Although comparing changes in the energy mix over three years may seem a heterodox idea, to highlight the differences, we created Figure 7.8, which shows that while solid fossil fuels, oil, and nuclear energy consumption decreased in 2019–2020 (due to the COVID-19 crisis), natural gas consumption decreased only in 2020–2021. Unfortunately, the official EU data source (Eurostat) does not provide more recent data across the entire energy mix

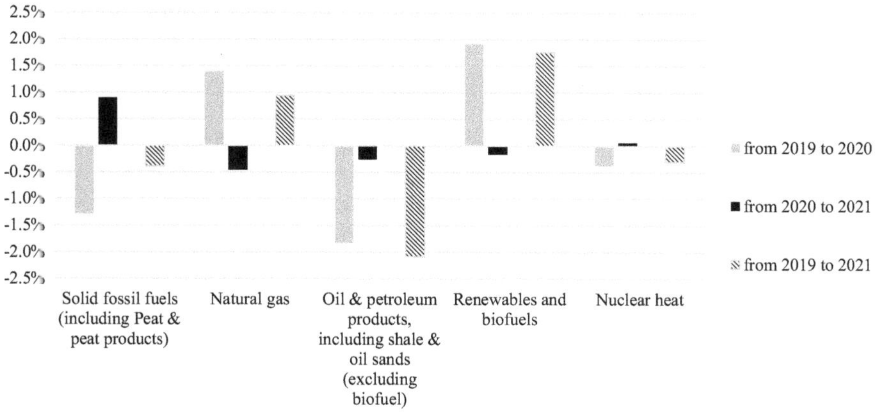

Figure 7.8 EU changes in the composition of gross available energy (energy mix).

to facilitate comparison for the years after 2021, for which we would expect more dynamic effects to be apparent.

7.5 Discussion: EU energy transition at a (blank-)gun point?

The aggressive Russian invasion of Ukraine on 24 February 2022 provoked a strong international response but did not deter Russia from continuing the invasion. The EU joined forces with other Western actors and introduced unprecedented sanctions to limit Russia's access to international goods and services, as well as to limit its revenues from goods sold internationally. Nonetheless, fossil fuels continue to be Russia's main revenue source; thus, discussions began almost immediately regarding a suitable target for smart EU sanctions. Russia depends on revenue from energy exports, and the EU is its main export destination (European Commission 2015). Elite voices within the EU have argued that the community must impose sanctions in areas where they have the greatest impact – the export energy sector, which is the Achilles' heel of the Russian economy.

The EC called for a common EU position, but member countries, aware of the domestic political fallout from rising energy prices and increasing energy poverty within the EU (Widuto 2023), were not supportive, and fossil fuel sources did not feature in the immediate sanctions after the invasion. The EU countries argued that energy sanctions would worsen the already difficult situation in the common energy market. The EU is the biggest economy in the world, but it struggles to translate this economic strength into a robust bargaining position, although not for want of trying; for example, the 2015 Energy Union took account of this shortcoming (Andersen et al. 2017). The main point of the initiative was to develop a common EU position that would strengthen the EU and thereby prevent Russia from engaging in a 'divide and rule' approach to energy negotiations (Karlsen

2019). Indeed, the challenge of presenting a united position on external energy relations may lie at the heart of the EU's inability to devise a set of powerful economic sanctions (Mišík 2022).

The first fossil fuel to enter the sanctions list was Russian coal, which has been subject to full sanctions since August 2022 as part of the fifth round of sanctions, including an earlier transitional period since April 2022. Although coal is an important 'transition' fuel for Germany due to its political decision to prematurely decommission its nuclear power plants, coal represents only a fraction of Russian exports to the EU compared to oil or natural gas. The EU has an abundance of domestic coal, so Russian coal can be replaced by increasing imports from other sources and, to some degree (even if politically increasingly contentious), by increasing domestic production (or postponing planned production phase-outs) within the EU. However, coal has the most significant carbon footprint in the EU's energy mix, and its use has been steadily decreasing due to its decarbonisation goals (European Council 2019). Despite the weak position of coal in the EU's economy, imposing sanctions on Russian coal exports was not easy and was the subject of difficult negotiations that involved transition periods and exceptions for some member states. Even during the first rounds of the sanction negotiations, it was clear that it would be difficult to establish a common position on other energy sources.

EU member states were even less united and determined over oil sanctions than they had been over coal sanctions, sending signals about the inability of EU countries to agree on a sanctions regime that would effectively target Russian aggression. Problems emerged immediately after discussions on oil sanctions began. Since oil is the most important revenue source for the Russian Federation, sanctioning it would have presented the most visible sign of EU resolve, but several member states strongly opposed this move. To properly understand these positions, it is crucial to recognise the considerable investments and infrastructural dependencies that have influenced internal disagreements within the EU. Some EU member states argued that Russian oil was their only option at that time and that their oil industries needed more time to adjust to supplies from other countries. In the case of Hungary and Slovakia, it remains unclear whether this was due to successful lobbying by the MOL company – an important regional energy giant with refineries reliant on piped Russian crude and significant exports of refined products to the rest of the EU – which clearly benefited from the price premium and the ensuing windfall profit,[7] or whether it was also motivated by the tax that both countries levied on MOL's windfall profits. Nonetheless, they were joined by Germany since several refineries in the eastern federal states of the former German Democratic Republic were only equipped to process Urals/REBCO Russian oil. Overall, opposition to full oil sanctions was strong (Barigazzi and Kijewski 2022). Instead, a system of transition periods was created that effectively excluded oil transported via the Russian pipeline for a prolonged period.

The importance of gas supplies from Russia present an even greater challenge for the EU. While the oil sanctions were not as successful as hoped for, the EU's position in the natural gas sector vis-à-vis Russia was even weaker and more reactive.

The EC voiced its commitment to eliminating all Russian fossil fuel imports by 2027 (European Commission 2022), but natural gas remained untouched by sanctions. Nevertheless, pipeline gas imports have fallen by four-fifths following Russia's weaponisation of gas supplies (McWilliams et al. 2023). The largest reduction in gas imports resulted from Gazprom naming various 'maintenance' and 'technical' issues as reasons for disruptions to the natural gas flow via some of its pipelines in the first half of 2022. However, it completely halted supplies via the Yamal and Nord Stream pipelines during the summer of 2022, when three of the four Nord Stream 1 and 2 undersea pipelines were irreparably damaged by sabotage explosions committed by an unknown but probably state-sponsored actor (Adomaitis 2023). Given that Russia's LNG exports to the EU have increased since the invasion of Ukraine, limiting Russian LNG exports remains the focus of discussions in Europe at the end of 2023. There are proposals to restrict LNG imports by preventing Russian exporters from bidding up front for the infrastructure needed to deliver LNG to Europe (Gotev 2023).

While member states agreed on a price ceiling for oil, in the case of natural gas, they only agreed on a price mechanism to prevent the spikes and market instability that occurred in late 2021. Some member states also backed the EC's proposal for a natural gas price cap. There has been no deeper discussion among member states on sanctioning natural gas imports, and the steps taken so far are either internally focused (filling domestic storage tanks and reducing natural gas consumption; EC 2022b) or concerned with alternative supplies (finding new suppliers). Moreover, many member states have 'nationalised' their energy security and started to find ways to secure natural gas supplies for the coming winter or reduce prices for domestic consumers (the most striking example is Germany). Consequently, they have become competitors in the international energy market (for example, over LNG) and have displayed reluctance to commit to EU-wide stratagems, the commitment of reducing gas consumption remained voluntary.

7.6 Conclusion

In this chapter, we examined the complex relationships among EU sanctions against Russia, which have primarily targeted its energy export sector, and the EU's own path to energy transition in the context of the crisis (shock) triggered by Russia's massive military attack on Ukraine. We attempted to empirically assess how these sanctions affected Russia's energy exports and the EU's energy mix, focusing on the potential role of sanctions as indirect catalysts for the EU's energy transition. We focused our research on the impact of EU sanctions (particularly against the Russian energy sector) on the EU's energy policy and its green transformation efforts. Thus, we considered how the willingness/unwillingness to impose energy sanctions reflected EU countries' dependence on Russian energy supplies and their ability to transform their energy policies. A significant limitation of this study is the challenge in collecting data, mainly due to the scarcity of timely and reliable sources. Despite this, preliminary conclusions can still be drawn from the available data.

The highly multilateral nature of sanctions as instruments of hard power (economic warfare), considering their intended and unintended economic consequences for the EU countries themselves, influences the behaviour of states. The asymmetrically distributed impact of these consequences among the EU member states also represents the internal contradictions within the EU regarding energy imports and sanctions.

EU unity has not proved particularly effective in terms of energy sanctions. Even in areas where sanctions were adopted (coal and oil), negotiations were difficult, with some member states effectively exercising their veto powers. The resulting sanction regimes came with transitional periods and exceptions (for example, oil transported by pipeline was excluded from the sanctions for quite a long period, mainly until December 2023, but further exceptions survived even longer, and at the end of 2023 further prolongation of the existing exceptions on oil sanctions is being discussed). All these considerably reduced the effect of sanctions and gave Russia ample time to adapt. However, the EU's main challenge has been the need for unanimity among member states regarding EU-wide sanctions. Member states have been willing to use the threat of veto to pursue national interests, often connected to their political interests, which in some cases go against the EU's (and other member states') interests. This undermines the EU's ability to succeed and plays into Russia's hands, especially regarding its 'divide and rule' approach and alleged mingling and influencing of domestic political dynamics, exacerbating energy poverty and undermining energy transition policies targeting carbon reduction.

Preliminary findings suggest that EU member states' sanctions against Russia may have directly impacted the EU's energy transition, based on data regarding changes in the EU's energy mix, including increased investment in renewable energy sources (such as heat pumps or photovoltaic systems). However, attributing the acceleration of the green transformation solely to sanctions remains difficult due to the lack of comprehensive data on the one hand and the complexity of causality on the other. We observe changes to the energy policies and energy mixes of EU member states, that correlate with the imposition of sanctions in response to Russia's invasion of Ukraine. Nonetheless, we are not in a position to claim a direct causal link between these.

Given that the interplay between the EC, member states, and other actors is one of the central elements of this volume; in this chapter, we also aimed to examine changes in EU climate and energy policy in relation to the two crises. Has the Russian invasion of Ukraine and subsequent sanctions changed the EU's climate and energy policy? Such changes are observable, but the question of whether they have led to the deepening of European policy integration remains open. On one level, an important derogation may be seen as a way of keeping the EU united in the face of member states focusing on securing their national solutions. In other words, Russia's aggression has put the EU's unity and decarbonisation resolve, including domestic politics within the member states, to a real test. Based on the data, it is too early to tell whether the EU and its individual member states will be able to maintain their steadfast resolve.

A patient observer will know within a few months whether the cautious green awakenings seen five years ago during the European Parliament elections marked the beginning of a trend, or whether there will be a relapse, with member states turning inwards and searching for national solutions to the climate and energy challenges, with corresponding new representation being elected to the European Parliament in 2024.

Acknowledgements

This work was supported by the Slovak Research and Development Agency grant no APVV-20-0012.

Notes

1 Twelve packages of sanctions against Russia by the end of 2023, with EU and its member states representing almost a fifth of all sanctions against Russia (Castellum.ai 2023).
2 As of December 2023.
3 A VPN is a technology that encrypts and routes internet traffic through servers in a different location, allowing researchers to access online resources in a country that blocks foreign access by making their locations appear to be in an unrestricted region.
4 SITC codes are primarily used to report and analyse trade statistics, and they help to facilitate comparisons of trade data across countries and regions. The system classifies goods and services based on their characteristics, use, and composition. The SITC system is hierarchical, with a series of codes that become increasingly detailed and specific further down the classification structure. This allows for the aggregation of data at different levels of detail, making it suitable for various analytical purposes.
The SITC codes are typically four-digit codes, and the hierarchy extends down to more detailed levels with additional digits. The classification covers both goods and services, and it is periodically updated to reflect changes in the global economy and international trade patterns.
5 According to the UN, the term 'not elsewhere specified (NES)' for trade partners is used (a) for low-value trade and (b) when the partner designation is unknown to the country, or an error is made in the partner assignment. The reporting country does not send the details of the trading partner in these specific cases. Sometimes reporters do this to protect company information (UN 2021).
6 We are grateful to colleagues at CREA for making their valuable raw data available for our analysis.
7 When MOL's refinery margin increased tenfold in early 2022, MOL even stopped publishing this important indicator (MOL Group 2022).

References

Adomaitis, N., 2023. Q+A What Is Known about the Nord Stream Gas Pipeline Explosions. Reuters, 26 September 2023, sec. Europe. www.reuters.com/world/europe/qa-what-is-known-about-nord-stream-gas-pipeline-explosions-2023-09-26/

Andersen, S.S., Goldthau, A., Sitter, N., 2017. Energy Union Europe's New Liberal Mercantilism? 2nd edn 2017. http://lib.ugent.be/catalog/ebk01:3710000000922060

Barigazzi, J., Kijewski, L., 2022. EU's Russian Oil Ban Stalls as Hungary Holds up Sanctions. POLITICO, 8 May 2022. www.politico.eu/article/eus-russian-oil-ban-stalls-as-hungary-holds-up-sanctions/

BP, 2023. Energy Outlook 2023. www.bp.com/en/global/corporate/energy-economics/energy-outlook.html.

CAMS, 2020. Copernicus: Study Confirms Reductions in Emissions during the First Wave of COVID-19 in Europe. 17 December 2020. https://atmosphere.copernicus.eu/copernicus-study-confirms-reductions-emissions-during-first-wave-covid-19-europe.

Castellum.ai, 2023. The Castellum.AI Dashboard Provides Consolidated Russia Sanctions Data. Castellum.AI, 15 December 2023. www.castellum.ai/russia-sanctions-dashboard

CREA, 2023. Centre for Research on Energy and Clean Air Russian Energy Export Tracker. 2023. https://energyandcleanair.org/financing-putins-war/methodology/

Danis, E., 2022. High Sea Russian Oil Transfers Are Far from the Only Smuggling Method. Windward, 25 August 2022. https://windward.ai/blog/high-sea-russian-oil-transfers-are-far-from-the-only-smuggling-method/

Dyduch, J., Skorek, A., 2020. Go South! Southern dimension of the V4 states' energy policy strategies – An assessment of viability and prospects. *Energy Policy*, 140: 111372. https://doi.org/10.1016/j.enpol.2020.111372

EEAS, 2023. Ukraine: The High Representative, Together with the European Commission Submits Proposals for 12th Package of Sanctions against Russia. 15 November 2023. www.eeas.europa.eu/eeas/ukraine-high-representative-together-european-commission-submits-proposals-12th-package-sanctions_en

European Commission, 2015. A Framework Strategy for a Resilient Energy Union with a Forward-Looking Climate Change Policy. COM(2015) 80 Final. www.eea.europa.eu/policy-documents/com-2015-80-final

European Commission, 2022. Statement between the Commission and the US on energy. 25 March 2022. https://ec.europa.eu/commission/presscorner/detail/it/statement_22_2041

European Commission, 2023. 11th Package of Sanctions. 23 June 2023. https://ec.europa.eu/commission/presscorner/detail/en/ip_23_3429

European Council, 2019. European Council Meeting (12 December 2019) – Conclusions. www.consilium.europa.eu/media/41768/12-euco-final-conclusions-en.pdf

European Council, 2023a. Timeline – EU Restrictive Measures against Russia over Ukraine. 28 July 2023. www.consilium.europa.eu/en/policies/sanctions/restrictive-measures-against-russia-over-ukraine/history-restrictive-measures-against-russia-over-ukraine/

European Council, 2023b. EU Sanctions against Russia Explained. 12 October 2023. www.consilium.europa.eu/en/policies/sanctions/restrictive-measures-against-russia-over-ukraine/sanctions-against-russia-explained/

European Parliament, 2023a. EU Sanctions on Russia: Overview, Impact, Challenges. 3 October 2023. www.europarl.europa.eu/thinktank/en/document/EPRS_BRI(2023)739366

European Parliament, 2023b. Effectiveness of the EU Sanctions on Russia. 9 November 2023. www.europarl.europa.eu/doceo/document/TA-9-2023-0397_EN.html

Eurostat, 2023. Preliminary 2022 Data for Energy Show Mixed Trends – Products Eurostat News. 5 July 2023. https://ec.europa.eu/eurostat/web/products-eurostat-news/w/ddn-20230705-2

Gotev, G., 2023. EU Countries Seek Legal Option to Stop Russian LNG Imports. Euractiv, 29 March 2023. www.euractiv.com/section/energy-environment/news/eu-countries-seek-legal-option-to-stop-russian-lng-imports/

Homer-Dixon, T., 2023. Why so Much Is Going Wrong at the Same Time. Vox, 18 October 2023. www.vox.com/future-perfect/23920997/polycrisis-climate-pandemic-population-connectivity

IEA, 2022. World Energy Outlook 2022 – Analysis. www.iea.org/reports/world-energy-outlook-2022

Karlsen, G.H., 2019. Divide and Rule: Ten Lessons about Russian Political Influence Activities in Europe. *Palgrave Communications* 5(1): 1–14. https://doi.org/10.1057/s41599-019-0227-8

Lucarelli, S., 2007. The European Union in the Eyes of Others: Towards Filling a Gap in the Literature. *European Foreign Affairs Review* 12(3): 249–270. https://kluwerlawonline.com/journalarticle/European+Foreign+Affairs+Review/12.3/EERR2007025

McWilliams, B., Sgaravatti, G., Tagliapietra, S., Zachmann, G., 2023. The EU Can Manage without Russian Liquified Natural Gas. www.bruegel.org/policy-brief/eu-can-manage-without-russian-liquified-natural-gas

Metsola, R., 2022. Aggression Is Confrontation with Europe: Speech of President Metsola on Ukraine. 24 February 2022. www.europarl.europa.eu/news/en/press-room/20220224IPR24012/aggression-is-confrontation-with-europe-speech-of-president-metsola-on-ukraine

Mišík, M., 2022. The EU Needs to Improve Its External Energy Security. *Energy Policy* 165(June): 112930. https://doi.org/10.1016/j.enpol.2022.112930

Mitrova, T., 2022. Understanding the Impact of Sanctions on the Russian Oil and Gas Sector with Limited Data. Center on Global Energy Policy at Columbia University | SIPA, 29 September 2022. www.energypolicy.columbia.edu/publications/qa-understanding-impact-sanctions-russian-oil-and-gas-sector-limited-data/

MOL Group, 2022. 2022 – Publications – Investor Relations. MOLGroup. https://molgroup.info/en/investor-relations/publications/2022

Nosko, A., 2007. Economic Interdependence of New EU Member States and Russia. CEU Political Economy Research Group (PERG) Project, CEU Political Economy Research Group (PERG) Project, 1/2007: 53.

Nosko, A., 2021. Ceny Energií Zdvíha Dopyt i Rusko, Ktoré Chce Dať EÚ Príučku. Slovenská Spoločnosť Pre Zahraničnú Politiku (blog), 27 October 2021. www.sfpa.sk/zapost/ceny-energii-zdviha-dopyt-i-rusko-ktore-chce-dat-eu-priucku/

Nosko, A., Ušiak, J., 2023. Effects of COVID-19 on Civil Society Voices in European Energy and Climate Policy. *Energy Policy* 174: 113421, https://doi.org/10.1016/j.enpol.2023.113421

Perkins, R., 2022. Tanker Switching Surges for Russian Oil as Moscow Turns to 'gray Market' Playbook. 1 August 2022. www.spglobal.com/commodityinsights/en/market-insights/latest-news/oil/080122-tanker-switching-surges-for-russian-oil-as-moscow-turns-to-gray-market-playbook

Rácz, A., Spillner, O., Wolff, G.B., 2023. Why Sanctions Against Russia Work. *Intereconomics* 58(1): 52–55. https://doi.org/10.2478/ie-2023-0009

Roth, A., 2021. Russia Issues List of Demands It Says Must Be Met to Lower Tensions in Europe. *The Guardian*, 17 December 2021, sec. World news. www.theguardian.com/world/2021/dec/17/russia-issues-list-demands-tensions-europe-ukraine-nato

Russian Federal State Statistics Service, 2023. Indicators Characterizing Import Substitution in Russia [Показатели, Характеризующие Импортозамещение в России]. 2023. https://rosstat.gov.ru/folder/11188

Seddon, M., Sheppard, D., 2021. Putin Says Russia Could Deliver 10% More Gas If Nord Stream 2 Approved. *Financial Times*, 21 October 2021.

Sonnenfeld, J., Tian, S., Sokolowski, F., Wyrebkowski, M., Kasprowicz, M., 2022. Business Retreats and Sanctions are Crippling the Russian Economy. SSRN Scholarly Paper. Rochester, NY. https://doi.org/10.2139/ssrn.4167193

TASS, 2016. President Putin Approves Russian Budget for 2017–2019. TASS, 20 December 2016. https://tass.com/economy/920922?utm_source=google.com&utm_medium=organic&utm_campaign=google.com&utm_referrer=google.com

Torkington, S., 2023. We're on the Brink of a 'Polycrisis' – How Worried Should We Be? World Economic Forum, 13 January 2023. www.weforum.org/agenda/2023/01/polycrisis-global-risks-report-cost-of-living/

Triebert, C., Migliozzi, B., Cardia, A., Xiao, M., Botti, D., 2023. Fake Signals and American Insurance: How a Dark Fleet Moves Russian Oil. *The New York Times*, 31 May 2023, sec. World. www.nytimes.com/interactive/2023/05/30/world/asia/russia-oil-ships-sanctions.html

UN, 2021. Areas Not Elsewhere Specified – UN Comtrade – UN Statistics Wiki. 2021. https://unstats.un.org/wiki/display/comtrade/Areas+not+elsewhere+specified

UN Statistics Division, 2023. UN Comtrade. 2023. https://comtradeplus.un.org/TradeFlow

Widuto, A., 2023. Energy Poverty in the EU. European Parliament's Members' Research Service, September.

Zugravu, N., Millock, K., Duchene, G., 2008. The Factors Behind CO2 Emission Reduction in Transition Economies. Fondazione Eni Enrico Mattei Working Papers, September. https://services.bepress.com/feem/paper217

8 Structural development of the Slovak economy and the impact on the production of emissions

Jana Kajanova and Lukáš Veteška

8.1 Introduction

Economies dominated by the processing industry are currently facing the challenges of reducing emissions resulting from the European Green Deal, particularly in achieving carbon neutrality by 2050. The current structure of the Slovak economy, which is dominated by the manufacturing industry as well, is a major source of emissions and air pollution. To address this issue and reduce emissions, a structural change in the economy is essential, with a focus on transitioning to 'green' industries that produce value without excessive emissions. The introduction of Industry 4.0 technologies and procedures (for example Internet of Things (IoT), artificial intelligence, robotics, big data analytics, and cyber-physical systems) can be a catalyst for this transition, as it brings new opportunities for improving productivity and reducing energy dependence. It is also beneficial to look at more developed countries that have made progress in achieving higher GDP per capita, as they can serve as models for structural changes and economic development. Our previous article on the comparison of the structure of the Slovak Republic's economy with the most developed EU countries (Veteška and Kajanová, 2022), where we identified nine prospective industries, is a good starting point. To further quantify the potential for reducing emissions, we have conducted a comprehensive analysis of these prospective industries, considering their energy intensity and emission production in comparison with the current dominant industries in Slovakia.

The COVID-19 pandemic and especially the energy crisis after the outbreak of the Russia-Ukraine war showed us how necessary it is to switch to less energy-intensive forms of the economy, in which energy-efficient industries predominate, and to support projects that modernize technologies and focus on reducing energy consumption and thus emissions. Russia, as our main supplier of fossil fuels, became subject to sanctions, which caused energy shortages in the market. The main goal of this chapter is to conduct a comprehensive analysis of the position of the Slovak economy with regard to its carbon dioxide (CO_2) emissions. This analysis can help policymakers and stakeholders understand where investments and measures to improve conditions. It should be directed to promote the growth of green industries and reduce emissions. It is important to engage with experts,

DOI: 10.4324/9781032624839-11

research institutions, and industry representatives to develop and implement strategies for a sustainable transition towards carbon neutrality while ensuring economic growth and job creation. It may also involve setting clear targets, incentives, and regulatory frameworks to support the desired changes in the economy. The main research question that arises is whether the structural change of the economy can have an impact on the reduction of emitted emissions.

In the first section of this chapter, we describe the current state of the problem. Subsequently, we set the goal of the chapter, which is the analysis of the Slovak economy in connection with reducing CO_2 and meeting the obligations set by the EU. In the methodology, we described the work process, the method of data collection, their analysis and scientific procedures. In the following section, we present the results using a graphical representation (figures). Based on the results of the analyses, we have compiled several suggestions and recommendations, which we present in a separate section. To conclude, we summarize all the findings.

8.2 Slovakia on the way to carbon neutrality

Member countries, including Slovakia, have committed to achieving carbon neutrality by 2050 as part of the EU's efforts to combat climate change and align with the goals of the European Green Deal. Carbon neutrality, also known as net-zero carbon emissions, means that a country's greenhouse gas emissions are balanced by measures that remove an equivalent amount of emissions from the atmosphere. Achieving carbon neutrality is a significant undertaking that requires multifaceted efforts across various sectors of the economy. Slovakia's manufacturing industry has been successful in producing a substantial proportion of the country's GDP, and manufacturing workers constitute a significant portion of the labor force. Bratislava, Košice, and the towns along the Váh River are Slovakia's main manufacturing centres. The country's manufacturing industry includes automobiles, machinery, steel, ceramics, chemicals, textiles, food and beverage processing, arms, and petroleum products (Tokarcikova et al., 2022).

The most important component of Slovakia's GDP is the automotive industry, which falls into the category of manufacturing industry. Slovakia produces the most vehicles in proportion to the number of inhabitants (CEIC, 2023; International Trade Administration, 2020). However, the negative side of this industry is the high burden on the environment expressed by the production of emissions. The trend in the development of the Slovak economy is the opposite, employment in the manufacturing industry continues to grow, while just this year the arrival of another car manufacturer, Volvo, was announced, which will create thousands more jobs (Slovak Press Agency, 2023). The main goal of the Paris Agreement is to limit global warming to 2 degrees (Matemilola et al., 2023). Achieving carbon neutrality in 2050 is unrealistic with the current measures, so it is necessary increase measures on a global scale. During 2020, there was a 5 per cent decrease in CO_2 emissions caused by the COVID-19 pandemic and its associated restrictions (Klemeš et al., 2020).

A key measure is the transformation of the energy system, as most GHGs are released during energy production and use. The European Commission has set an ambitious goal to reduce emissions by 55 per cent in 2030 compared to 1990 levels (European Commission, 2022). In addition to the reduction of emissions in existing industries using technological progress and development, the structural development of the economy and the transformation from ecologically demanding industries to less demanding ones are also important. To achieve the maximum efficiency of the future energy system, it is necessary to optimize the economy as a whole, not by individual sectors (Potrč et al., 2022).

Industry produces the most emissions worldwide, and consumes approximately a quarter of the world's energy, of which up to 70 per cent comes from fossil fuels (IEA, 2020). Within the European Union, more than 40 per cent of emissions are produced by the energy and manufacturing sectors. Energy-intensive industries contribute approximately 64 per cent of all emissions from the manufacturing sector (Vieira et al., 2021). In the transition from industry to a low-carbon economy, it is crucial to decarbonize energy-intensive industries that have a specific need for energy to achieve high temperatures or chemical reactions; the long-life cycle of industrial equipment used in the production process is also an obstacle. These factors complicate the reduction of emissions (Pee et al., 2018). The decarbonization of energy-intensive industries was dealt with, for example, by Wesseling, who identified the main bottlenecks of decarbonization. According to his findings, these main limitations are the high cost of renewable resources, their availability, as well as insufficient infrastructure (Wesseling et al., 2016). Legislators should also focus on mitigating these barriers, by using legislative interventions to reduce the obstacles preventing businesses from decarbonizing (Napp et al., 2014).

In 2005 the European Union initiated the Emissions Trading System (EU ETS) which is a significant policy for decarbonization of the energetical and manufacturing sector. The ETS provides the most thorough, detailed database of air pollutants in these sectors (Teixidó et al., 2019). The transition from fossil fuels involves complex structural changes, which require technological development and a stable institutional environment (Geels et al., 2017). Vieira found that, despite the tightening of legislation and the development of the ETS phases, there has not been a sufficient reduction in emissions, and further measures will be needed to achieve carbon neutrality in 2050. Indeed, many entities have even increased their level of emissions (Vieira et al., 2021). However, a huge change was caused by the COVID-19 pandemic which altered the flow of the industry during lockdown and therefore slowed down global warming as factories were working under restricted conditions. The carbon footprint of many countries, including Slovakia rapidly changed during this time.

The COVID-19 lockdown influenced carbon footprints globally, resulting in a reduction in transportation emissions due to decreased air travel and commuting. Industrial disruptions and reduced energy consumption contributed to lower carbon emissions. Changes in land use and consumer behavior, resulted in temporary reductions. Specific impacts varied by region, and rebound effects occurred as economies reopened. The study by Le Quéré et al. (2020) concludes that the COVID-19 lockdown led to a temporary reduction in daily global CO_2 emissions. It emphasizes the need for sustainable strategies to achieve long-term emissions reduction goals, considering the interconnectedness of economic activities and environmental impact (Le Quéré et al., 2020). A study by Liu et al. (2021) underscores the importance of designing the next generation of air quality monitoring strategies to address challenges exacerbated by the COVID-19 pandemic. It emphasizes the role of sustainable approaches in mitigating air quality issues and combating climate change (Liu et al., 2021). Other research concludes that the COVID-19 pandemic has had both short- and long-term effects on energy and the environment. It highlights the complex interactions between economic activities, energy consumption, and environmental sustainability, emphasizing the need for holistic and adaptive policy responses (Gillingham et al., 2020).

The dynamics of the price of allowances had permanently halved after the subprime crisis, from a value of around €28 per tonne of CO_2 in summer 2008 to a value of around €15 per tonne of CO_2 from January 2019 to September 2011. The drop following the COVID-19 crisis has been less, and, above all, it seems purely transitory (Baudry, 2021). Identifying the key factors that cause changes in GHG emissions are important in designing effective policies and strategies leading to decarbonization (Wang et al., 2019). The environmental rationale for economic transformation is well-documented and is in line with the imperative to reduce greenhouse gas emissions and mitigate climate change. It is increasingly evident that economic sectors play a substantial role in global emissions. To limit global warming to safe levels, a shift toward low-carbon and sustainable economic models is imperative (Change, 2021). Transitioning to green sectors offers significant employment opportunities, as demonstrated by recent research (Veteška and Kajanová, 2022). Sectors such as renewable energy, including wind and solar, have proven to be substantial sources of job creation (Zeng and Xu, 2020). The yearly renewable energy flows surpass the maximum technological potential by a factor of 17, with the maximum potential being four times greater than the minimum potential (Krozer, 2022). Studies have highlighted the potential to generate millions of green jobs globally, addressing both environmental and employment challenges (International Labour Organization, 2018). Economic transformation encourages innovation and the development of green technologies. Recent research underscores the pivotal role of investments in green technologies in enhancing productivity and sustainability.

Innovation is recognized as a driver of growth in green sectors, contributing to economic progress (D'Amato et al., 2017). Recent studies such as Sovacool et al. (2021) highlight the robust employment growth in the renewable energy sector, which surpasses traditional energy industries. Job opportunities within renewable energy are diverse, spanning manufacturing, installation, and research and development (Sovacool et al., 2021). Green sectors encompass energy-efficient technologies and sustainable construction practices. Research by Blum and Hone (2020) underscores the role of energy-efficient retrofits and green building projects in job generation. These activities often require skilled labor for renovations and construction, contributing to local employment (Blum and Hone, 2020). Green sectors are characterized by rapid technological advancements and requires a skilled workforce. Research by Wei et al. (2021) emphasizes the importance of skills development in green industries, identifying a growing demand for professionals with expertise in clean technologies. This fosters innovation and knowledge transfer (Wei et al., 2021).

8.3 The objective of the work and methodology

Slovakia represents a traditionally manufacturing-oriented economy, therefore we decided to carry out a case study which will focus on examining the current position in the area of produced emissions, efficiency in produced emissions and employment. The main goal of this chapter is to conduct a comprehensive analysis of the position of the Slovak economy concerning its carbon dioxide (CO_2) emissions. Slovakia, like many other countries dominated by manufacturing industry, faces the challenge of transitioning to a more sustainable and environmentally responsible economic model. Central to this transformation is a critical examination of the nation's current carbon emissions profile and an exploration of how structural changes within the economy can lead to the reduction and eventual decarbonization of its industries. The initial focus of this chapter involves a meticulous examination of the CO_2 emissions generated by the Slovak economy. This includes a detailed breakdown of emissions by sector, with particular attention to major contributors such as manufacturing and energy production. By providing a clear picture of the country's emissions landscape, the chapter aims to underline the urgency of addressing the environmental impact of economic activities.

The heart of this analysis lies in exploring the profound impact of structural changes in the economy. The Slovak economy, historically driven by manufacturing and energy-intensive industries, must evolve to meet its climate commitments and reduce its carbon footprint. This chapter delves into the crucial role of 'green' industries, which produce value with significantly lower emissions, and how they can be integrated into the economic landscape. Drawing insights from more developed countries within the European Union, who have made substantial progress in reducing emissions and transitioning to green industries, is essential. The chapter will consider successful models and strategies of environmental policies and regulations that can guide Slovakia on its journey to decarbonization. In addition to identifying prospective industries, the chapter will quantify the potential for emissions reduction by contrasting these industries with the current dominant sectors in the Slovak economy. This quantitative analysis will help set clear targets for emissions reduction and decarbonization.

8.4 Methodology

Overall, the research employs a combination of data analysis, statistical methods, and empirical observations to investigate CO_2 emissions and economic efficiency in Slovakia. These scientific methods are used to generate insights, draw conclusions, and contribute to informed decision-making and policy development in the context of emissions reduction and sustainability. This comprehensive methodology is designed to provide a robust framework for investigating CO_2 emissions and economic efficiency within the Slovak Republic, encompassing data collection, analysis, comparative assessments, correlation studies, and efficiency evaluations to offer a complete understanding of the environmental and economic landscape. It ultimately contributes to informed decision-making and policy development in the context of emissions reduction and sustainability.

The methodology employed in this research aims to comprehensively investigate the issue of CO_2 emissions within the context of the Slovak Republic, with a focus on understanding the position of Slovakia in the European Union and exploring the potential for reducing emissions. The research methodology involves a combination of scientific methods and data analysis techniques commonly employed in environmental and economic research. A breakdown of the scientific methods used follows.

Research begins with the collection of relevant data. In this case, data on CO_2 emissions, GDP, employment rates, and renewable energy sources were collected from authoritative sources, such as Eurostat and national environmental agencies. This step aligns with the scientific method of gathering empirical evidence for analysis. The research conducts comparative analyses of Slovakia's emissions data in the context of the European Union. Comparative analysis is a scientific method that involves comparing data from different sources or periods to identify patterns, trends, and differences. The research examines trends in CO_2 emissions over a nine-year period. Longitudinal analysis, a common scientific method, allows researchers to assess changes over time and understand how variables evolve.

Calculating per capita emissions is a scientific approach that accounts for population size, enabling a more precise assessment of individual contributions to emissions. It also considers regional and economic variations, reflecting the use of scientific methods to refine data. The research explores the correlation between renewable energy adoption and emissions efficiency, using correlation analysis, a statistical scientific method. This helps identify potential relationships between variables. The research assesses emissions from various industries, using the NACE classification. This approach applies scientific categorization to better understand the sources of emissions. Calculating the emissions per percentage of employment, known as the CO_2 / Employment rate index, is a scientific method that quantifies the efficiency of industries in terms of emissions. This index allows for the comparison of different sectors based on emissions efficiency. Calculating arithmetic averages for reductive and prospective industries is a scientific method that provides summary statistics for comparisons and conclusions.

8.5 Analysis results

Initially, our attention is directed towards examining the standing of the Slovak Republic within the context of the European Union regarding total CO_2 emissions. This involves a comprehensive analysis of the country's contribution to the overall carbon emissions within the EU framework. By assessing the magnitude and nature

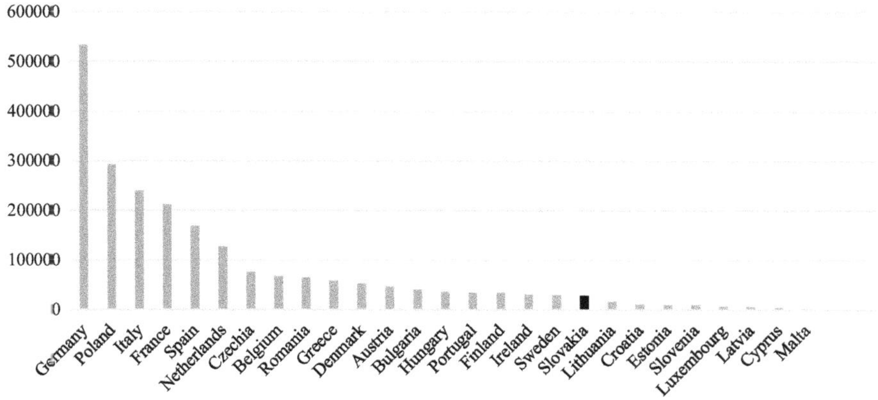

Figure 8.1 Total production of CO_2 in 2021 [thousand tonnes].

of Slovakia's CO_2 emissions, we aim to gain insights into its environmental impact and its comparative position among other EU member states. This examination provides a foundation for a nuanced understanding of Slovakia's role in the broader context of environmental sustainability within the European Union.

In terms of total production, Slovakia ranks 20th in the European Union with 28,478.60 thousand tonnes of CO_2 (see Figure 8.1). The leader in CO_2 emissions is Germany with 533,461.47 thousand tonnes of CO_2. Malta produces the least emissions, 1,485.53 thousand tonnes of CO_2. Our chapter deals with the development trend, so in the following figure we also focused on the development of emission production, where we selected neighboring countries of similar economic size as a sample, while we followed the development of the total CO_2 production in thousands of tonnes.

Compared to neighboring countries (see Figure 8.2), Slovakia achieved roughly comparable results, the development curve is roughly similar. All monitored countries have reduced their total CO_2 production over the past nine years. In 2012, the Slovak economy produced 30,415.07 thousand tonnes of CO_2, while in 2021 it was only 28,478.60 thousand tonnes of CO_2. In 2021 it was only 28,478.60 thousand tonnes of CO_2. From the point of view of the distribution of economies according to the size of GDP per capita from our above-mentioned previous research, Austria belongs to the category of highly developed countries, based on which we identified the trend of the structural development of the economy towards reducing emissions but, from this figure, we can see that the trend of the development of emission production is in Austria similar to other surrounding countries that did not belong to the category of highly developed countries. In the figure, we can also see the impact of the COVID-19 pandemic on emissions, which decreased in all countries. However, this was only a temporary effect and emissions increased again subsequently. Due to the different size of the economies, we focused on a

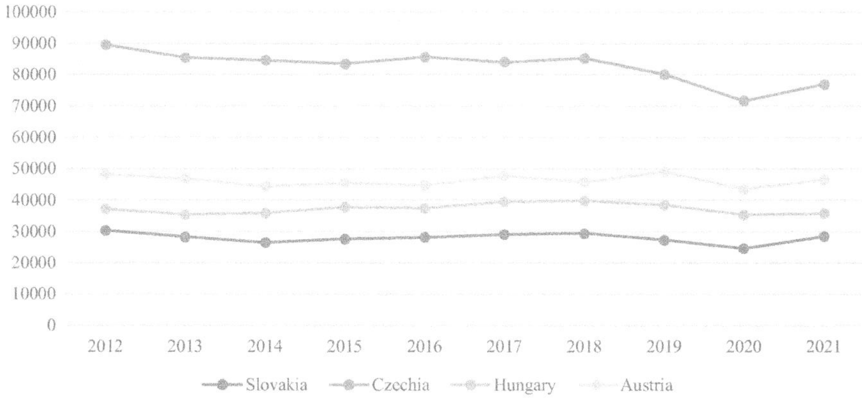

Figure 8.2 Comparison of the trend of produced emissions between neighbouring countries of comparable size in 2021 [thousand tonnes].

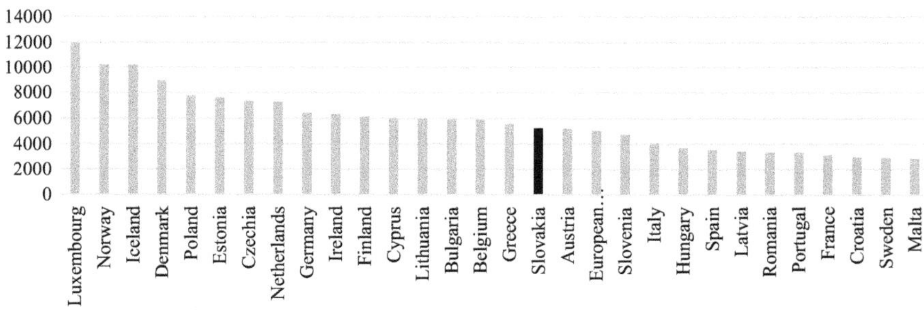

Figure 8.3 Emitted CO_2 emissions per capita in 2021 [Kg].

more accurate indicator, which is the amount of emitted CO_2 emissions per capita. In the following figure, we present these data based on Eurostat.

In terms of emissions per capita (see Figure 8.3), Slovakia ranks 17th, with 5,228 Kg per capita. Luxembourg produces the most emissions per capita with 11,959 Kg. Malta reaches the smallest value of 2,864 Kg. Based on this indicator, Slovakia is doing really well, but these data are significantly influenced mainly by regional specificities and the structure of the economy of the given countries. Geographical and climatic factors impact CO_2 emissions through variations in energy sources, climate-driven energy demand, topography affecting infrastructure, land use changes, industrial practices, water resource availability, urbanization levels, and susceptibility to natural disasters. Recognizing these influences is crucial for developing effective strategies to mitigate emissions based on a region's unique characteristics. For instance, a country with a high reliance on renewable energy sources may have lower emissions per capita compared to a nation heavily dependent on fossil fuels.

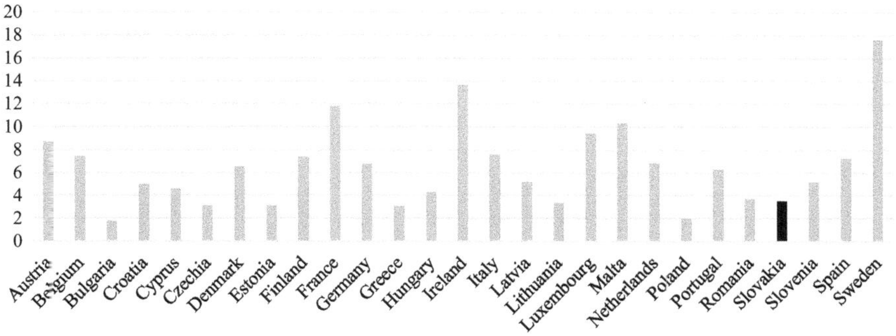

Figure 8.4 Index share of CO_2 emissions GDP [mil Eur].

Source: Eurostat (2021b).

The structure of the economy also plays a pivotal role. Countries with robust industrial sectors might have higher emissions due to manufacturing processes and energy-intensive activities. On the other hand, nations with a strong focus on service industries or those investing heavily in sustainable practices may exhibit lower emissions. For a more accurate determination of the emission efficiency of the economy, we put the GDP and emission production into context. The indicator in the following figure is the share of CO_2 emissions in thousands of tonnes on GDP in millions of Euros. In simple terms, it tells us how many million Euros of GDP the economy produced per thousand tonnes of CO_2.

The leader in the efficiency of the economy from the point of view of emissions is Sweden, noted for producing €17.59 million for every thousand tonnes of CO_2 emitted (see Figure 8.4). This metric reflects the economic output or value generated by a country per unit of carbon dioxide emissions. In essence, it assesses how effectively a nation is utilizing its resources to generate economic activity while minimizing carbon emissions. Contrastingly, Slovakia is one of the countries with relatively poor results in this efficiency indicator. The country generates only €3.52 million for every thousand tonnes of CO_2 emitted. This suggests that, in economic terms, Slovakia produces less value per unit of carbon emissions compared to Sweden. The disparity could be attributed to various factors, including the composition of Slovakia's economy, energy production methods, and industrial practices. Bulgaria is the worst-performing country in the European Union concerning this efficiency metric. It produces only €1.74 million for every thousand tonnes of CO_2 emitted. This indicates a significantly lower economic output relative to the amount of carbon dioxide released into the atmosphere. The wide variation in efficiency among these countries underscores the importance of considering not only the absolute levels of emissions but also how efficiently nations are converting those emissions into economic value. High efficiency in this context suggests that a country can maintain or increase its economic productivity while keeping its carbon footprint relatively low. The following figure is focused on the relationship between the share of energy from renewable sources in the total energy mix and

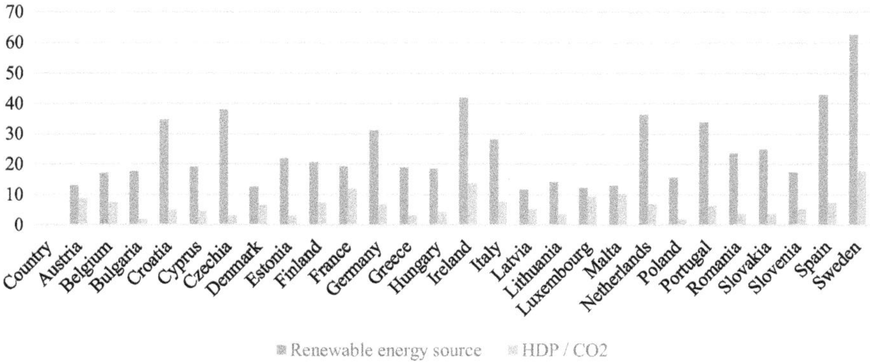

Figure 8.5 Relationship between the share of energy from renewable sources in the total energy mix and the GDP produced per thousand tonnes [%, mil Eur].

the index that we recalculated in the previous paragraph, which relates GDP and emissions exclusion.

Sweden is achieving the highest share of renewable energy sources at 62.57 per cent, it signifies a substantial commitment to sustainable and environmentally friendly energy practices (see Figure 8.5). This high percentage suggests that a significant portion of Sweden's energy needs is met through renewable sources such as wind, solar, hydro, and biomass. This emphasis on renewables aligns with global efforts to transition away from fossil fuels, reduce carbon emissions, and mitigate climate change.

In some cases, we can see indications of dependence of these two variables. Therefore, we analyzed these two variables using a correlation that resulted in a value of 0.46. This value, being positive, implies a moderate positive correlation between the share of renewable energy sources and the efficiency ratio. In simpler terms, as the share of renewables increases, there tends to be a moderate increase in the efficiency with which the economy utilizes carbon emissions to generate economic output. However, it is important to note that the correlation analysis did not reveal a close relationship between the share of renewable energy sources in the country's energy mix and the index of the share of CO_2 in GDP. In other words, while there may be a slight correlation between the share of renewable energy and the efficiency ratio, this does not necessarily translate into a direct correlation with the share of CO_2 emissions relative to GDP. This subtle finding highlights the complexity of factors influencing economic efficiency and carbon emissions beyond the share of renewable energy sources, including technological progress, overall energy consumption and policy frameworks.

In the following figure, we present the share of individual industries according to 'Nomenclature statistique des Activites economiques dans la Communaute Europeenne' – Statistical classification of economic activities in the European Community (NACE) in the emission of carbon dioxide in the Slovak Republic.

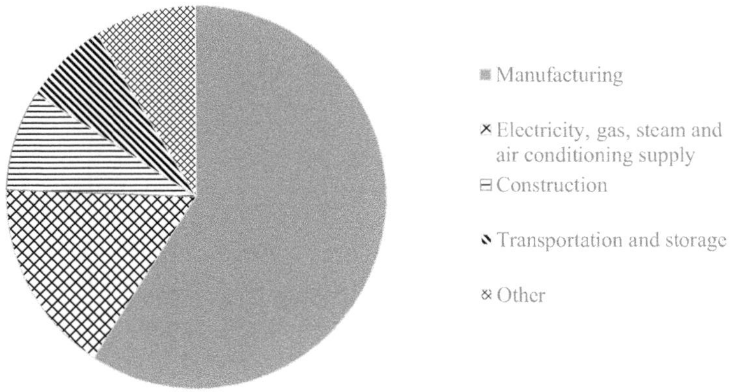

Figure 8.6 Share of individual industries according to NACE in the emission of carbon dioxide in the Slovak Republic [%].

The graphical representation shows that the main contributor to air pollution is the manufacturing sector, which is responsible for a substantial 58.11 per cent of CO_2 emissions (see Figure 8.6). This indicates that industrial production processes in the manufacturing sector contribute significantly to the release of carbon dioxide into the atmosphere. It is closely followed by the electricity, gas, steam and air conditioning supply sector, which accounts for 16.17 per cent of total emissions. The significant contribution of this sector highlights the importance of energy production methods in the overall carbon footprint. The third significant issuer is the construction sector, which represents a significant share of 8.37 per cent. This finding suggests that construction-related activities, including building and infrastructure development, contribute significantly to carbon emissions. In addition, the transport and storage sector appear to be a notable industry, responsible for 7.04 per cent of total emissions. Other industries with less than 2 per cent are grouped under 'other'. This underlines the impact of transport-related activities, such as the use of fossil fuels in vehicles and logistics associated with storage, on air quality and carbon emissions.

The sectoral breakdown provides valuable information on the sources of CO_2 emissions, enabling a targeted approach to the implementation of emission reduction strategies. By identifying the main contributors, policy makers and industries can formulate more effective and tailored measures to address the specific challenges presented by each sector. This comprehensive understanding of emission sources is critical to developing sustainable practices and mitigating the environmental impact associated with various industries. Since these are absolute values that do not reflect the size of the sector from the point of view of population employment, we also present the following table, which relates employment in the sector and the amount of emissions (Table 8.1).

Table 8.1 Employment in the sector and the amount of emissions

Sector	*CO_2 [thousand tonnes]*	*Share of Total CO_2 [%]*	*Employment rate [%]*	*CO_2 / Employment rate*
Manufacturing	16549.80	58.11	25.29	654.35
Electricity, gas, steam and air conditioning supply	4606.06	16.17	1.21	3811.71
Construction	2382.85	8.37	9.06	262.98
Transportation and storage	2005.60	7.04	6.38	314.20
Wholesale and retail trade; repair of motor vehicles and motorcycles	465.48	1.63	12.18	38.23
Administrative and support service activities	404.32	1.42	2.18	185.82
Public administration and defence; compulsory social security	247.01	0.87	8.66	28.51
Real estate activities	228.32	0.80	0.60	379.14
Agriculture, forestry and fishing	227.59	0.80	2.56	88.86
Human health and social work activities	161.22	0.57	7.46	21.61
Accommodation and food service activities	139.05	0.49	3.77	36.89
Other service activities	121.13	0.43	1.29	93.70
Arts, entertainment and recreation	101.42	0.36	1.33	76.32
Education	91.98	0.32	7.56	12.17
Water supply; sewerage, waste management and remediation activities	91.58	0.32	0.93	98.33
Information and communication	53.92	0.19	3.70	14.58
Financial and insurance activities	53.42	0.19	2.16	24.78
Mining and quarrying	48.33	0.17	0.29	169.55

Source: Own elaborate based on the data from the Eurostat (Eurostat, 2021d, 2021a).

The CO_2 / Employment rate index tells us how many thousand tonnes of emissions the industry produces for 1 percentage point of employment. This index tells us about the efficiency of industries and thanks to it we can compare individual industries with each other in terms of CO_2 emissions. The industry with the lowest emission efficiency per number of employees is Electricity, gas, steam and air conditioning supply with a value of 3811.71. The second least efficient sector is Manufacturing, where this index reaches up to 645.35 thousand tonnes. These industries are among those we have identified as reductive in previous research (Veteška and Kajanová, 2022). The manufacturing sector achieved the greatest difference compared to the structure of the economies of highly developed countries.

The most significant reductive industry that we identified, human health and social work activities, achieves an efficiency of 21.61 thousand tonnes of CO_2 per percentage of employment, which is significantly lower compared to reductive industries. We grouped reductive and prospective industries and performed an arithmetic average of CO_2 emissions per percentage of employment.

The data presented indicates a substantial difference in the average emitted emissions per percentage of employment between prospective and reductive industries (see Table 8.2). Specifically, prospective industries show an average of 58.40 thousand tonnes of CO_2, while reductive industries exhibit a significantly higher average of 1163.31 thousand tonnes. This disparity suggests that the structural composition of industries plays a crucial role in determining their carbon emissions per unit of employment. Prospective industries, which likely encompass sectors with forward-looking and environmentally conscious practices, emit

Table 8.2 Arithmetic average of CO_2 emissions per percentage of employment

Reductive		*Perspective*	
Water supply; sewerage, waste management and remediation activities	98.33	Human health and social work activities	21.61
Agriculture, forestry and fishing	88.86	Financial and insurance activities	24.78
Electricity, gas, steam and air conditioning supply	3811.71	Administrative and support service activities	185.82
Manufacturing	654.35	Other service activities	93.70
Average	**1163.31**	Information and communication	14.58
		Arts, entertainment and recreation	76.32
		Education	12.17
		Wholesale and retail trade; repair of motor vehicles and motorcycles	38.23
		Average	**58.40**

Source: Own elaborate based on the data from the Eurostat (Eurostat, 2021a, 2021d).

substantially less CO_2 per percentage of employment compared to reductive industries.

The statement puts forth a compelling argument: if the economy of the Slovak Republic undergoes a structural transformation in alignment with the observed trend in highly developed EU countries, there is a promising opportunity to achieve a substantial reduction in CO_2 emissions. This implies that strategically transitioning towards industries that prioritize sustainability, innovation, and reduced environmental impact can serve as a pivotal approach for effectively mitigating carbon emissions. By embracing and implementing such changes, the Slovak Republic has the potential not only to align with broader European sustainability goals but also pave the way for a more environmentally conscious and resilient economy.

8.6 Conclusion

Economic structural development involves the transformation of an economy from one dominated by 'dirty' industries, which often produce high levels of pollution and carbon emissions, to cleaner and more sustainable industries. This transition not only has environmental benefits but also positively impacts human health and social well-being. An example of such an economy based on 'dirty' industries is the Slovak economy, on which we conducted a case study focused on the analysis of emitted emissions in the context of GDP and employment. The analysis of the Slovak economy's CO_2 emissions and the profound influence of structural changes in the pursuit of decarbonization paints a roadmap towards a sustainable and environmentally responsible future. Slovakia, like many nations, stands at a crossroads, facing the dual challenges of economic growth and climate responsibility. This article has provided valuable insights into the intricacies of this transformation.

Structural changes in the economy emerge as the linchpin in achieving carbon neutrality. The embrace of 'green' industries, guided by advanced technologies associated with Industry 4.0, is the catalyst for a decarbonized future. The integration of sustainability and efficiency into economic activities is a promising path forward. The comparison with more advanced EU countries (like Sweden, Austria, Ireland, France) underscores the importance of learning from those who have already made significant strides in reducing emissions. Slovakia can glean inspiration from the experience of its European peers in setting emissions reduction targets and implementing policies that foster greener industries.

The journey towards decarbonization necessitates collaboration across sectors, a commitment to reducing energy dependence, and the implementation of progressive legislative interventions. It is not the responsibility of a single industry but a collective effort that will lead to success. In conclusion, the transformation of the Slovak economy from a high-emission, energy-intensive model to a sustainable, low-carbon economy is an achievable and necessary goal. The European Green Deal's ambition to reach carbon neutrality by 2050 is not unattainable; it is a challenge that can be met with vision, innovation, and dedication. This research has undertaken an in-depth investigation into the issue of CO_2 emissions within the context of individual industries, specifically focusing on the position of the Slovak Republic in the European Union. The examination encompasses several key dimensions to shed light on the nation's contribution to and potential for reducing CO_2 emissions.

In terms of total CO_2 emissions, Slovakia stands as the 20th largest contributor within the European Union. Germany takes the lead, while Malta produces the lowest. This initial assessment provides a crucial baseline for understanding Slovakia's environmental impact. To gain a more accurate understanding of the economy's emission efficiency, the research contextualizes GDP and emissions. The indicator that relates CO_2 emissions to GDP shows that Slovakia ranks lower. While Sweden emerges as a leader. The chapter underscores the need for Slovakia to enhance its economic efficiency in terms of emissions. The examination of the relationship between the share of energy from renewable sources and the efficiency of economies in relation to CO_2 emissions did not reveal a strong correlation. While Sweden excels in both areas, the analysis demonstrates that various factors influence emission efficiency, and renewable energy alone does not guarantee a significant improvement.

The chapter provides a breakdown of the share of different industries in carbon dioxide emissions within the Slovak Republic. The manufacturing sector emerges as the largest contributor. Electricity, gas, steam, and air conditioning supply follow. Examining the emissions in relation to the employment rate provides valuable insights into the efficiency of industries. The research highlights industries with potential for both emission reduction and economic growth. A comparison of emissions per employment percentage reveals that aligning with the trend in highly developed EU countries can lead to a significant CO_2 reduction. Prospective industries show much lower average emissions compared to reductive industries.

In sum, this research provides a comprehensive overview of Slovakia's CO_2 emissions landscape and the potential for reduction. While Slovakia's current emissions position within the EU is significant, the data and analysis offered here demonstrate that structural changes in the economy, inspired by successful models from highly developed countries, can lead to a more sustainable and environmentally responsible future. By optimizing economic efficiency, promoting renewable energy adoption, and reshaping the role of key industries, Slovakia can play a crucial role in achieving European climate goals and fostering a greener and more prosperous future. As Slovakia navigates this critical path, it must prioritize the reduction of emissions, foster green industries, and embrace cutting-edge technologies. Success in this endeavor will not only ensure environmental sustainability but also propel economic growth, create jobs, and enhance the country's resilience to global challenges. The shift towards a sustainable, decarbonized future represents an opportunity for Slovakia to lead by example in the broader European landscape and contribute to global efforts in combating climate change. The journey may be challenging, but the destination promises a more sustainable, equitable, and prosperous future for all.

8.7 Policy recommendations

Meeting the requirements of the European Green Deal is a significant challenge, but it is essential for addressing climate change and achieving environmental sustainability. Meeting the requirements necessitates a multifaceted approach involving government, industry, and civil society collaboration. Here are recommendations for Slovakia or any other country to work towards meeting the European Green Deal requirements. Increase investments in renewable energy sources, such as solar, wind, and hydropower, to transition away from fossil fuels. This should be accompanied by providing incentives and regulatory frameworks to make renewable energy projects more attractive for investors and consumers. Implement energy efficiency measures across various sectors, including residential, commercial, and industrial buildings. Encourage energy efficiency upgrades by offering financial incentives and tax benefits to businesses and individuals.

Encourage industries to adapt to cleaner technologies and practices by offering financial incentives or grants. Implement carbon pricing mechanisms to create economic incentives for industries to reduce emissions. The government can avail of various options which include grants, subsidies, and other schemes. To maintain GDP growth, we do not recommend the introduction of restrictive measures such as fines based on emissions, legislative restrictions, tax increases, bans, etc. A possible solution to this situation is also the modification of legislative frameworks, which would favor companies transforming their production towards decarbonization. From a financial point of view, such businesses could receive, for example, tax breaks or reduced tax rates. However, these measures must still be the subject of research so that they do not cause an outflow of investment and capital, which could slow down or even stop GDP growth. This issue must therefore be approached very sensitively, and interventions carried out only after an in-depth analysis of the environment.

Promoting circular economy principles to reduce waste, enhance recycling, and minimize resource consumption. Regulations and standards for sustainable product design and resource management should be enforced. Set clear, measurable emissions reduction targets for various sectors, including energy, transportation, and industry. These commitments should be legally binding to ensure accountability. Invest in research and development to create and implement new technologies and solutions for emissions reduction. Support startups and innovators in the green technology sector. Establish a robust system for monitoring and reporting on emissions, progress toward green goals, and the effectiveness of policies and initiatives. Transparency and accountability are crucial for ensuring that commitments are met. These recommendations provide a comprehensive framework also for other smaller countries to transition to a more sustainable and carbon-neutral future, aligning with the objectives of the European Green Deal.

Acknowledgements

This work was supported by the Slovak Research and Development Agency Grant No APVV-20-0012.

References

Baudry, M., 2021. Low-carbon transition of EU-ETS firms: Assessing the long-term effects of Covid-19, in: Belaid, F., Creti, A. (Eds), *Energy, Transition, Climate Change, and COVID-19*. Springer. Cham, pp. 45–72. Springer, ISBN 978-3-030-79712-6.

Blum, S., Hone, D., 2020. Green building and energy efficiency in the building sector: A review and analysis of recent policies and programs. *J. Clean. Prod.* 244, 118758.

CEIC, 2023. Slovakia Motor Vehicle Production, 1997–2023 | CEIC Data [WWW Document]. URL www.ceicdata.com/en/indicator/slovakia/motor-vehicle-production (accessed 1.26.24).

D'Amato, D., Droste, N., Allen, B., 2017. Sustainable business model innovation: Exploring an integrated value perspective. *J. Clean. Prod.* 147, 44–56.

European Commission, 2022. 2050 long-term strategy. https://climate.ec.europa.eu/eu-action/climate-strategies-targets/2050-long-term-strategy_en (accessed 11.6.23).

Eurostat, 2021a. Air emissions accounts by NACE Rev. 2 activity [WWW Document]. URL https://ec.europa.eu/eurostat/databrowser/view/env_ac_ainah_r2__custom_8341828/default/table?lang=en (accessed 1.26.24).

Eurostat, 2021b. GDP and main components (output, expenditure and income) [WWW Document]. URL https://ec.europa.eu/eurostat/databrowser/view/nama_10_gdp/default/table?lang=en (accessed 1.26.24).

Eurostat, 2021c. Energy supply and use by NACE Rev. 2 activity [WWW Document]. URL https://ec.europa.eu/eurostat/databrowser/view/env_ac_pefasu/default/table?lang=en (accessed 1.26.24).

Eurostat, 2021d. Employment by sex, age and economic activity (from 2008 onwards, NACE Rev. 2) – 1 000 [WWW Document]. URL https://ec.europa.eu/eurostat/databrowser/view/LFSA_EGAN2/default/table?lang=en&category=labour.employ.lfsa.lfsa_emp (accessed 11.21.22).

Geels, F.W., Sovacool, B.K., Schwanen, T., Sorrell, S., 2017. Sociotechnical transitions for deep decarbonization. *Science* 357, 1242–1244.

Gillingham, K., Knittel, C.R., Li, J., Ovaere, M., Reguant, M., 2020. The short-run and long-run effects of COVID-19 on energy and the environment. *Joule* 4, 1337–1341. https://doi.org/10.1016/j.joule.2020.06.006

IEA, 2020. Energy technology perspectives 2020. *Catal. Energy Technol. Transform. 182.*

Intergovernmental Panel on Climate Change, 2021. Climate Change 2021: The Physical Science Basis. Intergovernmental Panel on Climate Change.

International Labour Organization, 2018. World Employment and Social Outlook: Greening with Jobs. International Labour Organization.

International Trade Administration, 2020. Slovakia Automotive Market.

Klemeš, J.J., Van Fan, Y., Tan, R.R., Jiang, P., 2020. Minimising the present and future plastic waste, energy and environmental footprints related to COVID-19. *Renew. Sustain. Energy Rev.* 127, 109883.

Krozer, Y., 2022. Economics of Renewable Energy: An Assessment of Innovations with Statistical Data. Springer International Publishing. https://link.springer.com/book/10.1007/978-3-030-99480-6.

Le Quéré, C., Jackson, R.B., Jones, M.W., Smith, A.J.P., Abernethy, S., Andrew, R.M., De-Gol, A.J., Willis, D.R., Shan, Y., Canadell, J.G., et al., 2020. Temporary reduction in daily global CO_2 emissions during the COVID-19 forced confinement. *Nat. Clim. Change* 10, 647–653. https://doi.org/10.1038/s41558-020-0797-x

Liu, D., Zhou, Y., Wild, O., Bartlam-Brooks, H., Boucher, O., Jones, A., Vaughan, A.R., 2021. Air quality and climate change: Designing the next generation air quality monitoring strategies towards a sustainable future. *Environ. Pollut.* 278, 116832. https://doi.org/10.1016/j.envpol.2021.116832

Matemilola, S., Fadeyi, O., Sijuade, T., 2023. Paris Agreement, in: Idowu, S.O., Schmidpeter, R., Capaldi, N., Zu, L., Del Baldo, M., Abreu, R. (Eds), *Encyclopedia of Sustainable Management*. Springer International Publishing, Cham, pp. 2555–2559. https://doi.org/10.1007/978-3-031-25984-5_516

Napp, T.A., Gambhir, A., Hills, T.P., Florin, N., Fennell, P.S., 2014. A review of the technologies, economics and policy instruments for decarbonising energy-intensive manufacturing industries. *Renew. Sustain. Energy Rev.* 30, 616–640.

Pee, A. de, Pinner, D., Roelofsen, O., Somers, K., 2018. Decarbonization of industrial sectors: The next frontier. McKinsey & Company. New York. www.mckinsey.com/business-functions/sustainability/our-insights/decarbonization-of-industrial-sectors-the-next-frontier.

Potrč, S., Nemet, A., Čuček, L., Varbanov, P.S., Kravanja, Z., 2022. Synthesis of a regenerative energy system–beyond carbon emissions neutrality. *Renew. Sustain. Energy Rev.* 169, 112924.

Slovak Press Agency (Slovenská tlačová agentúra), 2023. Investícia automobilky Volvo na východe Slovenska je v ďalšej fáze – [WWW Document]. SITA.sk. URL https://sita.sk/vpriemysle/investicia-automobilky-volvo-je-v-dalsej-faze-planuju-u-nas-vyrobit-500-tisic-aut-rocne/ (accessed 1.26.24).

Sovacool, B.K., Burke, M., Baker, L.A., Kotikalapudi, C.K., Thompson, L.R., Kahumbu, D., 2021. Global employment and job creation from renewable energy, energy efficiency, and clean technology activities. *Energy Res. Soc. Sci.* 76, 101670.

Teixidó, J., Verde, S.F., Nicolli, F., 2019. The impact of the EU Emissions Trading System on low-carbon technological change: The empirical evidence. *Ecol. Econ.* 164, 106347.

Tokarcikova, E., Kucharcikova, A., Janosova, P., 2022. The relationship between environmental and economic aspects for measuring the sustainability of the enterprise: A case study of Slovak manufacturing enterprises. *Int. J. Environ. Res. Public. Health* 19, 7784. https://doi.org/10.3390/ijerph19137784

Veteška, L., Kajanová, J., 2022. Comparison of the structure of the Slovak economy and the most developed EU countries. *Acta Oeconomica Univ. Selye* 11, 73–86.

Vieira, L.C., Longo, M., Mura, M., 2021. Are the European manufacturing and energy sectors on track for achieving net-zero emissions in 2050? An empirical analysis. *Energy Policy* 156, 112464. https://doi.org/10.1016/j.enpol.2021.112464

Wang, Q., Zhao, M., Li, R., 2019. Decoupling sectoral economic output from carbon emissions on city level: A comparative study of Beijing and Shanghai, China. *J. Clean. Prod.* 209, 126–133.

Wei, X., Wu, G., Zhang, X., 2021. Skills development in green sectors: A comparative analysis of the photovoltaic and wind power industries in China. *Energy Policy* 149, 112082.

Wesseling, J.H., Lechtenbohmer, S., Ahman, M., Nilsson, L.J., Worrell, E., Coenen, L., 2016. How to decarbonise energy-intensive processing industries?: Survey and conceptualisation of their specific innovation systems. *Proceeding ECEEE Ind. Effic.* 1–16.
Zeng, S., Xu, B., 2020. Renewable energy and employment in China. *Appl. Energy* 276, 115462.

9 A quantitative assessment of energy security in EU member states following COVID-19 and the energy crisis

Ivana Gondášová

9.1 Introduction

Throughout the past two decades, European Union (EU) energy security policy has made significant strides, adapting to fast-changing geopolitical dynamics and the climate crisis along the way. The EU, notably, has forged considerable progress in diversifying its energy sources, bolstering energy efficiency, and reducing dependency on external suppliers. The bloc's commitment to renewable energy and stringent emissions reduction targets has, furthermore, contributed to enhancing its energy security by mitigating climate-related risks. Accordingly, the latter half of the 2000s witnessed a discernible rise in the prevalence of climate mitigation policies, which began to intersect with the domain of energy policy (Mišík, 2022). Since the ratification of the Lisbon Treaty in 2009,[1] the EU has displayed a high level of engagement in crafting legislative packages and shaping policy frameworks that align energy and climate policy objectives under newly introduced specific legal bases for EU energy policy, which has been categorized as a 'shared competence' between the EU and member states (MSs).[2] The EU has since solidified its position as a significant international actor[3] in the climate and environmental policy arena (Oberthür & Kelly, 2008).

Despite this success, challenges have persisted, including the impact of geopolitical tensions on energy supply routes (Kuzemko, et al., 2020) and the ongoing transition towards a sustainable, decarbonized energy system. Criticism, for instance, has mounted against the EU's greater dependence on fossil fuels, particularly energy sourced from Russia, with Moscow responsible for 43 per cent of natural gas imports (European Commission, 2022a) and 29 per cent of oil imports (Eurostat, 2023) into the EU in 2021. In a similar vein, the establishment of ambitious targets in the Paris Agreement[4] and the European Green Deal[5] as part of the EU clean-energy transition was interrupted by the COVID-19 pandemic and a subsequent energy crisis. Russia's invasion of Ukraine on 24 February 2022, has further exacerbated the energy crisis and significantly affected the state of energy security in the EU's member states.

Due to the unavailability of data for 2022 and 2023, this chapter focuses on the period until 2021. In 2020 and 2021, the primary focus of governments worldwide

DOI: 10.4324/9781032624839-12

revolved around addressing the implications posed by the pandemic and an energy crisis. Although the outbreak of the pandemic had a profound impact primarily on public health and the global economy, it nonetheless also constituted a substantial setback for the energy sector (Abu-Rayash & Dincer, 2020; Karakosta, et al., 2021). Even meticulously crafted and firmly established energy policies were put into question (Steffen, et al., 2020). Stringent containment measures broadly reduced demand throughout the first quarter of 2020, with energy production levels, in turn, significantly adjusted. The IEA called the decline in energy demand in early 2020 "the biggest shock since the Second World War" (International Energy Agency, 2020). However, the challenges thrust on the table by the COVID-19 pandemic were further compounded by the onset of an energy crisis in 2021. The rebound from the economic slowdown experienced in 2020 has been attributed as a primary cause of the energy crisis, with such a crisis defined as a situation characterized by an imminent risk of resource scarcity, restricted availability of resources, compromised security of supply, and elevated environmental apprehension (Simmons, et al., 2014). On that account, the energy crisis in the EU has been characterized by a compromised security of supply, with lower-than-expected supply from Russia[6] amid a strong recovery in energy demand, and several weather-related factors also contributing to soaring energy prices.

The implications of these crises have been examined by a range of scholars (von Homeyer, et al., 2021; Mišík & Nosko, 2023b; Sovacool, et al., 2020) and will likewise be the subject of scrutiny in this chapter. The primary objectives of this research, can be delineated into two distinct aims. The foremost objective involves a quantitative assessment of energy security across a subset of EU MSs. These 25 EU MSs encompass Austria, Belgium, Bulgaria, Croatia, the Czech Republic, Denmark, Estonia, Finland, France, Germany, Greece, Hungary, Ireland, Italy, Latvia, Lithuania, Luxembourg, the Netherlands, Poland, Portugal, Romania, Slovakia, Slovenia, Spain, and Sweden. Cyprus and Malta were excluded from the analysis, as these two member states do not report data for several indicators because of their energy portfolios, hindering comparative analysis. This assessment has been conducted by measuring the values of countries on the Energy Security Index (ESI), which stands as the cornerstone contribution of this study.

The second objective pertains to a longitudinal analysis of the evolution of the ESI over a decade (2012–2021), with an examination of performance before and after destabilizing events (the outbreak of COVID-19 and the energy crisis). The rationale for the 2012–2021 scope pertains to the availability of data. In this regard, the chapter analyzes year-to-year progress, focusing on 'near real-time' events to assess the short to medium-term stance of EU energy security. Furthermore, this chapter endeavors to seamlessly integrate the EU's climate and energy policy initiatives targeted towards promoting the energy transition and combatting climate change (such initiatives are embedded within the European Green Deal (EGD) or its Energy Union predecessor) into the energy security analytical framework. This is achieved through a test of the following hypothesis: The implementation of three key principles of the clean energy transition results in the enhancement of energy security. This analysis is directed toward an evaluation of the implementation of clean energy transition objectives, such as the integration of renewable energy sources (RES), advancements in energy efficiency, and reductions in carbon dioxide (CO_2) emissions, across the designated countries. In the context of the crises, EGD attained an instrumental role. Firstly, it was characterized as a "lifeline out of the COVID-19 pandemic" (European Commission, n.d.). Moreover, in the context of the energy crisis, which has been exacerbated by the Ukrainian conflict, the European Commission (EC) has called for "higher or earlier targets for renewable energy and energy efficiency" (European Commission, 2022b). The hypothesis tests, therefore, are tailored toward ascertaining the extent to which the implementation of these strategic actions contributes to ESI changes, particularly during periods of energy crises. This analysis, engaging with several key questions, further endeavors to contribute to the assessment of EU energy security and appropriate policy responses, alongside the broader domain of EU energy and climate policy.

The chapter, firstly, interrogates how the energy security performance of EU member states has changed over the past decade. The analysis, in this regard, examines a decade-long period to determine whether changes are positive, i.e. the EU entered a path towards becoming (more) secure, or the reverse. The analysis subsequently sheds light on whether these changes are characteristic of a uniform approach across the EU or, on the contrary, a divergent approach related to individual country-specific approaches. Secondly, taking into account the stated hypothesis, the chapter scrutinizes whether the implementation of energy transition policy initiatives has resulted in a distinct change in the ESI over a ten-year period. Finally, emphasizing the assessment of impacts from the COVID-19 pandemic and the subsequent energy crisis, the chapter explores how these events influenced the energy security performance of EU member states.

The chapter proceeds as follows. The next section introduces the current state of EU energy security and policy and discusses the primary research objectives and questions against this backdrop. This is followed by a discussion of the conceptualization and operationalization of energy security in this research analysis. This section also expounds on the use of z-score standardization as the key methodology for the calculation of ESI scores. The chapter subsequently explains the findings of the quantitative analysis, focusing on the energy security performance of EU MSs over one decade. Finally, the conclusion summarizes the main findings of the research.

9.2 Developing an Energy Security Index

Energy security is a widely discussed notion in academic literature. Despite its significance to contemporary political agendas, the absence of a universally accepted definition of energy security among the international community underlines the muddle involving the concept. Correspondingly, several authors have highlighted the confusion regarding the term's definition, characterizing it as 'polysemic' (Chester, 2010), 'blurred' (Löschel, et al., 2010), and 'elusive' (Kruyt, et al.,

2009). This observation is particularly intriguing given that the term itself has evolved over more than four decades (Zhiznin, et al., 2020). However, a comprehensive review of the existing literature underscores the intricate nature of the energy security concept (for instance, see Winzer (2012), Cherp & Jewell (2014), Sovacool & Mukherjee (2011), Kruyt, et. al (2009), Sovacool & Brown (2010)), which is contingent upon a multitude of factors. Given the focus of this research, which centers on conducting a quantitative assessment of energy security performance within the EU, the examination here draws on the conceptual framework and methodology developed by Sovacool and Brown (2010) and further substantiated by Brown et al. (2014).

The framework proposed by Brown et al. (2014) delineates energy security as "equitably providing available, affordable, reliable, efficient, environmentally benign, proactively governed and socially acceptable energy services to end-users" (p. 65). Four dimensions of energy security emerge from the definition, namely: 'Availability', 'Affordability', 'Energy and economic efficiency', and 'Environmental stewardship', with the authors underscoring the imperative of addressing all four dimensions holistically. Their analysis stresses the prudence of embracing a comprehensive approach to energy security that refrains from prioritizing supply security and affordability to the detriment of stewardship and efficiency, or vice versa. This suggested strategy instead confers equitable significance on every criterion rather than granting preferential status to specific dimensions. In light of the broad deployment of this approach in the literature (Sovacool & Brown, 2010; Sovacool, 2011; Sovacool, 2014), this chapter similarly refrains from delineating the core attributes of each energy security dimension or delving into the causal linkages between them. Nonetheless, it is imperative to explain the twofold rationale underpinning the selection of this conceptual and methodological framework.

First, the operationalization of the four dimensions is facilitated by the availability of pertinent data, enabling the construction of a comprehensive ESI and facilitating the quantitative assessment of each dimension and the subsequent measurement of energy security performance within distinct countries. Second, the use of z-score normalization enables the identification of discernible trends and trajectories. This methodology further permits the normalization of indicators characterized by diverse units of measurement, aligning suitably with the exigencies of this chapter. The z-score normalization approach has indeed been frequently used within scholarly literature. For instance, Brown, et al. (2014) deployed the method to analyze the energy security performance of 22 countries in the Organization for Economic Cooperation and Development (OECD) while Bogoviz, et al. (2017) assessed the energy security performance of Eurasian Economic Union (EAEU) member states and, in 2019, assessed the energy security of BRICS countries (Bogoviz, et al., 2019). Lobova, et al. (2019), moreover, used the z-score standardization method to quantitatively assess the energy security of the member countries of CIS. Obadi and Korcek (2020), for their part, used the method to quantify the energy security of selected EU countries. As with the research presented here, these scholarly works used z-score standardization to quantitatively assess the energy security performance of countries united by their common membership of a union or a group of states.

Within the scope of this chapter, the analysis delves into the assessment of the energy security of individual EU MSs. This approach is justified by the fact that most energy planning and policymaking occurs at country level, with important energy statistics also collected and specified as "within country". Despite the EC's increasing involvement in the energy sector, key political decisions still predominantly lie at the state level. Consequently, member states serve as the units of analysis for the index, potentially overlooking the significance of energy policy decisions made at different levels. The final ESI consists of a comprehensive set of indicators selected to encapsulate the multidimensional approach towards energy security. The principal objective lies in the selection of indicators that are readily accessible and could function as reliable proxies for the four dimensions within the ESI. This endeavor sought to mitigate the risk of overweighting through extraneous indicators. All data were derived from Eurostat based on the 2012–2021 scope of the study.

First, the dimension of 'Availability' consists of three indicators, namely 'oil import dependency', 'gas import dependency' and 'solid fuels import dependency'. The focus on major fossil fuels is justified by the fact that they account for most energy use in EU countries over the past decade. Dependency on fossil fuels has been calculated using the Eurostat solid harmonized methodology, ensuring high comparability between EU MSs (Eurostat, n.d.). The 'natural gas prices for household sector' and 'electricity prices for household sector' indicators were selected as proxies to measure the dimension of 'Affordability'. The indicators represent the prices for household consumers, rather than non-households, providing a more appropriate assessment of how energy is used by populations.[7] In addition, both indicators reflect the values in purchasing power standard (PPS) to ensure comparability. The dimension of 'Energy efficiency' consists of three reliable metrics, namely 'energy productivity', 'energy', and 'share of renewable energy sources'. These three indicators aptly depict the extent to which the respective countries have incorporated the key principles of the green energy transition and, correspondingly, how successful they have been with respect to the enhancement of energy efficiency. Lastly, the dimension of 'Environmental stewardship' is measured through the 'greenhouse gas emissions by energy sector' metric. This indicator provides a measurement of the performance of individual countries on environmental protection and climate change policies aimed at the reduction of greenhouse gas (GHG) emissions. The calculation of z-scores for each indicator from 2012 to 2021 involved subtracting the mean value for each data point and dividing it by the indicator's standard deviation. The resulting z-score is a dimensionless quantity, which indicates how many standard deviations an EU MS deviates from the mean value of the 25 EU MSs analyzed herein (Brown, et al., 2014). The z-scores were then summed for each year, providing a total energy security score for each country over the 10-year period selected. On that account, the variables were structured in a manner such that higher values correspond to an enhanced degree of energy security.

In addition, z-scores are effective in distinguishing between 'common cause' variation in the data, when all countries experience similar changes, versus 'special cause' variation in the data, when specific steps taken by a single country leads to significant changes in the energy security performance of the respective state. A focus on common cause and special cause variations is particularly important for evaluating ESI values, so as to discern whether EU MSs performance has been shaped by shared factors or whether the final ESI values represent special cause variations, i.e., changes at the national level within a single state. In accordance with the abovementioned conceptual and methodological framework developed by Sovacool & Brown (2010) and Brown et al. (2014), it is essential to recognize the limitations that this approach yields. As the authors note, construction of such an index

> is not meant to imply that quantitative measures of energy security are perfect or that reducing complex situations to numbers is without problems. Numerical indices often highlight not what is most significant or meaningful but merely what is measurable. Quantitative measurements, especially those taken out of context, can also conceal important nuances and variability.
>
> (p. 87)

Furthermore, the composition of the ESI and indicator selection are constrained by data availability. The absence of data prevents the establishment of an optimal set of indicators. Additionally, it should be noted that, due to the variance in the number of indicators across dimensions, an inherent bias exists towards putting undue weight on dimensions consisting of a greater number of indicators. Given that the indicators were attributed equal weighting and the scoring technique was relatively crude, it is important to note that the employment of more sophisticated multivariate statistical analyses has the potential to generate more nuanced and potentially divergent outcomes, thus providing a promising avenue for future investigation.

9.3 A decade of energy security performance among EU MSs

This section outlines and evaluates the results obtained from the quantitative assessment of energy security within EU MSs and puts forward findings with respect to the abovementioned research questions.

9.3.1 Has the EU entered a path towards becoming (more) secure?

The quantitative assessment of energy security has revealed the final ESI score for each of the 25 EU MSs analyzed herein and their development patterns throughout 2012–2021. Figure 9.1 presents a graphical illustration of the final annual ESI scores from 2012 to 2021.

Quantitative analysis underlines notable disparities in the ESI scores of EU MSs. Denmark is consistently ranked as the most energy-secure country from 2012

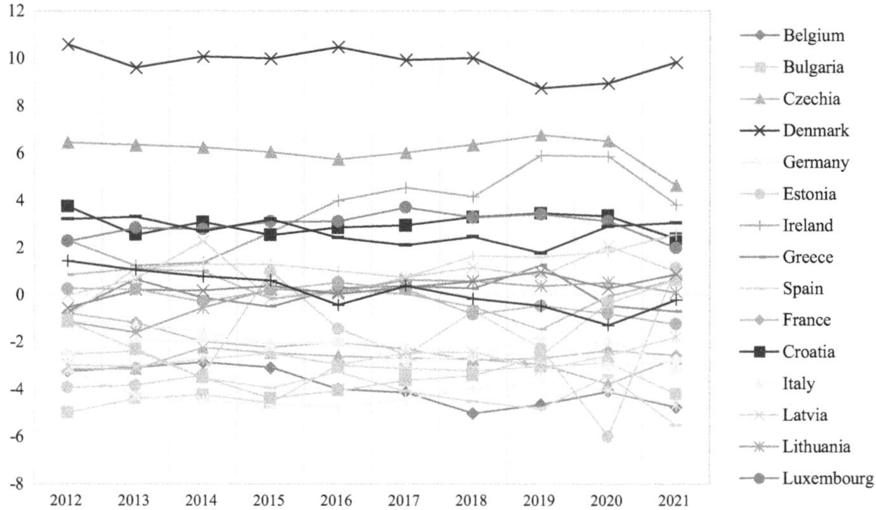

Figure 9.1 Final scores of ESI for 25 EU MSs from 2012 to 2021.

to 2021, owing to its low reliance on fossil fuel imports and high energy-efficiency scores. Similarly, Romania maintained the second-highest ESI scores during this period, attributed to its low energy-import dependence and strong energy-efficiency indicators. Ireland, meanwhile, recorded the third-highest ESI score in 2021, displaying a significant improvement since 2012 (nearly doubling its score), largely due to advancements in energy efficiency. Conversely, Germany, Belgium, and Spain ranked lowest in ESI, indicating room for improvement in their energy security measures. From 2012 to 2021, the ESI scores of these countries worsened significantly, with each facing distinct challenges. Germany saw its ESI score decline primarily due to exceptionally high greenhouse gas emissions from energy production, coupled with increasing fossil fuel imports and rising prices. Belgium, for its part, struggled with notably poor energy efficiency, ranking second lowest in the EU, after Bulgaria. Finally, Spain had the lowest ESI in the EU during this period, primarily due to an increasing reliance on fossil fuel imports, declining energy efficiency, and escalating energy costs.

Among the 25 EU MSs assessed here, three distinct trends have emerged over the period analyzed. First, ten states, including Bulgaria, the Czech Republic, Estonia, Ireland, Latvia, Lithuania, Hungary, Portugal, Slovenia and Slovakia, improved their energy security. While these improvements were noteworthy, their ESI scores still lagged behind those of the EU leaders. For instance, Slovakia, the Czech Republic, and Bulgaria saw enhancements in ESI, but their scores remained in negative territory, signifying the need for further progress. Lithuania, Latvia, Portugal, Slovenia, Hungary, and Estonia demonstrated more substantial improvements, turning negative 2012 ESI values into positives by 2021. Latvia

Table 9.1 Development of individual dimensions: A comparison 2012–2021

	Availability	*Affordability*	*Energy efficiency*	*Environmental stewardship*	*Energy security performance*
Bulgaria	↓	↓	↑	↓	improved
Czech Republic	↓	↓	↑	↓	improved
Estonia	↓	↓	↑	↑	improved
Ireland	↓	↓	↑	↓	improved
Latvia	↓	↑	↑	↑	improved
Lithuania	↑	↓	↓	↓	improved
Hungary	↑	↓	↑	↓	improved
Portugal	↓	↓	↑	↑	improved
Slovenia	↓	↓	↓	↑	improved
Slovakia	↓	↓	↑	↓	improved

Source: Author's own data.

Note Table 9.1 displays the development of individual dimensions among the 10 EU MSs, whose ESI improved from 2012 to 2021. Note that a decrease in the Availability, Affordability and Environmental Stewardship dimensions indicates improvement, whereas an increase indicates weakening. Conversely, a decrease in the Energy Efficiency dimension reflects deterioration, while an increase indicates improvement.

made the most remarkable improvement, followed by Hungary. Ireland, initially with a positive 2012 ESI, continued to strengthen its energy security, securing the third-highest ESI ranking in 2021. Table 9.1 outlines the diverse pathways taken by these states to enhance their ESI across four dimensions between 2012 and 2021.

Some countries achieved a better ESI score through improved affordability (e.g., Latvia, Lithuania, Bulgaria, Hungary), while others benefitted from a combination of lower prices and enhanced energy efficiency (Slovenia, Czechia). A few reduced their dependence on fossil fuels, alongside either heightened energy efficiency or lower prices (Estonia, Slovakia, Portugal). A second group of countries, however, experienced only minimal changes in their ESI scores. Although Denmark, Austria, Luxembourg, and the Netherlands witnessed slight declines in their ESI, they maintained positive scores. Interestingly, Greece's ESI path showed a positive trend over the 10-year period; however, its score remained the same in 2021 as in 2012. Poland's ESI score deteriorated only slightly yet slipped into negative territory. Lastly, nine countries experienced worsening ESI scores throughout the decade. The ESI scores of Romania and Croatia declined but remained positive. Sweden and Finland, by contrast, shifted from positive ESI scores in 2012 to negative values in 2021. France, Italy, Germany, Belgium, and Spain experienced a sustained decline in their ESIs. The causes of these negative trends varied, with some attributed to higher prices (Sweden, Romania, France) and others the product of higher prices and increased import dependency (Spain, Germany, Luxembourg). Some countries recorded a rise in their dependence on fossil fuel imports, paired with declining energy efficiency and/or higher prices (Croatia, Poland).

Based on these quantitative data, this section contributes to the main objective of this volume inquiring into (1) whether the EU has become (more) secure and (2) examining whether ESI changes are the result of common cause variations experienced uniformly across the EU or special cause variations distinct to individual countries. Figure 9.1 illustrates that ten EU MSs improved their energy security although some still report negative values (an indication of energy insecurity).[8] By contrast, fourteen countries exhibited a declining ESI trend, signifying a failure to enhance their energy security performance. However, as portrayed in Figure 9.1, it is worth noting that six EU MSs[9] saw a minor decline in their ESI scores from 2012 to 2021, with their overall placement still remaining on the positive end of the spectrum. Conversely, the remaining 8 EU MSs[10] experienced a steady decline in the ESI, indicating a failure to enhance energy security.

The ESI findings underscore the presence of special cause variation, suggesting that specific actions taken by individual countries prompted changes in their respective final ESI scores, such as national initiatives to enhance energy security. The evolution path of energy security performance across EU MSs, in fact, indicates the lack of a unified approach among member states. In this regard, the EU's shared competence in energy policy, as stipulated in the Lisbon Treaty, has not translated into a uniform strategy; countries are pursuing their own paths towards achieving energy security. The national variations in the development patterns of ESI scores indeed underscore that the EU's energy policy continues to be shaped by member state decisions and distinct domestic factors. Other scholarly work, such as the research by Maltby (2013) and Tagliapietra (2014), has produced similar findings.

This analysis now turns to further concentrating on an assessment of the relationship between the energy security of EU MSs and the green energy transformation through hypothesis testing. While this sub-section evaluated the energy security performance among EU MSs over a decade, the following section focuses on an assessment of the interplay between energy security and the implementation of the three key principles of the clean energy transition.

9.3.2 Green energy transformation vs energy security: what is the relationship?

The green energy transition presents a promising opportunity for MSs to simultaneously achieve carbon neutrality and enhance energy security. The EU, to this end, has sought to pivot away from fossil fuels and towards the widespread adoption of RES. Against this backdrop, this sub-section aims to ascertain the extent to which the implementation of green energy transition policy initiatives is genuinely impacting ESI scores. In other words, the objective here is to establish whether energy security is enhanced by the enactment of clean energy transition principles. This is to be achieved through a test of the following hypothesis: *The implementation of the three key principles of the clean energy transition results in the enhancement of energy security* (as indicated by distinct changes in final ESI scores).

The initial analysis, employing Eurostat data, reveals a positive trend across the selected indicators, all indicative of improvements in energy efficiency. Over the decade's research scope, the indicators for energy production and share of renewable energy sources demonstrated consistent growth, while the energy intensity indicator gradually decreased. Additionally, a majority of countries successfully reduced their greenhouse gas emissions from energy, though some member states, such as Hungary and Ireland, faced challenges in this regard. Despite these positive developments in indicators, which underscore the EU's progress towards decarbonization and enhanced energy efficiency, this analysis indicates that the focus on the implementation of green energy transition initiatives has not led to a distinct change in the ESI for most MSs.

However, comparing Sweden, Luxembourg, and the Netherlands to other MSs, it is noteworthy that their z-scores for the energy efficiency dimension exhibited considerable growth over the period analyzed. Simultaneously, the z-scores for GHG emissions from energy in these three countries recorded an incremental positive trend. Despite these improvements, the final ESI scores for this triad declined over the research period, hindered by a growing dependence on energy imports. It is also notable that the z-scores for the energy efficiency and environmental stewardship dimensions have undergone minimal or no changes over the ten years for many MSs. As a result, these marginal shifts have had little impact on the overall development pattern of the final ESI scores. An unfavorable z-score trend over a decade was apparent in some cases, with 2021 values receding compared to 2012. These declines were accompanied by negative shifts in the final ESI scores.

Nevertheless, the ESI scores of two EU member states offer compelling evidence that a concentrated effort on enhancing energy efficiency while concurrently decreasing greenhouse gas emissions can result in notable advancements in energy security performance. First, Ireland provides an exceptional case, demonstrating a substantial enhancement in energy security performance over a decade. Ireland's ESI performance in 2012, notably, lagged behind other countries. A considerable improvement in in energy efficiency, with its z-score nearly doubling from 2012 to 2021, coupled with reduced import dependency on fossil fuels, nonetheless, led to an overall improvement in the energy security of the country. Estonia, similarly, showcases how the amplification of energy efficiency, a reduction in GHG emissions, and a decrease in import dependency on fossil fuels can contribute to a positive trajectory in energy security performance.

However, despite concerted efforts to enhance energy efficiency, promote RES, and mitigate CO_2 emissions, a majority of MSs have struggled to reduce their dependence on fossil fuel imports. This challenge has limited the effectiveness of initiatives aimed at improving energy efficiency and emissions reduction, thereby impeding their potential to positively impact their overall energy security performance. However, it is worth noting that two MSs, Ireland and Estonia, serve as notable exceptions, demonstrating that accelerating the energy transition through measures like enhanced energy efficiency, reduced emissions, and restrictions on fossil fuel consumption can indeed lead to improved energy security. Hence, while energy efficiency measures are essential, reducing fossil fuel dependence remains a significant challenge.

9.3.3 Implications of the COVID-19 pandemic and the energy crisis on the energy security performance of EU MSs

The far-reaching consequences of COVID-19 and the unprecedented energy crisis have catapulted energy security to the top of the agenda for the EU and countries worldwide. Although the impact of the current energy crisis is likely to be profound, this section concentrates on the assessment of final ESI scores for the period spanning 2019–2021. It examines the development pattern of the ESI and scrutinizes energy security both before and after the pandemic and the energy crisis to determine the impact of these two destabilizing events on the energy security performance of MSs. The analysis revealed that the crises had divergent implications on the ESI scores of MSs. Some countries witnessed a significant decline in their ESI scores, while others saw notable improvements. Additionally, in some cases, the ESI displayed variable tendencies, such as an initial increase followed by a subsequent decrease or vice versa during the 2019–2021 period (see Figure 9.1). The destabilizing events negatively impacted the energy security performance of seven countries, whose ESI had been on a declining trajectory from 2019 to 2021.

These countries include Germany, Ireland, Greece, Croatia, Luxembourg, Romania, and Finland. Their energy security performance declined in 2020 and continued to deteriorate in 2021. Conversely, Denmark, Hungary, the Netherlands, Austria, Portugal, and Slovakia managed to enhance their energy security performance despite the crises. The steady decline of ESI within the first group of states was primarily driven by higher import dependency and increased energy prices, reflecting negative changes in the 'Availability' and 'Affordability' dimensions. Therefore, the drop in ESI placement can be understood through the lens of geopolitical issues, including a significant rise in energy demand in 2021 following a deceleration sparked by COVID-19 and sharp price increases in 2021 related to the energy crisis. In contrast, the ESI of countries in the second group improved, primarily due to reduced import dependency, reflecting positive changes in the 'Availability' dimension, with minor changes or improvements in the 'Affordability' dimension. This stands in contrast to the dynamics observed in the former group.

The implications of the pandemic and energy crisis on the ESI scores of the remaining countries have been variable. Initially, some MSs experienced a decline in their ESI from 2019 to 2020. However, in 2021, there was a notable reversal, with ESI scores showing an upward trend. Therefore, the temporary decline in the ESI observed in Czechia, Estonia, Poland, Slovenia, and Sweden in 2020 had no lasting impact, as the z-scores for 2021 indicated a return to pre-COVID-19 values or even higher. In contrast, Belgium, Bulgaria, Spain, France, Italy, Latvia, and Lithuania witnessed positive changes in their year-to-year ESI scores between 2019 and 2020. However, in 2021, their energy security performance regressed to levels similar to, or lower than, those observed in 2019.

The outbreak of the COVID-19 pandemic and the subsequent energy crisis had varying impacts on the final ESI scores of MSs. For some, the recovery in global demand and the surge in prices has led to adverse developments in availability and affordability because of higher import dependency and increased energy prices. Similarly, the implementation of anti-pandemic measures throughout 2020 and 2021 (Chong, et al., 2022; Steffen, et al., 2020) has had an adverse effect on ongoing energy transition and support for deepening energy security. This was particularly evident in certain MSs (e.g., Germany and Romania) where energy security performance deteriorated, due to a considerable decline in energy efficiency. Conversely, the MSs that have seen growth in their ESI scores, despite multiple crises, underscore the crucial role of government intervention in facilitating economic recovery in the post-pandemic era, as emphasized by Kuzemko, et.al. (2020), as well as the need to focus on measures to boost investments in energy efficiency, thereby converting challenges posed by the pandemic and energy crisis into opportunities (Karakosta, et al., 2021).

9.4 Conclusion

This chapter has expounded on the approach and findings of a comprehensive assessment of EU energy security that was conducted via the calculation of ESI scores. The overall aim was directed at analyzing index trends during 2012–2021 to identify and scrutinize changes in EU energy security, with an emphasis on the final two years, which were affected by destabilizing events. On that account, the first part of the quantitative evaluation provided an overview concerning the development of the energy security performance of MSs, steered towards ascertaining whether the EU entered a path towards becoming (more) secure. The findings indicate that ten MSs indeed managed to enhance their energy security. While notable, the ESI scores of this sub-group still lagged behind the EU leaders, with the final scores of some MSs remaining in negative territory. Despite some headway, there is an urgent need for further progress.

On the contrary, the energy security performance of 14 MSs declined between 2012 and 2021. As a result, a greater number of EU MSs failed to enhance their energy security, with the overall energy security of the EU correspondingly failing to assume a positive trajectory towards becoming (more) secure. Moreover, the findings shed light on substantial variations in energy security outcomes and the implementation of diverse energy policy measures among MSs. There is, in fact, no single path towards enhancing energy security, with different countries able to employ diverse strategies depending on their energy sector histories (Pérez, et al., 2019; Figulová & Gondášová, 2023). Despite an evident need for greater EU integration in the energy sector, the quantitative assessment conducted here indicates that a common approach towards achieving this objective is lacking. The landscape of the EU's energy policy remains characterized by a lack of cohesion, shaped rather by the sovereign decision-making of its member states. However, as noted by Mišík & Nosko (2023a), a unified approach would enable member states to project a much stronger position collectively, both politically and economically, especially in times of crisis.

The analysis further concentrated on the implications of the outbreak of COVID-19 and the energy crisis on the energy security of MSs. Significantly divergent energy markets and varying approaches to energy policy inevitably influenced the energy security of MSs throughout the crises, which had varying effects on their energy security performance. Even though a sharp rise in energy demand during the post-pandemic recovery, coupled with supply shortages and price spikes, had a detrimental impact on the energy security status of some MSs, others managed to elevate their energy security. This finding underlines the pivotal role of government support in fostering crisis recovery – or converting challenges posed by the pandemic and energy crisis into opportunities.

This chapter has further noted that the implementation of the three key principles of the clean energy transition has not resulted in a distinct change of ESI scores for most MSs. The struggle to reduce energy import dependency has limited the effectiveness of green initiatives and impeded their potential to positively impact overall energy security performance. The analysis revealed that Ireland and Estonia may serve as notable exceptions, demonstrating that accelerating measures like enhanced energy efficiency, reduced emissions, and constraints on fossil fuel consumption can indeed contribute to improved energy security. Apart from the climate change imperative, MSs are confronted with a pressing need to mitigate energy security concerns and dependencies. The past few years have reminded energy security actors about the need to accelerate decarbonization, while simultaneously preserving energy security. Prioritizing energy security, in other words, is essential until indigenous low-carbon energy resources can be reliably sustained (Mišík, 2022). The specific energy sources that may ultimately prevail remain uncertain at this juncture (Mikulska, 2023). Nevertheless, the EU community currently enjoys an opportunity to formulate a unified approach to its external energy security by using a strategy aimed at achieving a stable transitional phase, underpinned by a resolute commitment to decarbonization.

Acknowledgments

This chapter was supported by the Slovak Research and Development Agency Grant No APVV-20-0012.

Notes

1 Official Journal C 306, 17/12/2007 P 0001 – 0271.
2 Official Journal 115, 09/05/2008 P 0051 – 0052
3 A noteworthy illustration of this lies in the EU's pivotal role in shaping the United Nations Framework Convention on Climate Change (UNFCCC), as well as its contributions to the formulation of both the Kyoto Protocol and the Paris Agreement. Furthermore, the EU is firmly committed to the United Nations' Sustainable Development Goals (SDGs).
4 FCCC/CP/2015/10/Add.1
5 COM/2019/640 final
6 The exports to Europe in 2021 decreased from their 2019 level, and further the IEA called on Russia to increase gas imports to Europe, as the Agency believed that Russia could do more to increase the availability of gas to Europe and ensure that storage facilities are adequately filled (International Energy Agency, 2021).

7 Finland does not report prices for household customers of natural gas, only non-household (it is the only EU country to report the data this way). Finland's measurements, therefore, exceptionally include data representing non-household natural gas prices.
8 Bulgaria, Czechia, and Slovakia improved their energy security performance, however, their final ESI scores in 2021 remained in negative territory.
9 A more significant drop in ESI was recorded in the case of Croatia and Romania, yet their final ESI scores in 2021 were still positive. Denmark, Austria, Luxembourg, and the Netherlands saw only marginal deterioration in their final ESI scores, holding onto positive values.
10 These are Spain, Belgium, Germany, Italy, Poland, France, Finland, and Sweden.

References

Abu-Rayash, A. & Dincer, I., 2020. Analysis of the electricity demand trends amidst the COVID-19 coronavirus pandemic. *Energy Research & Social Science*, 2 July, 68, pp. 1–11.

Bogoviz, A. V., Lobova, S. V., Ragulina, Y. V. & Alekseev, A. N., 2017. A comprehensive analysis of energy security in the member states of the Eurasian Economic Union, 2000–2014. I*nternational Journal of Energy Economics and Policy*, 5(7), pp. 93–101.

Bogoviz, A. V., Lobova, S. V., Ragulina, Y. V. & Alekseev, A. N., 2019. A quantitative analysis of energy security performance by Brazil, Russia, India, China, and South Africa in 1990–2015. *International Journal of Energy Economics and Policy*, 25 March, 5(7), pp. 244–250.

Brown, M. A., Wang, Y., Sovacool, B. K. & D'Agostino, A. L., 2014. Forty years of energy security trends: A comparative assessment of 22 industrialized countries. *Energy Research & Social Science*, 4, pp. 64–77.

Cherp, A. & Jewell, J., 2014. The concept of energy security: Beyond the four As. *Energy Policy*, 75, pp. 415–421.

Chester, L., 2010. Conceptualising energy security and making explicit its polysemic nature. *Energy Policy*, February, 2(38), pp. 887–895.

Chong, C. T., Fan, Y. V., Lee, T. C. & Klemeš, J. J., 2022. Post COVID-19 energy sustainability and carbon emissions neutrality. *Energy*, 15 February, pp. 1–17.

European Commission, 2022a. Quarterly report on European gas markets. [Online] Available at: https://energy.ec.europa.eu/system/files/2022-01/Quarterly%20report %20on%20 European%20gas%20markets%20Q3_2021_FINAL.pdf [Accessed 2 September 2023].

European Commission, 2022b. REPowerEU: Joint European Action for more affordable, secure and sustainable energy. [Online] Available at: https://eur-lex.europa.eu/legal-content/EN/TXT/HTML/? uri=CELEX:52022DC0108 [Accessed 1 August 2023].

European Commission, n.d. Energy supply and pandemics. [Online] Available at: https://energy.ec.europa.eu/topics/energy-security/energy-supply-and-pandemics_en [Accessed 10 September 2023].

Eurostat, 2023. EU trade with Russia – latest developments. [Online] Available at: https://ec.europa.eu/eurostat/statistics-explained/index.php?title=EU_ trade_with_Russia_-_latest_developments [Accessed 5 September 2023].

Eurostat, n.d. Energy imports dependency (nrg_ind_id). [Online] Available at: https://ec.europa.eu/eurostat/cache/metadata/en/nrg_ind_id_esmsip2.htm [Accessed 5 September 2023].

Figulová, A. & Gondášová, I., 2023. Energy transition in Slovakia – Destiny in/and change. *European Journal of Transformational Studies*, November, 11(1), pp. 169–187.

International Energy Agency, 2020. Global energy demand to plunge this year as a result of the biggest shock since the Second World War. [Online] Available at: www.iea.org/news/global-energy-demand-to-plunge-this-year-as-a-result-of-the-biggest-shock-since-the-second-world-war [Accessed 4 September 2023].

International Energy Agency, 2021. Statement on recent developments in natural gas and electricity markets. [Online] Available at: www.iea.org/news/statement-on-recent - developments-in-natural-gas-and-electricity-markets. [Accessed 4 September 2023].

Karakosta, C., Mylona, Z., Karásek, J. & Papapostolou, A., 2021. Tackling the Covid-19 crisis through energy efficiency investments: Decision support tools for economic recovery. *Energy Strategy Reviews*, 38, pp. 1–12.

Kruyt, B., van Vuuren, D. P., de Vries, H. J. & Groenenberg, H., 2009. Indicators for energy security. *Energy Policy*, June, 6(37), pp. 2166–2181.

Kuzemko, C. et al., 2020. Covid-19 and the politics of sustainable energy transitions. *Energy Research & Social Science*, 2 July, 68, pp. 1–7.

Lobova, S. V., Ragulina, J. V., Bogoviz, A. V. & Alkseev, A. N., 2019. Energy security performance: A dataset on the member countries of the Commonwealth of Independent States, 2000–2014. *Data in Brief*, 29 August, 26, p. 1.9.

Löschel, A., Moslener, U. & Rübbelke, D. T., 2010. Indicators of energy security in industrialised countries. *Energy Policy*, April, 4(38), pp. 1665–1671.

Maltby, T., 2013. European Union energy policy integration: A case of European Commission policy entrepreneurship and increasing supranationalism. *Energy Policy*, 18 January, 55, pp. 435–444.

Mikulska, A., 2023. Climate action meets energy security: The Russian invasion of Ukraine adds a new dimension to energy transition. [Online] Available at: www.fpri.org/article/2022/06/climate-action-meets-energy-security-the-russian-invasion -of-ukraine-adds-a-new-dimension-to-energy-transition/ [Accessed 10 September 2023].

Mišík, M., 2022. The EU needs to improve its external energy security. *Energy Policy*, 1 April, 165, pp. 1–5.

Mišík, M. & Nosko, A., 2023a. Each one for themselves: Exploring the energy security paradox of the European Union. *Energy Research & Social Science*, 99, pp. 1–5.

Mišík, M. & Nosko, A., 2023b. Post-pandemic lessons for EU energy and climate policy after the Russian invasion of Ukraine: Introduction to a special issue on EU green recovery in the post-Covid-19 period. *Energy Policy*, 14 March, pp. 1–5.

Obadi, S. M. & Korcek, M., 2020. Quantifying the energy security of selected EU countries. *International Journal of Energy Economics and Policy*, 5 January, 2(10), pp. 276–284.

Oberthür, S. & Kelly, C. R., 2008. EU leadership in international climate policy: Achievements and challenges. *The International Spectator: Italian Journal of International Affairs*, 20 August, 3(43), pp. 35–50.

Pérez, M. d. l. E. M., Scholten, D. & Stegen, K. S., 2019. The multi-speed energy transition in Europe: *Opportunities and Challenges for EU Energy Security*. November, 26, pp. 1–6.

Simmons, R. A., Coyle, E. D. & Chapman, B., 2014. Global energy policy perspectives. In: E. D. Coyle & R. A. Simmons, eds *Understanding the Global Energy Crisis*. Indiana: Purdue University Press, pp. 1–318.

Sovacool, B. K., 2011. Evaluating energy security in the Asia pacific: Towards a more comprehensive approach. *Energy Policy*, 27 October, 39(11), pp. 7472–7479.

Sovacool, B. K., 2014. What are we doing here? Analyzing fifteen years of energy scholarship and proposing a social science research agenda. *Energy Research & Social Science*, 1, pp. 1–29.

Sovacool, B. K. & Brown, M. A., 2010. Competing dimensions of energy security: An international perspective. *Annual Review of Environment and Resources*, 35, pp. 77–108.

Sovacool, B. K., Del Rio, D. F. & Griffiths, S., 2020. Contextualizing the Covid-19 pandemic for a carbon-constrained world: Insights for sustainability transitions, energy justice, and research methodology. *Energy Research & Social Science*, 15 August, 68, pp. 1–12.

Sovacool, B. K. & Mukherjee, I., 2011. Conceptualizing and measuring energy security: A synthesized approach. *Energy*, 8(36), pp. 5345–5355.

Steffen, B., Egli, F., Pahle, M. & Schmidt, T. S., 2020. Navigating the clean energy transition in the COVID-19 crisis. *Joule* 4, pp. 1137–1141.

Tagliapietra, S., 2014. Towards a European Energy Union. The need to focus on security of energy supply. *Fondazione Eni Enrico Mattei* (FEEM, 1 January, pp. 1–16.

von Homeyer, I., Oberthür, S. & Jordan, A. J., 2021. EU climate and energy governance in times of crisis: Towards a new agenda. *Journal of European Public Policy*, 9 June, 7(28), pp. 959–979.

Winzer, C., 2012. Conceptualizing energy security. *Energy Policy*, 46, pp. 36–48.

Zhiznin, S., Timonov, V. M. & Dineva, V., 2020. Energy security: Theoretical interpretations and quantitative evaluation. *International Journal of Energy Economics and Policy*, 10(2), pp. 390–400.

Part III

Renewables as energy security tools

10 Wind energy in Poland

A successful restart or another false start?

Wiktor Hebda, Katarzyna Leśniak and Marek Stolorz

10.1 Introduction

The Polish energy sector has been undergoing modernisation for many years now, primarily towards the increased use of renewable energy sources. This process is a direct result of the energy-generation structure, which is still dominated by coal. Legal regulations of the European Union, as well as Polish legislation, clearly indicate the need to accelerate efforts towards a low-carbon economy, for which a gradual reduction in fossil fuel consumption is a necessary condition. It is also necessary to consider that the Polish energy sector has experienced great difficulties in recent years. The effects of the COVID-19 pandemic and the destabilising impact of the Ukrainian-Russian war on the energy security of Poland and other European countries are still being felt. Unfortunately, most Central European countries were or are still dependent on Russian fossil fuels (Hebda, 2023; Kratochvíl and Mišík, 2020; Tichý and Dubský, 2020). EU sanctions successively imposed on the Russian regime are intended to curb the financing of the war in Ukraine, but they have also forced many countries to seek alternative supplies of hydrocarbon. A series of adverse economic and political events has made Central Europe a region with a high risk of an energy crisis. Surely the situation that has occurred should send a signal to policymakers about the need to step up efforts towards ensuring regional energy stability.

Undoubtedly, the decarbonisation of the Polish energy sector requires increased investment in green energy, particularly wind energy. This sector has been a key renewable energy source in Poland, due to not only the potential of wind energy (both onshore and offshore) but also legal regulations that favoured investment in wind turbines. The implementation of the 10H rule in the Polish legal system in 2016 changed the current state of affairs to such an extent that further development of wind energy was halted (Sokołowski, 2017). It defines the minimum distance of a wind turbine from residential buildings as equal to 10 times the height of the turbine. This sector, which is extremely important for Poland's energy transition, stagnated during the next few years. Despite doubts raised by the wind energy industry about the strict provisions of the Wind Turbine Act, it remained unchanged. It was not until an amendment drafted by the government in July 2022

DOI: 10.4324/9781032624839-14

that the 10H rule was relaxed, as a result of which wind farm investments were supposed to be unblocked. Eventually, in April 2023, the amended Wind Turbine Act came into force, which admittedly relaxed the 10H rule. However, it has raised concerns as to whether the new provisions are appropriate enough for the wind energy industry to experience an effective restart.

The main research objective of this chapter is to consider the development of the wind energy sector in Poland from the perspective of ongoing legal changes. This chapter attempts to answer the following question: Which legal regulations have inhibited investment in onshore wind farms, and why? Which laws have made it difficult to invest in onshore wind farms, and why? To answer these research questions, the dogmatic legal method was used, through which a linguistic and logical analysis of normative acts was carried out. The theoretical-legal method was used to examine wind energy legislation from a theoretical perspective, while the sociological method allowed it to be approached from a practical point of view. In addition, the historical-legal method was used to illuminate the genesis and evolution of the 10H rule. The considerations were based on the most important legal acts that regulate wind energy in Poland (Polish legislation, EU directives), and analyses and reports of state and non-governmental institutions (in particular the Polish Wind Energy Association), as well as scientific and specialist publications.

The first part of the chapter presents the current state of the Polish energy sector, indicating the role of the wind energy sector. Next, the legal regulations regarding wind energy in Poland are discussed, with a particular focus on the 10H rule, which is part of the Wind Turbine Act of 2016. The next part of the chapter analyses the development of wind energy during the last two decades, with an emphasis on the effects of the implementation of the 10H rule. Then, reference is made to attempts to relax the provisions of the Wind Turbine Act and its 2023 amendment. The final part of the chapter refers to the role of offshore wind energy in Poland.

10.2 Current structure of electricity production in Poland

Poland has been decarbonising its energy sector for many years; however, its consumption of fossil fuels is still high. Unfortunately, in recent years there has been a noticeable dependence on the Russian Federation, so there has been heavy investment in infrastructure that would allow the broader diversification of oil or natural gas suppliers. Certainly, the commissioning of the Świnoujście LNG terminal in 2016 and the increased capacity of the Gdańsk oil terminal were milestones. Despite increased investment in the fossil fuel and renewable energy sectors, the Polish power sector was still dominated by coal at the end of 2022. This fuel (hard coal and lignite) accounted for as much as 70.7 per cent of electricity production (Dusiło, 2023). It should be noted, however, that the use of coal by power plants has generally been declining over the past several years (86.6% in 2010, 71.2% in 2021) (MCE, 2022). The opposite trend can be seen in the natural gas sector, which met approximately 6.5 per cent of its electricity needs in 2022. Nevertheless, it is worth mentioning that natural gas consumption has increased significantly compared to previous years.

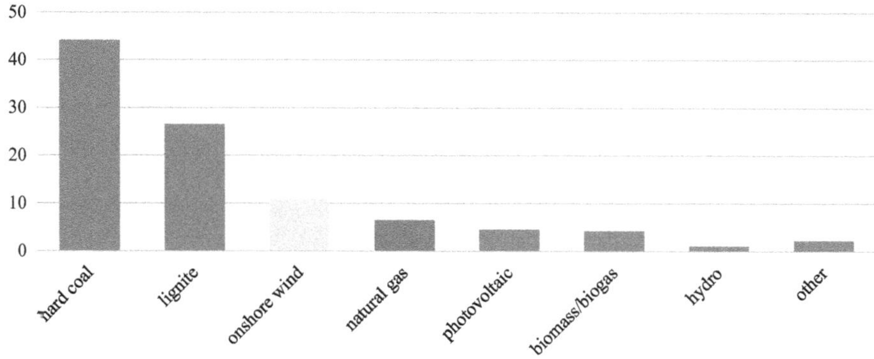

Figure 10.1 Structure of electricity production by source in 2022 (in percentage).

Unfortunately, Poland's natural gas reserves can supply only about 20–25 per cent of its needs, so a large share is imported (until 2022, mainly from Russia) (Hebda, 2021). When it comes to fossil fuels, we must not forget about crude oil, which, while not used by Polish power plants (except for the combined heat and power plant in Płock), is a crucial resource for transportation. Poland's energy transition is taking place through the increased use not only of natural gas but, above all, renewable energy sources (RES), which are expected to replace fossil fuels in a few decades. The dynamism of the green energy sector is evidenced by the fact that it accounted for only 8 per cent of the energy mix in 2011 while, in 2022, it accounted for nearly 21 per cent (Statistics Poland, 2022). The largest increases in generation capacity were achieved by wind power (especially between 2010 and 2016) and solar power (after 2018). In 2022, onshore wind power supplied 10.8 per cent, PV 4.5 per cent, biomass and biogas plants 4.2 per cent, and hydropower plants 1.1 per cent of electricity (Jakubiec, 2023). Undoubtedly, the greatest contribution to the development of green energy has been made by investments in wind power, which is a consequence of not only technological advances but also its considerable potential in Poland.

10.3 The potential of wind energy and its place in the Energy Policy of Poland until 2040

The wind energy potential in Poland is currently estimated at around 77 GW, of which more than 44 GW is onshore wind energy (Czyżak et al., 2021). From a geographical point of view, the most favourable conditions are in the northern coastal belt and the Suwałki region and central parts of Poland (Greater Poland, Mazovia) (Talarek et al., 2022). In terms of offshore wind energy potential, some discrepancies are noticeable. The Energy Policy of Poland until 2040 (EPP2040) indicates that the potential is approximately 11 GW; however, according to the Polish Wind Energy Association's report from the end of 2022, it is three times higher (33 GW).

Thus, if the estimated potential of the Polish part of the Baltic Sea is used, offshore wind energy could meet as much as 57 per cent of Poland's total demand for electricity by 2040. As part of the work undertaken for this report, 20 new sites with a total area of 2,171.5 km^2 were identified, including 18 in the exclusive economic zone (Polish EEZ) and two in the territorial sea; these sites have a combined potential of as much as 17.7 GW to be used for offshore wind power development (PSEW, 2022).

Wind energy occupies an important place in EPP2040. It is worth recalling that the use of RES in electricity generation will steadily increase, especially after 2025, due to the expected technological and economic maturity of individual technologies. It is estimated that by 2030 the share of RES energy in the electricity sector will be at least 32 per cent; by 2040 it will be around 40 per cent (EPP, 2021). To achieve these indicators, investment in wind power plants is indispensable; offshore plants are especially important because, as highlighted in EPP2040, they have a higher productivity than those located onshore. The possibility of receiving energy from these sources depends on the completion of work to strengthen the transmission grid in the northern part of the country. It is worth noting that the first offshore wind farm will be included in the electricity mix in around 2024/2025. In the area of the Polish Exclusive Economic Zone in the Baltic Sea, it is possible to deploy more wind power plants, but the development of the grid infrastructure is crucial. The installed capacity of these sources is expected to be up to 20 GW by 2040. Thus, production from offshore wind farms will account for the largest share of electricity generated from RES. In the case of onshore wind power plants, a significant complication is the lack of correlation between their operation and energy demand, so their rate of development will depend on costs (Sliz-Szkliniarz et al., 2019). Moreover, their construction is fraught with the risk of public disapproval (Bartczak et al., 2021; Igliński et al., 2016), which is why the 10H rule was intended to mitigate any potential social conflicts. The potential for the development of new onshore wind farms as both brownfield and greenfield investments is also significant. Furthermore, the popularisation of long-term RES power purchase agreements (PPAs) could contribute to the development of onshore wind power, among others, and potentially make regulating the above technologies more flexible (EPP, 2021). In April 2023, the Ministry of Climate and Environment proposed an update to EPP2040, which could result in increased investment in wind power

Table 10.1 Wind energy installed capacity according to the Energy Policy of Poland until 2040

		EPP2040		*EPP2040 April 2023 update*	
Year	2023	2030	2040	2030	2040
Onshore	8.7 GW	10 GW	10 GW	14 GW	18 GW
Offshore	0 GW	5.9 GW	11 GW	5.9 GW	20 GW

Source: Own work based on (Stachura, 2023).

capacity. These will increase capacity to 14 GW onshore and 5.9 GW offshore by 2030, and 18 GW and 20 GW, respectively, by 2040 (Stachura, 2023).

10.4 Legal regulation of wind energy in Poland

The legal framework for the wind energy market is defined by two laws in Poland: the Energy Law and the Renewable Energy Act (RES Act). The latter is crucial for wind energy. The RES Act primarily regulates the rules and conditions for the production of electricity from renewable energy sources, including wind energy, as well as mechanisms and instruments supporting the production of electricity by installations, including the auction support system, a support system in the form of certificates of origin, and rules for issuing guarantees of origin for electricity produced in RES installations (RES, 2015). This Act implemented Directive 2009/28/EC of the European Parliament and of the Council in the Polish legal system (Directive, 2009). Currently, this Directive has been repealed by the Directive of the European Parliament and of the Council (EU) 2018/2001, the so-called RED II Directive (Directive, 2018). The partial implementation of the provisions of the Directive had to wait until 2023, when an amendment to the Act on renewable energy sources and other acts was announced, entering into force on 1 October 2023 (RES, 2023). The amendment introduced changes regarding, for example, the definitions of a renewable energy source and an energy cluster, modifications regarding hybrid RES plants, and modernisation and operational support for RES plants. There was also a change concerning offshore wind farms that will be discussed later in this chapter.

Another extremely important wind energy law is the Act on Investments in Wind Farms of 20 May 2016 (commonly called the Wind Turbine Act) (IWF, 2016). From the moment it was drafted, the Act created controversy, in particular regarding the criminal sanctions contained therein and the matter of the specified distance of wind power plants from existing residential buildings (Sokołowski, 2017). In view of the position of the energy sector, some of the objections of its representatives were finally taken into account, such as the abandonment of criminal sanctions. Initially, allowing a wind farm to be operated without receiving an approval decision was punishable by a fine or restriction of liberty, or even up to two years' imprisonment. The same penalty was imposed on persons modifying a wind farm without the consent of the authorities; however, many regulations unfavourable from the point of view of wind investors remained in the Act.

The distance at which a wind power plant must be located from existing buildings (the 10H rule) deserves a separate mention. This regulation, which found its final form in Article 4 of the above-mentioned Act, allowed for the possibility of locating and constructing a wind power plant at a distance equal to or greater than ten times the height of the wind power plant, as measured from ground level to the highest point, including technical elements, in particular the rotor with blades (i.e. the total height of the wind power plant). The legislator indicated safety considerations as the justification for this distance, arguing that this is a distance that ensures physical safety, as ten times the height of the centre of the rotor is the distance at which components ejected by rotor blades and broken blade fragments will most often fall. Taking into account the possibility of the ejected parts being carried over a longer distance, as well as the fact that the impact of the wind turbine on its surroundings is influenced by its overall height, it was decided to use the total height of the wind turbine as the basis for determining the minimum distance. Elements of particular relevance to the surroundings that may constitute nuisances in relation to residential development include noise and infrasound, electromagnetic radiation, vibrations, shadow flickering effects, and light reflections (Sejm, 2016).

Moreover, wind power plants had to be located based on a local spatial development plan (LSDP, local zoning plan), i.e., a legal act in the form of a resolution issued by a local self-government unit that determines the purpose of the land, the location of public-purpose investments, and the development methods and conditions for the land (SPD, 2023). The exception was wind power plants with a capacity of no more than a micro-installation (i.e., 40 kW at the time, which could be located under general rules, by means of both an LSDP and a decision establishing the location of a public-purpose investment). Before the entry into force of the Act, if there was no development plan in force for the planned location of a wind power plant, the investor could locate the power plant on the basis of an outline planning permission.

Another important change introduced by the Wind Turbine Act was an amendment to the construction law that resulted in a new definition of a structure, which, together with the introduced definition of a wind power plant, caused interpretational discrepancies as to the property tax due (Gnatowska, Moryń-Kucharczyk, 2019). In the original wording of the Wind Turbine Act, a wind power plant was defined as a structure within the meaning of construction law (i.e., consisting of at least the foundation, the tower, and the technical elements). The inclusion of the technical elements in the entirety of the structure resulted in the possibility of also taxing the part related to the power plant, which contributed to an increase in the tax burden as, according to the tax authorities, it was possible to impose a property tax on the entirety of the power plant conceived as such. It was not until the 2018 amendment to the definition of a wind power plant, which separated the building part of the power plant from its technical elements, that property tax was charged only on the building part (RES, 2018).

A relatively new legislative idea is to regulate offshore wind energy generation. The regulatory framework for wind energy in the Baltic Sea is set out by the Act on the Promotion of Electricity Generation in Offshore Wind Farms, which came into force on 18 February 2021 (OWF, 2021). Although it enabled the construction of offshore wind farms, the need for its amendment was pointed out from the outset, in particular the need to correlate the duration of investment support with the length of permits to limit the costs of extending a permit after the support period, to shorten procedures under Geological and Mining Law, and to make the investment safeguards set by the legislator more flexible.

Some of the demands were taken into account in 2022 in the Act on amending the Maritime Safety Act and the Act concerning the Maritime Areas of the Polish

Republic and the Maritime Administration, where changes were proposed with regard to obtaining permits, the local jurisdiction of the provincial governor, or the lack of the need to obtain water permits for laying cables in maritime areas (MSA, 2022). Meanwhile, the amendment to the Act on Renewable Energy Sources of 2023 made it possible to increase from 10.9 GW to 17.9 GW the permissible output of offshore wind farms that will be allowed to be built under the support scheme provided for in the legislation. The established legal framework for offshore wind energy stems from the government's ambitions to gain energy from this sector.

10.5 Wind energy in Poland – from boom to stagnation

The Polish energy sector is still characterised by the high consumption of fossil fuels, primarily hard coal and lignite. For this reason, the transition of the electricity sector has been ongoing for more than two decades, with the primary aim of developing a diversified and sustainable energy mix. Its driving force is still decarbonisation, which is to be achieved through the increased use of natural gas and, in the longer term, primarily renewable energy sources supported by nuclear power (Hebda, 2022). Over the first decade of the twenty-first century, the largest investments in green sources were made in the wind power sector (Michalak, Zimny, 2011; Brzezińska-Rawa, Goździewicz-Biechońska, 2014). It is enough to recall that between 2005 and 2010 alone, the capacity of Polish wind power plants increased from 83 MW to 1,180 MW, which translates to an increase from seven to 46 per cent of the share of wind installations in the installed capacity of RES. There has undoubtedly been a boom in the wind energy sector, making it an essential source of support for the energy transition. In the following years, the development of the sector in question was impressive, as demonstrated by the massive (by Polish standards) increase in wind power capacity from 1,616 MW in 2011 to 5,807 MW in 2016 (URE, 2022). The importance of this energy source in the Polish energy mix is evidenced by the increase in its share from 1 per cent in 2010 to over 7.5 per cent in 2016.

Unfortunately, the development of wind energy experienced a distinct deceleration in 2016 as a consequence of the entry into force of the Wind Turbine Act (Gnatowska, Moryń-Kucharczyk, 2019). The 10H rule inhibited investment in new wind farms over the next four years. It is worth noting that only onshore wind farms have been commissioned so far due to, among other things, the lack of relevant regulation. At present (as of October 2023), the installed capacity of wind power plants amounts to 9,107 MW, which is slightly more than 14 per cent of Poland's electricity generation capacity (Rynekelektryczny, 2023a). In this context, solar energy has become the leading renewable energy source in Poland. It should be noted that the installed capacity in photovoltaics has reached 14,994 MW (it was less than 200 MW in 2016), but this does not appear to have had much of an effect on electricity generation. This state of affairs is a consequence of the inefficient deployment of photovoltaic panels (micro-installations, mainly in households, with a total capacity of more than 8,500 MW) and the small number of large-scale photovoltaic farms (there are only three above 50 MW, including the

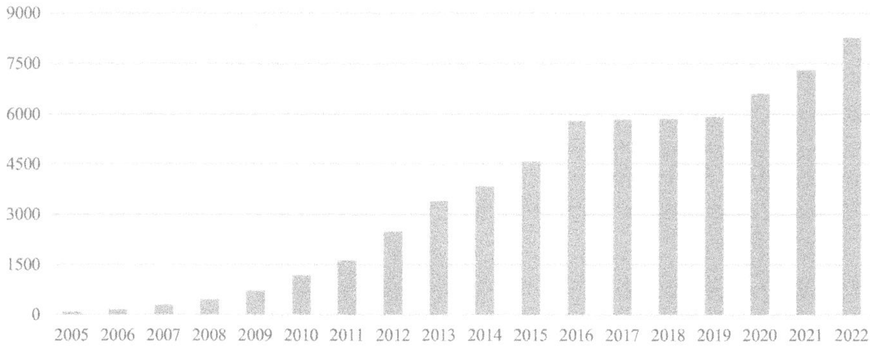

Figure 10.2 Wind farm capacities in Poland 2005–2022 (in MW).

largest in Zwartowo with a capacity of 204 MW) (Rynekelektryczny, 2023b). This has resulted in a clear imbalance in electricity production: wind turbines supplied more than twice as much energy as PV in 2022 (Jakubiec, 2023).

Wind power plants are scattered across the whole of Poland; however, the largest number are in the West Pomeranian and Pomeranian Voivodeships. In December 2020, the Energy Regulatory Office issued a licence for the largest wind farm in Poland, Potęgowo (to be located in Słupsk County). The Israeli investor, Mashav, commissioned 81 wind turbines with a total capacity of 219 MW (the previous record belonged to Margonin WF in the Wielkopolskie Voivodeship, which has been in operation since 2009 and consists of 60 wind turbines with a total capacity of 120 MW).

10.6 The 10H rule – regulations blocking wind energy

The consequence of the introduction of the 10H rule, i.e., only allowing the location and construction of a wind power plant at a distance equal to or greater than ten times the height of the entire wind power plant, was a significant limitation on Poland's wind power potential. In practice, such regulations meant locating a wind power plant at a distance of 1.5–2 km from residential buildings. This also prevented the expansion of existing wind power plants that did not meet this distance requirement, as these could only be renovated. Since 2016, there has been no new investment in the wind energy sector. The restrictions introduced mean that 99.7 per cent of Poland is now excluded from investment in wind energy (PSEW, 2017). Onshore wind energy was also deprived of further development opportunities. Consequently, this situation posed a serious threat to Poland's ability to meet the EU's 2030 climate targets, which include a 55 per cent reduction in greenhouse gas emissions compared to 1990 (Czyżak et al., 2021). The opposite problem should also be pointed out: as a rule, a residential building cannot be built within the distance specified by rule 10H even if one owns land with existing utilities – a problem that particularly affects areas with highly dispersed building developments.

Since the very beginning of the introduction of the 10H rule, there have been numerous criticisms pointing to the need for its relaxation. It was proposed that distances should be determined based on the provisions of the Act of 3 October 2008 on the provision of information on the environment and its protection, and public participation in the protection of the environment and environmental impact assessments, as well as the criterion of permissible noise levels set out in the Regulation of the Minister of the Environment of 14 June 2007 on permissible noise levels in the environment (PSEW, 2017). Here, it is also worth noting the opinions communicated during the legislative process concerning the Act on wind power plant investments. The Polish Chamber of Civil Engineers (24 March 2016), the Foundation for Sustainable Energy (10 March 2016), the Office of Studies and Analyses of the Supreme Court (15 March 2016), and the Union of Rural Municipalities of the Republic of Poland (18 March 2016) all expressed their negative opinion on the distance rule (the 10H rule). It has been unequivocally demonstrated that these stringent rules would either prevent or clearly limit the possibility of locating new wind power plants in Poland. Nevertheless, investors' growing concerns and the analyses of industry experts did not influence the fate of the Wind Turbine Act, which, as it turned out, remained unchanged and in force for several years.

10.7 Wind Turbine Act – attempts at relaxation

In 2016, it became clear that the 10H rule would negatively affect the development of wind energy in Poland. Although new infrastructure that was already being built and had received approval before the Act came into force could be completed, new projects had to comply with the 10H rule. It is worth noting that, according to the then-binding Polish Energy Policy until 2030, wind energy was supposed to be a key renewable energy source supporting the transition of the Polish energy sector (Igliński et al., 2016). Over time, there was increasing pressure from investors (e.g., PGE Group, EDP Renewables) to either abolish or relax unfavourable regulations.

The Ministry of Development, Labour, and Technology presented a draft bill amending the Act on wind power plant investment and certain other acts in mid-2021. The Act maintained the 10H rule but provided for derogations from it. The most important of these was the possibility of modifying the minimum distance of turbine locations from residential buildings based on the relevant local spatial development plan and reducing it to a distance of at least 500 metres. As a consequence, municipal authorities would decide on the location of wind power plants under local planning procedures and would bear the cost of the obligatory strategic environmental impact assessments. An important amendment was that residential construction in the vicinity of wind power plants was now permitted, and municipal authorities are now obliged to consult the public on the location of energy infrastructure (wind turbines) in LSDPs.

Certainly, the relaxation of the 10H rule has translated into increased investment in wind power plants. This is evidenced by the positions taken in May 2021 as part of the public consultation and opinion on the draft amendment to the Wind Turbine Act. Despite the need to revive wind energy as soon as possible, for the next several months the bill did not proceed. It is difficult to understand the reasons for this, although it seems to be a result of political disputes within the ruling coalition. Certainly, this delay was of great concern for the decarbonisation of the Polish energy sector.

In April 2022, the Ministry of Development and Technology (previously the Ministry of Development, Labour, and Technology) transferred the Wind Turbine Act to the Ministry of Climate and Environment. Three months later, the bill to amend the Act on wind power plant investments and certain other acts was unfrozen. Finally, on 5 July 2022, the Council of Ministers approved the draft amendment submitted by the Minister of Climate and Environment, thus allowing it to proceed. It should be noted that the most important relaxation provisions of the 10H rule were maintained. It was expected that, in the case of the Wind Turbine Act, the legislative process would not encounter any difficulties and would enter into force within a few months. However, the Sejm (the lower house of the Polish parliament) did not start work on the bill until the end of 2022.

At that time, the relaxation of the Wind Turbine Act appeared to be a necessity, not just because of the need to increase Poland's ability to generate renewable energy. An important factor that should now accelerate the legislative process is the European Commission's requirement that funds should be released from the National Recovery and Resilience Plan (NRRP). It should be stressed that the amendments to the Wind Turbine Act represented just one of the 37 milestones that Poland needed to achieve to meet its requirements under the Recovery and Resilience Facility (Perzyński, 2022). It is worth reiterating that, at the beginning of 2023, theoretically only one milestone (the amendment of the Wind Turbine Act) still had to be met to submit the first payment application under the NRRP.

10.8 The Wind Turbine Act and the 10H rule after amendment in 2023 – a revival of wind energy in Poland?

Unsuccessful attempts to relax the 10H rule have unexpectedly stretched out over time. Although the first negative effects on wind energy development in Poland were already noticeable in 2016, it was only in the first months of 2023 that steps were taken to change the legal landscape.

Proposed in July 2022, the government's bill on amendments to the Wind Turbine Act maintained the relaxed 10H rule, but with the possibility of changing it through local government (Sejm, 2022). Reducing the distance to 500 metres would allow for a 25-fold increase in the utilisation of wind energy potential in Poland because of the increase in the availability of suitable land to 7.08 per cent of the country's area (Czyżak et al., 2021). As a result of the referral of the project to parliamentary committees (the Committee on Energy, Climate, and State Assets and the Committee on Local Self-Government and Regional Policy), an amendment was made to the bill under which the minimum distance was to be 700 metres rather than 500 (Sejm, 2023a). This amendment was criticised by the energy industry as blocking Poland's energy potential. Increasing the minimum distance to 700 metres reduces the possible capacity to be installed by approximately 60–70 per cent (PSEW, 2023). The MPs of Solidarna Polska, a member of the governing coalition, also disagreed with an amendment proposing a minimum distance of 1,000 metres and greater support for the development of the biomass sector. In the end, the Sejm voted through the Act with a minimum distance of 700 metres. Although amendments were made by the Senate (the upper house of the Polish parliament) which assumed a return to 500 metres, these were rejected by the Sejm. The President of the Republic of Poland signed the Act, which came into force on 23 April 2023 (Sejm, 2023b).

The amendment to the Wind Turbine Act does not change the basic principle of locating new wind farms; this states that a wind power plant may only be located on the basis of a local spatial development plan, which means that the 10H rule still applies in the absence of a local zoning plan that reduces the distance to 700 metres. It is worth noting that LSDPs are updated, on average, once every few years, which may further delay investment in wind farms. Another disadvantage is that only 58.4 per cent of Polish municipalities include renewable energy sources in their spatial policy concept (Blaszke et al., 2021). The obligation to prepare or amend a local zoning plan to construct a wind turbine applies to the area of its projected impact and not, as before, to the entire area designated in accordance with the 10H rule. Making the minimum distance more flexible attracts additional obligations to consult with residents of these municipalities via public discussions.

Additionally, the amendment strengthens information obligations towards the residents of nearby communes, not just the commune hosting the wind farm. Importantly, local zoning plans will have to be adopted by all communes near which wind farms will be located. If the inhabitants of just one neighbouring commune do not agree to the investment, this can lead to a stalemate. Interestingly, an LSDP must specify the maximum total height of a wind turbine, the maximum diameter of the rotor and blades, and the maximum number of turbines (Sejm, 2023b). For this reason, before adopting an LSDP, it is necessary to carry out an analysis to obtain the appropriate technical specifications for a potential wind farm. There is some doubt as to whether this is a task for the investor or the commune authorities.

The obligation to carry out a time-consuming procedure for assessing the environmental impact of a given project will also be an obstacle to the rapid construction of wind turbines. Strategic environmental impact assessments (SEIA) analyse, among others, the impact of noise emissions on the health of residents. Commune authorities will not be able to waive an SEIA for an LSDP that includes a wind farm. It is worth emphasising that the 10H rule has been maintained for national parks. In the case of other forms of nature protection, the distance must be specified in an environmental permit. The amendment to the Wind Turbine Act also assumes that an investor should offer at least 10 per cent of the installed capacity of the wind farm to local residents, who could use it as virtual prosumers (Gajda, Sawicka, 2023).

In its current form, the Wind Turbine Act continues to be criticised by the wind energy industry as it still significantly limits development possibilities. This potential has therefore been released to some extent, but it is small and insufficient to achieve the targets set by the European Union by 2030, which would still be difficult to meet given existing administrative barriers (Czyżak et al., 2021). The compromise that sets a minimum distance of 700 m from residential buildings will not enable the wind energy sector to flourish quickly, but it will allow some development.

10.9 Conclusion

Energy transition is an indispensable part of the functioning of every country. However, it is important to bear in mind that this issue must be seen from a broader perspective. Thus, energy challenges should not only be considered individually by the state but also within the framework of regional or international organisations. This issue becomes particularly important in the event of international and sometimes global crises, of which certainly one of the most recent was the COVID-19 pandemic. During this period, clear symptoms of a threat to the energy security of many regions of the world were noticeable, including in the EU (Mišík and Oravcová, 2022). An even greater challenge is to ensure energy stability in the wake of Russia's aggression against Ukraine. Decarbonisation is an undertaking that could significantly reduce the risk of further energy crises in the EU over the next two to three decades. Reducing or eliminating fossil fuels in favour of renewable energy sources will achieve low-carbon economies and, most importantly, enable the majority of EU countries to become independent of imported energy.

Poland's energy sector undoubtedly requires a dynamic transition towards modern technologies based on renewable energy sources (Dzikuć et al., 2021). It is enough to mention that the current structure of electricity generation is about 70 per cent based on coal, whose share will probably decrease to approximately 56–60 per cent by 2030 (Li et al., 2020). Undoubtedly, the implementation of EPP2040's objectives will significantly change this unfavourable situation as one of the key sectors that will be intensively developed in the next two decades is RES. Meanwhile, wind energy is expected to be the most important source of green energy. The situation in Poland proves that in the context of investments in energy infrastructure, legal regulations are extremely important. The will of the legislator can sometimes be decisive for the development of a given energy sector. Unfortunately, the wind energy sector in Poland has encountered serious legal obstacles in recent years. The implementation of the 10H rule into the Polish legal order in 2016 prevented the development of onshore wind energy for several years.

It is worth highlighting that, since 2016, there has been a slight increase in the generating capacity of wind farms (especially in the period 2016–2019). As a result of the noticeable stagnation, attempts were made to amend the Wind Turbine Act, which, as it turned out, was not an easy undertaking. The main doubt remained the issue of relaxing the 10H rule, and specifically proposing new distance rules for the location of wind farms. Only in April 2023 was the Wind Turbine Act amended, with the intention of restarting wind energy in Poland. The 10H rule was relaxed, setting 700 m as the minimum distance between a wind farm and residential buildings. Certainly, reducing the distance by two or even three times is beneficial for new investment. Nevertheless, an obstacle to restarting wind energy may be the obligation to locate new wind turbines based on LSDPs – however, nearly half of Poland's municipalities still do not include renewable energy sources in their spatial development plans. In addition, a positive assessment about an investment's impact on the environment is now required. It must not be forgotten that changes to LSDPs and environmental impact assessment plans will be necessary for new wind farms, not only in the commune where the investment is implemented but also in those surrounding it. Thus, the long-awaited relaxation of the 10H rule has taken place, but the new requirements for the location of wind turbines may indicate another false dawn for wind energy in Poland.

Acknowledgements

This publication has been funded from the Anthropocene Priority Research Area budget under the program 'Excellence Initiative – Research University' at the Jagiellonian University. Translation/proofreading of this publication has been supported by a grant from the Faculty of International and Political Studies under the Strategic Programme Excellence Initiative at Jagiellonian University.

References

Bartczak, A., Budziński, W., Gołębiowska, B., 2021. Impact of beliefs about negative effects of wind turbines on preference heterogeneity regarding renewable energy development in Poland. *Resources, Conservation and Recycling*. 169, 105530. https://doi.org/10.1016/j.resconrec.2021.105530

Blaszke, M., Nowak, M., Śleszyński, P., Mickiewicz, B., 2021. Investments in renewable energy sources in the concepts of local spatial policy: The case of Poland. *Energies*. 14, 7902. https://doi.org/10.3390/en14237902

Brzezińska-Rawa, A., Goździewicz-Biechońska, J., 2014. Recent developments in the wind energy sector in Poland. *Renewable and Sustainable Energy Reviews*. 38, 79–87. https://doi.org/10.1016/j.rser.2014.05.086

Czyżak, P., Sikorski, M., Wrona, A., 2021. Wiatr w żagle. Zasada 10H a potencjał lądowej energetyki wiatrowej w Polsce. Instrat Policy Note 01. https://instrat.pl/wp-content/uploads/2021/05/Instrat-Wiatr-w-z%CC%87agle.pdf (accessed 5 December 2023).

Directive, 2009. Directive 2009/28/EC of the European Parliament and of the Council of 23 April 2009 on the promotion of the use of energy from renewable sources and amending and subsequently repealing Directives 2001/77/EC and 2003/30/EC (Text with EEA relevance). *Official Journal of the European Union*. L 140/16.

Directive, 2018. Directive (EU) 2018/2001 of the European Parliament and of the Council of 11 December 2018 on the promotion of the use of energy from renewable sources (recast) (Text with EEA relevance.). *Official Journal of the European Union*. L 328/82.

Dusiło, M., 2023. Transformacja energetyczna w Polsce. Edycja 2023. Forum Energii. www.forum-energii.eu/pl/analizy/transformacja-2023 (accessed 5 December 2023).

Dzikuć, M., Gorączkowska, J., Piwowar, A., Dzikuć, M., Smoleński, R., Kułyk, P., 2021. The analysis of the innovative potential of the energy sector and low-carbon development: A case study for Poland. *Energy Security Reviews*. 38, 100769. https://doi.org/10.1016/j.esr.2021.100769

EPP, 2021. Energy Policy of Poland until 2040. Official Gazette of the Government of the Republic of Poland. No. 264.

Gajda, G., Sawicka, D., 2023. Nowelizacja ustawy wiatrakowej. Bakertilly Legal Poland. https://bakertilly.pl/legal/wp-content/uploads/sites/18/2023/03/BTLP_Nowelizacja-ustawy-wiatrakowej_03.23-3.pdf (accessed 5 December 2023).

Gnatowska, R., Moryń-Kucharczyk, E., 2019. Current status of wind energy policy in Poland. *Renewable Energy*. 135, 232–237. https://doi.org/10.1016/j.renene.2018.12.015

Hebda, W., 2021. The North-South gas corridor in the context of Poland's gas transmission system – A perfect opportunity to diversify gas resources. *Energies*. 14, 7188. https://doi.org/10.3390/en14217188

Hebda, W., 2022. Energy Policy of Poland until 2040: The Challenges and threats to energy security in the next two decades. *Politeja*. 19, 4(79), 167–186. https://doi.org/10.12797/Politeja.19.2022.79.10

Hebda, W., 2023. Rosyjska agresja militarna na Ukrainę a bezpieczeństwo energetyczne Polski, in: Gruszczak, A. (Ed.), *The War Must Go On: Dynamika wojny w Ukrainie i jej reperkursje dla bezpieczeństwa Polski*. Księgarnia Akademicka, Kraków, pp. 115–124. https://doi.org/10.12797/9788381388801.11

Igliński, B., Iglińska, A., Koziński, G., Skrzatek, M., Buczkowski, R., 2016. Wind energy in Poland – History, current state, surveys, Renewable Energy Sources Act, SWOT analysis. *Renewable and Sustainable Energy Reviews*. 64, 19–33. http://dx.doi.org/10.1016/j.rser.2016.05.081

IWF, 2016. Act on investments in wind farms. *Journal of Laws of the Republic of Poland*. No. 961.

Jakubiec, M., 2023. Ponad 21% energii pochodziło z OZE! Miks energetyczny i struktura produkcji energii w Polsce w 2022 r. Globenergia. https://globenergia.pl/ponad-21-energii-pochodzilo-z-oze-miks-energetyczny-i-struktura-produkcji-energii-w-polsce-w-2022-r/ (accessed 5 December 2023).

Kratochvíl, P., Mišík, M., 2020. Bad external actors and good nuclear energy: Media discourse on energy supplies in the Czech Republic and Slovakia. *Energy Policy*. 136, 111058. https://doi.org/10.1016/j.enpol.2019.111058

Li, Y., Zhang, H., Kang, Y., 2020. Will Poland fulfill its coal commitment by 2030? An answer based on a novel time series prediction method. *Energy Reports*. 6, 1760–1767. https://doi.org/10.1016/j.egyr.2020.06.021

MCE, 2022. Statystyka elektroenergetyki polskiej 2021, Ministry of Climate and Environment, Energy Market Agency. www.are.waw.pl/badania-statystyczne/wynikowe-informacje-statystyczne/publikacje-roczne#2021-rok (accessed 5 December 2023).

Michalak, P., Zimny, J., 2011. Wind energy development in the world, Europe and Poland from 1995 to 2009; current status and future perspectives. *Renewable and Sustainable Energy Reviews*. 15, 2330–2341. https://doi.org/10.1016/j.rser.2011.02.008

Mišík, M., Oravcová, V., 2022. Ex ante governance in the European Union: Energy and climate policy as a 'test run' for the post-pandemic recovery. *Energy Policy*. 167, 113076. https://doi.org/10.1016/j.enpol.2022.113076

MSA, 2022. Act on amending the Maritime Safety Act and the Act concerning the Maritime Areas of the Polish Republic and the Maritime Administration. *Journal of Laws of the Republic of Poland*. No. 1604.

OWF, 2021. Act on the Promotion of Electricity Generation in Offshore Wind Farms. *Journal of Laws of the Republic of Poland.* No. 234.

Perzyński, M., 2022. Puda: Ustawa odległościowa pozostaje kamieniem milowym w negocjacjach o KPO. https://biznesalert.pl/grzegorz-puda-mfipr-kpo-ustawa-odleglosciowa/ (accessed 5 December 2023).

PSEW, 2017. The State of Wind Energy in Poland in 2016. Polskie Stowarzyszenie Energetyki Wiatrowej. http://psew.pl/wp-content/uploads/2017/06/Stan-energetyki-wiatrowej-w-Polsce-w-2016-r.pdf (accessed 5 December 2023).

PSEW, 2022. Potencjał Morskiej Energetyki Wiatrowej w Polsce. Polskie Stowarzyszenie Energetyki Wiatrowej. https://konferencja-offshore.pl/wp-content/uploads/2022/11/FarmyMorskie_RaportShort_Prev.pdf (accessed 5 December 2023).

PSEW, 2023. 700 metrów w ustawie wiatrakowej: mała poprawka – drastyczne zmiany. Polskie Stowarzyszenie Energetyki Wiatrowej. http://psew.pl/700-metrow-w-ustawie-wiatrakowej-mala-poprawka-drastyczne-zmiany-analiza/(accessed 5 December 2023).

RES, 2015. Act on Renewable Energy Sources. *Journal of Laws of the Republic of Poland.* No. 478.

RES, 2018. Act amending the Act on Renewable Energy Sources and certain other acts. *Journal of Laws of the Republic of Poland.* No. 1276.

RES, 2023. Act amending the Act on Renewable Energy Sources and certain other acts. *Journal of Laws of the Republic of Poland.* No. 1762.

Rynekelektryczny, 2023a. Moc zainstalowana farm wiatrowych. www.rynekelektryczny.pl/moc-zainstalowana-farm-wiatrowych-w-polsce/ (accessed 5 December 2023).

Rynekelektryczny, 2023b. Fotowoltaika ma już 15 GW mocy zainstalowanej. https://www.rynekelektryczny.pl/moc-zainstalowana-fotowoltaiki-w-polsce/ (accessed 5 December 2023).

Sejm, 2016. Justification for the Parliamentary Project of Act on Investments in Wind Farms. www.sejm.gov.pl/sejm8.nsf/druk.xsp?nr=315 (accessed 5 December 2023).

Sejm, 2022. Government bill amending the Act on Investments in Wind Farms and other acts. www.sejm.gov.pl/sejm9.nsf/agent.xsp?symbol=RPL&Id=RM-0610-95-22 (accessed 5 December 2023).

Sejm, 2023a. Druk nr 2962. www.sejm.gov.pl/sejm9.nsf/druk.xsp?nr=2962 (accessed 5 December 2023).

Sejm. 2023b. Act of March 9, 2023 amending Act on Investments in Wind Farms and other acts. https://isap.sejm.gov.pl/isap.nsf/DocDetails.xsp?id=WDU20230000553 (accessed 5 December 2023).

Sliz-Szkliniarz, B., Eberbach, J., Hoffmann, B., Fortin, M., 2019. Assessing the cost of onshore wind development scenarios: Modelling of spatial and temporal distribution of wind power for the case of Poland. *Renewable and Sustainable Energy Reviews.* 109, 514–531. https://doi.org/10.1016/j.rser.2019.04.039

Sokołowski, M.M., 2017. Discovering the new renewable legal order in Poland: With or without wind? *Energy Policy.* 106, 68–74. https://doi.org/10.1016/j.enpol.2017.03.033

SPD, 2023. Notice of the Marshal of the Sejm of the Republic of Poland of April 7, 2023 on the announcement of the uniform text of Act on Spatial Planning and Development. *Journal of Laws of the Republic of Poland.* No. 977.

Stachura, J., 2023. Aktualizacja PEP2040: Więcej OZE i atomu. Gaz zejdzie na drugi plan. BiznesAlert. https://biznesalert.pl/pep2040-oze-atom-gaz-energetyka-polska/ (accessed 5 December 2023).

Statistics Poland, 2022. Energia ze źródeł odnawialnych w 2021 r. https://stat.gov.pl/obszary-tematyczne/srodowisko-energia/energia/energia-ze-zrodel-odnawialnych-w-2021-roku,10,5.html (accessed 5 December 2023).

Talarek, K., Knitter-Piątkowska, A., Garbowski, T., 2022. Wind parks in Poland – New challenges and perspectives. *Energies*. 15(19), 7004. https://doi.org/10.3390/en15197004

Tichý, L., Dubský, Z., 2020. Russian energy discourse on the V4 countries. *Energy Policy*. 137, 111128. https://doi.org/10.1016/j.enpol.2019.111128

URE, 2022. Report RES. Energy Regulatory Office. www.ure.gov.pl/pl/oze/potencjal-krajowy-oze/5753,Moc-zainstalowana-MW.html (accessed 5 December 2023).

11 Nativist framing of energy issues in times of crises across the Slovak political spectrum

Andrea Figulová and Radka Vicenová

11.1 Introduction

Several major challenges to the global economy have surfaced in recent years, with the global COVID-19 pandemic and Russia's military invasion of Ukraine engendering palpable negative effects on the energy sector. These detrimental consequences pertain both to the economic aspects of energy (mostly related to the costs of energy resources) and the security implications in the context of energy supply security (Jirušek, 2023; Mišík and Nosko, 2023). The developments are also thrusting new issues onto the political agenda, with governments and political parties needing to make decisions on how to respond to and interpret such experiences in their different political systems.

Against this backdrop, this chapter scrutinises Slovak parliamentary debates between 2020 and 2022, examining the ways different political parties understood and communicated energy topics around the two crises (i.e. the pandemic and Russia's aggression). The central thesis is that the threat of crisis tends to be accompanied by the use of nativist and protectionist framings in the public discourse across the political spectrum (i.e. rather than focusing on deepening energy integration, responses generally favour adopting nationalist postures on energy security). *Nativist*, in this chapter, is understood in accordance with Mudde's (2007) definition as a xenophobic form of nationalism based on excluding the out-group to protect the in-group, thus connecting nativism to the state and its resources (including the environment and energy). Recent studies show that – in line with theoretical assumptions of 'the fourth wave' (Mudde, 2019a) – nationalist and authoritarian politics is gradually becoming the political mainstream in many (though not only) European countries (Mudde, 2019a; Weisskircher, 2023; Chytilek and Havlík, 2022). Moreover, nativist framings have been specifically observed in environmental narratives of far right and right-wing populist political parties across Europe, mostly regarding protectionist attitudes towards nature and the environment of specific areas, which are tied to the nation and consequently find compatibility with nationalist positions (Forchtner, 2020; Kyriazi, 2020; Tosun and Debus, 2021; Forchtner and Özvatan, 2022).

In conducting a case study on Slovakia, the analysis spans two levels. Firstly, it provides an opportunity to map the potential increase of nativist framings during the

DOI: 10.4324/9781032624839-15

two recent crises and their repercussions including the substantial impact on energy policies within the timeframe considered. Secondly, it also provides an opportunity to map the use of nativist arguments across the political spectrum, discerning any comparability between political parties from different ideological backgrounds. The key focus here is on political actors from various political orientations and the ways they differ in terms of how they perceive and incorporate energy issues in their political agendas.

The Slovak case provides an opportune vehicle for studying these phenomena for several reasons. This, firstly, includes the ability to explore the parliamentary debate in the National Council of the Slovak Republic (hereinafter also referred to as the Slovak parliament) throughout both crises. This analysis indeed examines a single parliamentary term spanning both the pandemic and the period of Russian aggression, ensuring continuity of political representation (explained later in the text) over time. It also enables the adoption of a comprehensive approach regarding changes in reasoning across the Slovak political and ideological spectrum, with continuity in the composition of the Slovak parliament and debates/parliamentary speeches in the plenary throughout both crisis periods, thus offering a unique opportunity for comparability across the political spectrum. Finally, the composition of the National Council of the Slovak Republic after the 2020 elections was heterogeneous and contained a wide range of ideological positions, including far-right, right-wing populist and right-wing conservative political actors (Gyarfášová, 2020; Kerekeš, 2020), i.e. including but not limited to those political parties where protectionist framings could be expected from their ideological profiles.[1] This further reinforces the comprehensibility of the analysis as well as the complex approach, especially given the theoretical assumption of the theory of 'the fourth wave' and the 'mainstreamisation' of far-right ideas.

This chapter starts with an introduction of recent research on populism, energy issues and crises, with a special focus on the linkage between the key concepts of the far right, populism and energy. The third section introduces the methodological framework along with the central thesis and key argument based on Mudde´s definition of populism and nativism. The fourth section presents the findings of the parliamentary speech analysis, adopting the central two-pronged approach: a subsection focused on the analysis of the presence of nativist framing across time followed by a section on an analysis across the political spectrum. The conclusion summarises the key findings based on the two levels of analysis, placing these insights into the wider geopolitical context of the CEE region.

11.2 Research context: Energy issues and populism

The academic literature examining the intersection between populism and environmental topics, which are closely related to energy issues, has grown markedly. Such interwoven topics are part of ongoing debates, with their significance rising during the pandemic. This burgeoning literature has connected populist ideas and green energy issues, focusing on the right/far-right of the political spectrum. Right-wing populist rhetoric is indeed the focal point of studies (Lacatus and Meibauer,

2023; von Bülow and Abers, 2022) focused on narratives of prominent populist leaders, for instance, in the US and Venezuela. This literature affirms the pathway for further possible narratives in use across the EU political spectrum and elsewhere. However, global climate change and environmental protection are topics usually examined in the case studies with a focus rather on the far right (Boecher et al., 2022; de Nadal 2022) or on fairly popular Populist Radical Right Parties (PRRP), e.g., Schwörer and Fernández-García (2023).

Climate denialism by the far right and related climate scepticism based on the rejection of elites is described by Lockwood (2018). Yazar and Haarstand (2023), for their part, draw attention to political parties in Western Europe and their use of specific discursive tactics that the far right uses to hinder the decarbonisation process. Huber et al. (2021) worked with six countries (both left- and right-leaning) and contrasted their differing populist attitudes towards energy and climate policies. Meanwhile, Right-Wing Populism (RWP) in Polish *PiS*, Hungarian *Fidesz* and Italian *Lega* – and the political opportunities that environmental discourses are bringing – are the core focus of Caiani and Lubarda (2023). Forchtner and Lubarda (2022), finally, open a new Pandora's box in naming a variety of conceptualisations derived from studying the far right and their views on the environment (ecofascim, far right ecologism, green nationalism, etc...), providing a future research agenda to be pursued.

We understand populism here as we (the people) versus them (the elites), as described in the next section, and follow the formulation of definitional features of the far right developed by Mudde (2002, 2007, 2019b) and others (Vaughan and Heft, 2023; Frič and Gyárfášová, 2019; Lockwood, 2018; Giurcanu, 2017). Additional research connects the far right and the COVID-19 pandemic through the analysis of the policies and narratives primarily of Europe's far-right parties (Wondreys and Mudde, 2020). From doctrinal characteristics – nativism, authoritarianism and populism – the authors found that nativist discourse was in place; however, it was applied differently depending on the positions of the political parties in their political systems. That also may lead, then, to hypothesising (Mudde, 2020) about the impact on populism and the effects of such major crises herein.

A further strand of literature, not robustly developed yet, has examined energy topics vis-à-vis Russia's invasion of Ukraine from a populist perspective. Goldthau and Boersma (2014) alerted European leaders about the need to view gas infrastructure with their 'eyes wide open' after the gas crisis in 2014. Osička and Černoch (2022) put forward the argument that 'the fate of Europe's energy transition will be decided in the suburbs of Ukrainian cities' (p. 4). Their perspective is based on four policy paradigms arguing that the EU should act cooperatively and leverage current momentum, thereby avoiding repeating mistakes from the 2010 crisis and averting a resurgence of populism.

An innovative study by Forchtner and Lubarda's (2023) analyses the far-right position in plenary debates and voting in the European Parliament (EP), spotlighting the 'scepticism' of the parties about the way the message on the environmental agenda is handled. This engagement with a variety of arguments advanced by the far-right found in EP communications is relatively novel and unique in the literature.

Of even greater value – the article demonstrated that the extreme/radical far right are leaning towards climate 'pro' communication somewhat more than others. In this vein, we also seek to contribute to this body of knowledge by conducting a case study on the communication of energy issues in the Slovak parliament, broadening the theoretical and empirical field. Parliamentary debates in democracy in fact serve as a key communication tool within electorates by legitimising ideas. According to Steiner et al. (2005), parliamentary discussions matter because they are crucial to the functioning of institutional rules and mechanisms. Proksch and Slapin (2015) additionally claim that parliamentary speeches are critical for the policy decision-making process and can prove informative about the strategies of different political representatives. In our research, we regard speeches as a vehicle for understanding energy issues and the performance of political representatives in the political system rather than scrutinising government views.

Though our focus is on Slovakia, several studies explore the CEE region more broadly (see more in Fagan and Buzogány, 2022) from various perspectives. Szulecki (2017) explains how Poland's membership of the European Union has influenced the status of Renewable Energy Source (RES) instrumentalisation. A study of Polish right-wing media pertaining to populist narratives and climate action went beyond a general illustration of this discourse in Eastern Europe (Żuk and Szulecki, 2020). Vicenová et al. (2022, 2023) have also scrutinised the Slovak far right, *Kotlebovci: People's Party Our Slovakia*, analysing their communication on green issues during the 2016–2020 parliamentary term. Specifically, Kevicky (2023) focuses on PRRP differentiation in Slovakia and the Czech Republic and its links with three concepts: nationalism, globalism and populism. Učeň (2023) also investigates political rhetoric and the radicalisation of political discourse in Slovakia in the context of the Russia-Ukraine war, claiming that Smer-SD is following a path to 'the functional equivalent of the Radical Right for members of these constituencies that identify as left-wing' (p. 284).

The limited studies combining the use of qualitative research methods and scrutiny of parliamentary speeches on energy policy, in particular in the context of the CEE region, represents a significant gap in the academic literature. Our theoretical understanding is based on Mudde's concept of the nativist character of populist radical right political parties; we are thus avoiding the latest academic debates on the definition and clarity of the concept (see more e.g. in Figulová and Dénešová, 2021).

11.3 Research question and methodology

This section analyses political positions and presumed use of nativist framing on energy issues across the Slovak political spectrum in parliamentary debates between March 2020 and December 2022, i.e., during two major crises: the COVID-19 pandemic (which started in March 2020) and Russia's invasion of Ukraine (which started in February 2022). The timeframe of this analysis, therefore, encompasses the 2020–2023 parliamentary term, which concluded in September 2023 when early elections were held.[2] The central thesis is that the threat of crisis tends to elevate nativist and protectionist framings into the public discourse across the political spectrum, premised on the theoretical assumption that crises serve as accelerators of nativism, which could further weaken the ability of governments to address international issues at the global level. Engagement with the Slovak case, meanwhile, can elicit a fresh perspective in two notable ways. Firstly, the use of the country's parliamentary speech database offers novelty from both methodological and empirical perspectives. Secondly, framing such utterances from the populist perspective across the political spectrum can respond to what Forchtner and Lubarda (2022) marked as an 'opportunity for experimental research' (p. 101) – we seek to achieve this through empirical evidence (still relatively rare in terms of far-right research) and data from parliamentary debates.

Energy policy is recognised as a cross-cutting issue that has been highly relevant throughout both crises explored here. For instance, the COVID-19 pandemic discussions were initiated on the sustainability of energy costs in addressing the consequences of COVID-19 restrictions and their impacts on national and international economies. Similarly, Russia's invasion of Ukraine has sparked major questions about energy price impacts and Slovakia's energy diversification and self-sufficiency. External threats, whether in the form of rising energy prices or endangered energy autarky/self-sufficiency provide an opening for nativist narratives that emphasise national security or national interest angles in the context of energy policies.

This chapter has two theoretical starting points. The first concerns the interrelations between the concepts of nativism and the environment and, through the related issues of natural (energy) resources and energy self-sufficiency, nature and natural resources as symbols of (energy) independence and autarky (Forchtner, 2020; Forchtner and Özvatan, 2022). The latter are symbols of territorial ownership as well as affiliation to the in-group (i.e., the nation) and its distinction from foreigners, or aliens. This is reflected in the definition of the term 'nativism' by Mudde (2007) as one of the core features of current populist radical right parties. This is also closely related to core elements of anti-EU and anti-European attitudes, also considered to be emblematic of the European far right, with EU policies traditionally a target of far-right political figures (Mudde, 2002). Research also suggests that the far right has recently intensified its attention towards environmental topics and other related green issues with a traditional focus of the far-right agenda on symbolism (Kyriazi, 2020; Forchtner, 2019; Forchtner and Kølvraa, 2015; Vicenová et al., 2022) and ties between the nation and the land (Mudde, 2007).

This is particularly relevant in terms of the response of far-right political figures to crisis moments, with research findings, for example, indicating that nationalism, or more precisely nativism, was the key common feature of far-right political actors across Europe at the beginning of the COVID-19 pandemic (Wondreys and Mudde, 2020). Nativism is integral to the far-right political agenda, particularly through claims about the security, prosperity and wellbeing of the in-group (mostly nation). It has also been considered the key factor in driving the increased intensity and agitation of the agenda of far-right political parties – mostly the vision of the nation or its symbols as in danger (Wondreys and Mudde, 2020; Wodak, 2023; Vachudová,

2020). This theoretical assumption is especially relevant to both the COVID-19 pandemic and the energy crisis spurred by Russia's invasion of Ukraine, where the notions of security, prosperity and wellbeing of the in-group are highly pertinent. For instance, recent research has concentrated on examining dissenting positions that simultaneously tend to support Russia and oppose the European Union, with energy policy front and centre due to its national security repercussions undergirded by the high level of energy dependence of some countries on Russian natural gas (Russel, 2020). Similarly, such security and protectionist undertones are apparent with regard to the tendencies of some countries to essentially fence off their national economies in response to crises; this is also part of the definition of 'energy nationalism' (Conversi, 2020) or 'energy securitisation' (Wilson, 2020).

The second theoretical starting point of this section is connected to recent research suggesting a continuous increase in public support for right-wing extremist or right-wing populist ideas across European society. Moreover, this research argues that the far-right and right-wing extremist agenda is becoming an integral part of the mainstream or, in some countries, even of the government (Mudde, 2019a) while resorting to nativist narratives. This includes not only a continuous strengthening of the extreme right political ideas (rooted in nationalism), reflected in extreme right parties gaining important elective positions in various countries, but also in the adoption of certain elements of the far-right ideology, such as nationalism, by other political parties, mostly those labelled as right-wing populist or right-wing conservative parties. This is referred to as the 'fourth wave' of the far right (Mudde, 2019a).

A crisis of any kind thus represents a key opportunity for exploitation by far-right political actors. At the same time, according to the fourth-wave theory, it is reasonable to expect such exploitation based on nationalism and xenophobia by other political actors. Therefore, the central thesis of this chapter is that the threat of crisis tends to bring nativist and protectionist framings into the public discourse across the political spectrum. The analysis was conducted on two levels: *across time* (i.e., analysing the presence of nativist narratives throughout two different crises) and *across the political spectrum* (i.e., analysing the presence of nativist arguments in parliamentary debate by all parliamentary political actors).

The coding was done in three stages. Firstly, using the keyword 'energy', a database of 1,255 parliamentary speeches across the 2020–2022 timeframe was assembled heeding the complexity of the energy policy context. Irrelevant occurrences of the word 'energy' – use of a different meaning of the word – were eliminated in this phase (365 entries). The final database of 910 speeches contained basic information for each parliamentary speech, including the date, time, the MP's name and political affiliation and bills it concerned. In the second step, the central arguments within the speeches relevant to energy policy and used in the collected parliamentary speeches were categorised. One central argument for each speech was identified, categorised according to the sector to which the argument relates, with the presence of nativist framing finally coded. The database was analysed across two levels: time and political affiliation (spectrum). In the final step, the sub-database of 121 speeches with detected nativist framing was additionally subjected to more detailed content analysis to provide greater insight with regard to both the time and political spectrum levels of analysis.

11.4 Results and findings

The results are presented in two subsections. The first summarises the distribution of the analysed speeches and their core arguments over time. Specific attention is given to the relevance of the arguments, particularly those labelled as nativist, over time and in relation to key topics, events and developments regarding the two crises examined. In the second subsection, closer insight is provided into the content of the nativist arguments with regard to the respective MPs and their political affiliations.

11.4.1 First level: Across time (and crises)

The distribution of the dataset of 910 parliamentary speeches, including the sub-database of 121 speeches with nativist arguments, over three years from 2020 to 2022 by month (Figure 11.1) shows that there are four episodes with a noticeable rise in the number of references to 'energy' issues in parliamentary debate, with a fifth episode starting at the end of 2022 and continuing beyond the time scope of this chapter. At the same time, a noticeable uptick in nativist framing is apparent in four of the upswings of energy mentioned. In other words, at crucial moments related to the two crises, with public discussions focused more intently on energy issues, the share of nativist framing in the discourse generally saw spikes as well. This finding supports the central thesis of this chapter that crises indeed amplify nationalist or protectionist framings in the political discourse; when crises arise and debates on energy issues intensify, nativist framing therein is also augmented. In this subsection, we provide more insight into the content of parliamentary debates

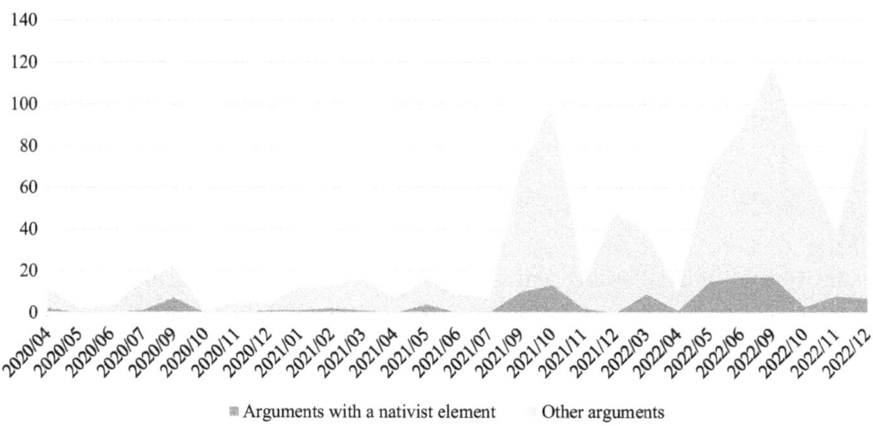

Figure 11.1 Analysed speeches over time.

in these crucial moments (peaks), with a focus on which bills were discussed the most and brought nativist framings into the discussions.

The September 2020 (the first peak) debate was constituted mostly by economic[3] arguments, with nativist claims present particularly through discussions on energy self-sufficiency, such as the debate on energy-related consequences of the COVID-19 pandemic, effects ostensibly compounded by the foreign ownership of strategic energy companies in Slovakia (National Council of the Slovak Republic, 2020). September and October 2021 (the second peak) reinforced the energy-related debate in parliament in response to a looming international energy crisis. Nativist arguments were mostly advanced in the context of debates on developments on the international energy scene and the situation with Nord Stream 2 (National Council of the Slovak Republic, 2021a), as well as the debate on removing the Minister of Economy for his alleged failure to handle the negative consequences of surging energy prices from prior months (National Council of the Slovak Republic, 2021b), with financial and social arguments prominent in the latter case.

Early 2022 (the third peak) analysed speeches that primarily reflected energy security issues via ongoing discussions on energy impacts related to the persisting external situation, with nativist arguments present through, again, the lingering effects of COVID-19 on the energy sector (National Council of the Slovak Republic, 2021c), but also through the debate about the Ukraine situation (National Council of the Slovak Republic, 2022a). This peak, occurring shortly before Russia's military aggression, stood at the intersection between the two crises, encompassing both the consequences of the COVID-19 pandemic and the potential energy implications of an impending Russia-Ukraine conflict in the country's immediate neighbourhood. The latter, in turn, further contributed to an increase in nativist arguments.

The most fundamental increase in the intensity of the energy debate and the corresponding rise in nativist framing was measured between May and October 2022 (the fourth peak). The debate was dominated by social issues in relation to rising energy prices, most notably discussions about pensions (National Council of the Slovak Republic, 2022b), various forms of social support (National Council of the Slovak Republic, 2022c), social security (National Council of the Slovak Republic, 2022d), or, again, removing the Minister of Economy because of rising energy prices and his handling of the situation in the wake of the sanctions against Russia (National Council of the Slovak Republic, 2022e).

11.4.2 Second level: Across the political spectrum

The second and more important part of the central thesis concerns the growing inclination towards adopting nativist arguments across the political spectrum, in line with the theoretical assumptions of the fourth wave of the far right and the 'mainstreamisation' of the far right in politics. Amongst parliament political parties throughout the 2020–2022 timeframe, Smer-SD, a social democratic party with expressive nationalist narratives, and *Kotlebovci-ĽSNS*, a far-right party, were among the parties with the highest numbers of nativist framings used in parliamentary speeches related to energy topics. *Kotlebovci-ĽSNS* also recorded the highest share of nativist arguments (34.4%) delivered by their MPs compared to their speeches without such framing.

It is, however, notable that the single largest number of nativist arguments in the given timeframe (Figure 11.2) was recorded in the group of *non-affiliated MPs*[4] (i.e., either ex-*Kotlebovci-ĽSNS* MPs or ex-Smer-SD MPs).

The detailed chart on the use of nativist framings by different MPs (Figure 11.3) underscores that most nativist arguments (in absolute numbers) were promulgated by either the most visible far-right politicians (namely, Marian Kotleba of *Kotlebovci-ĽSNS* and Milan Mazurek and Tomáš Taraba, non-affiliated MPs and

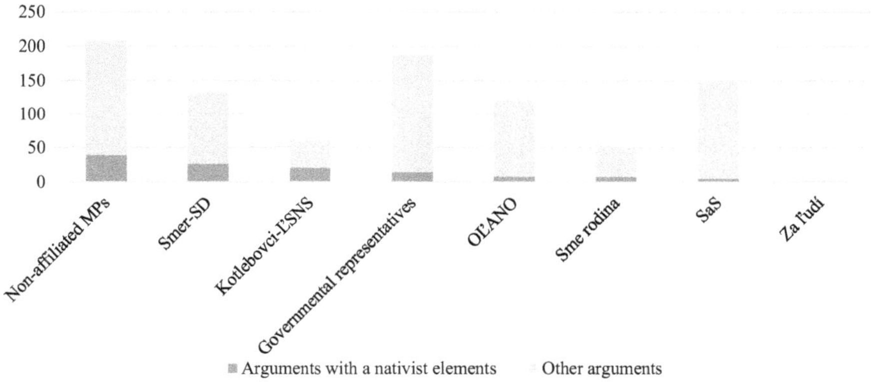

Figure 11.2 Speeches with and without nativist arguments by affiliation.

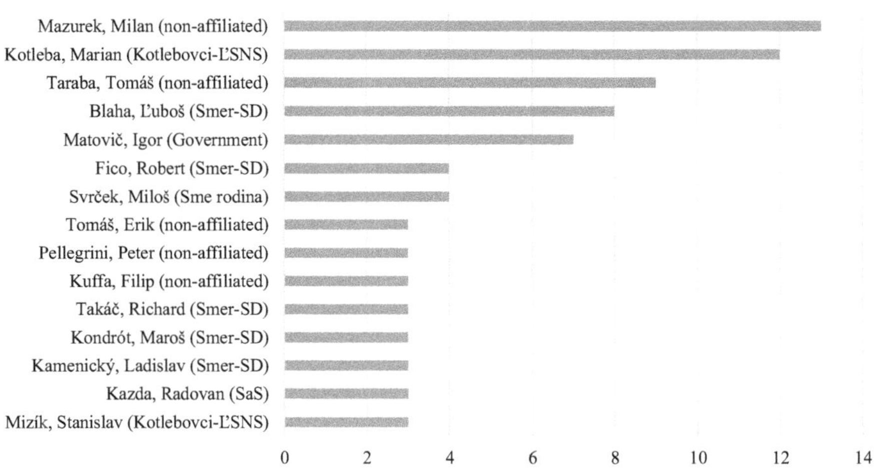

Figure 11.3 MPs with the largest numbers of nativist arguments.

ex-*Kotlebovci-ĽSNS*) or politicians infamous for spreading extremist narratives (namely, Ľuboš Blaha, Smer-SD).

11.4.3 Nature of nativist energy arguments

In scrutinising the dataset of nativist arguments or public policy sectors to which they relate (Figure 11.4), financial and economic arguments (i.e. arguments using nativist or protectionist framing in relation to either finances or the economy) appear to be prevalent across the political spectrum in nativist argumentation (Figure 11.5).

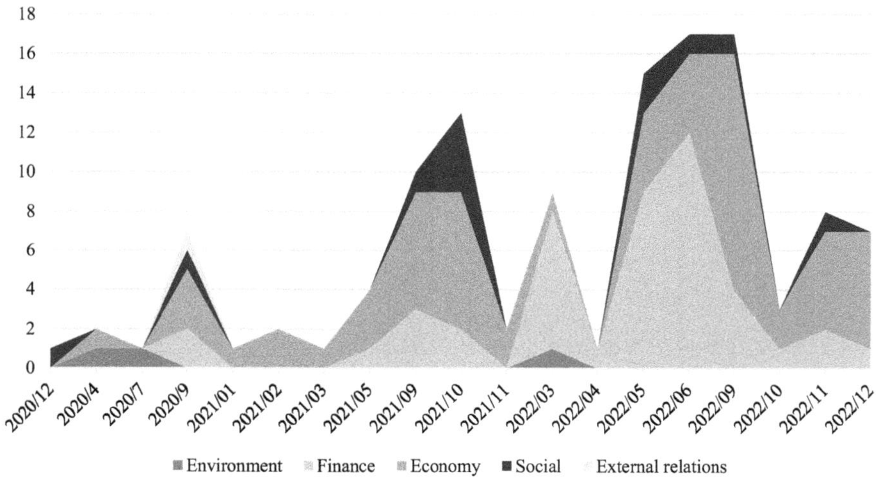

Figure 11.4 Nativist arguments over time by sectors.

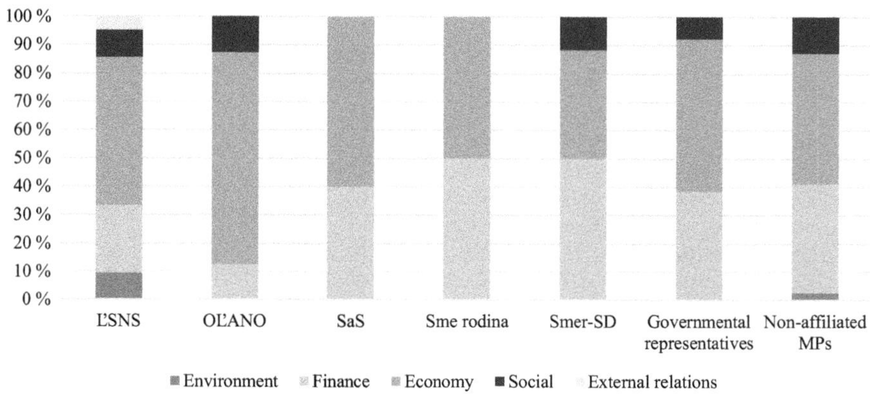

Figure 11.5 Speeches with nativist arguments based on sectors to which they relate and based on political affiliation.

An illustrative example of the use of economic arguments in nativist framing concerns the portrayal of energy as national property: 'the mission of Slovak electricity producers *Slovenské elektrárne* is, in the first place, to generate energy for consumption in Slovakia. For household consumption, for consumption in business, simply for the entire aggregate consumption of electrical energy in the Slovak Republic. And when you, as the government, are unable to make it happen any other way, start to nationalise' (Kotleba, (*Kotlebovci-ĽSNS)*, 2021a). MP Kotleba, in this vein, called for prioritising the nationalist cause over market elements, framing energy as a national interest and a national resource belonging first and foremost to Slovaks.

Furthermore, Kotleba (2020a) also reflected on the foreign ownership of energy and strategic enterprises, arguing that foreign management purportedly poses a threat to national interests and the national economy as 'these foreign co-owners don't know what to else to charge, don't know how else to rip off the nation'. Similarly (though from a different part of the political spectrum), MP Ľuboš Blaha (Smer-SD) employed the foreign ownership as a threat to the national economy and sovereignty frame: 'We have given up our sovereignty and we rely on our big American brother and big German brother to protect us every time. They will throw us in the trash just like that, whenever they need to. That is what geopolitics is about (…) we must protect ourselves. But here we are, throwing ourselves in the trash, we are throwing away all our tools to retain our national sovereignty' (Blaha, 2021a). Nativist narratives are also present in protectionist statements about the national ownership of strategic resources, such as wood/logging, as suggested by MP Rastislav Schlosár (*Kotlebovci-ĽSNS*). Arguing for the protection of national economic interests, he proposed that

> wood be constitutionally declared a strategic resource for the Slovak Republic, protected by the Constitution of the Slovak Republic, and this as the first step enabling us to subsequently adopt the appropriate legislation that will heavily constrain or, if needed, directly prohibit exports of Slovak wood.
>
> (Schlosár, 2022)

In all cases, the involvement of foreign actors and entities is weaponised in discussions on national sovereignty and (energy) independence.

Another example of nativist framing employing economic arguments pertained to criticism towards the European Union's unified approach in response to Russia's military invasion of Ukraine. For instance, critics argued that then-prime minister Igor Matovič was endangering Slovak security by 'blabber[ing] to the international media on how Slovakia has to be brave and set an example even though disconnection from energy from Russia would devastate us completely' (Pellegrini (non-affiliated/ex-Smer-SD), 2022). Distinguishing EU interests from Slovak interests and claiming they are in contradiction is thus another example of how nativist framing operates on economic matters. MP Milan Mazurek (non-affiliated/ex-*Kotlebovci-ĽSNS*) admonished the Slovak government and reassured his supporters that he was 'not involved in these absurd rules that will result in a heavy impoverishment of the population of the Slovak Republic', while also adding that EU actions were 'damaging the interests of the population of the Slovak Republic' (Mazurek, 2021). From the same segment of the political spectrum, MP Eduard Kočiš (non-affiliated/ex-*Kotlebovci-ĽSNS*) stressed that Slovak citizens and taxpayers should be predominantly prioritised, adding: '(…) and we can, if you excuse me, fuck off the whole Leipzig stock market' (Kočiš, 2022).

Furthermore, anti-EU sentiment is reflected in statements suggesting that EU policies by default stand in contradiction to Slovak national interests and lambasting the Slovak government for not having 'the courage to promote national solutions' as it tolerated 'nonsense from the European Union' (*(OĽANO)*, 2022). Further statements lampooned the government for 'waiting for an all-European energy solution while not giving a damn about the national interest' (Tomáš (non-affiliated/ex-Smer-SD), 2022). The speeches of far-right politicians in the Slovak parliament particularly called for the protection of Slovak interests and energy security, with a strong anti-EU sentiment identified. Kotleba (*Kotlebovci-ĽSNS)*, for instance, derided EU membership as the main source of [this whole] 'energy insanity, this energy inflation, which the population of the Slovak Republic will pay for this coming winter … under those disadvantageous terms that the Union dictated to us' (Kotleba, 2021b). These examples provide insight into nativist framings that have been used to highlight the sovereignty narrative in the context of foreign elements and simultaneously promote anti-EU narratives.

The threat that Russia would use the energy sector as a weapon following its military aggression provided another justification for propagating nativist framings in parliamentary discussions on Slovak energy security. This line of reasoning was deployed especially by government MPs, such as Juraj Krúpa (*SaS*): 'We have the steps taken by Russia here, which in effect destabilize or takes steps to undermine energy security, using it as their weapon' (Krúpa, 2022). Veronika Remišová (*Za ľudí*, then Minister of Investment, Regional Development and Informatisation) similarly remarked:

> Eduard Heger [PM then] who has never wavered in his service for the people of Slovakia, nor in fighting corruption, nor in defending Slovakia's foreign policy interests, nor in ensuring the energy security or security as such of people in Slovakia.
>
> (Remišová, 2022)

The economic rationale used in parliamentary speeches mostly concerned energy prices on (global) markets and other related variables. A nativist dimension was also apparent in the populist contrast between the interests of foreign corporations and those of the Slovak people in relation to the entire economy, as argued by Ľuboš Blaha (Smer-SD): 'Mr Fico cared about the Slovaks, but you care only about business deals of international corporations and banks' (Blaha, 2021b). The anti-EU finance-related frame was significant in the context of the energy market as well, suggesting that the energy inflation situation was the result of dependency on EU markets: 'some other countries, that is, not Slovakia, introduce various measures to prevent these wild energy price increases' (Kotleba (*Kotlebovci-ĽSNS)*, 2021c). Moreover, in addition to anti-EU narratives, attempts to interweave these issues with migration, a pressing and polarising political topic, have been apparent too: 'Slovakia is really a peculiar country; it prioritises the interests of migrants, the interests of Brussels and other organisations over the interests of Slovaks and, in my opinion, this is also related to energy' (Urban, (non-affiliated/ex-*Kotlebovci-ĽSNS*), 2022).

The energy price hikes spurred by Russia's military aggression against Ukraine served as another purported justification for folding nativist framings into the energy debate. Support for Ukraine, for instance, was problematised as contradictory to national energy stabilising policies:

> none of us can stop the war in Ukraine, but we can help the people who need help, but I would like to see you [government] presenting, in a summary legislative procedure, also some bills that will concern help for the heavily tried Slovak nation.
>
> (Mazurek (non-affiliated/ex-*Kotlebovci-ĽSNS*), 2022)

After the invasion of Ukraine, energy issues were often depicted in a manner that suggested a link between the concept of energy poverty and nation: 'households whose housing costs exceed 40% of their disposable income can fall into energy poverty. (…) The housing costs overburdening people therefore concern more than 178,000 Slovak men and women' (Svrček, (*We Are Family*), 2022). This pattern suggests the constant adaptation of key nativist arguments was at work against the backdrop of evolving geopolitical developments.

To a lesser extent, nativist framings are also associated with rhetoric on social issues, as evidenced by arguments suggesting that foreign corporations controlling strategic energy companies were engendering detrimental financial consequences on national social policies: 'the only thing they have offered as a solution is absurd neoliberal deregulation through which they will increase energy prices even more and distribute national assets to international corporations' (Blaha (Smer-SD), 2021c). The nativist framing of energy arguments in relation to social issues also recurred in speeches mainly of far-right politicians, for instance, through Eduard Kočiš's (non-affiliated/ex-*Kotlebovci-ĽSNS*) insinuation that there was a lack of protection of Slovak citizens from foreign policy decisions: 'If German nuclear power plants remain closed down, that dumping price on world markets will simply be so untenable that Slovak pensioners and Slovak households will really consider when and why they should switch on the lights' (Kočiš, 2021). Moreover, the closure of Slovak nuclear power plants provided another target for protectionist and anti-EU framings, paired with arguments about energy and social issues:

> had we not closed down the two units [of the nuclear power plant in Jaslovské Bohunice] thanks to the rotten European Union and, of course, the treacherous governments, we would be energy self-sufficient today (…), but you will never understand this because Brussels is a new deity for you.
>
> (Kotleba (*Kotlebovci-ĽSNS*), 2021d)

MPs affiliated with far-right party *Kotlebovci-ĽSNS* and, to a more limited extent, also to non-affiliated MPs/ex-*Kotlebovci-ĽSNS* also pushed nativist framing into the discourse via opposition to environmental protections and European green policies that they allege contradict Slovakia's national interests. This includes, for instance, anti-EU framings focused on the use of alternative energy sources in railways and the environmental consequences of market liberalisation on national policies: '[... I know that while the European Union is forcing us to liberalise the railway market, it has created enormous room for trades, corruption, business; and rather than addressing transport, various artificial investments and business models are being addressed' (Kotleba, (*Kotlebovci-ĽSNS*, 2020b). Similarly, MPs from far-right parties sought to differentiate European and national interests in relation to EU policies, including environmental and energy policies: 'this is the way to protect own nation, and this is the way the politician should behave towards its own nation. Not the way you are doing it, while not defending Slovak interests in Brussels' (Kočiš, (non-affiliated/ex-*Kotlebovci-ĽSNS)*, 2020). These insinuations strongly imply that foreign, often EU-linked, influences on national and environmental policies are engendering grave consequences on national policies.

External relations in energy policies were framed in a nativist manner only peripherally and recorded only once in relation to the consequences of Slovakia's EU and NATO membership for the energy sector:

> I too am asking whether our membership of the European Union and NATO actually multiplies the options for promoting and defending the Slovak Republic's interests (...) I am asking whether the designation as a reliable and responsible partner does not merely disguise the fact that we are nothing but obedient servants of geopolitical lords.
>
> (Mizík (*Kotlebovci-ĽSNS*), 2020)

11.5 Conclusion

Our chapter sheds some light on the puzzles in this volume, specifically the notion that crises *do* constitute and/or bring opportunities for framing certain policies, such as energy, in nativist and protectionist ways. The focus here paired an emphasis on populist and nationalist narratives. Returning to our central thesis, both the threat of a crisis and crises themselves promote nativist and protectionist framings in the Slovak public discourse. The adoption of such narratives spans the political spectrum – not only far-right parties. This chapter underscores that increased attention placed on energy issues in the political agenda has corresponded with a rise in the use of nativist arguments in the political discourse (Figure 11.1).

At the same time, the findings here provide backing to Učeň's (2023) argument that geopolitical issues, especially energy matters associated with Russia's military aggression against Ukraine, have significantly contributed to the polarisation of the political discourse recently. Energy topics have indeed been incorporated by the far right and other parties of the political spectrum as integral parts of their radicalised narratives. Most importantly, it also provides evidence for Mudde's (2019a, 2019b) theoretical assumption of a fourth wave of the far right and 'mainstreamisation' of far-right ideas that are gradually adopted by other ideological segments of the political spectrum. For instance, the Slovak parliamentary debate shows that in response to the crises, nativist framings have been increasingly present in the parliamentary discourse and incorporated into speeches of left-wing figures in the political spectrum (Smer-SD) and, in individual cases, also by other political actors. Nevertheless, the data also underlines that nativist framings are predominantly the purview of the far-right, as evidenced by the nativist arguments used by the *Kotlebovci-ĽSNS* MPs.

A palpable anti-European and nationalist narrative concerns the idea that solutions to energy resource issues should rest solely in Slovak hands despite a globalised energy space, an approach that accords with prototypical populist politics (Mudde, 2019a). The experience with the EU crises, such as migration and COVID-19, is heterogeneous; the Slovak case study serves as an example of the paradox of ardent (predominantly right-wing populist) criticism of EU involvement in policies that are not, in fact, decided primarily at the EU level but rather remain under the purview of national governments. This paradox is misused for further reinforcing anti-European narratives, the outcome of which is also visible in the results of the September 2023 Slovak general elections. The utterances of Slovak politicians are a testament to the fact that Slovakia is not contributing to a more decarbonised, secure and integrated EU and that, despite the EU's policies, the 'mainstreamisation' of energy issues is increasingly bolstering support for national solutions spanning the Slovak political spectrum. Further research should, therefore, further examine our finding that nativist arguments were presented across the political spectrum, particularly by formally non-affiliated MPs who changed their affiliation during the monitored period and formed new political entities. This suggests that the political spectrum in the Slovak parliament was experiencing a political tussle that may have significant implications for the country's political system and elections in the future.

Acknowledgements

This work was supported by the Slovak Research and Development Agency Grant No. APVV-20-0012.

Notes

1 After the 2020 parliamentary elections, six political parties entered the National Council of the Slovak Republic: *Obyčajní ľudia a nezávislé osobnosti* (Ordinary People and Independent Personalities, *OĽANO*), Smer – *sociálna demokracia* (Smer – Social Democracy, Smer – *SD*), *Sme rodina* (We Are Family), *Kotlebovci – Ľudová strana Naše Slovensko* (Kotlebovci – People's Party Our Slovakia, *ĽSNS*), *Sloboda a solidarita* (Freedom and Solidarity, *SAS*) and *Za ľudí* (For the People). During the 2020–2023

parliamentary term, several of these parties disintegrated and their former members either changed their political affiliation to other existing parties or created new ones or stayed "non-affiliated". Due to this and based on parliamentary rules, two political parties (*Za ľudí* and *Kotlebovci*) did not have their own parliamentary club (the formation of which requires six MPs).

2 Regarding the development of the Slovak political discourse, it should be noted that the results of the general elections in September 2023 have brought about a change in Slovak parliamentary representation: the political spectrum has been deprived of a far-right political party, though many former members of ĽSNS made it into parliament on the ballot list of SNS (Slovak National Party), which has returned after four years out of government and parliament after falling below the election threshold for seats in the 2020 elections.

3 In the text we are working with the notion of economy, such as in Ministry of *Economy*, while the term financial is meant rather as in Ministry of *Finance*.

4 The non-affiliation category does not indicate political independence or lack of political affiliation; on the contrary, this category contains those MPs who left the parties they were elected for and formed new political entities that failed to form official parliamentary club. A clear majority of the non-affiliated nativist arguments presented in this chapter are linked to the ex-*Kotlebovci-ĽSNS* MPs (who later affiliated with the successor movement *Republika*), with the remainder of the non-affiliated nativist arguments linked to ex-Smer-SD MPs (who later affiliated with the successor political party Hlas-SD).

References

Blaha, Ľ. (2021a). Speech in the parliamentary debate. National Council of the Slovak Republic. https://tv.nrsr.sk/archiv/schodza/8/43?id=249828

Blaha, Ľ. (2021b). Factual note. National Council of the Slovak Republic. https://tv.nrsr.sk/archiv/schodza/8/43?id=249729

Blaha, Ľ. (2021c). Factual note. National Council of the Slovak Republic. https://tv.nrsr.sk/archiv/schodza/8/43?id=249764

Boecher, M., Zeigermann, U., Berker, L. E., & Jabra, D. (2022). Climate policy expertise in times of populism – knowledge strategies of the AfD regarding Germany's climate package. *Environmental Politics*, *31*(5), 820–840. https://doi.org/10.1080/09644016.2022.2090537

Caiani, N., & Lubarda, B. (2023): Conditional environmentalism of right-wing populism in power: Ideology and/or opportunities? *Environmental Politics, 33*(4), 591–611 https://doi.org/10.1080/09644016.2023.2242749

Chytilek, R., & Havlík, V. (2022). The voters of populist radical right parties in CEE: How radical are they? In S.Hajdiniak (Ed.) *Behind the Illiberal Turn: Values in Central Europe pp.* 41–73. https://doi.org/10.1163/9789004514041_004

Conversi, D. (2020). The ultimate challenge: Nationalism and climate change. *Nationalities Papers*, *48*(4). 625–636 https://doi.org/10.1017/nps.2020.18

de Nadal, L. (2022). Climate change: Bad news for populism? How the *Rassemblement National* used COVID-19 to promote its environmental agenda. *Nationalities Papers*. https://doi.org/10.1017/nps.2022.104

Fagan, A., & Buzogány, A. (2022). Beyond Europeanization: Political ecology and environmentalism in Central and Eastern Europe. *Environmental Politics*, *31*(7). 1203-1213 https://doi.org/10.1080/09644016.2022.2147652

Figulová, A., & Denéšová, M. (2021). Governance of the COVID-19 pandemic in Slovakia. *Partecipazione e Conflitto, 14*(3). 1256–1273 https://doi.org/10.1285/i20356609v14i3p1256

Forchtner, B. (2019). The far right and the environment: Politics, discourse and communication. In *The Far Right and the Environment: Politics, Discourse and Communication.* https://doi.org/10.4324/9781351104043

Forchtner, B. (2020). Far-right articulations of the natural environment. An Introduction. In B. Forchtner (Ed.). *The Far Right and the Environment. Politics, Discourse, and Communication* (pp. 15–27). Abingdon and New York: Routledge.

Forchtner, B., & Kolvraa, C. (2015). The nature of nationalism: Populist radical right parties on countryside and climate. *Nature and Culture, 10*(2), 199–224. https://doi.org/10.3167/nc.2015.100204

Forchtner, B., & Lubarda, B. (2022). Far right and environment: Past-present-future. In B. Forchtner (Ed.). *The Far Right and the Environment: Politics, Discourse and Communication* (pp. 85–111). Abingdon: Routledge.

Forchtner, B., & Lubarda, B. (2023). Scepticisms and beyond? A comprehensive portrait of climate change communication by the far right in the European Parliament. *Environmental Politics, 32*(1), 43–68. https://doi.org/10.1080/09644016.2022.2048556

Forchtner, B., & Özvatan, Ö. (2022). De/legitimising Europe through the performance of crises. *Journal of Language and Politics, 21*(2). 208–232 https://doi.org/10.1075/jlp.21064.for

Frič, P., & Gyárfášová, O. (2019). The rise of the politics of emotions: Anti-elitism and Anti-corruptism as traits of Czech and Slovak populist parties. *Politické Vedy, 22*(4) 221–246. https://doi.org/10.24040/politickevedy.2019.22.4.221-246

Giurcanu, M. (2017). Trouble on the far right. Contemporary right-wing strategies and practices in Europe. *East European Politics, 33*(4). 572–573 https://doi.org/10.1080/21599165.2017.1369406

Goldthau, A., & Boersma, T. (2014). The 2014 Ukraine-Russia crisis: Implications for energy markets and scholarship. *Energy Research and Social Science, 3*(C). 13–15 https://doi.org/10.1016/j.erss.2014.05.001

Gyarfášová, O. (2020, March 6th). '*Slovenské voľby 2020: potvrdenie 'stabilnej nestability*'. HBS Prague. https://cz.boell.org/cs/Slovak_elections_2020

Gyimesi, G. (2022). Factual note. National Council of the Slovak Republic. http://tv.nrsr.sk/archiv/schodza/8/72?id=272114

Huber, R., Maltby, T., Szulecki, K., & Ćetković, S. (2021). Is populism a challenge to European energy and climate policy? Empirical evidence across varieties of populism, *Journal of European Public Policy*, 28(7), 998–1017.Jirušek, M. (2023). The Czech EU presidency: Strengthening energy security amidst the crisis. *Czech Journal of International Relations / Mezinarodni Vztahy, 58*(1). 147–157 https://doi.org/10.32422/mv-cjir.702

Kerekeš, D. (2020, February 26). 'Je volebné Slovensko rozdelené na Bratislavu verzus zvyšok krajiny? Ani nie.' *Denník N.* https://dennikn.sk/1754264/je-volebne-slovensko-rozdelene-na-bratislava-verzus-zvysok-krajiny-ani-nie/

Kevicky, D. (2023). 'We will protect our countryside without a Green Deal': The populist radical right and the environment in Czechia and Slovakia. *European Journal of Geography, 14*(2). 32–43 https://doi.org/10.48088/ejg.d.kev.14.2.032.043

Kočiš, E. (2020). Factual note. National Council of the Slovak Republic. Available at http://tv.nrsr.sk/archiv/schodza/8/9?id=22562

Kočiš, E. (2021). Factual note. National Council of the Slovak Republic. Available at http://tv.nrsr.sk/archiv/schodza/8/48?id=252765

Kočiš, E. (2022). Factual note. National Council of the Slovak Republic. Available at http://tv.nrsr.sk/archiv/schodza/8/72?id=272131

Kotleba, M. (2020a) Factual note. National Council of the Slovak Republic. Available at https://tv.nrsr.sk/archiv/schodza/8/4?id=220390

Kotleba, M. (2020b). Factual note. National Council of the Slovak Republic. Available at http://tv.nrsr.sk/archiv/schodza/8/6?id=221776

Kotleba, M. (2021a). Factual note. National Council of the Slovak Republic. Available at https://tv.nrsr.sk/archiv/schodza/8/48?id=252499

Kotleba, M. (2021b). Factual note. National Council of the Slovak Republic. Available at https://tv.nrsr.sk/archiv/schodza/8/43?id=249917

Kotleba, M. (2021c). Factual note. National Council of the Slovak Republic. Available at http://tv.nrsr.sk/archiv/schodza/8/48?id=252568

Kotleba, M. (2021d). Factual note. National Council of the Slovak Republic. Available at http://tv.nrsr.sk/archiv/schodza/8/48?id=252790

Krúpa, J. (2022). Speech in the parliamentary debate. National Council of the Slovak Republic. Available at http://tv.nrsr.sk/archiv/schodza/8/75?id=273963

Kyriazi, A. (2020). The environmental communication of Jobbik: Between strategy and ideology. In B. Forchtner (Ed.). *The Far Right and the Environment: Politics, Discourse and Communication* (pp. 184–200). New York: Routledge.

Lacatus, C., & Meibauer, G. (2023). Crisis, rhetoric and right-wing populist incumbency: An analysis of Donald Trump's Tweets and press briefings. *Government and Opposition, 58*(2). 1–19 https://doi.org/10.1017/gov.2021.34

Lockwood, M. (2018). Right-wing populism and the climate change agenda: Exploring the linkages. *Environmental Politics, 27*(4). 712–732 https://doi.org/10.1080/09644016.2018.1458411

Mazurek, M. (2021). Factual note. National Council of the Slovak Republic. Available at http://tv.nrsr.sk/archiv/schodza/8/48?id=252709

Mazurek, M. (2022). Speech in the parliamentary debate. National Council of the Slovak Republic. Available at http://tv.nrsr.sk/archiv/schodza/8/60?id=262567

Mišík, M., & Nosko, A. (2023). Post-pandemic lessons for EU energy and climate policy after the Russian invasion of Ukraine: Introduction to a special issue on EU green recovery in the post-Covid-19 period. *Energy Policy, 177.* 113546 https://doi.org/10.1016/j.enpol.2023.113546

Mizík, S. (2020). Speech in the parliamentary debate. National Council of the Slovak Republic. Available at http://tv.nrsr.sk/archiv/schodza/8/12?id=229237

Mudde, C. (2002). *The Ideology ofthe Extreme Right.* New York: Manchester University Press.

Mudde, C. (2007). *Populist Radical Right Parties in Europe.* Cambridge, UK Cambridge University Press.

Mudde, C. (2019a). *The Far Right Today.* Cambridge, UK: Polity.

Mudde, C. (2019b). The 2019 EU elections: Moving the center. *Journal of Democracy 30*(4), 20–34. https://doi.org/10.1353/jod.2019.0066

Mudde, C. (2020). Will 'the Coronavirus' kill populism? Don't count on it', *The Guardian.* [Online]. www.theguardian.com/commentisfree/2020/mar/27/coronavirus-populism-trump-politics-response

National Council of the Slovak Republic. (2020). Information from the Minister of Economy of the Slovak Republic on the conditions for the sale of 49% of the shares of VSE, a.s. to the German company E.ON. National Council of the Slovak Republic. www.nrsr.sk/web/Default.aspx?sid=schodze/

National Council of the Slovak Republic. (2021a). A proposal of a group of Slovak MPs for Slovak parliament to pass a resolution on the serious social impacts of the surging electricity, gas, and heat prices for Slovak households and small and medium-sized enterprises in 2022 and on the risk to the Slovak Republic's financial interests in connection with the opening of the Nord Stream 2 international gas pipeline. National Council of the Slovak Republic. www.nrsr.sk/web/Default.aspx?sid=zakony/cpt&ZakZborID=13&CisObdobia=8&ID=687

National Council of the Slovak Republic. (2021b). A proposal of a group of Slovak MPs for Slovak parliament to pass a vote of no confidence on Richard Sulík, a cabinet member in charge of managing the Ministry of Economy of the Slovak Republic. National Council of the Slovak Republic. www.nrsr.sk/web/Default.aspx?sid=zakony/cpt&ZakZborID=13&CisObdobia=8&ID=747

National Council of the Slovak Republic. (2021c). The Cabinet's bill to amend Act No 67/2020 on certain extraordinary measures in the financial sector in connection with the spreading of the dangerous contagious human disease Covid-19, as amended. National Council of the Slovak Republic. www.nrsr.sk/web/Default.aspx?sid=zakony/cpt&ZakZborID=13&CisObdobia=8&ID=808

National Council of the Slovak Republic. (2022a). The Cabinet's bill on certain other measures in connection with the situation in Ukraine. National Council of the Slovak Republic. www.nrsr.sk/web/Default.aspx?sid=zakony/cpt&ZakZborID=13&CisObdobia=8&ID=948

National Council of the Slovak Republic. (2022b). A proposal of Slovak MPs Peter Pellegrini, Denisa Sakova, Richard Raši, Erik Tomáš, and Matúš Šutaj Eštok for the promulgation of a law to amend Act No 296/2020 on the 13th old-age pension and on amending certain other laws, as amended. National Council of the Slovak Republic. www.nrsr.sk/web/Default.aspx?sid=zakony/cpt&ZakZborID=13&CisObdobia=8&ID=993

National Council of the Slovak Republic. (2022c). The Cabinet's bill on financing children's leisure time and on amending certain other laws. National Council of the Slovak Republic. www.nrsr.sk/web/Default.aspx?sid=zakony/cpt&ZakZborID=13&CisObdobia=8&ID=1028

National Council of the Slovak Republic. (2022d). A proposal of Slovak MPs Peter Pellegrini, Erik Tomáš, Denisa Sakova, Richard Raši and Matúš Šutaj Eštok for the promulgation of a law to amend Act No 461/2003 on social security, as amended. National Council of the Slovak Republic. www.nrsr.sk/web/Default.aspx?sid=zakony/cpt&ZakZborID=13&CisObdobia=8&ID=913

National Council of the Slovak Republic. (2022e). A proposal of a group of Slovak MPs for Slovak parliament to pass a vote of no confidence on Richard Sulík, a cabinet member in charge of managing the Ministry of Economy of the Slovak Republic. National Council of the Slovak Republic. www.nrsr.sk/web/Default.aspx?sid=zakony/cpt&ZakZborID=13&CisObdobia=8&ID=1068

Osička, J., & Černoch, F. (2022). European energy politics after Ukraine: The road ahead. *Energy Research and Social Science*, *91*. 1–6.https://doi.org/10.1016/j.erss.2022.102757

Pellegrini, P. (2022). Speech in the parliamentary debate. National Council of the Slovak Republic. Available at http://tv.nrsr.sk/archiv/schodza/8/65?id=265917

Proksch S.O. and Slapin J.B. (2015) *The Politics of Parliamentary Debate: Parties, Rebels, and Representation,* Cambridge: Cambridge University Press.

Remišová, V. (2022). Speech in the parliamentary debate. National Council of the Slovak Republic. Available at http://tv.nrsr.sk/archiv/schodza/8/79?id=278556

Russell, M. (2020). *Energy security in the EU's external policy*. European Parliamentary Research Service [online]. www.europarl.europa.eu/RegData/etudes/IDAN/2020/649334/EPRS_IDA(2020)649334_EN.pdf

Schlosár, R. (2022). The presenter is making a point. National Council of the Slovak Republic. Available at http://tv.nrsr.sk/archiv/schodza/8/75?id=274156

Schwörer, J., & Fernández-García, B. (2023). Climate sceptics or climate nationalists? Understanding and explaining populist radical right parties' positions towards climate change (1990–2022). *Political Studies. 0(0)* https://doi.org/10.1177/00323217231176475

Steiner, J., Bächtiger, A., Spörndli, M., & Steenbergen, M. R. (2005). *Deliberative Politics in Action: Analyzing Parliamentary Discourse*. Cambridge: Cambridge University Press (Theories of Institutional Design).

Svrček, M. (2022). Speech in the parliamentary debate. National Council of the Slovak Republic. Available at http://tv.nrsr.sk/archiv/schodza/8/72?id=270694

Szulecki, K. (2017). *Poland's renewable energy policy mix: European influence and domestic soap opera*. CICERO Working Papers. https://papers.ssrn.com/sol3/papers.cfm?abstract_id=2964866

Tomáš, E. (2022). Factual note. National Council of the Slovak Republic. Available at https://tv.nrsr.sk/archiv/schodza/8/77?id=276644

Tosun, J., & Debus, M. (2021). Right-wing populist parties and environmental politics: Insights from the Austrian Freedom Party's support for the glyphosate ban. *Environmental Politics*, 30(1–2), 224–244.

Učeň, P. (2023). The Russia-Ukraine war and the radicalization of political discourse in Slovakia. In G. Ivaldi & E. Zankina (Eds). *The Impacts of the Russian Invasion of Ukraine on Right-Wing Populism in Europe* (pp. 78–288). European Center for Populism Studies (ECPS). Brussels. https://doi.org/10.55271/rp0029

Urban, M. (2022). Factual note. National Council of the Slovak Republic. Available at https://tv.nrsr.sk/archiv/schodza/8/77?id=27650

Vachudova, M. A. (2020). Ethnopopulism and democratic backsliding in Central Europe. East European Politics. https://doi.org/10.1080/21599165.2020.1787163

Vaughan, M., & Heft, A. (2023). Anti-elitism in the European radical right in comparative perspective. *Journal of Common Market Studies*, *61*(1). 76–94 https://doi.org/10.1111/jcms.13347

Vicenová, R., Oravcová, V., & Mišík, M. (2022). What do far-right parties talk about when they talk about green issues? ĽSNS in 2016–2020 Parliamentary Debates. *Sociologia (Slovakia)*, *54*(6). 569–594 https://doi.org/10.31577/sociologia.2022.54.6.20

Vicenová, R., Oravcová, V., & Mišík, M. (2023). Not so green after all: Visual representation of green issues by the far-right Kotlebovci – People's Party Our Slovakia. In B. Forchtner (Eds). *Visualising Far-Right Environments: Communication and the Politics of Nature*. Manchester Press, 146–165.

von Bülow, M., & Abers, R. N. (2022). Denialism and populism: Two sides of a coin in Jair Bolsonaro's Brazil. *Government and Opposition*. https://doi.org/10.1017/gov.2022.14

Weisskircher, M. (2023). *Contemporary Germany and the Fourth Wave of Far-Right Politics: From the Streets to Parliament.* Abingdon: Taylor & Francis Group.

Wilson, J. D. (2019). A securitisation approach to international energy politics. *Energy Research and Social Science*, *49*. 114–115 https://doi.org/10.1016/j.erss.2018.10.024

Wodak, R. (2023). The politics of fear: The shameless normalization of far-right discourse. *The Politics of Fear: The Shameless Normalization of Far-Right Discourse*. London: Sage https://doi.org/10.4135/9781529739664

Wondreys, J., & Mudde, C. (2020). Victims of the pandemic? European far-right parties and COVID-19. *Nationalities Papers*, *50*(1). 86–103 https://doi.org/10.1017/nps.2020.93

Yazar, M., & Haarstad, H. (2023). Populist far right discursive-institutional tactics in European regional decarbonization. *Political Geography*, *105*. 102936 https://doi.org/10.1016/j.polgeo.2023.102936

Żuk, P., & Szulecki, K. (2020). Unpacking the right-populist threat to climate action: Poland's pro-governmental media on energy transition and climate change. *Energy Research and Social Science*, *66*. 101485 https://doi.org/10.1016/j.erss.2020.101485

Conclusion

A decarbonised, secure, and united EU?

Matúš Mišík and Andrea Figulová

When we started work on this edited volume in mid-2022, the EU was in the midst of a never-before-seen energy crisis (Mišík, 2022). The price of natural gas on spot markets had increased ten-fold compared to long-term averages (Kotek et al., 2023) and the import of supplies to the EU from its then main supplier – the Russian Federation – had been interrupted as a consequence of the bloc's support for Ukraine (Bruegel, 2022). There were also widespread worries about whether there would be sufficient quantities of natural gas available for winter 2023/2024 (European Commission, 2022). Now, two years later, the situation is markedly different – the EU has successfully addressed the crisis, with the price of natural gas approaching near pre-crisis levels. While governments are still adopting a cautious approach for winter 2024/2025, the overall expectation is that the EU will survive next season without major energy disruptions. This development has been possible due to actions by the EU and its members to exert influence on factors over which they have some control (e.g., an agreement to lower gas consumption, measures adopted to source more LNG from the US and elsewhere, investment in the strong growth of renewable energy sources and the establishment of new rules for underground storage), but also partly owing to factors outside the EU's reach (especially the exceptionally warm winters that lowered natural gas consumption). All of this has been taking place alongside the EU's ongoing efforts to restart its economy after the COVID-19 pandemic, a process that within the EU has been closely connected to energy and climate policy as part of a green (and digital) recovery (Crnčec et al., 2023; European Parliament, 2022) aimed at achieving EU climate neutrality by 2050 (European Council, 2019).

This edited volume has focused on the consequences of the two crises for the EU's climate and energy policy since 2020. More specifically, it has explored the interplay between the Commission, which presented its own (predominantly 'green') solutions to both crises (see the Introduction), and member states, which have not always agreed with Commission's proposals for a variety of reasons (Mišík and Nosko, 2023). This dynamic has engendered an impact on EU governance as such and the individual chapters of the volume explored its various aspects. To secure homogeneity and consistency of the volume, the introduction presented two main research questions that framed examination of the crises and their impact on the

DOI: 10.4324/9781032624839-16

climate and energy policy of the EU: (1) Have the two crises caused changes to the EU climate and energy policy? (2) If so, have these changes led to the deepening of European integration in these policies or have member states opted for national solutions instead? Or, in other words (reflecting the title of the volume): have the crises contributed to EU unity, decarbonisation, and security of energy supply or have they prompted member states to turn inwards and search for national solutions to climate and energy challenges? We first present the conclusions of the individual contributions before responding to these broader questions, identifying research limitations, and suggesting avenues for future examination.

This volume is divided into three sections that scrutinise various issues connected to the development of EU climate and energy policy and the ways in which they have been impacted by the two crises. In Part I of the book, 'EU Energy transition at a crossroads', contributors identified several challenging aspects towards achieving the energy and climate goals of the EU. In Chapter 1, Navrátil and Grigelová studied the European Commission's governance strategies connected to the European Green Deal initiative. They pinpointed three types of strategies (cross-sectoral, legislative, and infrastructural) employed by the Commission to widen its influence on green governance, thus tilting the scales between itself and member states in its favour. Chapter 2 by Mattera, Panarello, and Gatto examined various factors that impacted the perceptions of EU citizens towards the energy transition. The authors explain cross-country differences in public perceptions, arguing that various factors play crucial roles in different regions of the EU, while factors such as political preferences impact perceptions across the entire EU. In Chapter 3, Oravcová and Šafaříková analysed the regional dimension of climate and energy policy. Focusing on one region, they examined how Visegrad Group countries (Czechia, Hungary, Poland, and Slovakia) are contributing to addressing the energy transition and climate change. They argued that, contrary to the national level, Visegrad Group countries are not always laggards on energy policy at the regional level and that at least some of the governments in these countries can significantly contribute to EU goals connected to climate neutrality by 2050. In Chapter 4, the last one in the first section, Gál scrutinised the development of nuclear energy in Central and Eastern Europe. He argued that nuclear energy is a key element of the energy transition for this part of the EU; however, development herein is significantly vulnerable to dependence on Russian nuclear technology and fuel.

Part II of the book, entitled 'Russian invasion and European energy security', encompassed five chapters that investigated various aspects of EU energy security following the 2022 Russian invasion of Ukraine. In Chapter 5, Marušiak, examined the cooperation of the Visegrad Group countries in the energy security area, arguing that they focus on two dimensions: developing the security of supply of energy raw materials, particularly natural gas, and responding to the EU's green transition. While the Visegrad Group countries welcomed EU initiatives in the energy infrastructure area (i.e. the former), they were rather cautious in the latter area (see also Chapter 3 by Oravcová and Šafaříková). Following the Russian invasion, cooperation has, however, weakened, as the individual countries of the group have espoused different positions on the conflict. In Chapter 6, Deák, Szabo, and Weiner examined the responses of three countries from Europe that can be considered friendly to Russia (Bulgaria, Hungary, and Serbia) to the Kremlin's use of natural gas as a foreign policy tool (the so-called 'gas weapon'). Utilising a theoretical framework examining models of influence, the authors argue that the responses of these three countries varied according to what, in their view, amounted to Russian sanctions in the natural gas sector.

Nosko and Ušiak, on the other hand, looked at EU energy sanctions against the Russian Federation and how they have influenced the energy transition within the EU in the seventh chapter. Their point of departure rests on the argument that an external shock (i.e. crises discussed in the book) can accelerate the energy transition. Based on the available preliminary data, the authors claimed that the EU energy transition has been impacted by the sanctions, though more data is necessary to advance more robust conclusions. Kajanová and Veteška, in the eighth chapter, examined the connection between emissions and economic efficiency in the case of Slovakia, arguing that such analysis can identify areas where investment is most needed in the future. Their case study can therefore serve as a guide for the effective utilisation of post-pandemic recovery funds. The last chapter of this section (Chapter 9), by Gondášová, examined the energy security of EU member states over a ten-year period prior to the Russian invasion of Ukraine. The chapter argued that while some member states managed to increase their energy security in the examined period (2012–2021), the energy security of most EU member states declined. The COVID-19 pandemic had varying impacts on the energy security of EU member states, which were partly contingent on the different approaches adopted in response to the crises.

Part III of the book, 'Renewables as energy security tools', shed light on energy security aspects of renewable energy sources. In Chapter 10, Hebda, Leśniak, and Stolorz examined the development of Poland's renewable energy policy, with a focus on wind energy. While the country can be considered a forerunner in the development of offshore wind energy in the Central and Eastern Europe region, the development of onshore wind energy was significantly constrained, until 2022, by a 10H rule preventing the presence of wind turbines in proximity to human dwellings. This rule was relaxed in 2022, with expectations that this change will foster renewable energy growth in Poland. In Chapter 11, Figulová and Vicenová, explored whether mainstream political parties have adopted the nativist argumentation typical of far-right and extremist parties when discussing energy policy following the crises. They argued that this has, indeed, happened and that mainstream political parties have started to present solutions to energy security challenges via nationalist and anti-European perspectives, an approach that was typical mostly of far-right political parties before the crises.

This volume asked two main research questions: First, have the two crises caused changes to EU climate and energy policy? Second, if so, have these changes led to the deepening of European integration in these policies or have member states opted for national solutions instead? Although not all contributions in this volume reflected directly on these two research questions, all of them contributed to answering them from their specific perspectives: these included EU, national, regional, and local levels.

The answer to the first research question is rather straightforward. Yes, the EU and its climate and energy policy have undergone changes, and these were connected to the crises. As Navrátil and Grigelová argued, the Commission has developed a new system (that they call 'creeping supranationalism') that enables the Commission to exercise pressure on member states to support 'green' solutions to problems. Moreover, as Nosko and Ušiak claimed, the crisis connected to the Russian invasion of Ukraine and subsequent sanctions against Russia have prompted changes to the EU's energy mix. These are, however, not viewed in negative terms by these authors, but more as an opportunity for the energy transition and climate change mitigation efforts. This is very good news especially vis-à-vis findings presented in chapter nine by Gondášová, who argued that the energy security level of most EU member states had experienced a downwards trajectory throughout the decade prior to Russia's invasion of Ukraine. While these chapters looked at the first research question from an EU-perspective, others have examined it from the vantage point of member states. Hebda et al. claimed that domestic rules on the development of renewable energy sources (wind energy) were modified following the Russian invasion to support the growth of domestic energy sources; Figulová and Vicenová, meanwhile, argued that the same crisis led to the spread of an argumentation style highlighting nationalistic elements by political parties across the spectrum, from far-right to mainstream.

Kajanová and Veteška presented several lessons that countries with a less energy efficient industrial sector could heed from more energy efficient countries. Scrutinising the countries of Central and Eastern Europe, Gál argued that the Russian invasion increased the vulnerability of this region in the nuclear energy area as several countries in the region depend on Russian nuclear technology and fuel. Marušiak, in chapter five, argued that the Russian invasion of Ukraine caused a weakening of cooperation among the Visegrad Four countries in many areas, including energy, following their disagreements on Russia. Looking beyond the EU, Deák et al., in the sixth chapter, claimed that Russia has applied its 'energy weapon' against European natural gas importers. They argue that the Russian approach worked in many cases and the analysed countries changed their energy policies. While Oravcová and Šafaříková stressed the importance of the regional and local level in achieving a successful energy transition, Mattera et al. examined the factors impacting public support for the energy transition and regional differences therein.

Pertaining to the second research question of the volume, there is no clear-cut answer – we cannot discern for now if the crises caused the deepening of integration or the 'nationalisation' of energy policy by member states. While Navrátil and Grigelová claimed that the Commission used the opportunity provided by the crises to gain more control over climate and energy policy and Nosko and Ušiak employed provisional data to argue that the crises have fostered an energy transition at the EU level, Figulová and Vicenová showed how political discourses in

Slovakia became more nationalistic and anti-European. Gál, similarly, claimed that only some EU member states are keen on further developing nuclear energy while others hold negative stances towards nuclear power, with the divide a source of friction at the EU level. The crisis connected to the Russian invasion of Ukraine, which increased demand for domestic energy, has not changed the position of all EU member states on their anti-nuclear policy (the most visible case is Germany). Russian policy has been devised to 'divide and rule' and at least some EU member states have succumbed to this approach, though their position towards Russia had been essentially friendly (chapter six by Deák et al.). Oravcová and Šafaříková stressed the importance of the local level in the energy transition and climate mitigation efforts while Marušiak argued that the Visegrad Group has weakened following the Russian invasion due to disagreement between its members. The group, consequently, will probably not be as strong an advocate as before of its climate and energy preferences, which has sometimes gone against the majority within the EU. In other cases, member states have changed their domestic energy policies to become more energy resilient (Hebda et al.).

There are, undoubtedly, also some research limitations to the scholarship included in this edited volume. First of all, although we repeatedly refer to the EU energy crisis connected to the Russian invasion of Ukraine in the past tense, the crisis is not fully over. Not only is Russia continuing its aggression in Ukraine, but also energy markets have not completely stabilised yet and continue to be very sensitive to international developments. More than before, the price of natural gas and oil on the spot markets is fluctuating and reacting strongly to almost all supply chain changes. This includes planned and unplanned maintenance of energy infrastructure, weather changes, etc... While this edited volume, therefore, represents one of the first efforts to shed light on the consequences of both crises, contributions were limited by the ongoing nature of one of the crises and consequent restricted availability of data. Several chapters mention this explicitly. Future research should therefore work with data covering both crises in their entirety. Second, while it was not our goal, this book does not cover all actors that play a significant role in EU climate and energy policy. Indeed, the contributions in this edited volume refrain from examining all EU institutions and all member states. This should be a task for future research, however, that builds upon the findings of this book.

To conclude, based on the research presented in this edited volume – with the abovementioned limitations in mind – we can say with confidence that the European Union has become more decarbonised and somewhat more secure following the two crises (COVID-19 and the Russian invasion of Ukraine). The EU, however, is still not united when it comes to climate and energy policy.

Acknowledgements

This work was supported by the Slovak Research and Development Agency Grant No APVV-20-0012.

References

Bruegel, 2022. European natural gas imports. Brussels.

Crnčec, D., Penca, J., Lovec, M., 2023. The COVID-19 pandemic and the EU: From a sustainable energy transition to a green transition? *Energy Policy* 175, 113453. https://doi.org/10.1016/j.enpol.2023.113453

European Commission, 2022. Save gas for a safe winter. Brussels.

European Council, 2019. European Council meeting (12 December 2019) – Conclusions. Brussels.

European Parliament, 2022. EU recovery instrument. Brussels.

Kotek, P., Selei, A., Takácsné Tóth, B., Felsmann, B., 2023. What can the EU do to address the high natural gas prices? *Energy Policy* 173, 113312. https://doi.org/10.1016/j.enpol.2022.113312

Mišík, M., 2022. The EU needs to improve its external energy security. *Energy Policy* 165, 112930. https://doi.org/10.1016/j.enpol.2022.112930

Mišík, M., Nosko, A., 2023. Each one for themselves: Exploring the energy security paradox of the European Union. *Energy Res Soc Sci* 99, 103074. https://doi.org/10.1016/j.erss.2023.103074

Index

Note: Figures are indicated by italics. Tables are indicated by bold. Endnotes are indicated by the page number followed by 'n' and the endnote number e.g., 20n1 refers to endnote 1 on page 20.

For Product Safety Concerns and Information please contact our EU
representative GPSR@taylorandfrancis.com
Taylor & Francis Verlag GmbH, Kaufingerstraße 24, 80331 München, Germany

www.ingramcontent.com/pod-product-compliance
Ingram Content Group UK Ltd.
Pitfield, Milton Keynes, MK11 3LW, UK
UKHW020147200926
475702UK00016B/2588
* 9 7 8 1 0 3 2 6 2 4 8 1 5 *